The Underground Stream

Esoteric Tarot Revealed

by Christine Payne-Towler

edited by Tina Rosa

Noreah Press
Eugene, Oregon
1999

Noreah Press
1991 Garfield St.
Eugene, OR 97405

Grateful acknowledgment is made for permission to print:

Illustrations from Tavaglione Tarot, Visconti-Sforza, Rider-Waite, Medieval Scapini, Knapp-Hall, Papus, Egyptian Tarot reproduced by permission of U.S. Games Systems, Inc., Stamford, CT 06902 USA, Copyright © 1982,1984, 1985, 1986, 1983, 1982 respectively by U.S. Games Systems Inc. Further reproduction prohibited.
Illustrations from Ibis Tarot reproduced by permission of AGM AGMuller, CH-8212 Neuhausen, Switzerland. © 1991 AGM AGMuller. Further reproduction prohibited.
Illustrations from Oswald Wirth Tarot reproduced by permission of AGM AGMuller, CH-8212 Neuhausen, Switzerland. © for the German edition 1995. AGM AGMuller. Further reproduction prohibited.
Permission for Tarocco Delle Stelle by Teodomiro Dal Negro.

Charts and illustrations created by Barbara Bryan Gleason

Cover graphic: *Plants,* from Grand Oracle des Dames Tarot

Printed in the United States of America

ISBN 0-9673043-0-X

Acknowledgments

To those whose blood, sweat, and tears have mingled with mine in the creation of this book, I could not be more thankful. To Dr. Lewis Keizer and his wife Willa Esterson-Keizer, who between them have been holding up the Templar torch to light my path on this work, I extend my profound thanks for all the spiritual and intellectual support. To Mary Greer, long-time exemplar and esoteric friend, who read most of the manuscript before its first apearance on the CD and who kept me contained to what I could defend, you have my deepest appreciation, for your high standards and your generosity. To Paul O'Brian, founder of Visionary Networks, who published the bulk of these essays in their first form on the Tarot Magic CDRom, endless thanks go out for taking me on for that wonderful project, which led to this book. To Tina Rosa, co-conspiritor, friend, and most excellent editor, you know I could never have done this without you, and it has been the fulfillment of a fifteen year dream to put this book out with you. To Steve Rogers, who transcribed endless hours of tapes that we might have text. I am blessed to have had the pleasure of being your friend in this and many other adventures. And to Solala Towler, my dearest life partner and the singlehanded creator of this book's look and style, doing this with you has lifted a lifetime of fear about telling my truth to the world. Our partnership is another confirmation that the wisdom of the Eternal Feminine will never die.

Archeology must be divided into two schools. The first, composed of strictly materialistically minded men, classifies but never attempts to interpret or apply even, for that matter, to fit together the fragments of old civilizations and cultures. The second is the intuitional school, generally regarded as unorthodox by the fanatics of the first group. The intuitionalists attempt to build some reasonable pattern out of the wreckage. They dare to speculate, using their mind as an instrument of exploration and research. It is this last group that, to some measure, sense the significance of the old metaphysical systems. They realize almost intuitively that a broad learning, at the same time deep and lofty, existed among ancient nations.

Manly P. Hall, *Freemasonary of the Ancient Egyptians*

Contents

INTRODUCTION

Words cannot describe the great joy and gratitude I feel at being able to release this book to the world. The work of writing it has been sublime, a continual revelation of the inherent order that sustains us all, despite superficial chaos.

I have an agenda with this book that extends beyond "pure history", so it is appropriate that I state myself clearly at the outset. My motive has been, like a good Libra, to bring together different factions among the millions of Tarot-lovers in America, factions which have continually polarized over whose version of Tarot is the "real" version. This argument echoes between the lines of most of the modern Tarot manuals currently in print, and is even more explicitly articulated in the monthly and quarterly magical/occult/esoteric magazines which are so popular today. I have not been a published voice in the debate until my CD *Tarot Magic* was published in December of 1998.

This, then, is my position—that the great river that is Tarot on the verge of the twenty-first century is so wide, encompassing so many separate streams, lineages, and traditions, that there is no one Tarot, no singular authentic and immutable Tarot, but a great flood of tarots. Standing at the mouth of the river and arguing does not illuminate what Tarot was at its source. Even traveling upriver to the Tarot of a century ago does not take one far enough back in time and history to get a clear view of the topic. In order to understand the whole river of Tarot, we have to perservere to it's source, tracing its course even when it disappears "underground" and flows invisibly below the threshold of collective consciousness for a century or two.

Some modern Tarot writers believe that this is an impossible dream, due to the unfortunate first few centuries of Tarot's existence, when the Church of Rome was purging variant forms of Christianity out of Europe. During those troubled years, many books, artworks, Tarot decks, and private manuscripts were burned along with their unfortunate owners, forcing these wisdom teachings into the Secret Societies, where membership was guarded with tests and fearsome oaths.

The Chronological Approach

The approach we have taken with this project has been designed to minimize the problem of those "underground years". The truth is, our esoteric understanding of numbers, the elements, the planets, signs of the Zodiac, traditional god-forms, the so-called natural and theological Virtues, and other symbols traditional to Tarot each have extensive histories reaching back into the roots of western culture.

Tarot is much like a layer-cake, built up from historical substrata which were laid down up to three thousand years before the cards were first printed. By starting from that earliest time — back with the first codification of the Hebrew alphabet — and moving forward in time using documented historical sources, the layering of these ideas can be traced era by era, as additional wisdom, symbolism, and magical potency is laid down, each in its stratum.

While the first early Tarot decks had their symbolism subtly veiled to appease the Church, there is plenty of evidence to substantiate what these images, symbols, and codes meant to those who assembled them on the icons of Tarot. When tracing the transmission of the Mysteries from antiquity to the present, the sketchy evidence left from the thirteenth to the fifteenth century is not really so inscrutable. Numerous scholarly sources are named in this text to bolster my conclusion that Tarot is the continuation of a long and rich cross-cultural conversation, carried on through the generations between mystics of the western tradition.

The cards are just one relatively recent manifestation of transmission of various wisdom lineages and the memory arts that have helped preserve them. The fact that the church felt so moved to suppress Tarot is strong evidence itself for esoteric content in the earliest Tarots!

A scholarly fraternity, drawn from both the priesthood and the laity and from every culture with representatives in Europe, had the philosophical vision and technical vocabulary to communicate about the larger spiritual issues which concern humanity down through the generations. Their direct and indirect participation in the creation of Tarot invests its images with layers of wisdom traditions, practices, and beliefs. The immortal ideas pictured on the cards have changed in details, symbols, or correspondences through the ages, but the numinous original ideas live on despite costume-changes and arguments over who has them "just right" on their deck. Even the last century of experimentation and creativity with historical revisionism cannot erase the fingerprints of Tarot's earliest creators.

Of course, these are not my conclusions alone...I am a Libra, after all! So at every opportunity, I call upon the words of experts in their fields, past and present, to elaborate and sustain my personal opinions with their respected views. I believe that we have enough graphic, linguistic, and manuscript evidence available to clarify the lacunae in the documented history of Tarot. What I hope is that these chapters will stimulate those who have answers and proofs to come foreward and help us all figure out the missing pieces of the puzzle of Tarot. My eternal gratitude goes out to my mentors and teachers, historical elders and contemporaries, whose published wisdom has enriched my own understanding. When I visualize the links in the sacred chain of the wisdom teachings I thank the Great Mother!

I offer this book up, as an *homage* to the perennial philosophers, who since the beginning of time have protected and preserved the sacred knowledge of number, geometry, sound, astronomy, alchemy, and ritual technology. It has gone by different names in different places and times, but the core teaching of the Mysteries is always the same. I am eternally grateful to be able to serve in that transmission, tracing and documenting the Mystery teachings on the faces of the cards, as they shape-shift through Tarot's past and future history.

PART I
INTRODUCTORY CHAPTERS

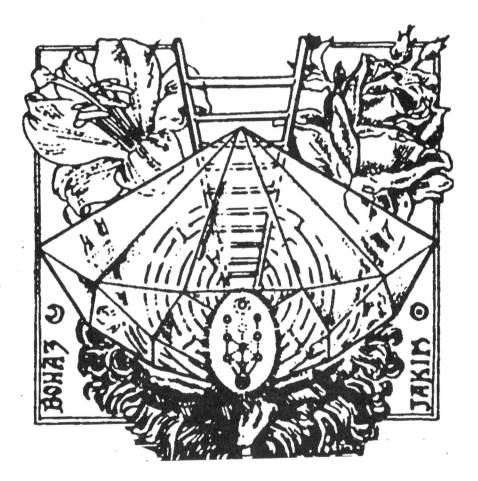

THE MIND OF THE PHILOSOPHER BY GIORGIO M.S. TAVAGLIONE FROM THE STAIRS OF GOLD TAROT BOOKLET

(WE ARE LOOKING DOWN AT THE TOP OF HIS HEAD AND IN HIS THIRD EYE IS A KABBALAH TREE FROM WHICH RISES THE LADDER OF LIGHTS, AT THE TOP OF WHICH IS THE 78-FACETED GEM OF TAROT.)

AN APPROACH TO TAROT HISTORY

The work you are reading started in 1970 when I purchased a used deck of the 20th Century Tarot in a book shop in Salem, Oregon. I was a freshman in college. With parents who were both therapists, I instantly recognized that Tarot was a tool with great potential for helping people grapple with the changing circumstances in their lives. Soon I returned to the book shop to buy Volume 6 of the Brotherhood of Light Encyclopedia, entitled *The Sacred Tarot*. From there I learned about the connections the cards have with letters, numbers, astrology and a host of other symbol systems from antiquity. Naturally, I sent for C.C. Zain's deck and began memorizing all the correspondences.

Finding others who were using different Tarot decks made me conscious of the need not to put all my eggs in one basket, so I started searching for other decks that were constructed with these correspondences in mind. Soon the Book of Thoth Tarot and the New Tarot for the Aquarian Age joined the first decks on my table, and I was plunged into a timeless passion that continues to this day.

When I discovered that I could buy Tarot decks directly through U. S. Games Systems, I became a collector. I also employed all the decks I could make sense of in my private practice with clients, students and study groups. Playing with them in terms of real-life situations as I conducted readings gave me the opportunity to see how their similarities and differences operated with different psyches and mindsets.

But collecting decks only multiplied my questions about which versions were traditional and which were innovative. Since my first exposure to Tarot reflected the Hermetic influence of the Brotherhood of Light, which is closely associated with the ancient self-initiation paradigm of the Mysteries, I could see that many decks were diverging from or just plain ignorant of Tarot's history. Thus, I found myself somewhat isolated from beloved colleagues who were for the most part satisfied with what they found in American bookstores.

Over time I managed to collect the books cited by the authors of the decks as well as the books *those* authors cited, ad infinitum. After all these years of study and practice, I have emerged from the confusion with confidence and would like to share with you the themes I have discovered.

The Difficulties of Tarot History

Studying the history of Tarot is no easy task. For one thing, because it first appeared in Europe in the early 1400s in the form of cards, the early evidence is understandably altered and fragmented. Political and religious forces in the 1400 and 1500's forced Tarot into a situation where it had to be camouflaged to obscure its radical content. Generations of students and scholars have had to join secret lodges and take binding oaths to earn the right to have information that we in the twentieth century can access on the Internet and

buy outright. As we shall see, some of Tarot's brightest lights have had to accept anonymity or damage to their reputations as the price of entry into the Arcane Teachings.

We latecomers to the scene have little understanding of or appreciation for the extreme sacrifices behind the preservation of our seventy eight card Tarot deck. To make matters more confusing, over the last three centuries, the gradual easing of cultural pressures to maintain secrecy led to distortions in the Tarot tradition and some wildly creative but revisionist "innovations" . Many different versions of Tarot's origins were postulated and evangelized, often with political or commercial gain in mind. What competing claims from differing viewpoints can we credit? How can we know which "expert" to trust? Is there a way to separate the truly historical part of the Tarot mythos from the oft-repeated but never documented "received wisdom"?

No. 19 THE SUN
IBIS TAROT

If I had fallen in line with most modern Tarot historians, there would have been no great insights coming from me on any of these topics. Commercial emphasis in the last several decades has been upon collecting documentable minutiae that can be proven about the charismatic personalities who have left a bit of themselves in the public record. While I am grateful to those who make it their mission to dig up the facts on these people, I cannot pursue that tack. My attraction to the traditional imagery didn't leave me the time!

I regularly find myself back at my Tarot table in the middle of the night, researching the pictures on the cards. While sorting them and laying them out, I am imagining the conversations between their originators about the details they contested versus those they held in common. Ultimately attracted to their Mystery School content, it is with the cards themselves that I have wrestled.

The Context In Which Tarot Appeared

The cards themselves have shown me an ongoing intergenerational and international dialogue amonst a stream of highly educated mystics and occultists. We can no longer name the earliest contributors to this stream. The teachings enshrined in the Tarot, most especially the Hebrew alphabet mysteries, astrology and the core concept of self-initiation itself, draw from very ancient sources. These teachings were driven underground during the era following the Christian victory over the Mysteries in the fourth century AD.

During that repression, people who wanted to preserve those ancient teachings had to be very secretive. The Church forbade the common folk the right to read and write, hoping that these teachings could be wiped out if the majority were illiterate. That very strategy, however, drove the teachings into visual form—painting, sculpture, architecture and needlework. By the end of the Dark Ages, Europe was filled with the imagery that would eventually appear on the cards. Over time, private clubs formed, like invisible churches, to allow interested parties to pursue these studies with peers who were trustworthy. In this way the Church's policies forced its enemies to get together within what became known as the Secret Societies.

Because of the persecutions, the Tarot had to be promoted as a game for social amusement and distraction. That way, teachings could be revealed in the imagery which if spoken would seriously jeopardize a person's reputation as a Christian, a dangerous proposition in superstitious times. Secret Society members, using pseudonyms, produced occult and philosophical works that hinted at the teachings contained in the Tarot, but veiled them in confusing terms or contradictory details to throw non-lodge members off the track. So although these strategies were necessary at the time, historians are left with a confusing maze of false leads and distortions to unwind. In addition, if historians or researchers do not think like occultists and lodge members of the fifteenth to eighteenth centuries, they are simply lost at sea. It was not until I committed myself to a thorough study of the Secret Societies and their histories that I began to understand the inner dimensions of the Tarot.

No.15 The Devil
Esoterico Tarot

Luckily for all, the faces of the cards never lie, testifying to their origins if ever so quietly. In the earliest decks, discernibly Kabbalist elements appear, commingled with classical Hermetic themes, spiced with Cathar and Gugliemite heresies, and unified by an overlay of Renaissance detail. In just a few generations, the cards became so rich with associations that it was impossible to reference them all in one deck, so Tarot decks had to proliferate. This led to different "schools" or families of related Tarots based on the emphases favored over others by any given deck's creator.

The paradox is that Tarot, our seventy eight card deck of distinct and definable Arcana (twenty two of which have their own names, along with their fifty six suit cards in four divisions), appeared in Europe nearly overnight, like Ve-

nus emerging from the foam, with no apparent antecedents. The European psyche birthed Tarot late in the 1300's, and although there were a few experimental exceptions (the Mantegna Arcana, for example), and a few variants (decks with shortened suits, or extra royalty, or an extra set of planetary gods, graces, or zodiac signs), Tarot decks today are essentially the same in internal structure as they were when they first appeared. Brighter minds than mine have asked, "How is this possible? Where did it come from?"

My Theory

Throughout this work I will be refferring to the "astro-alphanumeric" achetypes, those number/letter/astrology correspondences which allow a sounded letter to also stand for a number and also refer to a planet or sign, all at the same time. All sacred alphabets have these correspondences, from Sanskrit to Hebrew to Latin. This is one method people used to tabulate number values before the spread of the Arabic numerals.

I feel certain that the astro-alphanumeric archetypes linked to the Greek alphabet at the Greek alphabet reforms (approx. 500 BC) survived the Dark Ages, most especially in Southern Europe. This body of correspondences would have detailed the numerical links uniting the Greek alphabet to the older alphabet of the Hebrews, along with the astrological values that the Alexandrian Hermeticists assigned to those letter/numbers. Certain Hermetic texts were circulating in Europe even before the rediscovery of the *Corpus Hermeticum*. Those values became the basis for the medaieval magical alphabets which we find scattered through the folios of the alchemists, Kabbalists, astrologers, and Magi of the Renaissance.

This body of astro-alphanumeric archetypes, with or without images to accompany them, became property of the Secret Societies before the appearance of the earliest woodblock and handmade Tarots of the early 1400s. These archetypes, likely elaborated from the Mystery School teachings attributed to Pythagoras (again, 600 BC), later became disseminated around the Mediterranean through the spread of Alexandrian culture. These correspondences were regarded as controversial and spiritually dangerous in Europe during the Dark Ages, but were never entirely lost to scholars of the Mysteries.

Tantalizing clues point to multiple ways this body of astro-alphanumeric codes could have survived. Dr. Lewis Keizer notes the presence of Roman-Hellenistic Serapis temples in Italy, relics of the - cult, one of which was excavated by the tenth century and reputedly contained images that could double as illustrations of the Major Arcana in "Egyptified" form (see The Esoteric Origins of Tarot). He also details the contribution made by the Gypsies in keeping these correspondences alive during the Church persecutions. Assertions abound in the writings of the Tarot masters of the 1700s that the Jews used these alphabetically keyed archetypes in their Mysteries, and that these archetypes found their way into the Secret Societies through this avenue as well. We can also expect that the Moslem libraries in Spain, and the Orthodox monasteries in Eastern Europe possessed similar tables of correspondence as well, as these communities never experienced the orgy of book-burning inspired by the Roman Christians.

A preexisting body of codes and correspondences, coming to us from late antiquity, is the skeletal structure upon which Tarot is formed, as I hope these essays begin to demonstrate. Based on the Hebrew alphabet, Kaballah, Pythagorean number and harmonic theory, and the signs and planets of astrology, this structure is as old as Western civilization. Before there were Tarot cards, these astro-alphanumeric correspondences between related systems were firmly in place.

No. 2 The Popess
Visconte-Svortza Tarot

I have no doubt that the first Tarot cards were a reflection of these early archetypes, but for safety's sake they were stripped of the letters, numbers and other pagan symbols offensive to the Church. Unfortunately, even in this humbler form, Tarot was considered incendiary because of the Cathar-influenced images they contained, and two centuries of bans and persecutions followed.

In addition to variations on some Major Arcana imposed by Papal order, the trivializing effect of formatting Tarot as a game diluted the pointedness of the earliest images. Nevertheless the interior, divinatory body of correspondences kept growing through the Gypsy usage cited by Dr. Keizer in his excellent chapter. After the appearance of the Marseilles Tarot in the late 1600s, new versions of several Major Arcana marked a fresh restatement of the old Arcana. It still was not safe to blatantly put Hebrew letters and astrology on the faces of the cards, but the especially loaded changes that appeared at this time revealed more detail about Tarot's internal structures and relationships.

I cannot prove my theory with manuscript evidence (although some very interesting quotes by Manly P. Hall of Madame Blavatsky make my case very nicely). The decks of the 1660s themselves demonstrate that the primal Arcana archetypes re-emerged at that time, and every contemporary stream of Tarot was impacted. This includes the Marseilles-style decks, the de Gebelin school and the Etteilla variants (see chapter entitled The Continental Tarots).

At the end of the 1800s another emergence of that inner-school material spurred the reforms of the French school and the emergence of the English and Spanish lodges. We have more documentation (and more opinions) about this wave of Tarot "reforms" than any previous emergence. But there is little concensus on which of the competing versions of Tarot's history to believe. Dissension among different

"schools" or "lineages" has become more public as Tarot has grown more popular. A little study makes clear that the images we now generally associate with Tarot are relative latecomers to the earlier astro-alphanumeric archetypes inherited from Alexandrian culture.

The Arcana images, no matter who their earliest illustrator, are hung on a preexisting structure that dictates their intrinsic order. Even if a Tarot artist later decides to change the names, the ordering or the imagery, it makes no difference. The fact that Tarot is structured with 22 Major Arcana (the Hebrew letters) plus the Kabbalah Tree in the four elements (10x4, the numbered suit cards) plus the twelve signs and four seasons (12+4, the Royalty) gives it away as an ancient artifact. Tarot is the set of flash cards for the astro-alphanumeric Mysteries of late antiquity, and it is those Mysteries which are the Prima Causa of the deck itself and all its images, names, numbers and other correspondences.

The Situation in America

No. 1 The Magus
Waite Tarot

Since the turn of the twentieth century, received wisdom in the English-speaking world about Tarot is that the Waite-Smith deck is the definitive pack against which all others should be measured. It has stood like a monument in the history of Tarot, supposedly representative of the best of the tradition but newly revealed for the modern age, summing up the past but pointing to a brave new future for Tarot. America took this well-documented and beautiful pack to its heart, and to this day those images remain the common denominators people generally refer to when they think of Tarot.

This has not been a bad way for Tarot to be introduced to America, but it has caused a problem for the Tarot historian. The problem is that Tarot did not originate in England or America, but in Italy, Germany, France, and later Spain. The Waite-Smith Tarot, for all its popularity and attractiveness, cannot truly be considered as "traditional" when compared to the older and original Tarots.

The people and circumstances that originally shaped the Arcana were centuries older than those whose names we know and whose histories we now recite. Between the 1400s and the present, generations of decks have come and gone, with America hearing little about the older Tarots and what they meant to the people who used them. Unless one has been assertive enough to develop a relationship with U. S. Games Systems and buy the "foreign" decks the bookstores didn't carry, one would never know that there was a history

ries about the authors and their histories, the decks themselves can appear inscrutable. But like it or not, Tarot is too old to worry about personalities, and we are going to have to take on the work of evaluating it on its internal structures and symbolic elements alone.

Nor can we afford to hold out for manuscript evidence before we decide where Tarot "came from." Unfortunately, many of the manuscripts where we would expect to find records that are contemporary with the earliest cards and their underlying images have been destroyed. This was a calculated effort undertaken by the Roman Church over several centuries, designed to keep the European people from turning away from Catholicism and toward the Gnostic heresies of the Middle Ages. The devastation that the Church visited upon the culture of southern France in the twelfth century obliterated the conditions that germinated the Tarot as we know it now. We are infinitely lucky that the cards themselves survived.

Now we have to learn how to "read" the surviving images in all the glory and variety that they still show. In them we can see the ideas flowing and evolving in "pictures worth a thousand words." *We must cease viewing the images and symbols on the faces of the cards as secondary evidence, and learn to follow the protocols of the Art Historian when we investigate the Tarot. Insisting on text evidence for proofs of our theories is illogical given the underground status of its originators and the persecutions that Tarot engendered.*

Toward that goal, students and fans of Tarot would benefit from having full-color volumes at their disposal that would be filled with each and every Arcana from the earliest centuries. For example, researchers deserve to see every card from works like the Lazzarelli Codices (from 1471) which are in the Vatican Library. These are an exquisite set of tarocchi images, artistically resembling and named after the Mantegna cards, but confined to twenty two prints like the Major Arcana of the Visconti-Sforza (see Kaplan's *Encyclopedia*, p. 27). Between 1496 and 1506, Albrecht Durer, a German painter and engraver, made a set of 21 tarocchi images patterned after the E-series tarocchi of Mantegna cards. These images are exquisite and would make a very fruitful study (*Encyclopedia*, p. 47). As well, it would be a joy to see the remarkably beautiful circular pack of seventy two cards in five suits engraved at Cologne in 1470, a few of which are shown in the Fournier *Playing Cards* encyclopedia (Volume 1, p. 165).

Along those lines, it would also be beneficial if researchers could access a pack of cards reproduced from the Rosenwald Tarot cards as well as the related 15th century Italian Tarocchi whose cards are split between the Metropolitan Museum of Art and the budapest Museum of Fine Arts (see Vol. II of Kaplan's *Encyclopedia of Tarot*, p 291.). The oldest deck currently in print, the Pierpont Morgan-Bergamo Visconti-Sforza Tarocchi deck, is just the beginning of the collection we need to scrutinize once we come to understand what we are looking at.

We can also make better use of those creditable historical sources whose writings have proved to contain a high

*EUTERPE FROM THE LAZARELLI CODEX
IN THE VATICAN*

of Tarot before the twentieth century.

In my early years of study there was little published in English about those older decks, so there were no helpful teachers to consult when I needed a question answered. Even now, with Stuart Kaplan's *Encyclopedia of Tarot*, plus the books by Giles, Gad, Cavendish, Gettings, Knight and Tomberg (among others—see Bibliography), a clear focus on Tarot origins still eludes us.

Fortunately the evidence of Tarot's origins is all over the faces of the cards, and the diligent seeker can develop an "eye" for the clues once they line up the images and compare for themselves. With Stuart Kaplan's *Encyclopedia* in hand, and the works of the authors cited above, it has been possible to piece together a creditable history of the European Tarot which I hope can serve as a standard resource for English-speaking students and scholars alike. In the future we can carry on our Tarot debates with better grounding in the fundamentals, with an expanded knowledge about the larger, original world of Tarot.

Changing Our Attitudes

Our twentieth century love of personality makes the early centuries of Tarot look dull. Without names and sto-

proportion of accurate information, according to the hindsight of modern scholarship. Bearing in mind that we in the late twentieth century have more information available to us on the Internet than kings and Magi could amass in bygone days, we can now understand even more what the old masters were trying to tell us in the Tarot Arcana. Especially interesting are the chain of esotericists from the eighteenth and nineteenth centuries, detailed in the chapter *The Continental Tarots*, who revealed again the dormant esoteric content of the folk-style Tarots of their day, reinvigorating Tarot's ancient linkages with new presentations of Hermeticism, Kaballah and theurgy.

A Plea for Objectivity
About Eliphas Levi

In this context I have to highlight Eliphas Levi, a French esoteric scholar of the 1800s whose voluminous writings have fueled this century's Tarot revival. Because he did not write in English, we in America have been dependent upon translators if we want to follow Levi's ideas. Levi's primary translator is A. E. Waite, a well-known British occultist from the early 1900s who positioned himself as an expert in all matters esoteric, especially Tarot.

To give credit where credit is due, Waite and his compatriots Wescott and Crowley have, between them, translated much of Levi's occult catalog. There is no way to deny the great benefit which the English-speaking world has received from the dedication of these three translators. In the meantime, however, they made sure to load Levi's work with enough mean-spirited forewords, footnotes and afterwords that we struggle to see Levi through the thicket of discounts. I urge everyone who loves Tarot to study Levi and the Continental esoteric masters who followed him, ignoring all inserted material from translators, and *take these authors seriously*. Inaccuracies and distortions can be found in the works of every Tarot author, but we cannot discourse rationally about Tarot history until we can see through the smoke screen put up by the English occultists from the turn of this century.

I do not make these statements lightly, and dear friends in the Tarot community may wince at my bluntness. Nevertheless I simply differ with much of the received wisdom on Tarot lineages. The "party line" is that the English school was sincere in attempting to "correct" what they thought were ambiguities in Levi's works. My response is that those ambiguities were created by Levi's translators as part of the ongoing feud between the French (traditional) and English (upstart) branches of the European Secret Societies. (see accompanying essay "Esoteric Origins of the Tarot" by Dr. Lewis Keizer).

Let me state for the record that I do not fault any modern proponents of the English schools for this problem. I trace the origin of this issue to Levi's translators, who knew their actions would destroy Levi's credibility in the New World. It was necessary for them to do so because their version of Tarot was so radically different from its historical, Continental roots. To promote the Order of the Golden Dawn and its offshoots, they could not avoid casting doubt upon those who had gone before. Unfortunately, in trivializing Levi, they have deprived many sincere Tarot students of the readily available scholarship of Levi, reknowned French magus of the 1800s.

Even despite the cruel misrepresentations of his translators, Levi's works contain a treasure trove of hints, clues and historical facts of interest to any who claim to love the Tarot (see Bibliography). His style is old-fashioned, and he is prone to poetic flights of pun-filled metaphor that present a challenge to translators. But he represents the pinnacle of scholarship in his day and is a respected voice in the traditional stream as well as an exceptionally subtle thinker. As we relinquish our biases, I hope we can begin to appreciate the man for who he was.

Ample evidence exists to place the French Masons, exemplified by Etteilla and his Tarot correspondences, squarely at the center of the reformulation of the Secret Societies after the French Revolution. Levi inherited that tradition with the Supreme Grand Mastership of the Fraternitas Rosae Crucis of Europe, which he occupied from 1856 to his death in 1875. Levi went to great lengths to document the transmission of these already ancient alphanumeric correspondences in his excellent writings. His students Papus and Wirth in their turn reconfirmed the edifice of esoteric scholarship that is the French School. One cannot claim to be an expert on Tarot, or on Levi and the French School, and then dismiss those Tarots as "incorrect." This alone is proof that the most influential scholars in this field were "hidden in plain sight," like the Tarot itself for so many generations.

It is a signature of Secret Society style to make the fewest waves possible in the mundane world unless it is strategic to The Work. Levi's modesty in life has been appallingly repaid by those who have been intellectually, not to mention financially, enriched by his legacy. Yet nobody from the various orders with which he was involved has ever stepped forward in a public way to defend his name until now. A close study of Volume 2's biography of Eliphas Levi, found in E. Swynbourne Clymer's three-volume tome on the lives of the *Rosicruciae*, finally helped me put Levi's contribution to the history and transmission of the Tarot in perspective, but this wonderful work is unfortunately not readily available to all.

All this being said, I am fully aware that I am raising as many questions as I answer. It is the nature of knowledge to expand. My ignorance today will be glaring tomorrow, and I accept that fact in advance. If by presenting this information I provoke a buzz of responses (hopefully pro as well as con), trigger a few knowledgeable people to publish their books, even if to refute mine, and excite a few more souls toward the teachings that Tarot presents, then I will have been successful. I encourage everyone of such a mind to find and fill the holes in the presentation you find here, and we will all be the better for it.

CRITERIA FOR ESOTERIC TAROT

The term "esoteric Tarot" embodies the defining criteria by which we evaluate the unfolding history of Tarot. Throughout this book, it is the key concept and watchword. So the reader can follow the discussion, I have listed the following characteristics that must be met to qualify a deck as an esoteric Tarot:

1) The Tarot must have seventy-eight cards. This is not to say there is no esoteric content in the decks with other card counts. Many decks with fifty-two cards, or those with a few more or less, reveal the inherent structure of a Minor Arcana deck and contain imagery that refers to or reflects Major Arcana themes from larger decks. One can often see a King of Cups who looks like a minor Pope, or echoes of the Justice on the Queen of Swords, for example. Other decks have extras of both the Major Arcana and the Minors to serve the needs of the game for which the decks were constructed.

The seventy-eight card deck, however, encompasses the full spectrum of correspondences that fill out an esoteric Tarot as discussed in the "Confluence of Ancient Systems" chapter. A few of the odd-numbered Tarots feature royalty or Major Arcana so beautiful or magically constructed that we felt we had to include them despite eccentric numbers of Minor Arcana. But the "perfect" Tarot for esoteric work is one with seventy-eight cards containing twenty-two Major Arcana, sixteen royalty and forty suit cards. In this way you get the full Hebrew/Greek alphabet, the Kabbalah Tree in each of the four directions, the twelve signs of the zodiac in the Kings, Queens and Horsemen, and four Pages to mark the solstice and equinox points at the cusps of the seasons. Having fewer cards forces us to drop the zodiac angels that align with the numbered suit cards. Extra cards are either redundant or change the system the Tarot was designed to express.

2) An esoteric Tarot is literate. It demonstrates the hallmarks of its creator's exposure to the archetypes behind the modern forms of the Arcana. At very least, it signals awareness of the historical stream of images from which our modern decks emerge. It must be grounded to some extent in the intergenerational conversation about these timeless archetypes which has been passing from century to century.

This is not to say there is no place for entirely "new" decks, because some of the modern Tarots have reinvented the medium for wonderful, rich new uses. (In particular, I refer to Isha Lerner's therapeutic Inner Child Tarot, which has been translated into fifteen languages because it is so helpful to counselors of children and teens worldwide. Also note the Alchemical Tarot, entirely without Hebrew, Greek,

astrological assignments or any other controversial matter, but which provides a treasure trove of Renaissance imagery culled from alchemical journals of the period.) I celebrate the creativity that reformats Tarot for modern needs and uses, and many modern Tarots share space with the "research decks" on my Tarot table.

Unless Tarot authors make their affiliation with the ancient esoteric paradigm clear and detailed, however, their Tarot decks cannot be rightly called esoteric decks. They may be fabulous catalysts for intuition and deep emotional healing, they may be an innovative synthesis of modern themes, but they are not "the flash cards of the Mysteries."

In the course of this text we have laid out several different avenues whereby the relevant Greek, Egyptian and Hebrew symbol systems could have seeped into Europe in the centuries before Tarot appeared in card form. Tarot decks are the flash cards for this ancient worldview. The proofs are everywhere that the Hebrews, Pythagoreans, Christians, Moslems, alchemists and Rosicrucians were mining the same vein. In other words, the cards did not appear first and the esoteric correspondences second. Historically, the correspondences came first and dictated the structure of the Tarot deck. If a person has created a "Tarot" that ignores this inherent, innate historical foundation, then by definition that Tarot is not esoteric.

No one can know how many layers of meaning we will ultimately discover to be hidden in Tarot's structure, but it seems reasonable that a Tarot created to be used to its fullest will be designed with respect for the known history of this tradition. It will show Hebrew letters on the Major Arcana, the matching letters from the Alphabet of the Magi, or the matching Greek letters in order to establish a base upon which to place the related astrology correspondences. It will give us enough clues in the art and titles to declare its "pedigree," the historical stream from which it is quoting, if there is one. The presence of signs and planets could be optional if the other details are arranged consciously.

If any authors depart from the historical Hebrew, Alexandrian or French esoteric correspondences (for example, into one of the "modern traditions" like that of Dali or the English Magikal Tarots, which is the most well known contemporary pattern), they would do us all a favor to publish a complete table somewhere in their support material to delineate exactly what set of correspondences they are following. It would be wonderful if Tarot creators felt more obligated to research and explain where their images and correspondences came from and/or the idea motivating their emergence. There is nothing dishonorable or demeaning in saying "I am doing this on my own authority. I made these images and correspondences up myself." We who care about these simply want to know what the correspondences are so we know what we are working with when we pick up a deck.

It seems inevitable that there will be more true and authentic "ancient lineage" material yet to appear in the future as scholars sort out and date the various cultural strata included in the Tarot, even as it first appeared in the 1450s. Now that we can more clearly differentiate the truly ancient Hebrew and Hermetic/Alexandrian Mysteries of the handmade and woodblock Gnostic Tarots, the Renaissance Christian Cabbalist Mysteries of the Continental school, and the "modern Magikal Mysteries" of the English school, we can make even fuller use of the treasure trove of esoteric lore left us by our illuminated ancestors, both ancient and modern.

The Minor Arcana should also show forthrightly their correspondences to signs, planets, or zodiacal degrees. If they are including the traditional Hebrew angels which rule the zodiac six to a sign, (72 in all), or any other esoteric symbol sets, it is a kindness to make it clear how these values are distributed among the cards. Please do not assume that everyone already knows this stuff; they don't! Plus, it is so much easier to work with a Tarot whose authors respect the built-in symmetry between the Major Arcana and the Minors, being conscious of the traditional Mysteries of the Decave when constructing their numbered suit cards (see the chapter on The Minor Arcana).

3) Esoteric Tarots attempt to universalize rather than particularize. Beyond being founded upon or linked to either one of the three very closely related ancient lineages (which hopefully will be explicitly represented on the faces of the cards), or one of the "modern traditions" which have become elaborated for the twentieth century, esoteric Tarots are designed to be a scientific tool for examining energies, situations and psyches. They report without judgment. Like a microscope or a set of measuring devices, Tarot is impartial. It works best when it does not inflame the emotions overmuch or induce such flights of fancy that one cannot deduce practical instructions from its use. An excess of fanciful speculations can obscure the dynamics the card was created to reveal in its number/suit identity.

The images which have in this century become associated with the Alexandrian astro-alphanumeric correspondences make little use of elaborate art or brilliant color, avowedly because such embellishments influence us emotionally and affect our powers of judgment. The St. Germaine Tarot and the Brotherhood of Light Tarot both illustrate this principle admirably, as they are both emotionally neutral, although not lacking in information. Because they are esentially flash-cards, Tarot was made to hold layers of meaning condensed into cryptic symbols arranged in meaningful patterns. Those symbols have standard meanings which are geometric, astrological and alphabetical. They are not designed for "free association" but for calculation, like the equations that make sense of your tax statements or determine the placement of the beams that hold up your house. Their original meanings were not based on the "opinion" of any Tarot author, but were built upon the principles of numbers, elements and astrology.

For this reason, traditional esoteric Tarots do not usually show human images on the numbered suit cards. When the principle represented by a given card's place in the grid (see chapters on the Major and Minor Arcana) is illustrated with a sketch of humans in a given predicatment, the interpretive scope of that card is often diminished. This is not such a drawback in respect to the royalty cards because those cards were originally designed to carry the personalities of the related zodiacal signs. But the numbered suit cards are not people cards. They represent the play of forces and circumstances impacting human lives and the best strategies for not being swept away by them. They denote esoteric equations, not personalities.

In terms of the modern, fully illustrated Tarots, instead of being shown the formula that represents a certain natural law operating at a certain stage of the cycle in a distinct elemental realm, the Tarot user encounters a cartoon of people enacting specific behavior and undergoing a particular emotional experience. This overemphasizes the sense of self in the situation, narrowing the possibilities of meaning and interpretation for that card. The resulting reductionism has occurred gradually throughout the Major and Minor Arcana (over the centuries.)

Although a case can be made that Tarot needs to be allowed to change and evolve, each such departure takes a deck further and further from being an esoteric Tarot. I do not mean to say that fully illustrated Tarots are a bad development in the history of Tarot, only that they tend to obscure the underlying grid with editorializing. This is a human trait from which I am not free either, but it is out of harmony with traditional esoteric Tarot design principles.

A few Tarots manage to skirt this problem by imaging seasons, plants or animals, geometric figures, landscape features, special colors, signs or planets, or other mnemonic devices which keep these cards from seeming too simplistic. Excellent examples are the Ibis, Neutzheit, Masonic, and Knapp/Hall Tarots.

THE ESOTERIC ORIGINS OF TAROT:
More than *A Wicked Pack of Cards*
Lewis Keizer, Ph.D.

Foreword

Modern Tarot is not a card game. It is a form of divination. As such, modern Tarot does not originate in medieval Italian card games, although they eventually became mediums through which cartomantic divination was done. Modern Tarot has a much more ancient derivation in the phenomenology of religions, iconography, and in Western esoteric tradition.

Christine Payne-Towler has provided me with most of the motivation and much of the research for this essay. She could have written a much more comprehensive tome, as she is an expert on Tarot iconography and symbology. But she wanted a scholar to look over her materials and lend credence to the esoteric origins of Tarot. I am honored to comply.

The So-Called "Propaganda Campaign"

Decker, Depaulis, and Dummett make the following statement in Chapter One of *A Wicked Pack of Cards*:
"(The Tarot pack) . . . is the subject of the most successful propaganda campaign ever launched. . . . An entire false history, and false interpretation, of the Tarot pack was concocted by the occultists. . . ."

[The book *A Wicked Pack of Cards* is a carefully researched history of the *exoteric* history of Tarot. The authors have exhaustively explicated the *outer* events pertaining to Tarot but seem to lack all understanding of the world of the Secret Societies. Dr. Kiezer proceeds as if you, the reader, are aware of Tarot history.]

A statement such as this is as false as the misguided histories of Tarot presented by Gebelin, Etteilla, and the other founders of Tarot occultism in Western Europe. There was no conspiracy to misrepresent Tarot—only an attempt to understand and explain it. Eighteenth-century science was at the mercy of its own limitations, just as twentieth-century scholarship will later be recognized to be.

A Wicked Pack of Cards provides us with an excellently researched history of medieval and modern Tarot schools, but it does not attempt to understand and explain its significance. It understands Tarot as part of the history of European games, but it has no appreciation of the origin of modern Tarot in the history and phenomenology of the Western esoteric tradition, or as a sophisticated development of effective divination technique. *A Wicked Pack of Cards* provides a great deal of information, but the authors do not have a thorough enough background in the Western mystery tradition to properly interpret their information.

This article is intended to refocus academic discussion of Tarot to its significance and meaning within the context of real historical development in the Western esoteric tradition.

The Power of Tarot

When I was a young academic teaching Religious Studies at the University of California in Santa Cruz during the sixties and seventies, I was chagrined at the gullibility of students for naïve occultist theories about history, scripture, and emerging new-age fads like Tarot.

Like the authors of *A Wicked Pack of Cards*, I knew that modern Tarot decks were merely a development of medieval Italian *Tarocchi*. Tarot was not the secret *Urim* and *Thumim* of the Old Testament or the hieratic Egyptian Books of Hermes described by Clement of Alexandria. Yet not only young, impressionable students, but often even intelligent, educated adults *wanted* to believe that the Tarot was sanctified with hoary antiquity.

#10 Papa
The Tarocchi of Mantegna

As I began to have deeper experience and understanding of Eastern and Western esoteric tradition, however, I found myself using Tarot and other forms of divination to touch more deeply into my own interior life. I began to understand the spiritual phenomenology of dynamic psychism, magic, and theurgy. I found that even some of the most recent decks, like the *Alchemical Tarot*, were extremely helpful to me. The readings I did for myself and for others clarified the invisible currents and subtle influences associated with important decisions and life crises.

Many times the Tarot has warned me away from pathways that I later realized would have led to disaster, or it has given me confidence to pursue directions that have proven to be true to my purposes in life. At crucial times the Tarot has confronted me with hard advice that I could have never accepted from my closest friends. Again, it has cheered me with encouragement for which there seemed, at the time, no basis—and yet, it was true.

Can all this come from a pack of playing cards? Let us examine the historic esoteric influences associated with the iconography of the Tarot trumps.

The Popess

The earliest extant trump images date from the fourteenth century, and they include a female Pope. Today we know her as the High Priestess or Isis Veiled. The Popess was a remarkable image to use during an era when Knights Templar, Cathars, and other religious heretics were being tortured and burned in the Inquisition. We know that the Popess and other images fell afoul of the Catholic Church, which successfully suppressed *Tarocchi* for two centuries, while the game itself was often castigated by Protestant preachers. Why did the image of the Popess exist before the foutreenth century, and why was the Tarot suppressed after this period?

The issue raised by the Popess was theological dualism—the Albigensian heresy—which was the enemy that the Inquisition sought out either among the Cathars of Southern France, the Bogomils of Bulgaria, or other sects like the Patarenes. These were all survivals of a form of early Christian Gnosticism known as Manichaeism. The religion of the martyred saint Manes became anathema after St. Augustine of Hippo, a Manichaean of the fourth century, converted to Catholicism and became a founding theologian for Roman Catholic theology.

The teachings of the "dualist" sects allowed women to be clergy and to even hold office as a Pope. During the period of European history from which the image of the Popess survives, the Bogomils were loyal to their own mysterious Pope in Bulgaria, who may well have been a woman saint. Many of the heretical communities of the time relied upon prophetesses and female channels of Spirit to guide them, just as the early Montanists had done.

In the Visconti-Sforza *Tarocchi* deck we find a Popess dressed in the habit of the Umiliata Order of the Guglielmites whose female leader, a Bohemian Lombard, died in Milan in 1281. The image in the deck represents Popess Sister Manfreda, who was elected Pope by her sect. She was regarded as an avatar of the Holy Spirit sent to inaugurate the New Age of Spirit prophesied by Joachim of Flora. This Popess was burned at the stake in autumn of A.D. 1300, the year that the New Age ending male domination of religion was supposed to begin. Later the Inquisition started proceedings against Matteo Visconti for his slight involvement with the sect

In addition to the dualist heretical communities, there was a great proliferation of apocalyptic and new-age theology that had occurred with the advent of the millenial year A.D. 1000. Isolated scholars translated the Latin Bible, and especially the Book of Revelations, into their vernacular languages and read them as ciphers for their own age, which was one of ecclesiastical privilege and corruption. Their insights were privately promulgated, and secret societies formed to spread reform and revolutionary religious ideas.

From seminal movements like those of Joachim Flora, the German mystics in the line of Meister Eckhart, and the Brethren of the Free Spirit, there developed the greatest political ground-swell that was ever to threaten the Roman Catholic hierarchy—Protestantism. It now dominates much of Christianity, but is still theological heresy in Rome.

The early protesting or "protest-ant" sects were fiercely persecuted by Rome, which lumped them together with Albigensians, keepers of pre-Christian pagan religions, and the Jewish and Islamic infidels. All of these groups were theologically "dualist" in the perspective of Rome either because they recognized a feminine or Mother aspect of Godhead (Cathars, Jewish Kabbalists, Bogomils) or because they preserved a Gnostic cosmology and anthropology. The Christian dualists were especially targeted because their Christologies were based on the mystic *Imitatio Christi*, a discipleship aimed at ultimately becoming a Christ. It would have been more correct to call them "unarians,"

THE POPESS
LOMBARDY I TAROCCHI

because ultimately they viewed humanity as an emanation of God that contained a spark of diety and would eventually return to Godhead, rather than a mere creation of dust doomed ever to be subordinate and inferior.

The Cathars preserved the Merovingian ideal of the Wife of Jesus (Mary Magdelene) and his physical offspring through their concept of Holy Blood, against which the Carolingian revolution had presented the ideal of the Mass and Eucharist as the Holy Blood of Christ. The Eucharistic Sacrament was the priestly means through which the Church maintained authority over the laity. If personal mysticism and spiritualized allegories were to triumph over physical sacraments, the Church would lose its power. That is why later Protestantism renounced Priesthood and sacraments as "Popish" tools of Satan. But the ideal was originally that of the Gnostic heresies, who viewed human love as the Divine Sacrament *par excellence* and maintained the symbolism of a male and female Christ.

Under circumstances of political suppression and threat of the Inquisition, the wave of revolutionary spirituality that swept over Eastern and Western Europe in the tenth to fifteenth centuries was transmitted in heretical ballads sung by Bogomil troubadors and in other forms of art, imagery, and iconography. Very clearly, part of this trend is preserved in the iconography of the early *Tarocchi* trumps. The most evident aspect of this iconography is the Female Pope.

Tarot innovator Edgar Waite was the first modern scholar to propose that the trumps were originally a series of images to convey the philosophy of the Albegensians. It is ironic that Waite should make this observation, since he radically altered the images of the Tarot trumps, adhering to the sweeping changes made by the English occultists of the Golden Dawn to the traditional European images. Waite's altered Tarot images are those most familiar to lay persons, and yet they are many steps removed from the original iconography. Perhaps the best example of the original iconography to survive the Inquisition is the Marseilles deck, which synthesizes alchemical and other imagery with an Egyptian theme that I'll later address.

An excellent discussion of the influence of heretical religion on the original Tarot trump images is included in a book by Robert V. O'Neill entitled, *Tarot Symbolism* (Fairway Press, Ohio; ISBN 0-89536-936-2). His chapter on "Heretical Sects and Their Influence on the Tarot" is carefully researched and deserves a wide reading.

Tarocchi Iconography and Hermetic Philosophy

Tarot was far more than entertainment during the period from the 1300's to the 1500's when the game was suppressed. It appears among the luminaries of the Church as a means for contemplation and deep discussion. *Tarocchi* cards with trump images corresponding to Hermetic philosophical and cosmological ideals were used by Pope Pius II and Cardinals Bessarion and Cusa in the mid-fifteenth century during a church council in Mantua. The images of Mantegna's *Tarocchi* include Iliakos, representing the First Iliaster of Paracelsis and other metaphysicians, the Seven Planets, and other elements of the Hermetic-Platonic Hierarchy of Being. Nicholas of Cusa later wrote concerning a similar card game he had devised:

"This game is played, not in a childish way, but as the Holy Wisdom played it for God at the beginning of the world."1

The impact of Hermetic philosophy and iconography on the Church of the Counter-Reformation was considerable. There was a time when many of the intellectuals of Europe hoped that Hermetic philosophy would be the means through which Catholic theology could be reformed to meet the challenge of Protestantism, science, and secular thought. There is still a sealed room in the Vatican belonging to the Borgia Pope that is painted with images of Hermes Trismegistus and other occult symbology. Statues and printed images of Hermes Trismegistus, Pythagoras, and other legendary adepts proliferated. Hermetic thought struggled with church theology within the Vatican itself, but was overcome by the forces of conservatism by the middle of the seventeenth century, never to surface again.

However, during the oppression of heretical sects and the evolution of the Reformation, new venues for esoteric and occult thought developed within Protestantism and Catholicism. The Knights Templar had been driven underground, but the Priory of Sion lived on as an elite Catholic secret esoteric society with Grand Masters like Botticelli and

Da Vinci, whose art preserves the Hermetic cosmology and ideals. The Rosicrucian and Freemasonic movements of Protestant mysticism produced an esoteric Renaissance based on Hermetic thought and its synthesis with astrology, alchemy, magick, and a Christian version of Jewish Kabbalah that used not only Hebrew, but Greek and Latin alphabets. All this, in turn, was integrated with Greek philosophy and Pythagorean theory.

The scholar Frances Yeats' book, *Giordano Bruno and the Hermetic Tradition* demonstrates the importance of iconography, philosophy, and Hermetic idealism during the period crucial to the development of the Tarot imagery. Alchemists and other practitioners of the esoteric arts transmitted their most profound teachings, such as the evolution of the *Sophic Hydrolith* or Philosopher's Stone, by means of iconographical allegories. It would be naïve to think that Tarot images were devoid of such interpretation in the fourteenth to sixteenth centuries, even though they were suppressed.

*QUEEN OF CUPS
EL GRAN TAROT ESOTERICO*

During the eighteenth century, when the Inquisition was losing its grip on most of Europe, and both Europe and the New World were rushing toward violent democratic revolution, Tarot again surfaced, not merely as an Italian card game, but as a means of divination. It became a focus of interest for occultists who, like French and English Freemasons, wished to sanctify their alternative spirituality with the authority of hoary antiquity.

Divination, Cartomancy, and the "Egyptian" Gypsies

The earliest historical record we have of playing cards being used for divination is found in a memoire of the year 1765 by Casanova about the beautiful young Russian peasant girl named Zaire. She arranged twenty-five playing cards into a magical square and was able to read in them all the details of his amorous adventures of the previous evening.

On the basis of this account, the authors of *A Wicked Pack of Cards* speculate that cartomancy began with Russian peasants in the eighteenth-century. But to assign an origination date to an oral folk tradition, especially when it concerns magic, divination, or herbs and medicines, based upon the date of its first mention in European literature, is unrealistic and quite ignorant of the historical dynamics of oral tradition.

Where did Zaire get her knowledge of cartomancy? Not

from books, and certainly not from the French nobility, who in the eighteenth century had just began to discover occultism, divination, and spiritualism and relate it to their previous flirtations with Hermetic science. No, Zaire's knowledge came from an oral folk transmission totally independent of literacy and with a much greater antiquity than the literary products of Guttenberg's revolution. The source of Zaire's knowledge was ultimately *Gypsy folk tradition*.

The Gypsies were a unique nomadic nation that left India and wandered to Europe by way of Eastern Europe and Bohemia. They were erroneously considered by Europeans, including Russians, to be a survival of the ancient Egyptian people. They were also known as "Bohemians" because their annual traveling routes brought them into Europe by way of Bohemia, the Motherland of many European esoteric traditions.

Gypsies had their own kings and queens, their own initiatic traditions, and they were experts in forms of entertainment, animal training, and divination for wealthy clients. Methods of divination included "reading" various elements like tea leaves and scrying crystal globes, clouds, sand formations in stream beds, or reflections of the full moon on water. They read palms, used other physiognomic techniques, and they developed various psychic arts that were attributed to Rosicrucians, alchemists, and other occultists of Prague and Bohemia.

No. II POPESS
SPANISH MARSEILLES

As interest in the Gypsy ("Egyptian") arts developed into European spiritualist fads of the eighteen century, as the Hermetic ("Egyptian") philosophy spread through publications of the *Corpus Hermeticum* and various alchemical and magical texts purchased by the nobility, and with the popularization of hieratic Egyptian artifacts like the *Mensa Isiaca* (Tablets of Isis) published by Kircher, all divinatory and esoteric knowledge was attributed to ancient Egypt. Everything from Freemasonry to Mesmerism claimed its roots in the hoary antiquities of Egypt. Gebelin, Etteilla, and the other eighteenth-century European popularizers of cartomancy attributed the Tarot to the ancient Egyptian Books of Thoth, and the trump images to symbolic frescoes on the walls of Egyptian temples used as part of instruction given during priestly initiation.

The iconography of Egyptian Serapian temples were familiar to Italians. The temples had been built in Italy and Asia Minor during the Roman-Hellenistic period, when Greek Revival of Egyptian Isis religion was popular throughout the Empire. A Serapian temple had been excavated as early as the tenth century, and Italians often traveled to see it and speculate upon the meaning of its frescoes and hiero-

glyphics. During the Italian Renaissance, classical culture was studied and idealized. It is quite possible that *Tarocchi* images were understood as allegories from the very beginning, since the game itself was a kind of medieval Game of Life with reference to archetypal human conditions. Since the Serapian temples were places of initiation into Isis cult, it is also reasonable to assume that their iconography related to initiatic journey through life. To this extent, it is not impossible that Tarot images, which had a similar purpose in *Tarocchi*, had some root in Egyptian temple iconography.

But cartomancy, or divination with playing cards, was not an Egyptian invention. There may have been other systems of divination parallel to the throwing of yarrow sticks for the *I Ching* in the ancient or Roman-Hellenistic world of Egypt, but there is no evidence of anything similar to playing cards. Fortune-telling with playing cards, or cartomancy, was popularized by the Gypsies in medieval Europe after the invention and publication of playing cards. Because the authorities and teachers of cartomancy were Gypsies, divination with Tarot cards was assumed to be "Egyptian."

The Sanskrit-related language of the Gypsies was called Romany, erroneously related to Roumanian. The Gypsies were considered to be spiritually allied to the heretical and protesting religions of Europe, especially the Bulgarian, Roumanian, and Bohemian villagers whose folk religion preserved Manichaean and Gnostic elements, and whose preoccupations in the eighteenth century included astrology, alchemy, and esoteric speculative Freemasonry. These included the descendants of the Bogomiles, Cathars, and Albigensians, who had become the objects of persecution and attempted genocide by partisans of the Roman Catholic Church, and whose cultures had produced the wandering Troubadors, who sang mystical, heretical songs to the Magdalene and told stories of the Holy Grail.

As a bridge to Eastern mysticism, European heretics had nurtured the European consciousness that would produce the institutions of Chivalry and Courtly Love. In the heyday of the Hermetic Renaissance and amidst the social upheaval of the Protestant Reformation, the mysterious Gypsies emigrated to Europe and wandered in large bands. They brought the ways of Indian mysticism and divination with them, and when they arrived in fifteenth-century Western Europe, the romance of the vanquished European heretical cultures was associated with them. They were welcomed for the entertainment they brought, feared and avoided because of the ferocity of their fighting men and women, and often expelled or forced to move on.

They were closely attuned to the animals they brought with them, developing skills in animal communication and training. They traveled in annual migration routes throughout Europe and the Slavic regions, moving South for the winters and North for the summers, providing carnivals or trained animal shows and various kinds of "fortune telling" for a fee. They stayed clear of the regions where the medieval Inquisition held sway, but were often accused of witchcraft.

By the eighteenth century the Inquisition was on the

wane. Gypsy lore was much in demand by both the nobles and middle class of Europe. The Gypsies were happy to oblige credulous Europeans with stories of their ancient origins in Egypt. In fact, they called their homeland "Little Egypt."

The Albigensian Paper Making Connection

Paper making was brought to Europe from the East by Templars and other Crusaders returning from the Holy Land or by Moors in Spain. The earliest paper making centers in Europe were in the South of France and in Lombardy and Tuscany—the areas occupied and controlled by the Albigensians or Cathari. After the massacre of the Cathari at Montsegur in 1244 by operatives of the Pope—perhaps the greatest act of genocide known to history previous to the slaughters of Armenian Christians by the Moslems in the twentieth century and Hitler's Jewish Holocaust in World War II—about four thousand survivors wandered Europe like the Gypsies as troubadors, pedlars, merchants, and journeymen paper makers. The persecuted Albigensian paper makers used a secret, symbolic watermark on their "Lombardy paper" by which means they communicated and kept track of each other in different areas.

Interesting evidence of the esoteric relationship between Gypsies, hidden Albigensians, hidden Knights Templar, and the operative Masons are indicated in manuscripts on guild practices created in the Rosslyn Chapel Manuscript Manufactory of the fifteenth century, which is now in the Scottish National Museum and exhibited in facsimile at Rosslyn Chapel which, as scholars are now finding, memorializes Gypsy, Rosicrucian, Templar, Freemasonic, and other hidden esoteric institutions of the period—all of whom were in contact. The St. Claire royalty of Rosslyn were both protectors of the Gypsies and Grand Masters of the operative Masons!

Given these facts, it is quite reasonable to assume that the first manufacture of tarocchi cards was done by partisans of the persecuted Albegensian tradition who maintained close relations with the Gypsies of India, the exiled Knights Templar, and the Scottish Masonic groups out of which Scottish Rite and other "speculative" forms of Freemasonic cult were emerging. This in itself points strongly to an esoteric origin for the Tarot images from the very beginning of their appearance as playing cards manufactured by guilds of Cathari paper makers who lived in hiding.

Divination and Other Spiritual Antiquities of the Gypsies

Gypsy tradition was Indian, but the traditions associated with the Gypsies in the European mind were directly derivative from Roman-Hellenistic Gnostic and Manichaean spirituality, which the Cathars were still practicing in the thirteenth century. The Roman Catholic polemic against magic and divination that had been successfully and brutally waged against the Greek mystery religions and the Neo-Platonic philosophical schools like that of Hypatia never influenced the Gnostic-Christian religious culture of southern France and Bulgaria. There many of the ancient divinatory practices of Greece, Asia Minor, Egypt, and the Hellenized world were not only tolerated, but developed and well integrated into daily religious practice.

We must acknowledge that Murray's theories about the Old Religion of the Witches and its survival in the folk practices of rural Europe have been shown to be unrealistic. Modern Wicca, like modern Tarot, is a recent production with yearnings to an ancient occult history. The European romances about Egyptian Freemasonry, Christian Rosencreuz and the ancient Rosicrucian Brotherhood, or the Theosophical Masters of Tibet were also, in great part, the creations of spiritual imagination. They tell us more about the spirit of their own times than about sacred antiquities.

However, in the case of the Western esoteric tradition and its interaction with Gypsy lore, *we do find strong evidence of historical continuity with ancient pagan and mystery traditions*. Gypsy traditions were strongly Indo-Iranian, thus extremely compatible with Manichaean and Gnostic culture. In their oral traditions concerning magic, spells, herbs, plants, stones, psychism, and divination, Gypsy communities preserved Eastern folk-magical and divinatory traditions that were essentially and qualitatively different from those preserved in Western Christian monasticism.

"There is general agreement among occult authorities that the use of the Tarot was popularized by the wandering bands of Bohemians—gypsies—who made their appearance in the late Middle Ages." (Doctoral dissertation of Thomas Williams for the University of Alabama, quoted in *A Wicked Pack of Cards*, Chapter One). Not only "occult authorities," but most scholars would agree that cartomancy and Tarot-card divination were introduced to Europeans by Gypsies.

In late antiquity, the Bohemians transferred and adapted their traditional forms of divination to the newly emerging form made possible by the invention of the printing press—the deck of cards. These more ancient forms of divination were compatible with a deck of cards because:

• they relied upon a complex set of symbols not unlike Chinese trigrams, Roman dice, Druidic runes, that could be

interpreted allegorically

• they operated by means of randomizing these elements through throwing or casting, as with lots, dice, or yarrow stalks

No. XVIII Moon
The Spanish
Marseilles

• they had numerological associations that could be used to amplify interpretation

The symbols of the Gypsies would have been pictographic, although they could have developed into more glyphic representations as did later demotic Egyptian or the Chinese trigrams of the *I Ching*. They would have been etched, drawn, or painted onto randomizable elements that could be cast or thrown, like runes or dice. The numerical system they used would have been similar to Pythagorean decimal number lore, as it was derived by Pythagoras from Indian Brahmin lore.

Since we can see that the original Tarot trumps were based, for the most part, upon Italian social images arranged in allegorical postures, and that only later were images altered to appear Egyptian or pre-Christian, it is easy to conclude that modern Tarot trump images have no relation to images or allegories that would have been used by the Indo-Iranian Gypsies. However, there are certain original trumps that simply do not have a basis in medieval Christian society, such as the Popess or female Pope (becomes the High Priestess). Moreover, this image certainly does have a basis in both Indian and Albigensian religion as the Gnostic Sophia, the Magdelen, the female Christ, and the Virgin Goddess. To what extent did the cartomancy of the Gypsies influence even the earliest Tarocchi trumps? Perhaps more than we can know. According to some authorities, the Gypsy migrations began as early as the ninth century and peaked in the fifteenth century.

Although Gypsies must have made many innovations when they began to adapt European playing cards for fortune telling, it is also clear that they were able to find attributions for suits and trumps that were recognizable and correspondent to their own traditions of divination. Thus the fact that the images of the Tarocchi trumps survive in various permutations into modern Tarot decks indicates that they were congruent with Gypsy folklore that served as the basis for divination.

Iamblichan Tarot Tradition in the French Occult Revival of the Eighteenth Century

The occultist Court de Gebelin theorized in 1781 that the Tarot trump images originated in the initiatic halls of Egyptian temples. His ideas were popularized by Alliette, later known as Etteilla. But these men were not the originators of such speculation. It was already common undertanding in French occult circles, which were essentially Freemasonic.

In the year 1798 there were six to seven hundred Masonic lodges in France containing perhaps 30,000 of the most educated citizens. Unlike modern American Freemasonry, which after WWII became mostly blue collar workers and lost much of its great intellectual patronage, the French lodges were (and still are) subscribed to by university professors and other intellectuals.

Lodges were split between those chartered by nobility and under a Grand Master for life appointed by nobility, and the new democratic form in which Masters were elected for a term. The first form was traditional, and its premise was that the Grand Master was a true adept with all the knowledge and powers of a master. Unfortunately, princes and dukes often chartered unqualified Grand Masters, and the democratic movement in Freemasonry was causing lodges to split into factions. This same movement was attuned to the emerging American colonial revolution and closely tied to its founders. Ben Franklin, for example, was the elected Grand Master of a Lodge in Paris as well as in Philadelphia.

An extreme wing of the democratic Masons were the Fratres Lucis, Brothers of Light. Under the leadership of university free-thinkers, they were active architects of the French Revolution. They used forms of initiation that could result in death, based on their ideas of ancient Egyptian priestly initiation. A document probably translated by the nineteenth century occultist Jean-Baptiste Pitois (Christian) and published recently in English by Weiser entitled, *Egyptian Mysteries*, is an example of Illuminist initiatio practice in the guidance of Egyptian lore. During one part of the ordeal, in which the candidate must work his way through a dark labyrinth, he finds himself in a lighted chamber with a bed, food, and a beautiful unclad woman. He has vowed not to tarry, but if he does make the wrong choice, he is immediately set upon and killed.

At this point in the eighteenth century the Lovers trump of the Tarot is reinterpreted according to the "Egyptian" initiatic ordeal, and we see a man with two women—one on his right who is chaste, and one on his left who is a coquette. Over his head is an angel aiming an arrow at him, to slay him if he makes the wrong moral choice. (I would have been dead in this situation!)

Allegorically, this represents the right-hand and left-hand paths, the Way of Life and the Way of Death of the Old Testament, the good and evil *yetzerim* of Kabbalah, or the Pythagorean Motion to the Left versus the Motion to the Right of Plato's *Timaeus* and the *Kore Kosmou* of Hermetic-Gnostic tradition. But among the Fratres Lucis, it represented something quite immediate and final. It is not known how many candidates met their doom in this form of Masonic initiation, but given the proclivities of Frenchmen, I am not optimistic.

Egyptian lodges were established also by Cagliostro who, according to legend, was initiated by the Grand Master, the Compte de St. Germain, in a Templar ceremony using hundreds of candles. Cagliostro introduced the Egyptian Rites, which paved the way for the later Rites of Memphis and of Mizraim, which competed with the Scottish Rite in nineteenth century America until it was finally banned or abondoned in different jurisdictions. There is now one chartered Lodge of Memphis-Mizraim in New York City that, like all of the later Ultra-Masonic orders, admits both men and women.

The Egyptian paradigm was justified by a medieval document claiming to be part of the body of writings by the NeoPlatonist Iamblichus, whose *Manetho* is the memoires of an Egyptian priest. The Pseudo-Iamblichan document describes initiatic images used in the hall of neophytes that correspond closely to the Tarot trump images known in the eighteenth century.

This, of course, is the Holy Grail of esoteric Tarot advocates—evidence that the Tarot images derive from ancient and archetypal Egyptian temple images. Currently [written in 1998, all internet postings are now gone as of 6/99.] there are many postings of a document by Michael Poe describing an Italian archeological description of images from a Serapian temple in Italy now under water. The images correspond exactly to modern trumps, with Veiled Isis taking the position for the Popess or High Priestess, etc. I have been unable to contact Poe, so I contacted the Italian archeological museum in charge of the sunken Temple of Serapis at Pozzuoli and asked for any information, as this is the only Serapian temple in Italy I know that is under water. As of this writing, I have no response. But if Poe's information is correct, we would have an excellent possible source for the earliest Italian Tarocchi images, devoid of Egyptian dress.

Pseudo-Iamblichus was part of Egyptian Freemason occultism that also revived Pythagorean theory and numerical symbolism as part of their synthesis of Christian Cabbala, usually spelled with a "C" to differentiate it from true Jewish Kabbalah. This in turn was linked to alchemical, astrological, theurgical, and magical departments of the Hermetic arts in the French occult revival.

The Cabbalistic Attributions to the Tarot Trumps

During this period of intense occult innovation, the Tarot was legitimized among French practitioners as a valid ancient Egyptian divinatory tool. It is not surprising, then, that it is in this period we find Hebrew and magical alphabet attributions made to the trumps. But the Hebrew alphabet, with its twenty-two letters, became the most important system of attributions.

The letters represented the twenty-two Paths connecting the ten Sephiroth. These Paths, then, were associated with each trump image. Some of the Paths were in the Lightning Flash series leading from Malkuth back to Kether, so

they were considered to be specifically associated with stages of initiation, while the others represented powers gained and obstacles surmounted at each of these stages.

The authority for the Paths was the Jewish *Sefir Yetzirah*, the Book of Creation. However, it existed in several redactions and versions, each differing on details. The oldest was the Gra version, but it may not have been accessible to French occultists, who depended upon Latin and French translations. However, the French occultists did have access to the Alexandrian/Hermetic attributions—those of the Renaissance magi and the *Fratres Lucis* document. With these, they were able to associate the correct Hebrew letter with the Cabbalistic Path number and image in the twenty-two card series.

These attribution were added to the Tarot trumps in eighteenth-century France and spread to Italian, Spanish, and other Continental decks by the nineteenth century. They were part of the general Freemasonic and Ultra-Masonic lodge occultism of all Europe.

ACE OF CUPS
THE SPANISH MARSEILLES TAROT

Tarot and Cabbala: Levi's Attributions

In his book, *Eliphas Levi and the French Occult Revival*, Christopher MacIntosh says, "Clearly Levi was in possession of no pre-Court de Gebelin material connecting the Cabala (sic. Ut.) and the Tarot. The connection was his invention."

This is the kind of fiction about Levi that English occultists have promulgated since the days of the Golden Dawn. English Freemasons declared French Freemasonry invalid in the late nineteenth century when the Grand Orient decided to expand their definition of theism to include Buddhist, scientific, and other non-Judeo-Christian concepts of Godhead or Utimate Reality. The bad blood between English and French occultism that divided Gnosticism into English and French ecclesiae, Martinism into English Masonic and French ultra- or non-Masonic schools, and resulted in the contemporary French requirement that anyone who joins a Golden Dawn lodge be demitted from French Masonic lodges, has been clearly evident in English attitudes toward one of the greatest French occultists—Eliphas Levi.

In his *Conspiracy Against the Catholic Religion and Sovereigns*, Levi said, "The true initiates who were Etteilla's contemporaries, the Rosicrucians for example and the Martinists, were in possession of the true Tarot, as a work of Saint-Martin proves, where the divisions are those of the Tarot."2

Saint-Martin had been a member of the occult lodge established by the adept Martinez de Pasqually in the mid-eighteenth century. He wrote his book divided according to the Tarot trumps before Levi's era. Later brilliant Martinists like Papus and Oswald Wirth would reaffirm Levi's assertion that the Tarot was the secret book of the eighteenth century Rosicrucians which existed as, "their criterion, in which they find the prototype of everything that exists by the facility which it offers for analysing, making abstractions, forming a species of intellectual world, and creating all possible things."3

Levi elaborated on what French occultists had already created perhaps a century before, and what was to become standard in all European Tarot decks of the nineteenth century—the correct attribution of Hebrew Path letters to the Tarot trumps. In this system, the Fool was attributed to Shin and the Magician was attributed to Aleph. The Hebrew letters were associated with their meanings as numerals in the Greek alphabet version..

Just as Etteilla had popularized Tarot for fortune telling based on Gypsy lore, Levi popularized what must have been secret lodge teaching in which the Tarot cards were used as tools of philosophical divination, probably in assumed likeness to the Book T of the seventeenth-century Rosicrucian *Fama*.

English Versus French Esoteric Freemasonry: The Golden Dawn

The founders of the Golden Dawn fabricated German Rosicrucian adepts who had supposedly transmitted profound esoteric and initiatic knowledge to them and given a charter to teach and initiate others. In fact, however, most of what Mather and Westcott had actually received came from a French source—not German adepts—through Kenneth MacKenzie, who received it directly from Eliphas Levi. Few scholars would seriously challenge this assertion.

Mathers was a brilliant creator and synthesizer who spend untold hours at the British Museum reading magical and Kabbalistic texts. He and Westcott, like all English occultists, were Freemasons. The synthesis they created for the Golden Dawn rituals combined Rosicrucian and Christian Cabbalistic doctrine with the kind of layout used on a Masonic floor. The floor and officers represented Sephiroth, and initiation from 0=0 to 5=6 represented the upward ascent from Malkuth to Tiphareth.

The initiatic instruction given to each Candidate on the Path from one Sephira to the next higher was allegorized on the Tarot trump associated with the Path number in the Hebrew alphabet. Mathers found that having the Fool in the position of Shin didn't work for his Masonic floor plan, so he decided to retain its number of Zero, but associate it with Aleph.

To justify this, he and later English occultists claimed one of two things: Levi had given a "blind," or purposely given a wrong Cabbalistic attribution to test people and make it possible only for adepts to discover the true attributions; or, Levi invented his own attributions and was wrong. After all, he was French, not English. How could he

be right? Such were the later claims of dark luminaries like Crowley and even the American Paul Foster Case.

As a result, the Waite deck and all other English decks from that time forward have used the Golden Dawn system of Cabbalistic letter attribution to the Tarot trumps, in spite of the fact that it is blatantly inaccurate. The practice continues because very few modern occultists know how to apply true Kabbalistic principles to Tarot interpretation. Only the European decks like those of Tavaglione use the correct trump attributions, and even Tavaglione presents the Golden Dawn Path attributions rather than those of the Gra.

The Tarot has a distinguished history in European esoteric tradition. It is not merely a card game that was adapted for fortune telling by Gypsies, and then sanctified with occultist illusions. It is a valid and powerful tool for divination that has roots in much older occult systems.

Author's Information and Footnotes

Dr. Lewis Keizer was one of the original scholars of the religious studies faculty at the University of California in Santa Cruz in the late sixties specializing in Biblical studies, Roman-Hellenistic religion, and the Nag Hammadi Coptic Gnostic Library. He received his M.Div. from the Episcopal Divinity School and a Ph.D. from the Graduate Theological Union in Berkeley. His doctoral dissertation, *The Eighth Reveals the Ninth: A New Hermetic Initiation Disclosure*, has become a standard work in Hermetic studies.

He and wife his Willa are presiding bishops of the Home Temple Priesthood and can be contacted through **http://hometemple.org**, where a list of his self-published writings and monographs is available. Keizer is also grailmaster of the Temple of the Holy Grail, which can be contacted at **http://hometemple.org/THG.htm**. Currently he is co-authoring an esoteric novel with Dr. Eugene Whitworth, author of *The Nine Faces of Christ*, and serves as academic dean for Great Western University in San Francisco, which specializes in distance-learning B.A. degree completion and graduate degrees with emphasis upon metaphysical subjects and the Western Mystery Tradition.

Lewis has written and taught widely in Western and European initiatic traditions, and he introduced male-female Freemasonry and other French initiatic societies to the U.S. Founder of the Popper-Keizer schools and Keizer Academy for gifted students (**http://hometemple.org/ACADEMY.HTM**), he also conducts orchestras and performs as an all-star jazz cornetist at international festivals. He is listed in *Who's Who in the World*, *Who's Who in Religion*, *Who's Who Among America's Teachers*, and many other standard reference biographies.]

1 Seznec, Jean, *The Survival of the Pagan Gods: The Mythological Tradition and Its Place in Renaissance Humanism and Art*, translated from the French by Barbara F. Sessions (Harper/Bollingen; NY 1986)
2 Quoted in MacIntosh, p. 148
3 Ibid.

PART II
ARCANA MAJOR AND MINOR

EMBLEM XLII, FROM ATALANTA FUGIENS BY MICHAEL MAIER, 1617

(THIS IS THE HERMIT FOLLOWING THE WORLD SOUL THROUGH THE LANDSCAPE OF THE MOON.)

A PREFACE TO THE MAJOR ARCANA

As has happened so many times over the years, a friend asked me in the course of putting together this book, "Isn't this all too encyclopedic for the average user to care about?"

Well, yes, such a project can seem near-impossible on the face of it. The detail is ponderous. In most books, authors are forced to concentrate upon one deck or at most, one family of related decks just to keep the material within one volume. They must of necessity not include scores of decks that are interesting in their own right but do not fit the pattern being presented in that work. By taking an historical perspective we have much more room to integrate the broad sweep of historical Tarot.

Another daunting factor for the modern researcher consulting the Tarot "experts" of the early twentieth century has been the chorus of official voices saying "Tarot has no real history. Don't even bother to look up previous generation's masters. The decks were all pretty generic before Eliphas Levi decided to make up correspondences between the Major Arcana and the Hebrew alphabet." Evidence proves that nothing could be further from the truth, but because it is scattered across multiple disciplines, requiring much cross-checking, it has seemed easier just to trust the "experts." Those turn of the century savants put up such a wall of denial about the origins of the Tarot that it has taken nearly a century to get over it.

In 1978, Stuart Kaplan published his first *Encyclopedia of Tarot*, and anyone who did not travel or read outside the English language could finally have access to the Continental Tarots. By far the most available Tarots in America have remained the English family of decks right up to the present, but Mr. Kaplan staunchly keeps many Tarots available from all branches of the tradition in his U. S. Games Systems catalog. It is entirely due to his single-handed commitment to providing a wide selection of decks for the American market that a person like myself can undertake a project like this one. Eternal gratitude goes out to him.

Because of these two situations—the lack of European Tarot decks circulating in the English-speaking world and the stonewalling by the "experts" of the early twentieth century—there have been numerous fads and styles of Tarot recently emerging that have little or no grounding in Tarot history. Most of these come from sources honest enough to admit that they are reinterpreting tradition, or departing from it entirely, without making inflated claims about the "authenticity" of their versions. However, some Tarot creators have played fast and loose with history to add cachet to their decks (and books about them). This phenomenon frustrates the sincere student who wants to understand the origins of Tarot. Various partisan groups, each with their hallowed interpreters, disavow other interpreters within the ebb and flow of countless variations. Who can decide where to start unraveling the threads?

We can start by making a historical scan of the Arcana. In this book, we have made available a representative range of European historical Tarot decks, with relevant commentary and divinitory support, so both the new and ongoing student of Tarot would have the fundamentals close at hand. The present revival of Tarot deserves to be supported with creditable information drawn from the faces of the cards themselves.

To do this I have had to take interpretive risks that an encyclopedist should not allow herself to make. However, I have not departed from material that is on the faces of the cards and in the public domain for all to see. With this approach I hope to level the playing field beneath the feet of the modern competing versions and schools of Tarot. I realize that this will result in a much greater emphasis upon the European Tarot decks than on the modern English-style decks that Americans and the British are so fond of. This presentation is about the history of Tarot, and we hope it will assist modern Tarot students to have a larger frame of reference to refer to, as they compare and contrast the esoteric frameworks inherant in their Tarot decks.

Lest we forget for a minute the value of these images and their related teachings, let's review the context in which Tarot was being explored in the centuries of its crystallization. It rested upon, and contained images from, a rich seedbed of ideas and images retained from the mixing of classical and pagan societies of Europe, Africa, the Near and Far East. Astrology, sacred geometry and Kabbalah were already very old by this time and fully exposed to each other. The symbolic grid that related the cosmos to humanity, and both to the world of Nature, had been taught in the sacred universities from their founding by Alexander the Great until the beginning of the Renaissance.

Petrarch's famous fourteenth century poem *I Triumphi* names six of the Arcana as stages of the mythological travails of Petrarch and Laura, his idealized and unconsummated love. Gertrude Moakley, in her study of the decks from the Bembo family workshop (a popular and prosperous artistic cooperative of the 1400s), thinks this poem served as inspiration for the Tarot, as it certainly did for the yearly Mardi Gras-like costume parades in which Italian nobles of the early 1400s played out the themes of the *Triumphi*. But we know from the history of art in Europe that the images of the *Triumphi* were in the public domain for centuries already, many integrated into official Church teachings because of their shared origins in Greek and Roman culture.

Coincidentally or not, the Visconti Tarots began emerging in 1440, with the Mantegna archetypes following right along in 1465. As Kaplan makes apparent in his *Encyclopedia,* there seems to have been a conversation going on between the creators of these two original streams of Arcana, because certain images from one echo the other so closely. There also exists a codex in the Vatican from 1471 with twenty-two Major Arcana (Visconti-style) that are obviously derivative of the Mantegna images in the art. These clues seem to indicate a high-level dialogue between both ordained and lay esotericists who were roughing out a consensus version of something they all knew in common, but possessed in differing versions.

I am inclined to think that the return of the Hermetic texts to Europe in the early Renaissance brought the prototypes of the Alexandrian Arcana to the Continental metaphysicians. The Renaissance artists then refashioned the ideas to look and feel European, muting the symbolism that demonstrated affiliation with the banned Secret Societies.. The result is the Marseilles stream of Tarot, which achieved its standard form after the Viville and Noblet Tarots were published in Paris in 1660.. Two more centuries passed before a complete text and images became available to "rectify" the traditional decks with the Alexandrian ideas again in the late 1800s. This is the conclusion reached by Oswald Wirth in his little booklet, *Introduction to the Study of Tarot,* and to judge by the character of the esoteric Tarot by Manly P. Hall and Augustus Knapp, one could not help coming to the same conclusion.

And don't let the fact that there were Tarot images in the Vatican lull you into thinking that students of the Arcana had a warm relationship with the external Church. This was the period when Rome finally managed to get astrology permanently banished from the ancient canon of the classical university curriculum in Europe. People were being imprisoned, tortured and sent to their deaths for being involved with groups who used these images. In particular, during the Cathar and Albigensian rebellions of the thirteenth century, the papermakers used heretical symbols (such as the intricate Grail cup shown as the Ace of Wands in the earliest decks) as their watermarks, risking persecution but unequivocally stating their politics. The Catalans of Spain used astrological symbols as trade logos in their businesses as well, and these same symbols show up on the very first Spanish Tarot decks (see Fournier's *Catalog of Playing Cards,* Volume 2, p. 9). Does it not seem natural then to think that teachings and beliefs repressed in one form might come up in another? Generations of souls lived and died for these images that you might have them to contemplate and meditate upon in this century. We do not want to be guilty of taking this hard won legacy from the philosophers of antiquity for granted!

This compilation of the Arcana has been arranged chronologically, so the reader can more easily visualize the unfoldment of the ideas inhabiting the Arcana in the minds of the Tarot illustrators and their teachers. Generally speaking, even though the Tarot had a roughly standard form from its appearance, each Arcanum (letter/title/number/sign or planet) was likely to have several different versions appear in the 1400s and 1500s. But by the 1600s, a standardizing force had appeared, which we explore in the chapters on the Major Arcana and the Continental Tarots. Another wave of creative proliferation happened between the late 1700s and the late 1800s, as overt esotericism replaced the veiled magical references of previous centuries. It is this progression which you will read about in the next chapter.

Over the years, even with my growing collection of decks and books, most notably Kaplan's *Encyclopedia,* I became increasingly convinced that there must be certain places I should look to get "insider information" that was not in the public domain. This is why I have included a chapter by my dear friend and ordaining Bishop, Dr. Lewis Keizer. He speaks as a scholar of the Mystery Schools, and as an initiated member of both the Martinists and the Order of the Golden Dawn. Dr. Keizer and I share a compelling interest in the cultivation of effective tools for operational magic and organized self-cultivation. Those who are similarly inclined will want to further investigate the means by which the cards leave prediction behind and enter into the domain of self-cultivation. This approach leads directly back to the mindset originally shaping the cards at their inception in Europe, widening the significance of Tarot to address the perennial quest for redemption, healing and transcendence.

My greatest frustration is that we cannot show each version of each card mentioned in the text. This is a case in which a picture is truly worth a thousand words. Because if this, you will enjoy this essay to the fullest if you have access to Stuart Kaplan's *Encyclopedia of Tarot,* Volumes 1 and 2, as nearly all the Tarot decks cited in this essay are illustrated there. A great resource for color and detail in the classical Tarots is the Tiny Folio™ called *The Art of Tarot* by Christina Olsen, published in 1995 by Abbeyville Press Publishers in New York.

With this I invite you to stroll through the chapter titled *The Major Arcana.*

THE MAJOR ARCANA

The Fool

This Arcanum has mutated profoundly throughout its history. Its original image was the Beggar, who appears sound of limb but vacant-minded, raggedly dressed, with feathers in his matted hair (Pierpont Morgan-Bergamo Visconti-Sforza tarocchi, mid-1400s). Stuart Kaplan (*Encyclopedia of Tarot*, Volume 2), in his essay on The Fool (pp. 158-9) explores the significance of the white shirt and pants, the droopy stockings and the feathers worn in his hair or on his belt, all associated with the spirit of Lent during the spring carnival in Renaissance Italy where Tarot was born.

The Mantegna Tarot of 1459 shows us Misery by portraying the lowest level of human life, an injured and exhausted beggar being attacked by a dog. Tarots from this same era used the image to editorialize about the causes of such misery: the Charles VI Tarot (1470) shows a Madman wearing a hat with bells and rabbit ears, tattered shirt and loincloth, teased by boys in the street, while Ercole d'Este (1475) shows him prey to lust, with the little boys pulling off his loincloth to reveal his insatiable arousal. Clearly, no respect was being accorded to anyone who embodied this archetype in the fifteenth century!

By the next century, this character harnessed his entertainment potential by becoming the more formal Jester with his trademark multicolored outfit and puppet-headed wand (anonymous Parisian deck, early 1600s). The village idiot image had not faded away, however (Mitelli, 1664).

The Marseilles image (1748) merges the entertainer with the idiot, giving us the multicolored costume and now-familiar walking away pose of the Fool, with a snapping dog pulling off his pants from behind. The Arcana of Court de Gebelin (1787) and Eteilla (late 1700s) repeats this image exactly. The Tarocco Siciliano cards of 1750 differentiate the Fool (No.0) from Miseria (unnumbered), including both for good measure.

A century later, Etteilla's Fool had mutated into the Alchemist, still dressed in his traditional jester garb but walking tentatively forward with his hands over his eyes. This concept is further revealed on the "Alexandrian" Blind Fool card, who stumbles his way between the shards of a fallen obelisk while a stalking crocodile lurks in the shadows.

All these versions of the Fool comprehensively depict a person who is ignorant, driven by the basest needs and urges, and who has fallen into the lowest human estate of poverty and deprivation. At best he is a carnival entertainer, a shyster; at worst he is lost and vulnerable because of his self delusion. Not until the twentieth century do you see the Waite image of the soul before its fall into matter, untainted by contact with the city and its ills. Modern decks take from this image the mountainside scene, the butterfly, the potential misplaced step that will send him tumbling, all on faith that this is a historical Fool image. In truth, the Fool was meant to represent already fallen humanity preparing to take the first step toward self knowledge, and eventually, The Gnosis.

No.0 The Fool
Ercole d'Este Tarot

No. 0 The Fool
Spanish Marseilles Tarot

Astro-alphanumeric Correspondences:
  "Gra" Hebrew: Fire (modern: Pluto), numbered 22
  Old Alexandrian: Sun, numbered 21
  Levi's Corrected Alexandrain: Fire, numbered 22
  Marseilles (Maxwell): Fire, unnumbered
  Modern Spanish (Dali): Scorpio, numbered 0
  Spanish Varient (Balbi):Scorpio, numbered 0
  English (Waite): Air (modern Uranus) numbered 0
  English Varient (Crowley): Uranus, numbered 0

The Magus

Earliest versions of the Magician can be seen in the Visconti-Sforza family of Tarots (mid-1400s). Named the Mountebank, he is seated on a cubic hassock, manipulating objects on the table before him. This image continues largely unchanged for centuries. Both hands are down close to the table, although the left hand holds a long, slender, upright wand.

No. 1 THE MAGUS
FROM DE GEBELIN

The d'Este Mountebank seems more active, leaning over his table, left hand reaching down, right hand raising his chalice (fifteenth century). Catelin Geoffrey's Tarot (1557) crowds the card with onlookers, and the Mountebank is clearly doing tricks with cups and dice, still with both hands down, again one holding a wand. In the Rosenwald images from the early sixteenth century, the interesting detail is the rabbit eared hat which we saw first in the 1470s on the Charles VI and d'Este Fool. Most Tarots of this century emphasize more or less the performance aspect of his workings by the presence or absence of an audience (anonymous Parisian Tarot, early seventeenth century, and later Piedmontese or Tarot of Venice, late seventeenth century). The anonymous Parisian Tarot shows a dog and a monkey at the feet of the Magus, another indication of his variety show.

The Juggler card by Mitelli (1664) assumes an entirely different aspect, the magician dancing with a dog and a drum. However, this version was not taken up in the common Tarots. The ubiquitous eighteenth century Marseilles deck brings us back to the traditional image, with the suit symbols on the table before the standing operator. Both the Marseilles and the contemporary de Geblin Arcana (1787) add the lemniscate hat, the "sideways 8" symbol of eternity crowning him. The Magus image from Etteilla (as in the Grande Oracle des Dames, 1890) continues the tradition of the prestidigitator working the crowd; he lacks the lemniscate and bears the dismal title Maladie.

In the earlier versions of this Arcanum a much stronger emphasis is placed upon the performance aspect of the Magician than in twentieth century Tarots. Although this card is named for the Magus, a person who could calculate astrology charts and shamanically enact magical rituals for special spiritual effects, by the debut of Tarots in Europe, this sense of the word "magician" was lost. The presence on the table of suit symbols, however, implies that

No. 1 THE MAGUS
WAITE TAROT

this person is adept at more than sleight of hand.

We are used to thinking of the Magus as one who can demonstrate true hands-on magic (as in healing, alchemical transmutation, charging of talismans and the like). The modern Magus is understood to be a person who can complete the circuit between heaven and earth. We sometimes forget that at the birth of Tarot, even a gifted healer who was not an ordained clergyperson was considered to be in league with the Devil. For protection's sake, the line between fooling the eye with hand jive and charging the world with magical will was left vague in the early Tarot imagery. Waite's image of the solitary ritualist communing with the spirits of the elements, with the formal arrangement of symbols and postures between left hand and right, is a token of the freedom we have in the 20th century to declare our spiritual politics without fear of reprisal. The older cards were never so explicit about what the Magus was doing. Keep your mind open with this card, and imagine yourself manifesting something unique, guided by evolutionary forces that emerge spontaneously from within.

Astro-alphanumeric Correspondences:
  "Gra" Hebrew:Air
  Old Alexandrian: Aor
  Levi's Corrected Alexandrain:Air
  Marseilles (Maxwell): Sun
  Modern Spanish (Dali): Sun
  Spanish Varient (Balbi): Sun
  English (Waite): Mercury
  English Varient (Crowley): Mercury

The High Priestess

Earliest versions of this image portray the Popess (Bembo's Visconti-Svorza, 1475) robed in gold, with triple tiara, holy book and bishop's staff. She lacks only the pectoral cross to complete her High Church costume. The various versions of the Mantegna proto-Tarot (1470) modify this image on the Pope card, but she remains unambiguously female. In the same pack, No. 40, Fede (Faith), shows a woman holding a cross on her left and elevating a chalice with the right over which a shimmering Host levitates. The Cary-Yale Visconti (1440-45) also includes an Arcanum called Faith, an enthroned woman with a large gold crucifix in her left hand, her right making the single-finger sign of the Monophosytes; an aging and shrunken Pope sits below the dais at her feet.

We can only gaze in awe at these images because at the time

No. 2 THE PRIESTESS
VISCONTE-SFORZA TAROT

No. 2 The Priestess as Eve
El Gran Tarot Esoterico

they were in circulation, the Catholic Church was waging holy war against the Gnostic sects who promulgated these pictures and allowed women to seek ordination to administer the sacrament. The idea of a female pope or priest was a heresy of high degree. The mere ownership of such an image could have a person condemned to death!

Volume 1 of Kaplan's *Encyclopedia* gives us some tantalizing clues about who this Popess might be in history. The Fournier Visconti-Sforza cards show her in a brown nun's habit. The Catelin Geoffrey Tarot from 1557 shows her with the key to St. Peter's Cathedral! Even the "Alexandrian" Tarots, whose provenance is unknown though definitely medieval if not older, show the Priestess as an educated, high ranking member of a temple community, with the same book and triple crown.

A number of Tarot artists took the noncontroversial option of dropping the High Priestess as such but substituting something else to fill the space. Moors and satraps replace the Popess and Pope, Empress and Emperor in the tarocchini di Bologna from the 18th century, and the Spanish Capitano replaces her in the Vandenborre Tarot, an eighteenth century Belgian pack. Another device used was the substitution of Juno and Jupiter for the Popess and the Pope (J. Gaudais pack, 1850). Mitelli's Tarot of 1664 doubles up on Popes, one bearded Pope sitting and the other standing, the beard a shorthand reassurance of maleness.

We see more triple crowned Popess cards reemerging through the sixteenth and seventeenth century Tarots (the Rosenwald Tarot and the anonymous Parisian Tarot in the Bibliothèque Nationale) as the power of the Church to suppress the spread of cards waned. This version of the High Priestess as Head Mother of a nunnery would be familiar to a Renaissance eye, representing a woman's one opportunity to become literate and powerful in her own right. In her role as teacher and guide, she would train new initiates in meditation and prayer in order to quiet their minds and develop receptivity to the boundless mind of God. Seated between the twin pillars of reason and intuition, she is a witness to all but partaker of none.

One remark from Volume 2 of Kaplan's *Encyclopedia* deserves special attention. On page 161 he states, "The Popess holds a book; in art, a sealed book often appears in the hands of the Virgin Mary after her ascension into heaven. The Virgin Mary enthroned with a book personified the Church." He also mentions that there is a painting of Isis in the Vatican wherein she sits between two pillars

that hold up a veil stretched between them; an open book rests upon her lap. This version of the Popess, whether Egyptian, Gnostic or Christian in origin, has had real staying power, as we do not see any significant mutations of this image again until the mid-1700s.

Etteilla's Tarots portray the Priestess as Eve, first mother of humanity, about to make the fateful decision that precipitates our kind out of mythical time and into history as we now know it. This image has several variations because the Etteilla Tarot was "adjusted" several times over its last three hundred years of existence. Earliest Etteilla decks show the Tree of Life beside Eve and a vortex of energy around her, the Magus being recast as Adam in such decks. Later printings changed the vortex into a snake twined around the tree.

This image intentionally casts the Priestess into the era preceding Christianity, reviving the ancient Snake and Bird Goddess from our preliterate past. Guler's El Gran Tarot Esoterico, commissioned by Fournier on the six hundredth anniversary of Tarot in Europe, also depicts the Priestess this way but puts a pomegranate into her hand to indicate the mysteries of Persephone. (Demeter is correspondingly portrayed as the Empress.) In keeping with the Gnostic character of earliest Tarots, there is no judgment placed on either the Eve archetype or the earlier Popess version despite the Church's ongoing campaign against women's involvement with matters sacred.

In overview, this Arcanum represents human Wisdom, whether as the Gnostic Popess, Priestess of Isis, the ancient Snake and Bird Goddess, Persephone or as Eve before the "fall" into historical time. For the accused heretics who revered her in the fourteenth and fifteenth centuries, she was the prophecy of the coming Age of the Holy Spirit, female personage within the Christian Trinity. On the journey of self transformation, once the Fool decides he wants the self mastery to become a Magus, The Priestess or Popess serves as his first teacher, representing the Inner Life and contemplative study of Nature and the Mysteries.

Astro-alphanumeric Correspondences:
"Gra" Hebrew: Moon
Old Alexandrian: Moon
Levi's Corrected Alexandrain: Moon
Marseilles (Maxwell): Moon
Modern Spanish (Dali): Moon
Spanish Varient (Balbi): Moon
English (Waite): Moon
English Varient (Crowley): Moon

The Empress

In the Visconti-Sforza Tarots, the Empress has nearly the identical attributes that she has today. Seated on her throne and robed sumptuously, she holds on her left side a shield with a black eagle emblazoned upon it and in her right hand

No. 3 The Empress
Grimaud Etteilla Tarot

a long, slender, golden wand. She is given four servants in the Cary-Yale Visconti deck but not in any of the others from this group. She always has a crown, occasionally large and ornamented. This image is near-universal among the early Tarots.

Starting with the Jacques Vieville Tarot from the 1660s, the image was reversed, and she seems to have stayed that way ever since. Court de Gebelin (1787) kept to the older arrangement. At this same time, the bulbous finial which had earlier been a mere detail on her wand (occasionally a fleur de lis) began appearing as the now-familiar orb and cross talisman, usually at the top of her wand. Stuart Kaplan tells us that this talisman "signifies sovereignty over the earth. Surmounted by a cross, it was used by the Holy Roman Emperor" (*Encyclopedia*, Volume 2, p. 161).

The title Empress has also shown remarkable constancy, although during the French Revolution, when titles were out of favor, she was occasionally given other monikers such as La Grande Mère ("the Grandmother" from the French Revolutionary Tarot by L. Carey, Strasbourg, 1791). Her image suffered far less erosion than the Priestess because it was more easily explained to the Church.

There have been two notable exceptions to this stability. Here they are mentioned in chronological order, based on when they first appeared in card form for mass production. However, the second could be older than the first, we just don't know (see "The Continental Tarots"). The Etteilla Tarot first appeared at the end of the eighteenth century, right on the heels of the Court de Gebelin/de Mellet manuscript, after the Tarot of Marseilles assumed its present form. Etteilla's Empress is not personified at all; we see instead an Eden-like image he calls "the Birds and the Fishes." This card has caused endless confusion among encyclopedists and is almost always misattributed. The title "Protection" tells us that Etteilla equated the Empress with wild nature, fertility and the stability of natural law.

The second exception is the "Hermetic/Alexandrian" stream of Tarots drawn from the *Fratres Lucis* document published by Paul Christian in 1870 (see The Continental Tarots). The Falconnier Tarot is the first public version of these images, used as illustrations for a book called *Hermetic Pages of the Divinitory Tarot* published in 1896. They were meant to be cut out, colored and applied to cardboard for a do-it-yourself Major Arcana pack. Here the Empress is Isis-Urania, barebreasted and in profile, sitting on a cubic throne covered with eyes (a reference to Hermes). Behind her is the glowing orb of the sun, twelve stars arch overhead, her feet

rest on an upturned crescent moon, and instead of a shield in her left hand, she holds the eagle itself. The staff in her right hand has a crossed orb on the top.

These two exceptions have been the primary inspirations for the modern Empresses of Waite, Wirth and Knapp-Hall. The men who created these decks were Tarot scholars attempting to present a "definitive" Tarot, yet all three were more influenced by the maverick Tarots than the very steady traditional image repeated so often from the 1450s to the present. All of them added the nimbus of solar light and the crown of stars; the Knapp-Hall even adds a live eagle on her arm.

No. 3 The Empress
Ibis Tarot

Wirth and Waite include various plant forms, perhaps in reference to Etteilla. Of the "traditional-style" modern esoteric Tarots, only the El Gran Tarot Esoterico has used the Marseilles as the foundation for her image, and in that deck she was given two lions from the Strength Arcanum, the four phases of the moon on her crown, an ear of corn (signature of Demeter), black bat wings and Mars as her planetary attribution (as in the Gra version of the Sephir Yetzirah).

It seems safe to say that this Arcanum, from ancient to modern, portrays the Great Mother, as in her title in the Revolutionary Tarot. This is the ancient, aboriginal, pre-Christian Goddess for whom the Priestess serves as handmaid. In medieval Europe it could have been argued that the Empress was a representation of whatever Queen currently ruled the land, an explanation that may have satisfied the Inquisitors. But the scholars of the Renaissance and beyond would have had no doubt about her inner identity, although she could not be shown as the "woman clothed with the sun" until after the French Revolution. The Empress is the fertility principle of the planet who feeds us all, delights us with flowers and fruit and terrifies us when her mood swings destroy our plans with heavy weather and plagues. She is the Mother of Embodiment, the source of natural law, and she who recycles us when we die; we upset her at our own peril.

Astro-alphanumeric Correspondences:
  "Gra" Hebrew: Mars
  Old Alexandrian: Venus
  Levi's Corrected Alexandrain: Venus
  Marseilles (Maxwell): Venus
  Modern Spanish (Dali): Earth
  Spanish Varient (Balbi): Mercury
  English (Waite): Venus
  English Varient (Crowley): Venus

No. 4 The Emperor
El Gran Tarot Esoterico

The Emperor

We find several versions of the Emperor among the earliest handmade Tarots: in the Brambilla Tarot, 1440-45, he is middle-aged, seated, holds the wand and crossed orb in his hands, and wears a long gold robe to the foot. In the Cary-Yale Visconti Tarot at Yale University, the Emperor is wearing armor and seems younger. His servants stand in the four directions. Both these Emperors show the imperial eagle on their clothing and/or hat.

In the Visconti-Sforza Tarot of 1450, the Emperor is older, has a long white beard and gloved hands, and the crossed orb is raised before him. He's not looking at it, though—his gaze seems to search the far distance. Perhaps these Emperors show a resemblance to the noblemen they were created for.

The Mantegna proto-Tarot (1470) includes several images that have influenced the Emperor Arcanum. Re (the King), a young, clean-shaven man, sits ramrod-straight on a hard, backless throne, wears a spiky crown and holds a narrow wand. Imperator (Emperor) is older and full-bearded and sits on a padded throne embellished with curtains. His long robe cocoons his slouched figure, but is pulled up to show his shins and feet crossed at the calf. One hand holds the crossed orb of sovereignty. An eagle stands at his feet. Elements of both these images have found their way to the Emperor Arcanum over time.

In the Charles VI Tarot of 1470, the Emperor is an amalgam with armored torso but the skirt of a long robe. His crown is smaller, the orb is lacking the cross, and his wand has a fleur de lis finial. Two small servant boys kneel at his left. The Rosenwald Emperor (early 1500s) is minimalist; he is face-front, crowned and bearded, and holds a wand on the left and orb at right. The Catelin Geoffrey Tarot cards from 1557 show the Emperor fully armed under his robe, holding a sword clutched against his breast and crossed orb on his knee. In all these cards so far, the Emperor either looks out of the card full-face or is turned away at a 45-degree angle.

In the Piedmontese or Tarocchi of Venice cards (late 1600s) the Emperor is shown for the first time in profile, a detail that may be linked to the proposed emergence of the Fratres Lucis manuscript or an earlier prototype version, to which the early Marseilles Tarots were adjusted in this very decade. This Emperor sits on a more chairlike throne with arm rests; the eagle is portrayed on the shield at his feet and his crown is now an elaborate helmet. He brandishes a very formal and decorated wand. For contrast, let's look at the Hermetic/Alexandrian images, (the Falconnier Tarot published in 1896 but quite likely older): Here we see the Emperor with body facing forward but face in profile, holding the usual wand with (uncrossed) orb at the top. His legs are crossed under a short pleated skirt, and the crown on his head represents his mastery over the material world. If there is a connection between these two, it is the head and face in profile and the different but equally odd-shaped hats they both wear.

The Mitelli Tarot (1664), in excluding both the Popess and the Empress, has added an extra Emperor and Pope. The first Emperor is seated, is bearded (older), and holds a geographical globe and a wand. The second Emperor is beardless (younger), is standing, and holds the usual wand and crossed orb. The anonymous seventeenth century Tarot from Paris (p. 135 in Kaplan's *Encyclopedia*, Volume 1) shows us a new view: The Emperor is standing, striding through the landscape, dressed in armor and carrying something that looks obscure but is more likely to be his shield than an eagle. His spiky crown has a long feather billowing from it.

Etteilla, a contemporary of de Gebelin in the late 1700s, eliminated the human imagery completely from the Emperor, and promoted it as No. 1 in his amended order, representing the first day of the divine creation described in the Hermetic *Pymander*. Stuart Kaplan would disagree with me, but I feel The Ideal (aka Chaos) is Etteilla's Emperor card, and he means it to represent "everyman," the male querant. It is alternately pictured as either a radiant sun beaming between parted clouds (late 1700s) or the earth surrounded by the rings of the planets (1800s).

The latter variant is an image of great antiquity, used by early Kabbalists and later Gnostics (it also appears in the Mantegna cards) to represent the descent of the soul into matter. Later variations of Etteilla's Emperor call it "Enlightenment," as in the dawning of higher consciousness (nineteenth century Etteilla version, p. 142 of Kaplan's *Encyclopedia*, Volume 1). Because we now know that Etteilla was a Mason and studied the Hebrew and Greek creation myths, I am inclined to rename his Emperor "Adam Kadmon" (see "Gnostic Tarot").

The Waite-Smith Tarot returns the image to more familiar territory except for the addition of ram's heads prominently displayed to override more traditional associations of the Emperor with Jupiter (as shown in the previous two century's Arcana from Etteillla, Levi, Papus and Wirth to the Falconnier family of decks). Variations in the intensely interesting Emperor

No. 4 The Emperor
Visconti-Sforza Tarot

from El Gran Tarot Esoterico include deer horns in a leather crown, a feathered cloak much like that of the Empress who preceded him, and a black bird sitting in a tree in the background. These trappings cast him into the deep pre-history of Christianity, as does the glyph of the sun hanging in the air (the earliest Hebrew correspondence to the number four and the letter Daleth). I see him as the Grain King who is sacrificed after a year of royal living, his limbs thrown into the fields in the fall fertility ritual.

In the development of this Arcanum, common themes of the historical stream of images are remarkably similar, with even the lone dissenter, Etteilla, opting for a more grandiose version of the same idea. The Emperor is the boss or leader, the head of state, the most exemplary and powerful person in the realm. His word is law, and the positive outcome in affairs of state is directly proportional to his well being and happiness. The more enlightenment and cosmic perspective he possesses, the better life is for all under his reign. He has mastered the realm of the Cube, the world of matter and of manifestation.

Astro-alphanumeric Correspondences:
   "Gra" Hebrew: Sun
   Old Alexandrian: Jupiter
   Levi's Corrected Alexandrain: Jupiter
   Marseilles (Maxwell): Jupiter
   Modern Spanish (Dali): Jupiter
   Spanish Varient (Balbi): Jupiter
   English (Waite): Aries
   English Varient (Crowley): Aquarius

The Heirophant or Pope

This image has been subject to several modifications due to the political and religious climate of the times in which Tarot first appeared. In the Visconti-Sforza Tarot from Bembo, the Priestess is called Popess and is often dressed in ecclesiastical finery, undermining the exclusivity of the Pope's role and making both genders of equal rank. The male, bearded Pope is shown in triple crown making ecclesiastical gestures, but holds no tokens of his rank. The Von Bartsch Visconti-Sforza (date unknown) at least gives him a proper papal staff. Among the published versions of the Mantegna cards, the Pope is unambiguously female, although referred to by the encyclopedists as if male. Perhaps that is because Albrech Durer's version of the Mantegna Pope (from the early 1500s) is so clearly masculine.

The Goldschmidt cards from the mid-fifteenth century show a more typical patriarchal Pope with the fascinating variants of a Catholic bishop's mitre, a mysterious anchor inlaid in the wall beside him, and a checkerboard black and white floor mosaic repeated in several cards from this deck (said to be from either Provence or Italy) and in the contemporary Guildhall cards (possibly German). One of the Visconti-Sforza tarocchi cards from the Victoria and Albert Museum also shows a checkerboard floor under the

Death card. We notice that in the early 1400s, this checkered pattern shows up several times in relation to Tarot, still a rare subject in those days. The two examples given by Kaplan in Volume 2 of his *Encyclopedia* show large scenes of Tarot players, either sitting in a room with a checkerboard floor (a fresco now at the Sforza castle in Milan, circa 1450) or framed in the checkered arches of a fresco in one of the arcades at the Issogene Castle in Val D'Aosta, circa 1415-1450. Perhaps the checkers on those early decks show a relationship to the "scene" those fifteenth century frescos represent. (We notice that the

No. 5 *Papa*
Montegna Tarocchi

checkered theme disappeared until it was recently revived on the Tarots of the French and English lodges of the late nineteenth century. I take it as a signal of their various Masonic affiliations, since their rituals were always played out on a floor similarly checkered in black and white.)

The Gringonneur Pope from the mid-fifteenth century is shown with cardinals flanking him. His profile is left-facing, and he holds the key to St. Peter's Cathedral in his right hand and the Gospel on his lap with his left. The contemporary Pope from the d'Este cards wears a more elaborate triple crown, holds up the two-fingered blessing with the right hand and grasps a chunky, gilt Grail Cup on his lap in his left hand. In the following century, the Rosenwald Tarot shows the Pope in face-front pose, with triple crown and scroll in right hand. Catelin Geoffrey's Tarot from 1557 gives us a triple-crowned Pope with the triple-crossed staff as well as the keys to St. Peter's Cathedral. The Mitelli Tarot from 1664 includes two Popes as mentioned in the Priestess entry, both bearded, both wearing the triple crown; one Pope is seated on a throne with a paper in his right hand, while the other stands empty-handed.

A refreshing break from all this Catholic symbolism appears upon the French Revolutionary Tarot by L. Carey (1791). Due to anti-royalist politics of the time, the Priestess became Juno and the Heirophant became Jupiter. He is nude save for a strategically floating scarf, and he straddles the back of an eagle, holding thunderbolts in both hands. (His counterpart, Juno, is tastefully dressed but barefoot, and riding on a peacock.)

Notes from Fournier's *Catalog of Playing Cards* Volume 1 tell us that, in regard to the contemporary tarocchino from Bologne (No. 36 in Fournier's section on Italy), "... the Popes and Emperors are shown with heads and shoulders of Negroes and satraps according to the dictates of the Papal Authority." Perhaps the Pope didn't want these Arcana to be

No. 5 The Pope
Goldschmidt Tarot

confused with any historical European peans past or present!

In the eighteenth century Tarots, two pillars appear behind the Pope, perhaps another clue to the timing of the appearance of the Alexandrian/Fatidic Egyptian Tarot which places the Pope between them (though in those decks he was called the Master of the Arcanes). Contemporary decks by Jean Payen, the Marseilles, the N. Conver Tarot and the Lando all seem to have adopted this device. Court de Gebelin repeats the pillars, puts servants at his feet, and introduces the name The Heirophant. The same Tarots that replaced the Popess with the Spanish Capitano (the Vandenborre and the pack by Jean Galler) have replaced the Pope with Bacchus astride a wine keg, with a headdress and loincloth made of grapevines, swigging from his bottle with evident glee.

Etteilla, ever the iconoclast, replaces the personification entirely with "Secrets," showing the zodiac filled with the stars of day and night. I believe that this was his way of emphasizing that the teacher of the Mysteries is not as important as the Sacred Sciences themselves. The Pope or Heirophant has from ancient times represented the head teacher in a sacred university, an institution that the Roman church had overtaken and co-opted to its curriculum by the fifteenth century. Etteilla chose to point the university of Nature from which his students should seek initiation and where they would not be denied.

As this Arcanum developed into the twentieth century, we see the older debate over the gender of the Heirophant returning. Knapp-Hall and Papus make it unambiguously female, while Waite-Smith and Wirth show him with full gray beard. In the end, there is no difference, really. The Heirophant teaches practical applications from the book of natural law, revealing those secrets hidden in everyday matter, the cycles of moons and tides, the links between the body and the cosmos. Because the monasteries were the only places a person could learn to read and write in the Middle Ages, the Heirophant is the one to whom a student would petition for entry, and s/he sets the curriculum for the neophytes' course of study. With right raised hand in the attitude of blessing, s/he links herself with the ancient lineages of Melchezidek, first initiator of the Hebrew priestly tradition, and passes on the lineage teachings. All self-generated shamans of any tradition inherently belong to this lineage.

Astro-alphanumeric Correspondences:
  "Gra" Hebrew: Aries
  Old Alexandrian: Aries
  Levi's Corrected Alexandrain: Aries

Marseilles (Maxwell): Mercury
Modern Spanish (Dali): Mercury
Spanish Varient (Balbi): Taurus
English (Waite): Taurus
English Varient (Crowley): Taurus

Lovers

The Pierpont-Morgan Bergamo tarocchi "Love" card (mid-1400s) shows a handsome young man advancing from the left and a beautiful woman standing to the right, both in medieval clothing reflecting royal status, as if they were reiterations of the Empress and Emperor. They are meeting and shaking hands below an upright, blindfolded Cupid who appears to be ready to drop an arrow onto the man's head. The contemporary Cary-Yale Visconti portrays the same couple but on opposite sides, in a manicured garden under a sumptuous canopy furnished with a bright red couch. A blindfolded cherub flying above is now about to drop the arrow on the woman. This image too was called Love. Kaplan, in Volume 2 of his *Encyclopedia*, likens these images to "betrothal portraits" popular in Germany and later in Italy. Such portraits typically show the couple linked by Cupid, who carries two arrows but no bow. The arrows are meant "that they might love each other equally" (p. 164).

The Charles VI Tarot from 1470-80 calls this Arcanum the Lovers, and shows several couples dancing and romancing; two cherubs are at the ready, bows drawn, to pierce some members of the crowd with their barbs of love. Kaplan, in Volume 1 of his *Encyclopedia*, says the Lovers card is represented in the Mantegna Tarocchi (1470) by cards No. 20, Apollo, and No. 43, Venus, suggesting the identities of the royal couple who come together under the auspices of this Arcanum.

The Rosenwald Tarot cards from the sixteenth century reveal a man on bended knee before a woman, while above them a blindfolded angel with female breasts and male genitals prepares to shoot the woman in the heart with an arrow of love. Note that this ambivalent gender association shows up a century later as one characteristic of the "new" Devil Arcanum influenced by the reforms of the 1660s. We know this angel is not meant to be a devil figure, however, because the wings are distinctly feathered rather than black and leathery as would be those of a demon.

In the mid-1600s we enter a time of mixed influ-

No. 6 The Lovers
Anonymous Parisian Tarot

No. 5 Secrets
modern Etteilla
Tarot

ences. This card tends to have a large numbers of variants through the years, giving us numerous subtle changes in interpretation from one pack to another. Several that might be especially interesting are mentioned below. But the image that eventually became standard, first on the Marseilles family of Tarots and later on Etteilla and all the French Esoteric cards, was the Two Paths, showing a young man at a fork in the road, standing between two women who represent different possible destinies for him. This image first shows up on the Jacques Vieville and Jean Noblet Tarots, both from the early 1660s in France.

By the early seventeenth century, the anonymous Parisian Tarot shows a very quizzical version of the Lovers. The woman appears on the right, human but with what seems to be gray angel wings that match those of the cherub overhead. Her gaze and hands are focused on his lap. We see him diagonally from behind as he straddles a hassock, looking at her face and embracing her chest. The cherub has an arrow ready to release, pointing at the man. Is he receiving sexual attention from an angel? Is this love or lust? Giuseppe Maria Mitelli's Tarot (1664) does not help us with this question, as he shows only the chubby cupid standing on earth though possessing wings, arrows holstered, wearing a blindfold. He holds a flaming heart in his left hand.

One Tarot from 1750 shows an interesting variation (Tarocco Siciliano cards). This pack presents the Arcana in a different numerical order than usual, so the Lovers image is numbered 8 instead of 6. A woman and a man are in the open landscape, the requisite cherub on a cloud above them. The cherub's bow is drawn, ready to shoot the man. This man is caught in a moment of shock, recoiling at what the woman is presenting. She is holding up another arrow, which has apparently already been released into her. It seems the man is not as receptive and peaceful with the prospect of love as the woman!

Aside from these amusing but inconclusive variations, the primary image for the Lovers goes forward as some variation on the "new" (in the 1660s) Two Paths image. In that formulation, the young man (the Magus?) who is standing at a fork in the road must choose between a modest angel and a primitively dressed nature girl (meant to imply sexual availability). Between them, the two women represent virtue and vice. The cherub is aiming the arrow at the man in the center of the image as if to imply that the responsibility for all consequences of this Choice will be borne by the chooser (meaning the person who draws this card).

The main variant of the Choice card is shown by the Jean Payen, Marseilles, Court de Gebelin, N. Conver and Vandenborre Tarots. All show a marriage ceremony being performed by an older priestess who stands in the same position the "vice" woman would have, to the left of the young man. This produces the same silhouette as The Choice, but the temptress image is replaced by the priestess (or Holy Mother) image.

This priestess is ceremonially uniting the couple at a crossroads in the manner of a pagan handfasting. The priestess sometimes has her back turned to the viewer of the card, which can make it unclear whether she is older and making a marriage or younger and competing with the bride for the attentions of the young man. Usually the artist will have taken the time to detail a headdress for the extra woman if she is meant to be more than a flirtatious competitor of the bride.

In each case, the cherub hovers overhead either targeting the groom or aiming between the bride and groom. Almost never are either of the women made the explicit target of the cherub's arrow. A modern version appears in the F. Gumppenberg Tarot, 1807-1815 (Kaplan's *Encyclopedia* Volume 2, p. 344). This card shows a beautiful young girl having to choose between a young king and a handsome warrior. The cherub is aiming at the warrior, while the young

No. 6 The Lovers
Spanish Marseilles Tarot

king is trying to pull her away with him. Even in this case, it is not the girl who is in the sights of the cherub! There must be an implicit lesson showing through in this Arcanum, implying as they all do that in this kind of situation the man (symbolically the ego and the will) is the deciding factor rather than the woman (referencing the heart).

Etteilla returns the Lovers to the church, now presided over by a priest in the nave of his chapel. We have no particular evidence to link Etteilla to the Church, although we can now be sure that he was a Mason and esteemed among his peers. He may be echoing the Adam C. de Hautot Tarot (1740s) or the Sebastian Ioia Tarot (mid- to late 1700s), both of which show the sacred marriage being performed by a man. But it is just as likely that Etteilla picked this version of the Lovers card because it allows him to transplant the Heirophant onto the Lovers Arcanum. In this way he frees up one card to name after himself: No. 1, Etteila (also called "le Consultant" and "Ideal") implying, it seems, that he is the Heirophant of the Tarot. In other Etteilla-style Tarots, this card gets the label Chaos, which in light of the *Poimandres* theme that Etteilla was following, was referring to the primordial state before creation began.

The Lando Tarot is less specific about which version of the Lovers we are seeing, but in any case it includes the classic "Two Paths" silhouette. Even the Milanese Tarot by F. Gumppenberg (late eighteenth or early nineteenth century), which is the deck the individual members of the Golden Dawn school were instructed to work with before they each created their own personal decks, shows the Two Paths/Marriage formula.

The Waite-Smith Tarot offers a surprising formulation of this Arcanum, depicting a naked Adam and Eve apparently before the events of the "fall." He stands on the right before a tree with ten flaming leaves (representing the Kabbalah Tree) and she on the left before a tree laden with red fruit and where a serpent is climbing into its branches. One can say that Waite is projecting the Bembo-style Royal Couple backward into the primordial myth, and reminding us of our august origins, our original divine natures, before we misused our powers of will. A similar Adam & Eva card exists from a card game called Labyrinth by Andrea Ghisi (1616), and perhaps that is what Waite is referencing.

In choosing to add these Gnostic and Hebrew implications to the meeting of the Queen and the King, he has superimposed a biblical mythos onto an otherwise pagan Sacred Marriage image. This has not been a bad thing in itself—Waite's Lovers card is one of my favorites in his Tarot. But in so doing he left aside the important lesson of The Choice at the crossroads, the challenge to mature and commit, which has been the dilemma of the young man on the Lovers Arcanum since the 1660s. He also eliminated the Priestess, representing feminine Wisdom, the link to the Sophia bonding force that draws the partners together and binds them over time.

The Lovers card in all its glory and variety has referred to the sex/love/commitment/consequences continuum and how to stay balanced within it. This card has been more variable than some because there are so many nuances of opinion about sex and relationship across cultures and centuries. But doubtless this Arcanum is about the issues raised by real human relationships, since the protagonist is shown in the act of making a life-changing choice. One cannot have it all. To partake of a higher ideal requires self discipline. The path of pleasure eventually leads to distraction from spiritual growth. The gratification of the personality eventually gives way to the call from spirit as the soul matures.

Astro-alphanumeric Correspondences:
  "Gra" Hebrew: Taurus
  Old Alexandrian: Taurus
  Levi's Corrected Alexandrain: Taurus
  Marseilles (Maxwell): Saggitarius
  Modern Spanish (Dali): Virgo
  Spanish Varient (Balbi): Virgo
  English (Waite): Gemini
  English Varient (Crowley): Gemini

Chariot

The Cary-Yale Visconti Tarot (1440-45) portrays a man directing a pair of horses who pull the Chariot, occupied by a robed noblewoman under a blue canopy with gold stars. She holds the Visconti dove that has a nimbus of energy around it. In the Visconti-Sforza Tarot, the horses are winged, and the lady seated in the cab gets along without a driver. In her gloved hands she holds a thin wand on the right and a crossed orb on the left.

The Charles VI Tarot (mid-1400s) changes the gender of the person in the Chariot. It shows an armored warrior wearing a red hat, holding an ornamental ax and standing on the dais of a float pulled by two white horses. They are coming at us full-front. The No. 45 Marte (Mars) card from the Mantegna cards seems directly related.

In the Rothschild Tarot (late fifteenth century or early sixteenth) at the Louvre in Paris, the Chariot shows a male figure with winged helmet on a raised platform. The horses pulling his vehicle, while looking at each other, are in fact diverging. With his hands full of the symbols of authority and victory and no reins in sight, one wonders how he will control the implicit dilemma. The Rosenwald Tarot from the early 16th century depicts the charioteer in the same dilemma, but standing.

The Catelin Geoffrey Tarot (1557) gives us more controlled image: The man is holding a bouquet of flowers and the groomsman is holding the horses' bridles. In the early seventeenth century anonymous Parisian Tarot, the laurel crowned man is piloted by a youth or cherub who holds a whip over the steeds. The bottom part of the card is difficult to read because of clumsy coloration over faint outlining, but it looks like the steeds may be swans.

Mitelli's Tarot (1664) shows Venus in the chariot, nude except for a golden ribbon around her ribs and a golden scarf billowing behind her. Her chariot has no steeds, consisting instead of a rolling throne with stairs leading down to ground-level in front. The "ground" in question is, however, a cloud, as evidenced by the birds at her feet. She pulls up on a set of reins which pierce downward through the cloud, presumably to the world below. Her empty right hand is outstretched, her expression benign. To my eye, this card has a distinctly Gnostic flavor.

The Tarots I have identified as the "turning point" from folk

No. 7 The Chariot
Mitelli Tarot

Tarot to esoteric Tarot are the Jacques Vieville Tarot and the Jean Noblet Tarot, both from the early 1660s. The Vieville pack shows the interesting detail of human faces upon the Chariot. This may show a relationship with the prototype manuscript for the eventual Falconnaire Tarot, which I have suggested started circulating in the Secret Societies at this time. In that stream of Tarots which has emerged from this source (including the St. Germaine Tarot and the modern Ibis Tarot), the Chariot is pulled by sphinxes with human faces.

Stuart Kaplan suggests that the Vieville Tarot is the prototype for the Belgian Tarots, but in those that he illustrates (Adam C. de Hautot, 1740s, Antoine Jar and Martin Dupont in the 1800s), the horses just

No. 7 THE CHARIOT
VIEVILLE TAROT

look like horses. The Jean Noblet form seems to represent the standard model from this time forward. Sometimes it is difficult to tell if the person in the Chariot is male or female, with the crescent-moon shoulder pads and the beardless face now becoming standard features. some, the arrangement of the armored breastplate could suggest a female figure.

By the eighteenth century, the male charioteer clearly outnumbers versions where the rider is a woman or a goddess. Occasionally the image proceeds away from the viewer or is in profile (as in some of the Etteilla Tarots), but more often it comes straight out of the card toward the viewer. The sense of dynamic motion is always emphasized, often with oversized, studded wheels which, it is implied, are whirling the Chariot along the road.

In the esoteric Tarots from the cusp of the twentieth century, for example the Oswald Wirth, Knapp-Hall, and the Waite Tarots, a lingam and yoni image, sometimes winged, appears on the front wall of the Chariot. This symbol often refers to the sexual mysteries of combining the opposites. But in this context, because only one person is riding the Chariot, the implication is that this one person is becoming androgynous. This approach is made distinct in a 1935 pack called the British Tarot, which shows a distinct pair of breasts on a seemingly male charioteer.

In every case of this card's appearance, there is a triumphal feeling, as if the charioteer is being celebrated for a victory at battle or is being paraded through the streets as a hero (or heroine). The card appears to congratulate high achievement, a signal of a soul empowered in the world. The huge wheels and frisky steeds speed up the rate at which the driver's will can be realized, and make more of

the world accessible to one ambitious enough to take the reins. There is real danger here because of the increased rate of change and its power to magnify mistakes in judgment, but like a seasoned warrior, the charioteer stays attentive to the road before him.

Astro-alphanumeric Correspondences:
"Gra" Hebrew: Gemini
Old Alexandrian: Gemini
Levi's Corrected Alexandrain:Gemini
Marseilles (Maxwell): Mars
Modern Spanish (Dali): Saggitarius
Spanish Varient (Balbi): Gemini
English (Waite): Cancer
English Varient (Crowley): Cancer

Justice

In the Visconti-Sforza Tarot of 1450, the seated image of Justice, her sword held upright on her right and scales held up in the left, is vaulted over by a fully armored, beardless knight with chin-length blonde hair who sits astride a skirted horse, unsheathed sword in right hand. I think what we are seeing here is the two sides of Justice—the contemplative side and the active side. Alternately, the Charles VI pack depicts the

No. 8 JUSTICE
ANONYMOUS PARISIAN TAROT

Justice seated on a cubic throne, holding an upright sword in her right hand and a hand-held scales in her left. Resemblance to the Justice Arcanum can be seen in the Mantegna card No. 37, Justicia (with both sword and scales, plus a leggy bird with a fruit held in one foot). The Rosenwald Tarot images present a version of the same thing (early sixteenth century).

In the early seventeenth century anonymous Parisian Tarot, Justice is shown standing in a field, sword and scales in hand but blindfolded, and with the Janus face (a young woman to the front, a bearded old man to the back). This device harkens back to antiquity and usually implies the benefit of hindsight that comes with long reflection. In this case both faces share the blindfold.

Mitelli's Tarot shows Justice unblinded in an outdoor setting, her one-shouldered dress flowing in the wind and revealing one breast. Her right hand holds the sword, the left the scales. In the intervening century separating this from the Sicilian Tarocco (1750), the only thing that has changed significantly in this Arcanum is that Justice is seated in the later pack, and her emblems have switched hands. From this

No. 8 Justice
El Gran Tarot Esoterico

point on she has almost no variations aside from the occasional pair of wings or a two-pillars allusion formed from the uprights of her throne rising behind her. Neither Etteilla (whose images we know were deliberately skewed from the usual order) nor Waite felt free to editorialize much on the image, although in the Waite Tarot, Justice was switched from position 8 to position 11.

One interesting image from the illustrious El Gran Tarot Esoterico shows Soloman as the figurehead instead of a female Justice. He is holding aloft a small infant by the feet. With a sword in his other hand, he prepares to cut the infant in half. This image represents a famous incident from the Bible in which Soloman was able to determine which of two women was the infant's real mother by their individual reactions to his proposal to divide the baby equally.

The standard meaning of this Arcanum is conscience, the moral sensitivity that is supposed to put us into others' shoes and evoke our compassion and sense of fairness. The great antiquity of this image has represented a standard for humane and equal treatment between humans of all kinds since the time of Soloman. By providing a fulcrum that helps balance competing needs against the greater good, and by using the two-edged sword to symbolize the exactitude necessary to make these adjudications, this Arcanum puts us all on notice that not one detail misses the inner eye of the conscience. The treatment we mete out to others will be received in our turn.

Astro-alphanumeric Correspondences:
"Gra" Hebrew: Cancer
Old Alexandrian: Cancer
Levi's Corrected Alexandrain: Cancer
Marseilles (Maxwell): Libra
Modern Spanish (Dali): Libra
Spanish Varient (Balbi): Libra
English (Waite): Libra
English Varient (Crowley): Libra

Hermit

The very oldest image we associate with the Hermit of Tarot is probably an illustration of the poem *I Triumphi* by Petrarch, composed during an 18-year period starting in 1356. Stuart Kaplan shows a set of fifteenth century illustrations of the Triumphs, and the Triumph of Time is a per-

fect prototype for the Hermit. He stands on his float or chariot on crutches, bald, bearded, robed and winged. Two stags pull him, and two hourglasses stand on either side of him. Stuart Kaplan tells us that "the hermit is well-known in medieval and Renaissance art as a man of great virtue and spiritual strength. Often in paintings his presence is a reprimand to sinners who are frolicking and carousing" (*Encyclopedia*, Volume 2, p. 167).

In the Visconti-Sforza Tarot of 1450, an old and bent but sumptuously dressed man with a tall staff carries before him an hourglass, contemplating the passage of time. The Charles VI version (mid 1400s) shows a similarly well dressed old man, lacking staff but still contemplating the hourglass, with cliffs rising beside him. The uncut sheet of Minchiate cards from the late fifteenth century (p. 128 of Kaplan's *Encyclopedia*, Volume 1) shows the well-dressed old man on crutches, bellypack at his waist. A pair of transparent wings rises behind him and between them rises a six-sided pillar along the line of his backbone. Another early sixteenth century image from the Rosenwald Tarot shows the bent old man on crutches, but it has left out the wings, hourglass, staff and/or pillar entirely.

No. 9 The Hermit
Rothschild Tarot

In Catelin Geoffrey's Tarot (1557), the Hermit is shown as an older tonsured (or balding) monk with rosary in his belt, walking away from us. He is entering a curtained doorway with a lantern held low before him. It doesn't appear to be an hourglass. In the anonymous Parisian Tarot from the early seventeenth century, the Hermit is now emerging from the curtained archway, and he has a cane as well as his hand-held lamp. (The shape of whatever it is he is carrying is indistinct, but it seems to have a lampshade over it.) The secret door in both cases would most probably represent a portal to the Inner Sanctum where the ineffable mysteries can be contemplated without interruption.

Gioseppe Maria Mitelli (1664) evokes the classical image of Father Time, a naked old man with flowing beard and large gray wings. He shows no visible infirmities, but leans on crutches anyway, reminding us again of our original image from *I Triumphi*. As of 1750 and the publication of the Tarocco Siciliano cards, the essential details had been codified as a robed and hooded old monk with flowing white beard, a lamp held up on the right; a short crutch on the left supports him.

In the late sixteenth century decks from Jacques Vieville and Jean Noblet, a new detail enters the picture—the arrangement of his cloak partially covers his lantern. This detail, found in all the Falconnier Tarots modeled on the *Fratres Lucis* document, which I think has been circulating since the 1660s, also appears on the Jean Payne Tarot (1743), the Marseilles (1748) and the Court de Gebelin images (1787). A serpent at the feet of the Hermit is a feature of the Egyptian-style Tarots as well, but that doesn't appear until the F. Gumppenberg Neoclassical Tarot from 1807.

Other contemporary decks followed the example of Etteilla, whose Hermit Arcanum reveals his light unshielded. The Tarocchini di Bologna cards (eighteenth century) sidesteps the issue by portraying the Hermit in his older form as a well-dressed old man on crutches, downcast but with large wings, standing in front of an unbroken, ornamented pillar.

No. 9 The Hermit
El Gran Tarot Esoterico

Another eighteenth century image from an uncut set of Minchiate cards (Kaplan's *Encyclopedia*, p. 52) reinstates the lame old man but adds an arrow piercing the hourglass and stag resting beside him. We see the stag again in the Spanish El Gran Tarot Esoterico, which we are using in this CD Rom to represent the ancient Hebrew correspondences. This image, attributed to Eliphas Levi, includes a serpent at the Hermit's feet leading him into hidden knowledge of the Kundalini.

Turn of the century Tarot "experts" differ as to which version they emulate. The Waite-Smith Tarot falls with Etteilla into the camp of the uncovered lantern, in a land where no serpent lurks. Both Oswald Wirth and Knapp-Hall show the occulted light of the Levi-inspired versions, complete with a stylized serpent at their feet. Few maintain loyalty to the oldest formulations, especially after the Marseilles became the prototypical "traditional Tarot."

Given the many parables to be found in spiritual literature about "entertaining angels unaware" (as implied by the Hermits with the angel wings), and considering also the interesting later variation of cloaking or uncloaking the light, it seems obvious that this Arcanum's major intergenerational theme reminds us that the most powerful and interesting souls will often appear unbidden in a "plain brown wrapper," wearing the simple garb of an anonymous monk, often appearing aged or infirm. The pillar or column behind him in some cards reminds us not to judge his power by his apparent fragility.

The challenge of The Hermit is to be able to recognize the Teacher in this humble disguise. He will not make it easy for the student to acquire his wisdom because it takes time

and long contemplation to fathom what he is illuminating with the lantern. He often speaks wordlessly or in ancient and barbaric tongues, communicating with the elements, the animals, the laws of Nature. While the hourglass was an identifying feature of the earliest Hermit cards, the more modern ones have shifted the metaphor, showing more or less light released from his lantern. But every Hermit card reminds us of the value of time spent away from the everyday hubbub of community life in order to destimulate the soul and learn to join with the mind of Nature.

Astro-alphanumeric Correspondences:
  "Gra" Hebrew: Leo
  Old Alexandrian: Leo
  Levi's Corrected Alexandrain: Leo
  Marseilles (Maxwell): Pisces
  Modern Spanish (Dali): Neptune
  Spanish Varient (Balbi): Neptune
  English (Waite): Virgo
  English Varient (Crowley): Virgo

Wheel

The Brambilla Tarot (1440-45) shows the classic blindfolded Dame Fortune at the center with four people around her on the stations of the Wheel, embodying the various States of Man. (In some cards with this formulation, the stations are labeled "I have reign" at the top, "I did reign" on the descending side, "I shall reign" on the ascending side, and "I have no reign" at the bottom.) This image holds steady through the numerous Tarots from the workshop of Bonifacio Bembo (1445-80). The blindfold indicates that Lady Fortune rewards people with no respect for their relative goodness or badness.

A deck of Minchiate Cards from late fifteenth or early sixteenth century (Kaplan's *Encyclopedia*, Volume 1, p. 128) shows the Wheel and its four riders but not the central figure. Standing atop the Wheel is a robed bear with a heavy club in the left hand and the crossed orb of power in the right. The other three stations of the Wheel are occupied with humans in their variations. The bear may allude to a royal lineage, a tribal or initiatory affiliation with the astrological Great Bear (totem of the mythical Arthurian clan.) If that were true, this Tarot could be representing its author's loyalty to the families who were still tracing their lineage back to the children of Mary Magdalen and Jesus.

No. 10 The Wheel of Fortune
Brambilla Tarot

An anonymous early seventeenth century Tarot at the Bibliothèque Nationale in Paris gives another spin on the image. It portrays the expected people rising and falling around the perimeter of the Wheel, but crowning the Wheel is a male monarch with a pitchfork or trident, apparently missing half his left arm. It is not clear whether this entity is human or demonic, as the clumsy coloring obscures the shape of his feet. If they were cloven or chickenlike, the reference would be to the Devil, which I would consider a strongly Gnostic statement.

By the mid-1660s most Wheel of Fortune cards had settled down around the Marseilles style of presentation. Here the rising and falling characters on the edge of the Wheel are dominated by a crowned creature with a sword who sits motionless at the apex. Sometimes the entity at the top of the Wheel is a sphinx, sometimes a monkey. As Stuart Kaplan mentions, the characters rising and falling on the Wheel vary in the amount of human and/or animalistic characteristics they portray from deck to deck.

Mixing animal and human forms is standard in alchemical and magical arts, indicating incomplete development on the part of the magician. Doglike characteristics represent greed, while references to the monkey indicate malice, vanity and cunning. The sphinx is a very old composite entity which represents the Gnosis within Greek mythology.

The later emerging Hermetic/Alexandrian Tarots, drawn from the *Fratres Lucis* document or its prototype, refine this metaphor. In them one can see the ascending force as Azoth, the dog-headed human, the person of desire. This person could become godlike if he worked on himself, and he can be seen carrying Hermes' wand, another symbol of the Gnosis (see "Confluence" essay). Meanwhile the descending force, called Hyle in Greek and Typhon in Coptic, is pictured with the qualities of a reptile, suggesting the unconscious, instinctive residue of our animal nature. So the visual formula is "change is certain; learn to control impulsiveness and embrace the law of cycle. Wisdom will grow through experience."

Mitelli (1664) changes the approach drastically, putting a wagon wheel under the seat of naked Lady Fortune. She is posing with it, holding up an open purse from which pour coins and jewelry. Her hair is blowing in the breeze. The logo for his card could be "easy come, easy go." This image was not taken to heart by the masses, and by 1750 and the Sicilian Tarocco, we have a fairly conventional image again.

Etteilla, on the other hand, uses the image of a crowned monkey on a tree branch, perhaps making a statement about inexpert leadership among the "royalist" lodges. A man, a serpent twined around him, is descending on the left while a little gray mouse is ascending on the right. The rolling hoop hovers mid-bounce above a rocky landscape. The angle at which the monkey holds the wand hints that it is he who is keeping the hoop rolling. When we think of the times in which Etteilla lived, a period that encompassed both the American and French democratic revolutions, one can imagine the poignancy Etteilla must have felt as he designed this card!

Eteilla's Tarots were the most popular of the end of the eighteenth century and the first part of the nineteenth, and a Catalan version was the first standard Tarot printed in Spain a century later. Because of this, variant images crept in, including a revival of blindfolded Lady Fortune, this time robed and standing on a wagon wheel (Delarue Etteilla, circa 1880-90).

No. 10 The Wheel of Fortune
El Gran Tarot Esoterico

In the nineteenth century the images return again to a more traditional look, but the creature at the apex begins to mutate afresh, showing variations of a crowned woman resembling Justice, a little king, or an indeterminate "beastie" that could be a variation on the Sphinx.

One "modern" concept of the Wheel has followed the Waite-Smith "wheel in the sky" image that includes the four creatures of the elements and quarters. Others have followed the Oswald Wirth version which uses a very stylized Wheel on an elevated frame in a crescent moon boat, bobbing on choppy waters as the Wheel turns with the action of Azoth (the rising force) and Hyle (the falling force). This image is a near-exact copy of the Egyptian-style Arcana, which I see as the influence for all the Wheel cards with a sphinx at the top. El Gran Tarot Esoterico combines the crowned monkey of the Etteilla with the white bear of the late fifteenth century Minchiate, here seen rolling a great stone Wheel of Time. This is the plight of the secret royalty of Europe, the clan of the Holy Blood, to patiently wait out the reign of the "crowned monkey"—the Church and its made-up royalty.

A simple explanation of this card from its most ancient form to the present is change; the Wheel will keep on rolling, churning events in a ceaseless progression of ups and downs. No one can escape its action, which feels good when we are rising and terrible when we are falling. The figure balanced on the top has a moment of eternal clarity, but the only unmoving part of the Wheel is the hub that pivots on the crossbar that holds it up. Whether it is moved by the action of the Angel of Time, a disembodied Hand of Fate turning a crank or the natural law of eternal return, we are each bound to occupy all the roles at one point or another in our life's journey. The predictability of the Wheel is its lesson, and that's something we can take comfort in. If you don't like the look of things right now, just wait a bit—it's bound to change. Of course, if you do like the look of things right now enjoy it while it lasts because it's bound to change!

Astro-alphanumeric Correspondences:
    "Gra" Hebrew: Virgo

Old Alexandrian: Virgo
Levi's Corrected Alexandrain: Virgo
Marseilles (Maxwell): Capricorn
Modern Spanish (Dali): Capricorn
Spanish Varient (Balbi): Capricorn
English (Waite): Jupiter
English Varient (Crowley): Jupiter

Strength

In the image called Fortitude from the Cary-Yale Visconti (1440–45), a beautiful lady with a corona-patterned aura rides the golden lion sidesaddle. The Pierpont Morgan-Bergamo Visconti-Sforza tarocchi (1475), also called Fortitude, shows a strong young giant, probably Hercules, swinging a club to kill the lion at his feet. The Charles VI Tarot of 1470–80 depicts a young lady with a dark halo, seated on a cubic throne, breaking a pillar with her hands. The Mantegna tarocchi (1470) presents us with a similar image called Force in which the woman is wearing a lion-embossed helmet and breastplate with a live lion in the background. She holds a wand with a knobby end in her right hand and breaks the pillar with her left.

No. 11 STRENGTH
ETTEILLA TAROT

In the Rosenwald Tarot from the early sixteenth century, a mild-looking woman sits next to an unbroken pillar, her arms wrapped around it. A contemporary deck, the anonymous Parisian Tarot found in the Bibliothèque Nationale in Paris, shows us the familiar image of a woman wrestling with and/or taming a lion. She leans down from her throne to handle the beast, and her scarf billows behind her.

Giuseppe Maria Mitelli's deck (1664) retains the woman standing with a broken pillar, although there is no indication that the woman broke it. Her one-shouldered dress exposes her left breast, and she holds a scarf in her right hand.

A French pack circa 1720 (see Stuart Kaplan's *Encyclopedia* Volume 1, p. 146) shows us a man of royal rank opening the jaws of a lion with his bare hands. This hearkens back to the Hercules image of yore. But the Tarocco Siciliano of 1750 prefers the symbol of the woman with the pillar instead of the lion. Etteilla's images are all versions of the lady with the lion, although the beast is usually asleep at her feet. This approach emphasizes the taming power of Lady Strength rather than the brute force of Hercules. This theme is also reflected in the Falconnier Tarot from 1896, first of the Alexandrian-style Tarots to be published, but quite possibly older than Etteilla's Tarots.

A most beautiful Major Arcana tarocchi with art from

1893, the Vacchetta, shows both the lion and the unbroken pillar with the calm and lucid Goddess standing between them. She looks away into the distance, while the lion frolics beside her and licks her hand. This synthesis combines the most non-violent elements of the earlier themes we can trace in this card.

No. 11 STRENGTH
VACHETTA TAROT

In the Strength Arcanum, the animal nature, so fierce and frightening in its primal form, has been tamed and brought to heel under the direction of our finer, more subtle (feminine, interior) self. The will and passion of our untamed nature does not need to be "broken" but instead refined and brought to consciousness so that all levels of creation, inner and outer, might come into harmony. The feminine soul-force shows a strength and persuasive power that can induce cooperation from others, stilling disruptive energies and bringing the planes of being into harmonious relationship.

Astro-alphanumeric Correspondences:
"Gra" Hebrew: Venus
Old Alexandrian: Mars
Levi's Corrected Alexandrain: Mars
Marseilles (Maxwell): Leo
Modern Spanish (Dali): Leo
Spanish Varient (Balbi): Leo
English (Waite): Leo
English Varient (Crowley): Leo

Hanged One/Prudence

Illustrated in one version of this card is the medieval custom of hanging traitors or their effigies by their feet. This shaming image represents punishment or, alternately, the state of debt and delinquency and its repayment. In the earliest Visconti-Sforza image (1450), a youth in his undervest with tie-on sleeves and hose is suspended, upside-down by his left leg, from a square frame. The right is crossed behind the left, and his hands are tied behind his back. He gazes pensively into the distance as his hair hangs around his face. Alternately, the Charles VI pack from the mid-1400s shows the Hanged Man holding bags of gold coins in his hands, hanging from his right leg, with an orange feather peeking from behind him like a tail.

The Mantegna (1470) introduces the first image of Prudence, a woman holding an elaborate mirror in her left hand, a caliper in her right. She has a Janus head—young female face looking forward, older bearded male face looking back. This symbol is usually employed to suggest sober reflection in the light of past experience. The same face also appears on the Mantegna Theologia card, implying that the state of mind behind those two faces participates in two worlds at once, presumably with the "feminine" side in the world of spirit and the masculine side in the world of matter.

The Rosenwald Tarot of the early sixteenth century shows the hanging man again, arms untied, holding a full bag in each hand, preventing the contents from spilling out. The Catelin Geoffrey Tarot (1557) also returns to this earlier image of a hanged man, but in this case the man is tied by both feet, hands bound behind him, swinging from an L-shaped gibbet. There appears to be a ruffle of red feathers around his waist which could refer to the Lenten Fool, No. 0, harbinger of the spring carnival. In keeping with the Hanged Man's traditional attribution to Libra, those feathers could symbolize the Spring Fool being sacrificed at the onset of fall.

In the early seventeenth century anonymous Parisian Tarot, the Hanged Man's hands are free, and with the right hand he holds something so it will not drop. The left hand makes an open-palmed blessing like a priest. He's hanging from his left leg with the right one crossed behind, and his foot is tied with a rope.

Never one to conform, Mitelli (1664) features a man asleep on a throne, with his head resting in his arms on a pillow. Another man stands behind him, arms raising a large mallet overhead, ready to strike a blow from which the sleeping man will never awaken. This image is so specific and so unique that it looks like an event from local history.

No. 12 *The Hanged Man*
Catelin Geoffrey Tarot

A card called Prudence in a French pack from the late eighteenth century (p. 337 of Kaplan's *Encyclopedia* Volume 2) shows us an effeminate or beardless youth standing like an upside-down Hanged Man on his left foot with the right leg crossed behind, hands on hips. The Vandenborre Belgian Tarot from the eighteenth century follows suit. But the Tarocco Siciliano cards from Modiano, Italy (1750) take the image to its lowest common denominator: We see the back view of a gentleman in frock coat, knee britches and hose, hanging dead from the branch of a tree, arms tied behind him. Versions like this violate the unwritten rule of this card, which is that however painful or tortuous the treatment of the Hanged Man at the time, it is specifically not fatal.

A most interesting form of the Prudence card emerges in Etteilla's Tarot, which we now know was an attempt at restating the Hermetic creation mythos as detailed in *The Pymander*. Here she resembles the Hebrew Matronit and the Gnostic Sophia, aware that the serpent at her feet is an initiator and teacher, not a demon. Her subtle smile and lifted skirt imply an understanding of the serpent's place in the great scheme of things. No longer does she contemplate only, but instead she actively accepts her fate and whatever are its natural consequences in the world in which she finds herself.

No. 12 *Prudence*
Mantegna Tarocchi

Both the Falconnier and the Waite packs represent the Hanged Man, as do the majority of Tarots in history. This seems to imply a certain fatalism compared to the Prudence formulation, with its suggestion of learning to work with our fallen state instead of against it. This shows again that the Etteilla Tarot was not just a whimsical distortion of the Arcana, but an attempt to upgrade the Arcana at the dawn of more liberal times. If he failed in some cards, he succeeded with others, including this one.

This card invariably indicates the lack of ability to help yourself through independent action. Whether this is because one is trussed and awaiting judgment or because one is female or too young to be taken seriously and therefore relegated to a passive role, there is no avenue for the will to win back its freedom until this situation has passed. This is a time to be philosophical, to study and meditate upon your circumstance, to make your resolutions for the moment when you become free again. Only those who possesses wisdom, patience and optimism will be able to see through the present humiliation and limitation in order to grasp the inspiration one can gain from such an experience.

Astro-alphanumeric Correspondences:
 "Gra" Hebrew: Libra
 Old Alexandrian: Libra
 Levi's Corrected Alexandrain: Libra
 Marseilles (Maxwell): Aries
 Modern Spanish (Dali): Uranus
 Spanish Varient (Balbi): Pisces
 English (Waite): Water (modern Neptune)
 English Varient (Crowley): Neptune

Death

In many of the oldest Tarot decks, including the Cary-Yale

NO. 13 DEATH
VISCONTI SVORTZA TAROT

Visconti from 1445, the reaping skeleton rides a pale horse over fields filled with the body parts and blood of various Arcana characters. Alternately, Death is an archer in the Pierpont Morgan-Bergamo Visconti-Sforza tarocchi (1450), with the curve of the bow articulated like a spine. He stands at the brink of a precipice, testing the edge with his bony toe. The Charles VI pack (mid-1400s) shows a skeleton dressed in a yellow smock riding a dark horse. His big deathshead grin expresses his glee as he chops away at the pope, cardinals, king and others who are being trampled underfoot. The early sixteenth century Rosenwald Tarot echoes the Charles VI image, but with less drama. In Catelin Geoffrey's Tarot (1557) the reaper is standing, shovel over the right shoulder and scythe skimming the ground on the left. A wan crop of straggly hair and empty eye sockets are especially ghastly. The landscape is unremarkable.

Stuart Kaplan, in Volume 2 of his *Encyclopedia of Tarot*, states that "beginning with Vieville's deck of the mid-seventeenth century, the figure of Death is seen on foot with his scythe. . . . This image persisted until Waite revived the old form with his depiction of Death as a skeletal knight on horseback, carrying a banner instead of a scythe." He seems to be correct on that; although we see one standing Death a century earlier, the convention changed precipitously after Vieville's Tarot. Several Arcana display this radical change appearing in the mid-1660s in the Vieville and Noblet Tarots, and I assume the Devil card is one example of this phenomenon. When we look at the Falconnier Tarot, which I am suggesting is one of several Alexandrian-inspired versions of the *Fratres Lucis* manuscript circulating in Europe since the Middle Ages (the manuscript I suggest inspired these changes), we see a standing Devil reaping a field of severed limbs, much like Vieville's modification.

By the early seventeenth century, Death had sprouted what looks like wings, as in the anonymous Parisian Tarot. Little gore is visible, and the scythe is the reaper's only tool.

NO. 13 DEATH
VIEVILLE TAROT

A lone plant grows in the background. In the Mitelli Tarot from 1664, the skeleton benefits from a better sense of anatomy, but seems bland, with scythe on the left and hourglass held aloft on the right. A little pyramid stands in the background on the left side. (The attributes of scythe and hourglass are also associated with Father Time as well as Death.)

In every case, Death represents the time of harvest, as the ubiquitous scythe testifies. Unless the fruits of summer are harvested, they are lost to winter's harshness and the people do not eat. This Arcanum portrays the action of winter on the landscape—lush greenery is cut back, revealing the bones of the earth. The season of dark and cold separates the annual plants, which live and die in one year, from the perennials, which can take refuge in their root systems until the following spring, then sprout anew. As the scythe cuts the cords that link us to the past, it liberates us to go forward without fear, because we have nothing to lose. We can see that everything pruned away is recycled for the fertility of the future, so there is no loss despite the changes the seasons bring.

Astro-alphanumeric Correspondences:
"Gra" Hebrew: Water
Old Alexandrian: Water
Levi's Corrected Alexandrain: Water
Marseilles (Maxwell): Saturn
Modern Spanish (Dali): Saturn
Spanish Varient (Balbi): Saturn
English (Waite): Scorpio
English Varient (Crowley): Scorpio

Temperance

In the Pierpont Morgan-Bergamo Visconti-Sforza pack (mid-1400s), the Temperance card depicts a long-haired blond woman in a blue dress covered with gold stars, pouring an invisible substance from a silver urn to a gold one. She stands at cliffside looking down as she pours.

The Charles VI Tarot of 1470–80 makes the substance pouring between the urns more visible, but that and the woman's dark halo are the only outstanding features. The Mantegna tarocchi shows Temperance pouring the invisible substance again, with a dog at her feet looking at himself in a mirror that has a snake eating its

NO. 14 TEMPERANCE
WAITE TAROT

own tail as a border.

In Catelin Geoffrey's Tarot (1557) Temperance pours from an urn to a basin, showing less association with alchemy than with washing up. She is at least making a significant health statement in her times! Another variant of the Temperance image in the early centuries of Tarot might show her seated, but it seems to make no difference to the meaning whether she is enthroned or afoot.

NO. 14 TEMPERANCE
VIEVILLE TAROT

The Temperance from the anonymous Parisian Tarot from the early seventeenth century seems unremarkable, unless you can make sense of the jumble of forms to the right of the woman. It is also difficult to read what happens to the stream pouring from the upper urn—does it land in a second one at her feet? The paint job makes the underlying image unclear. She may be standing cliffside or next to a body of water. Mitelli (1664) has turned her back to us, but otherwise she is as we would expect her, pouring from the right-hand urn to the left-hand urn.

The Vieville Tarot, which with the Noblet Tarot marks a turning point in Tarot history, gives us an interesting variant on the Temperance Arcanum. In this case, she holds a bird-topped wand (or a wand with an elaborate fleur de lis) on her left and pours from the urn in her right hand into another vessel at her feet. A banner imprinted with the words Fama Sol waves beside her, clearly an alchemical reference. This version persists among later Tarot decks, but less often than the image which the Marseilles Tarot immortalizes, that of Temperance pouring the liquid between vessels held in each hand.

Over time, Temperance acquired wings, although exactly when is difficult to pinpoint because Kaplan does not always include Temperance in the groupings of Arcana he displays. Vieville's Tarot lacks them, but Noblet's Tarot has embraced them. As Kaplan mentions in Volume 2 of his *Encyclopedia*, this Arcana has seen less variation than others in the first four hundred years, so he probably did not feel it necessary to display every single Temperance card.

The consensus on this card appears to be nearly complete. The female figure is a reference to the soul, and she is mixing a blend of subtle energies that will presumably be employed in the further evolution of the personality. The key to meaning in this card is its title, a pun on the process of tempering metals in a forge. The metals must undergo much violent handling, extremes of temperature and endless folding and pounding, but the end product is infinitely superior to the original raw ore, fresh from the earth and utterly unrefined. In this image, the soul volunteers the ego for a cleansing and healing experience which may turn the personality inside-out, but which brings out the gold hidden within the heart.

Astro-alphanumeric Correspondences:
  "Gra" Hebrew: Scorpio
  Old Alexandrian: Scorpio
  Levi's Corrected Alexandrain: Scorpio
  Marseilles (Maxwell): Aquarius
  Modern Spanish (Dali): Aquarius
  Spanish Varient (Balbi): Aquarius
  English (Waite): Saggitarius
  English Varient (Crowley): Saggitarius

Devil

Authentic early images of the Devil in the Tarot are extremely scarce. For some reason this card is missing from nearly all the oldest Tarots. Perhaps the controversial nature of the image made it more subject to abuse. A very early image of the Devil Arcana can be seen in the Rothschild Tarot or Minchiate cards at the Louvre in Paris. The image is of a composite demon with chicken feet and legs, a remarkably human face in its abdomen, wings, tail, horns, goat ears, shaggy fur or feathers, and a huge gobbling maw with the remains of several people hanging out of it.

A figure very similar to this appears on the Tower card of the Catelin Geoffrey Tarot (1557). This is a conception right out of the ancient stone churches dotting Europe, which were carved inside and out to represent the teachings of the Gospel (interwoven with pagan tradition) for the non-literate masses. The reference is to the "hairy wild man" of paganism, Pan the god of the wilds, and the animal side of ourselves. The image from a Parisian woodcut circa 1530 shows very clearly the same kind of creature. Kaplan says "He is the Devil of the folk, rather than fine art" (Volume 2, p. 172). The Hebreo Devil card from the sixteenth century, cited by Kaplan in his *Encyclopedia* (Vol. 2, p. 297), is another classic folk-style Devil. Later Tarot decks which want to reference this theme show the Devil and its minions covered with hair.

NO. 15 THE DEVIL
ROTHSCHILD TAROT

This image was predominant even into the seventeenth century, and expresses the traditional concept of the lamia, werewolf or vampire, the mon-

WOODCUT OF THE DEVIL

ster that haunts the superstitious mind in the dark of night, threatening to steal one's soul. This primordial fear was cleverly harnessed by the Church when it was equated with the biblical Satan. The anonymous Parisian Tarot features a terrifying Devil as a composite demon with chicken feet, goat legs, face in his abdomen, bat wings, hairy arms, tail and an insane expression. He holds a red pole with fierce raking claws at one end and a heavy iron chain hanging from the other. The red tongue sticking out of his gray beard completes the look. The Mitelli Tarot (1664) shows a powerfully built, nude man/demon with bird feet, pointed ears and curving horns growing from his hairline. He carries a trident, has leathery wings, and sits with his feet upon a dragon-snake.

On an alternative track, the Jean Noblet Tarot, one of the earliest examples of the Marseilles Tarot decks (this one published in Paris in the early 1660s) introduces important changes to the older demonic image. This shift adds a new gender alignment to the Devil, that of the androgyne. Female breasts and male genitalia introduce new information on the card. The Devil also acquires for the first time a male and female demon chained to the pedestal upon which s/he stands. It looks as if a distinctly new image began circulating among cartomancers at this time which influenced their thinking and showed up on nearly every Tarot after this pivotal date.

The Pierre Madenie Tarot of 1709 continues to make the Devil androgynous with the new feminine breasts just above a curvaceous waist, complimented with black bat wings and accompanied by the two primordial humans chained to his pedestal. Madenie and his contemporaries are a little ambiguous about what is below the beltline of this Devil, but the Claude Burdel Tarot of 1751, showing umistakable male genitalia, again makes explicit the issue of mixed or double gender for the Devil. The Grimaud Marseilles deck, first pub-

NO. 15 THE DEVIL
JEAN NOBLET TAROT

lished in 1748, presents the image we are now accustomed to see as traditional.

All the Tarot decks from this era seem to be reflecting this new, more esoterically composed version of the Devil. Court de Gebelin mirrors it nearly exactly, Etteilla has a rare moment of accord with the collective consensus, and we see a near-total agreement on this image right up to the twentieth century. Even among those dissenters who revert to the older, all-male lamia version of the Devil (e.g., Edoardo Dotti, 1862; the Tarot pack by J. Gaudais of 1860) often choose to include the later addition of the wild man and woman chained to the pedestal.

This card's sudden mutation in the mid-1660s is a powerful argument for a new source of inspiration entering the Tarot canon at just this time. And if we compare this new mutation to the Typhon card of the Alexandrian Tarots, one sees the salient details of the change prefigured; the female breasts and male phallus, the bat wings, the horn(s) on the head, the two figures, male and female, chained at Typhon's feet. Although the Westernization of this image thinned the Devil's waistline (in later times made very narrow and feminine) and gave it a goat-

NO. 15 THE DEVIL
IBIS TAROT

like rather than crocodile head, it would be very difficult to argue that the Typhon formulation had nothing to do with the transformation of the Devil Arcanum, from the shaggy figure out of a medieval bestiary into the refined Baphomet image of Levi, Papus, Wirth, Esoterico, Balbi, and the other Continental esoteric Tarots.

Scapini's modern restorations of the missing Devil cards from the Pierpont Morgan-Bergamo Visconti-Sforza tarocchi pack and the Cary-Yale Visconit tarocchi deck (fifteenth century) are wonderful, as is all his work, but it is not likely that the originals were similar. The Scapini images show the two people chained to the pedestal under the Devil, a detail which emerged only in the later 1600s in response to the Hermetic/Alexandrian document that inspired the Falconnier Tarot. Of the other modern Esoteric Devil cards, the Waite-Smith image is the most familiar, showing us the very early, male, bird-footed Devil but including the chained demons on the pedestal. Dali's image deliberately echoes the Fool, showing a hermaphroditic soul being pushed into his/her deepest desires—a very Gnostic image!

An overview of the Devil Arcanum shows us the realm of the Taboo, the culturally created, rejected and undigested shadow side that each of us is burdened with due to our acculturation. This is in fact the core of our individuality which we cannot get rid of but will never succeed in taming. From its earliest versions, showing the lamia or vampire-demon, this card evoked the Church-fueled fear that a person could "lose his soul" to this wild, animalistic force. The amended version that emerged in the mid-1600s shows us a more sophisticated version called Typhon, a hermaphroditic amalgam of the four elements, enslaving the animal nature in men and women.

By the 1800s the concept had refined into the scapegoated Goddess, whose esoteric name is Baphomet. Volcanic reserves of passion and primal desire empower her labor to overcome the pressure of gender-based role assignments and experience true freedom of soul. Tavaglione's fully realized image portrays the magical, theurgical formula for harnessing and transmuting primal and obsessive emotions into energy toward enlightenment. As a part of the Gnostic message of Tarot, this frightening but awesome passion and power must be reintegrated into the personality to fuel the soul's passage from mortal to immortal.

Astro-alphanumeric Correspondences:
  "Gra" Hebrew: Saggitarius
  Old Alexandrian: Saggitarius
  Levi's Corrected Alexandrain: Saggitarius
  Marseilles (Maxwell): Water/North Node of the Moon
  Modern Spanish (Dali): Mars
  Spanish Varient (Balbi):Mars
  English (Waite): Capricorn
  English Varient (Crowley):Capricorn

Tower

The Tower image, like that of the Devil, has not survived through history as well as the other Arcana from the oldest Tarots. This could be a side effect of the Church persecutions of all things occult or Gnostic. Then again, it may just be because the royalty who commissioned the earliest Tarots didn't want to be confronted with images of themselves in physical or political danger, or pursued by demons from the pits of Hell. Nevertheless, some ideas can be derived from looking at the earliest versions that we do possess.

A massive Tower is the only subject of the Charles VI Tarot (mid-1400s). Its front is shown intact, but the backside is cracking, dropping pieces and revealing flames licking from between the bricks. By the time of the Catelin Geoffrey Tarot (1557) we see only the door of the Tower, at ground level, with gray smoke and yellow flames belching out the windows. Three beings are crossing paths at this stone archway; a gray, chicken-legged demon with mad humanoid face is reaching out for, and locking eyes with, a man who has a viola on his shoulder, his bow ready to play. The musician is walking briskly into the melee, but looks back at the touch of the demon. A wailing woman with her arms in the air flees something she sees behind the door, oblivious to everything else around her. The Rothschild Tarot or Minchiate cards from the late fifteenth or early sixteenth century show

a pile of broken bodies before the door of the Tower, with another person ready to jump off the ramparts. Flames are licking out from all the windows. No demon is present to complicate matters.

The early seventeenth century anonymous Parisian Tarot shows a very disturbing image. Little is made of the Tower, but smoke and flames are everywhere. One nude woman crouches with her arms over her head, another runs screaming through the devastation. A gray faced demon with a man's body raises a red club, perhaps to dispatch the crouching person. Another dwarfish demon with what looks like a horn growing backward from his head appears to be straddling and/or embracing several amorphous flesh-colored forms slanting away from the top of the card. Everything is falling and askew, an impression increased by the sloppy coloring job. The Mitelli Lightning card (1664) is a revelation of clarity by comparison, dispensing entirely with the tower and showing a single man being struck by a zigzag bolt of fire.

NO. 16 THE TOWER
VIEVILLE TAROT

Two other images emerge in the pivotal 1660s, one of which becomes the Marseilles standard called the House of God, seen on the Jean Noblet Tarot circa 1660 (Kaplan's *Encyclopedia* Volume 2, p. 309). This shows the familiar crowned Tower being hit with a bolt of lightning from the sun, releasing a shower of falling sparks, knocking the top of the Tower right off, and plunging its two occupants to their deaths. Stuart Kaplan retells the Arthurian legend of the "Dolorous Stroke" as a possible subtext for this image (on p.174 of Volume 2 of his *Encyclopedia*), as well as cites the biblical story of the Tower of Babel, a traditional connection. We can assume there were other well known correspondences to this Arcana even in the 1600s, however.

Not only do we have the demonic images on the earliest Tower cards to factor in, but the Jacques Vieville Tarot, chronological and physical partner to the Noblet Tarot, shows another version of Arcanum No. 16, one which becomes the norm for the subsequent Flemish Tarots. In this version a young man expresses wonder at the sight of a large tree under a cloud containing the sun. Drops of something white or transparent fall through the sky, and neither a tower nor lightning are apparent. This image is named "Lightning" but evades entirely any of the ramifications that have to do with the House of God.

Perhaps the awestruck young man is contemplating the amazing powers of Nature at work in the landscape. Or could this be Adam, rediscovering the Tree of Life after winning his way free from the depredations of the Devil? In his caption for the pictures of the Adam de Hautot Tarot (1728–48), Kaplan tells us that "according to the Bibliothèque Nationale, [this image] may have once been The Star, portraying one of the shepherds on the night of the Nativity of Christ, with the star of Bethlehem blazing and sheep at the foot of the tree." This is a far cry from our original images from the 1400s, and never caught on with the majority despite its Gnostic evocativeness.

NO. 16 THE TOWER
CATELIN GEOFFROY TAROT

In the majority of these images, disaster is striking or has just struck. The demons of madness and despair are released from ancient hiding places, and Nature conspires with human evil to destabilize the people. One unwritten subtitle of this card is "The Act of God" because the upheaval is collective, impersonal. Yet let us remember the patrons for whom these images were created—nobles and clergy, the educated rich—and we realize just who will lose altitude fastest should the towers start to fall. In that sense, lightning is a fitting karmic response to the guilt of those whose fortunes come from abuse of the land and its residents. A more fitting modern subtitle could thus be "Revolution from Below," indicating drastic enough change that a poor person has new cause for hope of better times. Although the Tower comes packaged as a classic crash and burn experience, it also levels the playing field for everyone, providing all who survive with a fresh start as equals.

Astro-alphanumeric Correspondences:
"Gra" Hebrew: Capricorn
Old Alexandrian: Capricorn
Levi's Corrected Alexandrain: Capricorn
Marseilles (Maxwell): Air/South Node of the Moon
Modern Spanish (Dali): Aries
Spanish Varient (Balbi): Aries
English (Waite): Mars
English Varient (Crowley): Mars

Star

The Visconti-Sforza Tarot (1475) shows a long-haired blond woman wearing a blue dress embellished with golden stars, covered by a red robe lined with green. She is looking up and reaching out with her left hand to touch a star in the heavens. The Charles VI pack (mid-1400s) shows two mature men in robes, one with a star map in his hand, pointing up at a brilliant gold star with eight points in the heavens above them. These men epitomize the two earliest representations of this concept: the astrologer who charts the Star, or the Spirit of the Star, and bridges the gap between heaven and earth.

The Rothschild Tarot or Minchiate cards from the late 1400s to early 1500s now at the Louvre in Paris show us a fascinating image. Figures much like the Emperor and the Pope carry an elaborate crown between them. They bump into a Fool-like person who hails them with open arms, as if he is a long-lost brother. An eight-pointed star hangs overhead. Are these unlikely three about to become the Three Wise Men? The suggestion is that each of them is being led by the Star.

The anonymous Parisian Tarot from the early 1600s shows a learned professor in mortarboard hat sitting at his drafting table with protractor in hand, looking up at an eight-pointed star in the upper left corner of the card, partially obscured by the border.

NO. 17 THE STAR
VISCONTE-SFORZA TAROT

The Mitelli Tarot of 1664 uses an interesting variant of the Star. A man with a heavy load slung from the staff over his shoulder carries a lit lantern through the night. His head is down and his stride is long. Overhead are six small stars and one very bright one, all with six points, lighting his way. Another variation emerges with the Tarocco Siciliano cards from Italy in 1750. Here a man on horseback balances a giant sphere or covered hoop sporting the design of an eight-pointed star, of which we see the bottom half. There is a carnival or Triumphi feel to this picture, entirely at odds with the quiet, contemplative, meditative trend of the other Star cards considered. This formulation, like Mitelli's, did not catch on with the larger marketplace.

The form that did catch on and become standard is the young, nude woman by the bank of the water, pouring from two vessels into the water and onto the earth. The Marseilles, the Falconnier and the Waite image all align with this form of the Arcana, as does the Knapp-Hall Tarot, Oswald Wirth's Tarot, and El Gran Tarot Esoterico. We see this as the traditional image now, but it is in actuality one of many that have been named the Star.

Despite the changes from deck to deck, the overall idea of the Star is the reconnecting of one's soul with a larger

No. 17 THE STAR
ROTHSCHILD TAROT

frame of reference outside of personality, community or worldly accomplishments. The soul (always shown as female in Tarot) is responding to forces affecting it from outside this world, forces that provide the personality with such sureness and orientation that it can ignore what anyone else thinks. Remembering the Gnostic myth of the soul's descent from on high, the Star card implies a new remembrance of our exalted origins and attraction to the path of return. An alternate title for this card is "Celestial Mandate" in that it refers us back to our reason for being, our mission in this lifetime. This Arcanum reminds us that each of us is a secret agent enacting Divine Will through our moment to moment lives. If we let go of the idea that we are supposed to be in control of our lives every minute, we can study and reflect upon the synchronicities that are constantly nudging us through our days. Thus we become conscious of the invisible help focused on us, and we understand our place within and value to the larger cosmos in a new way.

Astro-alphanumeric Correspondences:
  "Gra" Hebrew: Mercury
  Old Alexandrian: Mercury
  Levi's Corrected Alexandrain: Mercury
  Marseilles (Maxwell): Taurus
  Modern Spanish (Dali): Venus
  Spanish Varient (Balbi): Venus
  English (Waite): Aquarius
  English Varient (Crowley): Aries

Moon

In the Visconti-Sforza Tarot of 1450, a long-haired blond woman wears a red slip over a blue dress bound with a silver cord for a belt. Her right hand grasps the moon in the sky while the left hand tries to control the belt ends, which are flapping in the breeze. She stands at cliff side but looks at the moon. In the Charles VI pack (mid-1400s) we see an older magus with a white beard, seated at his desk, with a zodiacal globe of the heavens on a stand behind him. He is using a compass to erect a chart of the Moon, whose image from the heavens is reflected in the paper under his hands. The Gringonneur Tarot (mid-1400s) shows not one but two magi, with compasses and sky map, "who measure the conjunctions of the stars and planets" (Stuart Kaplan's *Encyclopedia* Volume 1, p. 115). The Rothschild Tarot or Minchiate

cards (late fifteenth or early sixteenth century) show two philosophers crowned in laurel, the one on the left with a sophisticated astrolabe sculpture in hand. Each also holds a caliper or angle measuring tool, and the person on the right points to the moon above. There are no connotations of lunacy or disorientation here.

One early seventeenth century anonymous Parisian Tarot propounds a different idea for this card entirely. A nude woman in a tall tower lets down her hair and exposes her back for the man with a harp seated in the garden below. We see the archway and door he could enter to reach her, yet he stays and makes music. A full moon looks down benignly from above. In contrast to the Lovers from this Tarot described above, this card shows some restraint and an aesthetic sensibility. It could be referring to the growing tradition of courtly love saturating Renaissance culture at this time.

No. 18 THE MOON
ROTHSCHILD TAROT

Another idealistic Moon card is seen in the Mitelli Tarot (1664), where a young woman standing with a hound at her feet leans on her staff and looks into the heavens; she is crowned by a crescent moon. She seems to be making a reference to Diana or Artemis, goddess of the purity and natural sacredness of wild places.

The Tarocco Siciliano from 1750 gives us another variation. A man is asleep under a tree, and a woman stands over him making gestures as if to point out his limp state. Kaplan refers to the cloud around the moon as being ominous and the face on the orb as diffident, uninterested. Is she sad? Mad? Is he sick? Under the influence? The card does not specify. But we know that the Moon Arcanum has often been used to symbolize special shamanic states of mind, such as those reached through dreams or deep trance work, so there are multiple possibilities about what is going on in this image.

The Marseilles Tarot decks, which were emerging as a separate style in the late 1600s, show us the now-familiar Two Towers image in

No. 18 THE MOON
ANONYMOUS PARISIAN TAROT

which the path rises from a pool containing a crawfish or crab at the base of the card. The moon emanates an otherworldly glow to the tune of two baying dogs who stand at the base of the towers, between which the path runs to the horizon. Although this may seem to represent a departure from previous Tarots that we have evidence of, a similar Arcanum No. 18 image appears on the Alexandrian Tarots modeled from the *Fratres Lucis* manuscript (or its prototype) purportedly circulating in Europe since the Middle Ages. The difference is that in the Alexandrian-style version, called the Twilight, the towers are pyramids. In truth, these two Moon cards are more similar to each other than to any earlier images in the stream.

NO. 18 THE MOON
IBIS TAROT

The Moon Arcanum always refers to our deepest body-mind states, the ones where, within a protective cocoon of deep relaxation, we are brought to the finest pitch of sensitivity and imaginative impression-ability. Here we dream and trance, have visions and receive insights, wash in and out with the psychic tides and experience deep mystical and/or terrifying realities beyond our ordinary senses. The full moon and/or eclipse charted by the magi (as in some of the earliest Moon images) imply one mechanism that Nature uses to dilate the soul. The variants of the courtly lovers (representing right use of the sex force) or the man "sleeping it off" under the tree (use of drugs to alter consciousness) are also traditional avenues for touching the primal body/mind outside our conditioning. The human curiosity for knowledge of "higher states" has propelled us to the frontiers of consciousness, where we cannot always control what happens. This Arcanum represents the ultimate test of a soul's integrity, where the barrier is removed between the self and the unknown, and the drop reenters the ocean of being. What transpires next is between the soul and its Maker.

Astro-alphanumeric Correspondences:
  "Gra" Hebrew: Aquarius
  Old Alexandrian: Aquarius
  Levi's Corrected Alexandrain: Aquarius
  Marseilles (Maxwell): Camcer
  Modern Spanish (Dali): Cancer
  Spanish Varient (Balbi): Camcer
  English (Waite): Pisces
  English Varient (Crowley): Pisces

Sun

One of the earliest images of the Sun Arcanum is the one on the Gringonneur cards (agreed to be from the mid 1400s). A young and beautiful woman with fair hair is shown with a staff and drop-spindle, walking through an Eden-like landscape, complementing its beauty with her own. The sun looks down impassively from above. An uncut sheet of Minchiate cards, circa late fifteenth or early sixteenth century (Volume 1, p. 128, Kaplan's *Encyclopedia*) shows a seated version of the same spinning woman, although the Sun has a decidedly stern face in this card. The Charles VI Tarot from 1470–80 displays this theme as well.

This image did not become the standard form, however, giving way (or giving birth?) to other formulations within only a few decades. In the Visconti-Sforza Tarot of 1450, a muscular cherub on a leaden-green cloud holds up the red and radiant face of the Sun, which beams aggressively over the landscape below. Gareth Knight, in his book *A Treasure-House of Images*, mentions that this particular version "is an image that has resonance with the Mysteries of Orpheus and the Holy Grail, ancient Celtic Mysteries, and the esoteric Christianity associated with Salome and John the Baptist" (p. 72). I do wish he had explained that line of thought further!

Alternately, the Ercole d'Este cards (1475–80) shows an old man sitting on the edge of a huge overturned wine keg and carrying on a discourse with a man who is standing and facing him. A large gold Sun with silver emanations shines in the dark sky above.

NO. 19 THE SUN
CHARLES VI TAROT

The early seventeenth century anonymous Parisian Tarot takes a different tack, putting a blue ape in the image, which appears to startle a woman who was combing her hair. It is unclear to me what the ape is holding up between itself and the woman, but Gareth Knight says it is a looking glass. A radiant Sun shines down upon the scene impassively. On the other hand, the Mitelli Tarot, another unique pack from later in the same century, shows the Greek god Apollo with his lyre, haloed in golden light, his purple cloak tied loosely around him. Perhaps these two are mirroring each other, the truly beautiful and harmonious Apollo contrasted with the false beauty and glamour of vanity, truly the "ape" of our higher values.

The Tarocco Siciliano cards from 1750 seem to continue the innovative trend in this image, showing the Cain and Abel murder being enacted under an "ominous cloud" that surrounds the impassive Sun. This image reflects in human terms the dismal characteristics that guarantee our continu-

ing estrangement from Eden, damning humankind to generations of strife and fighting. It is here that "original sin" becomes personal.

The Marseilles image which became the standard by the early 1700s shows us two toddlers protected from wild Nature by a brick wall that stands protectively between them and the greensward. Being "back to Eden" after the global reconciliation to come is implied. This reconciliation, sacred to all the Old Testament believers from antiquity, resolves the tension between all opposites (symbolized by the two children, ambiguous in both gender and age).

The Alexandrian model of Arcanum No. 19, exemplified on this CD in the Ibis Tarot, is called "Love" in the Falconnier version and "The Beaming Light" in the Fatidic Egyptian Tarot from 1901. This image shows the two children grown, of opposite genders, holding hands within a circle of greenery. A symbol of sexual union hangs in the sky above them. If these two Sun cards were made in respect of each other, the Marseilles version represents a naive approach to the resolution of the opposites compared to the one portrayed on the Egyptian-style decks!

Etteilla chose the mixed image called "Enlightenment." The bottom half of the picture shows two naked infants playing around what looks like a sepulcher or monument in a woodsy setting. Perhaps their new lives represent the victory of life over death. In a sort of split-screen effect, the upper end of this image is a scene in deep space, at the birth of a star. He might be trying to say that when we become conscious of our true cosmic identities, we are no longer so tied to birth and death.

When his time came to represent esoteric Tarot for the twentieth century, Waite chose to hark back to the earliest versions showing a cherub, only this time riding a horse and carrying a banner, seen against the walled backdrop of the Marseilles image. We could infer that in this formulation, the opposites are united within the self, in the Divine Child Within.

Because The Sun Arcanum personifies the goal of self cultivation and self initiation in the classical scheme, the overall theme of this card is "back to Eden" or "reversal of the fall from grace." It is here that one's original nature or preconditioned being can be encountered in health and safety. The limitations of time and space are stripped away; the soul rests and is refreshed, protected from the chaos outside the garden walls. Life reassumes its primordial goodness, truth and beauty. If one person is portrayed, it is usually shown as a human incarnation of the Divine. When two humans are shown, they are usually designed to ex-

press a resolution of the tension between opposites on all levels. It is for this reason that this card is read in a spread as saying "you can do no wrong."

Astro-alphanumeric Correspondences:
"Gra" Hebrew: Pisces
Old Alexandrian: Pisces
Levi's Corrected Alexandrain: Pisces
Marseilles (Maxwell):Gemini
Modern Spanish (Dali): Gemini
Spanish Varient (Balbi): Uranus
English (Waite): Sun
English Varient (Crowley): Sun

Judgment

Called the Angel in the Cary-Yale Visconti, winged spirits blowing long trumpets hang in the blue firmament while below the earth is parting to release the souls of the dead into their resurrection. Most emerge naked, but one is emerging in full ecclesiastical regalia. The Visconti-Sforza Angel image, from 1450, shows a third entity in heaven with the trumpeting angels, this one a grand fatherly patriarch with blue robe, flowing white beard, red gloves, and an upright sword in his right hand. Another patriarch emerges from the tomb between two nude maidens who are also emerging. The Charles VI pack shows two angels with trumpets blowing a blast that raises seven nude men and women from their graves (mid-1400s).

Luckily the trend toward greater population on this Arcanum ended here. Catelin Geoffrey's Tarot (1557) scales it back to one trumpeting angel and three resurrected souls— two women and one man—all nude. Mitelli (1664) is so minimalist that he only presents the trumpeting angel, and viewers are left to come to their own conclusions about the results.

The Tarocco Siciliano cards from Modiano, Italy (1750) changes the Angel image into an image of Jove, and it is numbered to be the last card in the Major Arcana sequence in this family of Tarots. He sits on a throne with an eagle at his feet, his upraised hand full of descending thunderbolts. The robe wrapped casually around him reveals his strength and vigor. This could be seen as a very patriarchal image, implying continuing punishment for fallen

humanity rather than the reconciliation of opposites which often informs this Arcanum.

The Marseilles image is now our classic reference for

this card, and there is very little substantial difference between this and the Alexandrian version, the Etteilla versions, and the versions of Papus and Wirth. A settled consensus seems to inhabit this card through the last three centuries of Tarot, which seems to mirror the concern amongst most world religions: that believers be assured that this life, this body, this personality and gender, are not all there is to look forward to.

No. 20 Judgement
Tarroco Siciliano

This Arcanum, called Judgment but usually picturing the Resurrection, represents the great reunion that the ancients believed would happen once every world age, when the group of souls who had been reincarnating together is gathered up and taken "home" to the place of origin outside the solar system. Then the World is seeded with a batch of new souls and the process starts over. In this great reunion, every personality you have ever been and every soul you have done deep work with comes back together to consciously complete the process. In personal terms, this portrays you as becoming so spiritually transparent, so clear a channel, that the buried talents and gifts of past incarnations bloom through you in this lifetime. You can afford to open yourself trustingly because what emerges is of consistently high quality. You effortlessly manifest as a multi-talented, multi-dimensional being, and you assist in evoking that response in others.

Astro-alphanumeric Correspondences:
  "Gra" Hebrew: Saturn
  Old Alexandrian: Saturn
  Levi's Corrected Alexandrain: Saturn
  Marseilles (Maxwell): Scorpio
  Modern Spanish (Dali): Pisces
  Spanish Varient (Balbi): Saggitarius
  English (Waite): Fire (modern Pluto)
  English Varient (Crowley): Pluto

World

This Cary-Yale Visconti Arcanum from 1445 centers on a portrait of a Renaissance village, complete with little lake, people fishing from the bank and a knight errant riding by. We see the Goddess in the firmament above, rising from a crown whose headband hangs high above the scene. She presides over her World serenely, a thin wand in her right hand and the orb of sovereignty in her left, an upper-case Empress.

In the Charles VI pack (mid-1400s) a similar globe or world-ball showing towns and villages in the folds of a hilly landscape lies under the feet of a blond woman looking much like the Strength, Fortitude and Temperance figures from the same deck. She holds a golden wand in her right hand, a golden ball in her left. The Italian tarocchi cards of the early sixteenth century, which are divided between the Metropolitan Museum of Art and the Budapest Museum of Fine Arts, also show this configuration on its World Arcanum. The imagery appears to have started out feminine, pointing to a Gnostic inspiration.

In 1450 the Visconti-Sforza Tarot portrays two muscular male cherubs holding up a globe that shows a walled city on an island surrounded by a turbulent sea. The Ercole d'Este image again contains the rolling landscape with towns and trees dotting the hills. This time a chubby cherub with green wings sits above, and a golden eagle with outstretched wings holds up the ball from below. The Eagle has had esoteric connections since biblical times, and has also served as a totem of the Empress and her family.

The late fifteenth or early sixteenth century Minchiate cards in the Bibliothèque de l'Ecole Nationale Superieure des Beaux-Arts shows, in Kaplan's words, "a mythological god or warrior atop an ornate stone wheel" (Vol. 1, p. 128). His winged helmet has Hermetic associations. His right hand holds a wand topped with a winged, gold-trimmed orb and the left holds another orb, with the t-cross inscribed on it and surmounted by an equal-armed cross.

The anonymous Parisian Tarot from the early seventeenth century uses an androgynous figure covering itself with the drapery of a curtain held up on a rod behind it. This symbol, the "veil of the Mysteries," is an ancient Hebrew concept which is not usually illustrated though often mentioned by early Kabbalists. This idea can be related to the Ain-Soph-Aur or "triple-veiled nothing" of the Kabbalists. This self-complete being strides across a globe that seems to contain the sun, the planets and the signs, and which has the classic band-and-raised-cross trimming that is usually seen on the globe in the hand of the Empress or Emperor. Stylized faces in the clouds blow upon the globe, presumably to keep its contents rotating.

No. 21 The World
Cary-Yale Visconti Tarot

A bit later in the seventeenth century Mitelli shows the World as a huge stone which a burly naked man struggles to lift from a kneeling position. This could be Hercules or Sisyphus performing monumental labors to defend humans from the judgment of the gods. The Tarocco Siciliano (1750) echoes this image, but the boulder is banded with the glyphs of the zodiac signs, like a giant calendar-stone.

The Marseilles image, most familiar of all, is of a woman, haloed man, or androgyne dancing or standing in space, surrounded by an oval wreath of leaves. Usually the image is unambiguously feminine, but the Vieville World card from the early 1660s de-emphasizes the breasts and gives it a halo, like the familiar Christian images of Christ Triumphant. Stuart Kaplan reveals a wealth of detail about ways in which the Marseilles image resembles religious pictures of the Last Judgment (*Encyclopedia,* Volume 2, p. 179), and he also includes the Christ Triumphant image rendered on a beautiful piece of carved ivory from the eleventh century which could double as the World Arcanum without changing a detail. Kaplan also introduces the idea that the earliest female World cards might have been intended to represent a female Christ, which indicates a distinctly Gnostic mentality.

No. 21 The World
de Hautot Tarot

Another Marseilles variant, the modern El Gran Tarot Esoterico, which with its correspondences refers us back to the very ancient Hebrew versions of the Sephir Yetzirah, portrays a divine person with both breasts and male genitalia within a blossoming wreath, surrounded by the "four beasts of the Apocalypse," a popular formulation of this Arcanum. This Tarot may be chronologically modern, but the reference is to the same themes that Kaplan details in the slow slide of this Arcanum through both male and female forms over the centuries.

The Etteilla Tarots feature a substantially similar image, although the gender of the figure may be either male or female, depending upon the edition. When it is female, she is usually accompanied by two tall, narrow pyramids on either side. The image is called "Voyage," perhaps implying traveling around the world.

This Arcanum is called The Crown of the Magi in the Alexandrian Arcana, which resembles the Falconnier Tarot and is drawn from the *Fratres Lucis* manuscript purported to be from the Middle Ages. It shows a regal woman seated under the heavens. The skies are filled with a winged lingam and yoni symbol within a floating wreath, accompanied by the creatures of the four elements. The woman plays upon a three-stringed harp, each string representing one aspect of the human endowment—body, mind and soul.

We cannot see this detail on the Falconnier or the Fatidic Egyptian Tarots published between 1896–1901 because Kaplan left those Arcana out when he photocopied those Tarots for his *Encyclopedia.* But the Ibis, the St. Germaine Tarot, and the Sacred Tarot from the Brotherhood of Light all record this detail, so I feel safe to assume the older ones do too. If the Alexandrian-style Arcana do prove to have had an impact upon the Marseilles images of the late 1600s, this card would have to be cited as a counterargument. Perhaps the tension created by a female image appearing on the World Arcanum, after several centuries of Christ-centered iconography, was too great to allow a return to the older, Sophianic conception of the earliest Tarots.

Most of the images in our modern Tarots, made at the turn of the twentieth century, follow the Goddess-oriented line of thought from the earliest versions of the card. Oswald Wirth, Manly P. Hall and A.E. Waite all give us virtually the same idea. Interestingly enough, Hall's World card rearranges the suit symbols held by the four angels/animals of the elements in an intriguing and unexplained way. Perhaps the fact that his Tarot shows a strong leaning toward the Spanish style gives us the hint we need to further examine his elemental attributions, because the Spanish Tarots are the only ones that switch the elements on the suit symbols in their Tarots.

The predominating idea of the World Arcanum is the presiding intelligence, called Sophia or Wisdom, that upholds the platform for life on this and all worlds through infinity. A more accurate title would be "Soul of the World" because the (usually female) figure who has become our standard World image originates in Hebrew, Gnostic and alchemical lore. She stands between heaven and earth as the Cosmic Mother of Souls, the Wife of God who protects us from the karmic forces we have set loose on Earth in our immaturity and ignorance. Where the Empress secures and fertilizes our terrestrial lives, The World Arcanum's Goddess invites us into cosmic citizenship once we have come to know our soul's potential for it. Just as the Chariot (No. 7) stands for success in achieving a separate self, and the Temperance (No. 14) represents achievement of mental and moral health in the cauldron of culture, The World (No. 21) announces the stabilization of the soul's Immortal Being, accomplished without the necessity of dying. Hence this card, like the Sun, is reputed to have no negative meaning no matter where or how it appears. If the Hermetic axiom is "know thyself," this image represents what becomes known when the true nature of self is followed to its uttermost end.

Astro-alphanumeric Correspondences:
   "Gra" Hebrew: Jupiter, numbered 21
   Old Alexandrian: Fire , numbered 22
   Levi's Corrected Alexandrain, Sun numbered 21
   Marseilles (Maxwell): Virgo, numbered 21
   Modern Spanish (Dali): Taurus, numbered 21
   Spanish Varient (Balbi): Pluto, numbered 22
   English (Waite): Saturn, numbered 22
   English Varient (Crowley): Saturn, numbered 22

THE MINOR ARCANA

When the Major Arcana is removed from the Tarot, a pack of cards remains that comes close to replicating what we moderns know as a playing card deck. Earliest Tarot manuscripts make a clear distinction between the twenty-two Majors (Trumps) and the rest of the cards. Stuart Kaplan cites this as evidence that they originated as two separate entities.

Kaplan points us to a deck of cards called Mamluk, which may have originated in Turkey or come to Europe from Asia through Turkey. It has four suits numbering one through ten with four or five royalty each, for a total of fifty-two or fifty-six cards. A pack from the 1400s is in the Topkapu Museum in Istanbul, and may represent the originals from which the Italian suit symbols were drawn. Stuart Kaplan also mentions the Trappola decks as an alternate form of Minor Arcana Tarot; these have the expected four suits, but with only three royalty and six numbered cards each. Both these types of cards appear in Europe during the same time frame as the earliest Tarots, so it's difficult to say for sure if they preceded Tarot or sprang up along with it. Their presence suggests that the Minor Arcana can and did stand alone in some packs and that they possess an internal structure independent of the Majors.

Historians believe such cards as these may show us how the twenty-two Major Trumps became a seventy-two card deck. If the Mamluk was actually a progenitor of the modern Tarot, then we would have to assume that its authors were in harmony with the synthesis of the Kabbalah, Pythagorean number theory and astrology that you will read about in this essay. It would be very hard to retrofit the interface of these three distinct symbol sets over a pack of cards if those cards weren't originally designed to accommodate them.

If your deck is designed for divination, it has pictures of humans involved in various activities, and you do not notice the resemblance to playing cards nearly as much. But the striking and obvious feature of an esoteric Tarot is a stark geometric, numerical and elemental treatment of the numbered suit cards, along with royalty that exemplify the zodiac and the characters that enact its central mythos. As such, it looks almost exactly like a common bridge deck.

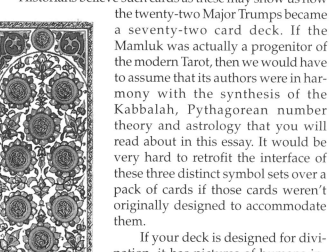

TEN OF COINS
MAMLUK TAROT

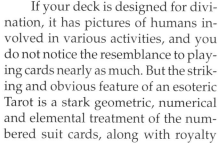

The Four Elements

The common denominator of the Minor Arcana from all decks is that they belong in suits—the traditional four suits of the bridge deck (hearts, clubs, spades, diamonds) or their earlier, more elemental forms (Cups, Wands, Swords and Coins). The Minor Arcana can be subdivided further to differentiate the royalty from the numbers, but they all participate equally in the four-way breakdown by element--water, fire, air and earth. Additionally, these four elements symbolize the four "worlds" of traditional magical practice: the worlds of the mind, heart, will and body. The four seasons, marked by the equinoxes and solstices, are also drawn into the symbolism of the suits by representing time and its passage through the quadrants of the year. In the case of the Spanish-influenced Tarots particularly, even though the symbols of the elements are occasionally interchanged one for another, there are still always four that embody the values of the elemental worlds.

In the course of examining the aces and the royalty of a number of older Tarots, I began to see patterns I now believe were part of the common knowledge shared by Tarot makers and practitioners from the first appearance of Tarot in Europe in the early 1440s. I want to suggest what I have come to see in these Tarots, but let us think of these ideas as working hypotheses rather than fixed theories. I hope they prove interesting enough to stimulate future publications from those who can enlighten us further.

ACE OF COINS
MAMLUK TAROT

The Suits and Their Symbolism

The four suits have been used as vehicles to carry symbols and images drawn from underground spiritual movements too controversial to stand in print in their own right. Each element represents its own mythos clearly enough for those who know how to look for it, but veiled enough to deflect the suspicion of the Inquisitors should a deck fall into their hands.

For example, the suit of Cups in some esoteric Tarots seems to be dedicated to the heresy of the True Royal Family of Europe, which asserts a bloodline purportedly stemming from the marriage of Jesus of Nazareth and Mary Magdalen.

This lineage was supposedly transplanted into southern Spain when Mary Magdalen fled the Holy Land after the crucifixion. Those Tarot decks which support this theme will show the cup in the hand of the King or Queen boiling, smoking, or full of blood. The knight may evoke echos of a Templar, and the Page may appear shackled or in front of an ancient toppled tree.

XXXVII.
MASTER OF CUPS

KING OF CUPS
IBIS TAROT

The suit of Wands can be seen bearing the Mason's marks which spell out the numbers one to ten, possibly representing grades of initiation in the secret lodges of Europe. Each grade would be a tempering achievement of the will toward the Divine, through the self-divining practices mapped out within the orders.

The suit of Coins has been attributed, card by card, to the planetary governors of ancient astrological pantheons, regularly invoked through Hermetic and later Renaissance talismanic magic. The numbered Coins are often inscribed with sigils drawn from Gnostic, Hebrew and Persian magical grimoires.

Only the suit of Swords seems to marginally evade this type of overlay of esoteric themes, although the Ace of Swords is regulrly embellished with either the laurel crown of a philosopher, or the iron crown of a warrior, or both, one at each end of the card. The Swords may have received different treatment because they carry the inherent meaning of ideological conflict, wars and communication problems, a universal dilemma in every generation, sect and situation. With careful scrutiny, one can see these themes riding alongside the regular, divinatory, simplistic meanings of the suit cards as agreed upon in the common tradition.

As we view the interior architecture of the suit cards,
you may be surprised at how much symbolism can be packed into such stripped-down imagery. It is easy to miss the profound depth built into the Minor Arcana if you do not know to look for it, because in the Hermetically inspired Tarots, the cards themselves seem so plain. Every attempt was made to refrain from stimulating emotions with the cards so the profundity of the symbols and interior correspondences could register on the unclouded mind. This approach allows the reader to construct a wide range of meanings for any given card rather than rely on a cartoon that may limit its significance and application to the current situation.

The cards 1-10 of each suit simultaneously embody the Gods of Number, the main energy centers in the human body (called Sephira by the Hebrews), and the planets in the solar system. Anyone who had procured the so-called classical education of the Renaissance would be able to recognize how each system corresponded to the cards, so that just seeing the suit symbols and the Arabic numerals on the faces of each card would bring up associations from sacred geometry, Kabbalah and astrology. The magi of the sixteeth or seventeenth century would have learned to "triangulate" between these three systems as they studied the meanings of the Minor cards, and their understanding of what any given card represents would be enhanced by that expanded view. Thus used by one who truly understands it, Tarot is truly a philosophical machine.

The Hermetics of Number Theory in the Minors

Inherent design principles, organic and repeated everywhere, attract the attention of thinking souls no matter what their language or culture. From very ancient times, philosophers recognized that Nature inclines toward certain arrangements and away from others, and canny thinkers began to see the ratios involved—literally, to "rationalize" the geometry of Nature. By the height of Egyptian culture, two thousand years before the life of Jesus, numbers themselves were seen as gods to be handled very carefully in order not to disturb their dispositions.

NUMBER	1	2	3	4	5	6	7	8	9	10
GEOMETRY	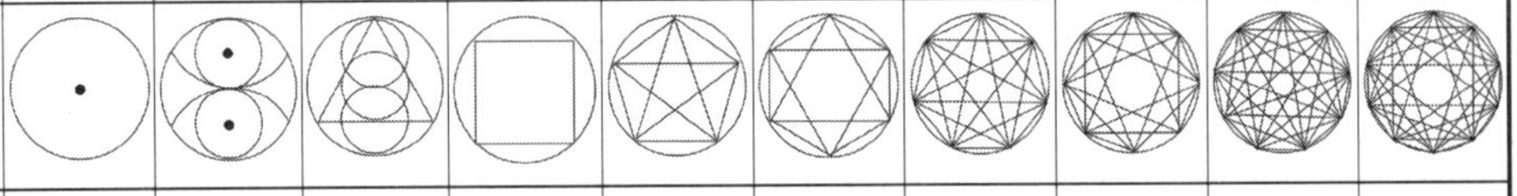									
ARCANUM	Magus	Priestess	Empress	Emperor	Heirophant	Lovers	Chariot	Justice	Hermit	Wheel
SEPHIROTIC CORRESPONDENCE	Keter	Chakmah	Binah	Chesed	Gevurah	Tiferet	Hod	Netzach	Yesod	Malkuth
RULING PLANET	△	▽	△	♃	♂	☉	☿	♀	☽	♄

The turning point between the mentality of antiquity, which envisioned humanity as the pawn of Nature and the gods, and the beginning of the modern worldview, which turned toward self-cultivation and the development of the human powers of mind, is marked by the work of Pythagoras, a sixth century BC teacher, scholar and prophet.

By the time of Pythagoras, mathematical thinking had penetrated the geometry hidden within whole numbers. An even more sophisticated symbolism emerged to portray the geometric solids proceeding from numbers, revealing the special properties of each number in its own world, resonating at its own frequency. From this perspective, the relations between numbers or their frequencies gave birth to harmonic theory, which Pythagoras revealed to the world through the medium of music, but which governs relations macrocosmically amongst the stars, and simultaneously, amongst the atoms. It would not be an exaggeration to suggest that all of Nature at every level is related through dynamics which could be expressed as interwoven harmonic ratios that are interacting.

Pythagoras used numerals as his first principles. In his philosophy, the whole numbers embraced and illustrated the Great Laws of Nature. He studied the properties of numbers and their relations not only in the realm of music but also in the realms of astronomy and philosophy.

The quintessential figure that Pythagoras invented to visually express his philosophy, called the Tetractys, is composed of ten discs arranged as a pyramid, each disk bearing the geometric figure of a whole number. We have shown it here in two forms—first as described above, and second with the internal relationships between stations in the pyramid lined out.

Call this the Mysticism of the Decave, the religion of base-ten enumeration. Contemplation of this remarkable doctrine leads right into sacred geometry and harmonic theory, and illustrates the classical understanding of beauty: symmetry, proportion, harmony, ratio and grace. Classical Greek culture reached a pinnacle in art and architecture in the century following Pythagoras, and his fame spread to what was then the ends of the world.

Every numbered card in a Tarot deck partakes of the innate geometry of the number that rules it. One is a whole, so every ace represents pure potential in one of the four elements. Two divides and polarizes, so each two expresses a dichotomy. Three gives polarity a fulcrum to balance upon, mediating extremism and harmonizing each of the elements. Four crystallizes and solidifies, so potentials acquire a framework on which to actualize. Five forces individuation and challenges creativity, eliciting vision and imagination. Six is yin and yang, two threes intertwined, fertile and furthering. Seven strives for the mastery depicted by the spiritual triangle surmounting the material square.

Eight is the test of interlaced squares, implying the wheel of the year and the challenge of survival from season to season. Nine is three threes, the "triple ternary," balance of balances, the so-called perfect number. Ten folds the circle of the numbers into a cycle, recapitulating the one at the next higher level. (In Tarot terms, the tens are each transforming into the ace of the next element in the chain of ascent/descent.) In the different elemental worlds, the numbers will appear with different emphases (like the difference between the Five of Swords and the Five of Wands), but the principles of the single digits rule the numbered suit cards of Tarot.

Extending this line of reasoning, the Major Arcana cards that bear the single digits are also reflected downward into the numbered suit cards. So, for example, the Hierophant, number five, rules the fives in all four suits, while the Chariot stands behind all the seven cards, the Justice underlies the eights, the Hermit upholds the nines, and the Wheel personifies the tens. You really are supposed to see, for example, the qualities of the Emperor embodied in the numeral four, implying the cube, the 90-degree angle, and the principle of materialization in each of the elements. These are all examples of the same principle at work. A student's job is to learn these correspondences until they are second nature.

Kabbalah and the Minors

The ancient Hebrews had their own Mystery of the Decave which Pythagoras was known to have studied in his travels around the Mediterranean. It was portrayed in many forms, but when it was described, it was called the "Doctrine of Emanations." In a nutshell, it expressed the way that the Origin of All opened itself and poured into successive vessels, one emerging from the last, in a series of ten great waves of creativity. As such, our entire world has been created by these great waves of energy emerging from the One, and humans are also constructed with this built-in tenfold pattern.

The creation of the world is conceptualized as a top-down procedure whereby the subtle forces at the top of the

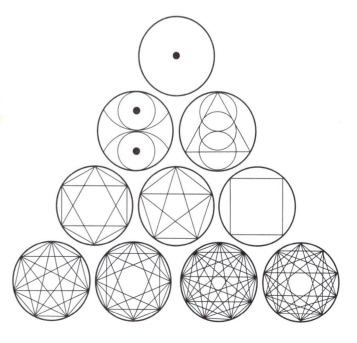

TETRACTYS

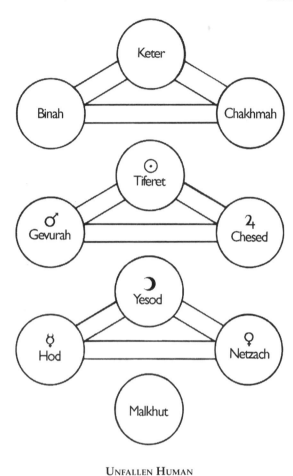

UNFALLEN HUMAN

plies deconstructing the mind map created by one's acculturation, so that consciousness can be free to ascend to higher and higher levels of mystical apperception.

The Kabbalah Tree's grid pattern that links the ten centers is a linear diagram made up of three vertical bars connected by a matrix of horizontal and diagonal bars interwoven to resemble the scientific drawing of a molecule. This diagram represents the way in which humans are "made in God's image." If you imagine this "molecule" superimposed upon your body, your backbone aligned with the Middle Pillar, it is easy to sense the nodes that appear at the points where the horizontals, diagonals and verticals converge. There's four in the "unfallen" diagram, and five in the "fallen" pattern. Two shorter pillars, each with three nodes, close the sides of the diagram, representing the left and right eyes, hands, and legs.

The system is similar to the Hindu chakra system, but the emphasis in the Hebrew Middle Pillar is on the number five rather than on the seven chakras of the East. The nodes

chain of creation are stepped down into successively denser and more material energies, to finally reach the tenth stage in the material world we experience with our senses. When the soul's descent is complete the energies reverse, and the soul begins to rise back up the Kabbalah Tree by the same path it descended (the combination of paths called the Lightning Bolt). The ascent of the soul is a classic theme occupying every aspect of the ancient Mystery School, and that path of ascent is mapped out by the 1-10 cards of the Tarot.

The logic is this: There is a complete Tree in each of the four elemental worlds, and we must climb each rung of this ladder to win our immortality and get off the Wheel of Incarnation. The ten rungs at the very bottom are represented by the earth cards (Coins). This suit involves the process of rising through the ten stages of material success, which culminates at the boundary of the emotional/psychic life. The next stage up is represented by the water cards (Cups). This level brings one to an understanding of the subjective life of fantasy, dream, sentiment and psyche. When that realm has been crossed, the fire cards (Wands) represent the next challenge in which the Will is tempered and tamed, like raw ore in the melting pot. The topmost reaches of the ladder are depicted by the air cards (Swords), the realm of the ideal or archetype, where the Mind of God contemplates the ideas behind the forms of matter. Passage through this sphere im-

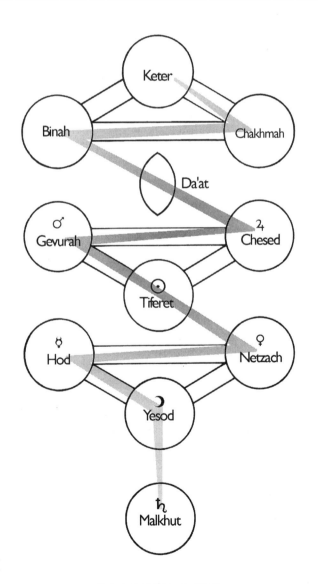

LIGHTNING-STRUCK TREE
"THE FALL"

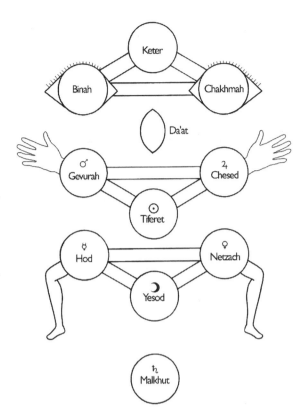

FALLEN HUMAN

nodes and directing will toward overcoming the distractions of the left and right pillar.

When divine order is restored, Saturn will occupy this center. As the last visible planet in the solar system, it is the symbol of limits, discipline, examinations and natural consequences. On a higher octave, Saturn is our representative of natures immutable laws, which hold us firm to the material plane while we work out our karmas through incarnation n this plane. In antiquity Saturn was known as the "ring pass-not" which prevented unripe souls from leaving the wheel of incarnation before they were mature. Stationed in the throat center, Saturn would restore the Power of the Word which the Creator used to materialize the world.

At the top of the Middle Pillar is Kether, which would correspond to a fusion of the third eye and the crown centers in the Hindu system. Actually, the point that Kether represents is the pineal gland deep in the brain, the organ that metabolizes light for the body. All the vertical channels—left, right and center—emerge from this point to descend into matter; conversely, all the channels converge on this point when ascending toward more refined states of being.

The set of three nodes on each pillar left and right represents the two eyes, two arms and hands, and two legs and feet. The three to the right in the diagram are called the Father Pillar, and their rising action is oriented toward contemplating the inner workings of God. The pillar to the left in the diagram, called the Mother Pillar, is directed in a descending manner, showering attention upon the outer world of things, beings, time and space. In relation to the distinct genders of the two outer pillars, the Middle Pillar is considered to be androgynous, neither male nor female, but partaking in the nature of the Divine Child Within.

What must be noted here, and what the Hebrew people managed to conceal from the Gentiles for several centuries after the invention of the printing press, is that you have to "back into" this diagram when superimposing it onto your body, so that the Mother Pillar stands on your right side and the Father Pillar stands on your left. Energy surges up the left side, over the top, and down the right before plunging into the earth below, only to surge up the left side again. This is part of the message of the Wheel of Fortune card in the Major Arcana: We each exist within a circulating vortex of lifeforce which we must learn to manage and utilize. The first organizing principle is that it all circulates around the heart.

Astrology and the Minors

Next for consideration is the zodiac of the 360-degree heavens wrapped around the Earth that has been distributed among the numbered Minor cards. For purposes of prediction and ritual applications, these could be the most well-used group of correspondences of the whole canon.

The great genius of the Babylonian numbering system is that Babylonian astrological priesthood devised a scheme whereby the fundamental unit of measurement is expressed

of the two side pillars express, distribute and administer the energies aroused and pooled in the Middle Pillar. The version of the Kabbalah Tree illustrated above represents a diagram of our energetic circuitry *after* the fall from Eden to eros. This "fallen" Tree no longer resembles the divine original, Adam Kadmon, which was the signature of the original creation (see essay on the Hebrew Kabbalah).

To restore ourselves and the fallen creations, according to the Kabbalists, our souls must retrace the steps we took in falling. Rising from the bottom of the Middle Pillar we first encounter Malkuth, the earth, foundation, root, body. Next up is the node called Yesod, which rests around the gonads and balances our hormones, emotions, feelings, psychic life and instincts. The Moon is traditionally equated with Yesod. The next node above is Tifareth, which encompasses what the Hindus would separate into two different chakras called Will and Heart. The Hebrews did not see a way in which an individual could have a personal will that contradicted divine will, so they lumped the two together in what was called the "heart." The sun of our solar system is equated to Tifareth, standing at the center unifying and organizing the whole, around which everything circulates.

Above Tifareth is Da'at, a node that exists as potential in everyone but which a person has to work on to activate. This corresponds to the Hindu throat chakra, the power of the Holy Word to create by fiat. This power is something that must be earned through effort and striving, aligning the lower

in both spatial and temporal terms simultaneously. To do this they had to:

(a) work within the ancient world's already-established preference for counting on our ten fingers

(b) determine a number which when multiplied by ten would express in whole numbers the full circle of the visible and invisible sky wrapped around the earth: the formula is $(10 \times 3) \times 12 = 360$

(c) harmonize the divisions of space marked out by the formula with the then-traditional Mansions of the Moon (an earlier, lunar division of the zodiac) and determine which twelve major constellations would be used to anchor the new zodiac for all future time

(d) develop the correspondence between one degree of movement in space and one unit of time elapsed in the course of making that movement. (This formula states that it takes four minutes of time to move the stars rising over the eastern horizon by one degree.)

In the process of inventing the modern paradigm of time and celestial motion, the Babylonians employed the Indian Brahmin concept of zero, so helpful in sophisticated calculations that go beyond the single, whole numbers. The entire world uses variations on this astrological system, and our modern space program would never have happened without this creative interpretation of the boundless distances and time scales presented by the spin of the Earth on its axis while pursuing its yearly trek around the sun.

When the Minor Arcana are drawn into this scheme, we again have to face the issue of fitting a 10-based form of counting onto the 360-degree sphere mapped by the ancients to track the ticking of the cosmic clock. The accommodation made was very clever: Taking into account the bias in this enumeration system for 3x10, each sequence of suit cards is divided into three threes, with each card representing ten degrees of zodiacal space, (five degrees for a card upright and a different five degrees for the card reversed). This leaves one card left over in each element to represent the equinoxes and solstices which mark out the four seasons. It's essentially the Wheel of the Year, with either the aces or tens standing in for the four high holidays celebrating the changing of the seasons. We see this system illustrated at the top of each Porta della Stella Minor Arcana card, to help the user "find themselves" in the zodiac.

Some schools of Tarot go even further into the astrology of the Minor Arcana, attributing a planetary ruler to each 10-degree segment of each sign, and including these subrulerships into the divinatory meaning of the card. The French esoteric group were the first to print the Hebrew angel-names for each 5-degree segment of the zodiac right on the cards. These angels are to be prayed to, contemplated upon, or evoked when asking for help with the issues represented by the cards in a spread and/or the hot spots in a person's birth chart (see the essay "Kabbalah/Cabbalah").

The Royalty

Now that we have covered the underlying constructs inherent in the numbered cards, let us turn our attention to the royalty who complete the Minor Arcana. It is well known that the zodiac is represented in twelve of the sixteen royal personages pictured through the four elements, but different Tarots deviate in how the twelve are derived from the sixteen. The most standard pattern, matching the method used in the 1–10 cards above, distributes the royalty around the seasonal calendar, placing the fire cards (usually the Wands) in the spring, the water cards (most often Cups) in the summer, the air cards (usually Swords) in the fall, and earth cards (mostly the Coins) in the winter. Used this way, the Kings are the cardinal signs starting into each season, the Queens are the fixed signs at the center of the seasons, and either the Pages or the Knights are used to symbolize the mutable signs that close out each season. (Whichever royalty is left over, whether the Knight or the Page, is used as a messenger or harbinger of change in each of the four suits.) Tavaglione's Tarots demonstrate this pattern on the royalty.

That scheme is simple and easy to remember, and quite possibly very old, but it is not likely to have much appeal to an astrologer because it glosses over the way in which the elements and the modes actually interact within the unfolding seasons of the natural year. If we start with Aries as the cardinal sign that initiates spring, we see the correspondence of the Wand (fire) with spring. But the sign that naturally follows Aries is Taurus, which is indeed a fixed sign yet is of the element earth, not fire. The next sign following Taurus is Gemini, a mutable sign indeed but of the element air, not fire.

In astrological fact, no element rules for an entire season uninfluenced by the other elements. So the more sophisticated, and possibly more modern, esoteric Tarots apportion the Wands royalty to the fire signs, the Cups royalty to the water signs, and so on, dropping the connection with the seasons and more accurately representing the flow of natural time around the wheel of the year. The English-influenced Tarots use a modified form of this pattern. As above, the Knights or Pages not corresponded to the mutable signs become messengers and bringers of change, like the stagehands between acts of a theater piece who rearrange the sets for the advancing plotline. I, for one, like to use the astrologically attuned method, with the Queens as the cardinal signs, the Kings as the fixed, the Pages as the mutable, and the Knights as the agents of change between the seasons.

Much profit can be had in studying the first ten Major Arcana lined up with the Tetractys, the Numbers 1–10, the Sephira of Kabbalah, and the planets of the solar system in their mythological personalities. After you have explored this expanded array of correspondences for your first ten Arcana, look again at how those Arcana/numbers might express themselves in the numbered cards of the four suits. The graph on page 3 will help you remember the parallel correspondences between the three systems as they apply to the Minor Arcana.

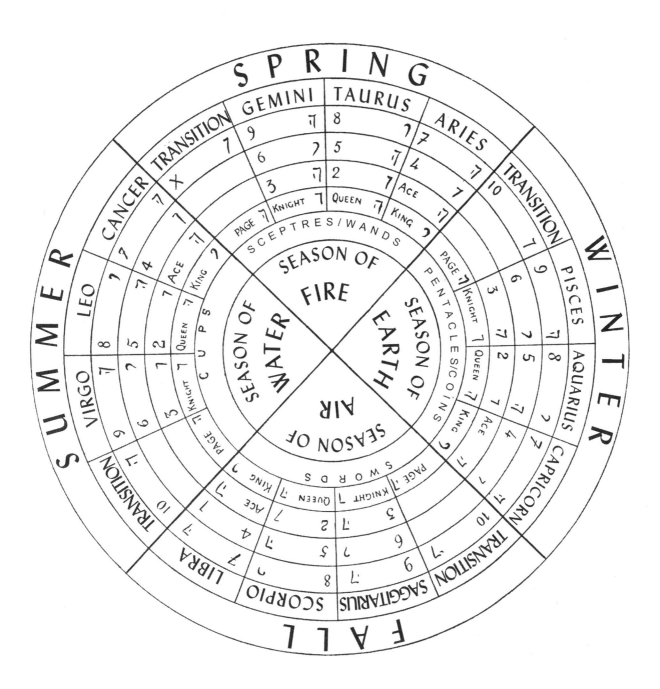

Suit Cards on the Wheel of the Year
Derived From Papus

PART III
ESOTERIC MOVEMENTS
IMPACTING TAROT

THE TREE OF LIFE AND DEATH (MINIATURE BY BERTHOLD FURTMEYER, 1481)
(THIS GNOSTIC IMAGE CONTAINS EVE, MARY DISPENSING THE EUCHARIST, CRUCIFIED CHRIST, THE SERPENT OF GENESIS, DEATH,
AND THE TEMPERENCE ANGEL. THE FALL AND THE RESURRECTION ARE BOTH CONTAINED IN THIS IMAGE.)

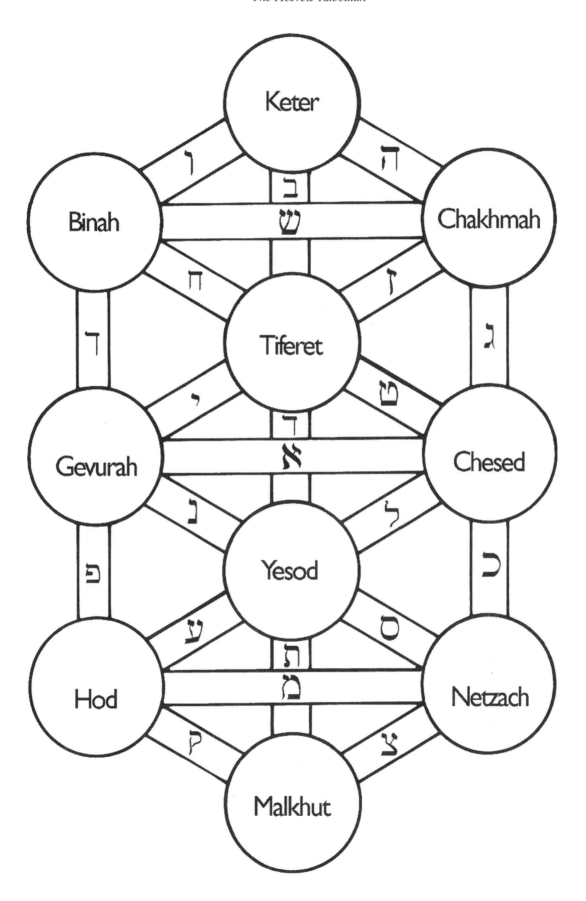

GRA TREE

THE HEBREW KABBALAH

For the nearly three decades during which I was assimilating information about Tarot, I avoided learning about the history of the Kaballah. Not only had it seemed too abstruse and foreign, but the teachings had apparently fragmented due to the many forced migrations imposed upon the Jews throughout their history. I did not relish the task of sorting out all the nuances, and I was intimidated by the volume of literature associated with this ancient study.

My attitude was a microcosm of the American approach to Tarot: Why do we have to drag in this other set of correspondences when the cards already hold so much information, what with their pictures, numbers, titles and the astrological references that are often on the faces of the cards? Isn't that enough to learn about already?

Well no, it is not. As a matter of fact, that attitude is exactly opposite of the approach requisite to understanding the core content of Tarot. The Hebrew alphabet and its associations with numbers, astrology, angels and a host of other correspondences provides the very skeletal structure upon which the cards have grown. Without the Hebrew astro-alphanumeric associations that were laid out so long ago by our ancient ancestors, the Tarot could never have taken its present shape. So even if we never learn how to pronounce the letters correctly or read any words in Hebrew, we must understand just what is going on with these twenty-two letters in order to truly deepen out understanding of Tarot.

Made in the Image of God

It is the position of the entire Western Mystery Tradition, the orthodoxy of Christianity, Islam and Judaism, and the unorthodox fringe dwellers like alchemists, astrologers and Gnostics that the human species is the capstone of creation. Tradition has it that we carry the Grand Plan within our constitution. Inside each of us is hidden a "little world," seed and reflection of the "big world," the cosmos. This is the sense in which humanity is "made in God's image." In the spirit of respect for the grand assignment which the human race is living out, the Hebrews developed their alphabet mysteries to try to articulate our place in the whole and to develop a method for utilizing our divinely inspired powers safely and morally.

The Hebrew nation, ancient tribe of sacred scholars, has been a force for literacy and spiritual cultivation in Western civilization throughout its stormy history. The Hebrew alphabet, derived from the Phoenician, became the prototype for all the Western languages. Hence the letters have accumulated myriad associations and correspondences through the eons. Research on each letter would disclose an encyclopedia's worth of teachings in hundreds of languages spread across Western history. This treasure trove of spiritual knowledge is a large part of what the European Secret Societies have been pledged to protect throughout the generations.

While enslaved among the Babylonians prior to the turn of the second millennium BC, the Jews absorbed the excellent mathematical and astronomical skills of their captors. They brought away an understanding of how numbers unfold from one another, the inner mechanics of Sacred Geometry. Their passionately mystical national psyche, no doubt mixed with the unique discouragement that ensued from being a designated slave nation in the Middle East, caused them to turn their scrutiny inward to examine their relation to the Divine and how it could be expanded. Over time, the Hebrew nation unfolded their mysticism of numbers to illuminate how the physical and energetic constitution of humanity mirrors that of Moses' God.

There is no way a short essay like this could be at all definitive, so it must be assumed that we are only skimming the tips of the icebergs of Kabbalah. Great help will be gained from turning to Aryeh Kaplan's wonderful contribution, *The Sefir Yetzirah*. This extraordinary book catalogs and comments upon every version of the Hebrew astro-alphanumeric system from Abraham into the 20th century, and has been endlessly helpful to me. We Gentile occultists need this exact information so we can understand what the Hebrew people have been discussing among themselves, aside from the controversies that have played out in astrological, cartological or alchemical circles in the name of Christian Cabbalah. I shall be quoting Kaplan quite a bit as you read along, so if your interest is piqued or if you care about these issues, you should own his book.

Origins of the Kabbalah

The first formal document to codify the alphabet teachings for posterity was called the Sefir Yetzirah. Tradition has it that it was taught by Shem (aka Melchezidek) to Abraham around 1800 BC. Abraham is known as the father of both the Hebrew and the Arab nations, as they were each dynasties founded by Abraham's two sons—one by his wife's servant (the Arabic tribes), and one by his wife (the Hebrews). His banishment of the servant and her son when his wife finally gave him a "legitimate" heir is the basis of the ancient grievance between these two immense and competing cultures.

Aryeh Kaplan explains that an eighteenth century BC dating for the Sefir Yetzirah "is not very surprising, since such mystical texts as the Vedic scriptures date from this period, and there is every reason to believe that the mystical tradition was further advanced in the Middle East than it was in India at that time. Since Abraham was the greatest mystic and astrologer of his age, it is natural to assume that he was familiar with all the mysteries of ancient Egypt and Mesopotamia. Abraham was born in Mesopotamia, and he also lived in Egypt" (p. xiv).

Scholars like to have more than legend to base their claims upon, so Kaplan looks further for proofs of the antiquity of the Sefir Yetzirah. Based on analysis of various historical strata within the text, he states that "the earliest parts of the book appear very ancient, possibly antedating the Talmudic era [first and second centuries AD]" (p. xxiii). The Hebrew content within the alphanumeric teachings of the neo-Pythagoreans in the first and second centuries AD also verifies for us an already complete system of correspondences (see next section).

Furthermore, according to Kaplan, "we find actual mention of Sefir Yetzirah in the Talmud [by 300 BC], and even though it is not absolutely certain that it is identical with our version, there is no real reason to doubt that they are one and the same" (p. xv). He also reminds us that "Sefir Yetzirah is one of the primary ancient astrological texts" which tells us that it is in harmony with the standard astrological paradigm used by both Hebrew and Gentile magi throughout the Western world.

The difficulty with dating this book's origins is that it came down through ancient history as an oral tradition, and was not formally written down until 204 AD. What we possess of it in the earliest times is legend, or hearsay evidence, references to it rather than the text itself. But other alphanumeric references, in both Psalms and Exodus, add evidence that a well known and nuanced philosophy existed for centuries in the ancient world before it ever was committed to writing.

The body of correspondences that Aryeh Kaplan is showcasing in his *The Sefir Yetzirah*, called the Gra pattern, is being given on highest Hebrew authority and validated by copious evidence as the original and extraordinarily ancient bedrock of Western Esoteric Tradition. The Gra is the baseline from which later developments, even competing versions, will be drawn. In it are defined the natural placements of the Sephiroth, the Paths, and their astro-alphanumeric correspondences. This pattern, taken altogether, is called the Gra Natural Array.

It should be noted that these correspondences are the ones we find on the illustrious Spanish Tarot, El Gran Tarot Esoterico, designed by Marixtu Guler and published by Fournier. These correspondences represent the tradition of Kabbalah, the ancient pure Hebrew stream of astro-alphanumeric mysteries. Remember, alphanumeric means numbers and letters, and when I add the prefix "astro," I mean signs , planets, and elements are included too.

Parallel Influences of Hebrew and Greek Thought

Inconveniently, at the point in history where we can finally find these ideas in written form, we already find ourselves at a fork in the road. Kaplan indicates that the Sefir Yetzirah was as well-known outside Hebrew circles as within because of its astronomical and astrological content. So we should not be surprised if we see it being quoted or even assimilated by scholars of later centuries. This is exactly what happened in the ancient world.

One such scholar was Pythagoras, whose life in the seventh century BC marks the inception of Hermetic philosophy and numerological mysticism among the Greeks. He traveled the world while still in his thirties and forties, studying with every priesthood and esoteric college he could reach and procuring the texts of those he couldn't physically visit. When he finally settled down to start his own school, he credited the Hebrew Kabbalists and Hindu Brahmans for enlightening him about their number mysteries in which his own teachings about the whole numbers and Sacred Geometry were grounded.

Pythagoras wrote many volumes, a good quantity of which still survive. But in the context of Tarot, what we are most interested in is his participation in the "reform" of the Greek alphabet, which happened in his lifetime. The objective was to bring the Greek alphabet back into harmony with the Hebrew, from which Greek had been derived. In the course of this scholarly labor, two pairs of planets were purposefully switched in relation to their respective letters.

This small shift created a second stream of authentic, ancient, esoteric correspondences that are no longer "pure" Hebrew. It is these Greek/Hermetic variants that came into European history from various sources. The magi of the Italian Renaissance passed them into the Secret Societies, where they were enshrined in the *Fratres Lucis* manuscript which Dr. Lewis Keizer suggests is the model for the earliest self admitted "esoteric" Tarots: Etteilla, Levi, de Gebelin, et al. (see "Esoteric Origins of Tarot").

The Tarots that use these correspondences have been grouped in the chapter The Continental Tarots and show two variants: those that were published before Eliphas Levi and those that came after. The difference is subtle, which is why it has escaped the attention of Tarot scholars of this century until now.

The Holy Word: An Alphabet of Numbers

I want to insert a reminder for those who are not used to the idea that spoken letters have a correspondence with numbers. This may seem like a made-up connection which could be changed at will to serve the needs of a particular code or cipher. But in the ancient world, the numbers associated with the letters, whether in either Greek or Hebrew, were not changeable according to whim. In both these languages, the numbers were letters. By that I mean any mathematical value or calculation in numbers would be written out *in letters*. Each letter also represented a literal number, thus simultaneously having both a sound and a value.

This fact has profound implications which we moderns often fail to understand. We can easily grasp that a letter represents a sound; that's phonics as we learned it in grammar school. But a sound is also a vibration, a frequency resonating the eardrum in a mathematically specific pattern, a ratio or bell curve of ratios. So in that sense, a sound is a number. The ancients already knew from their own experience that sound works magic on the world, both on the human psyche and on the interior structure of matter. Rightly applied sound, the Holy Word of old, can work miracles. This is one reason why the names of angels, choirs of angels, Sephiroth and other divine names in Hebrew were considered so powerful and sequestered so long from the Gentiles.

Hence it follows that any noun, verb, name or other part of speech activates energies along the pathways in this Natural Array, which represents the Body of God that humans share in. These words also can be converted to numbers, revealing the word's "true essence" or interior nature. In the Hebrew language, words that add up to the same or related numbers are considered to have a direct link in the energy-world, as if they were vibrating at octaves of the same frequency. Gematria is the ancient name for the study of words that have numerical or geometrical structure in common, and there are many and various techniques to employ in that study. Most of the magical codes and ciphers of the Western tradition are derived through one or another form of Gematria in either Greek or Hebrew.

Use of these and other magical techniques empowers a practitioner to achieve one's spiritual goals. A spiritual name or sacred number, written on a piece of paper with the right intention, can serve as a talisman for contact with that energy/entity. This is the key to an invisible but potent link-up with the Chain of Being whereby the operator can specify exactly which frequency s/he is trying to contact.

In Greek there were also preserved lists of ancient God-names from the Orphics, the Isis cult, the Serapis mysteries, traditional mythology, and dead languages from their antiquity. All these names would be analyzed and employed mathematically as well as mythically.

I cannot in these essays convey to you how important it is for Tarot esotericists to ground themselves in Greek and Hebrew number theory in order to fully appreciate the profundity of our (quite a bit more recent) Major Arcana. One perfect starting place would be to study David Fideler's *Jesus Christ, Sun of God*. Although to my knowledge Tarot is not mentioned once in the entire book, it is a thrilling immersion in the alphanumeric Mysteries of old.

So when the subject of the "ancient alphanumeric correspondences" comes up throughout this book, I am referring to a fixed body of beliefs whose values have not changed in three thousand years. A=1, B=2, and so on down the Hebrew and Greek alphabets. These correspondences are canonical, set in historical stone. Lists of correspondences abound that are used for various purposes, but "the ancient correspondences" are none other than either the Hebrew originals or the Greek variant, modified in the seventh century BCE by Pythagoras.

Is It Hebrew or Is It Greek?

Contributing to the confusion among Tarot scholars about the relationship between the Hebrew and Greek alphanu-

merics is that, although Pythagoras credited the Hebrews for refining his understanding of the number-letters, later Kabbalists of the first and second centuries were using the writings of the neo-Pythagoreans to help them reassemble their tradition after the fall of the second Temple. So we have the Jews of the second century AD studying second century revivals of Pythagoras' writings from the seventh century BC, to find out what their Hebrew ancestors were doing in the eighteenth century BC! Is there any wonder we get confused?

It did not help that the words the second century Jews were using to explain their Kabbalah were drawn from the vocabulary of the Greek philosophers. In following up to see what I could find on this stage in the development of the Sefir Yetzirah, I found this quote from Gershom Scholem's *Major Trends in Jewish Mysticism*: "The combination of late Hellenistic, perhaps even late NeoPlatonic numerological mysticism with exquisitely Jewish ways of thought concerning the mystery of letters and language is fairly evident throughout. . . . Various peculiarities of the terminology employed in the book, including some curious neologisms which find no natural explanation in Hebrew phraseology, suggest a paraphrase of Greek terms. . ."(p. 76).

I take these hints to imply that earliest redaction of the Sefir Yetzirah, which Scholem thought was assembled between the second and sixth centuries, was already cross-infected with the Hermetic/Alexandrian number mysticism which we now know first emerged with the Pythagorean school in the seventh century BC. So is it any wonder that the esoteric scholars of the Renaissance seized upon the Greek form of these correspondences rather than the older and much more obscure but original Hebrew ones? From the European point of view, even that of a Europeanized Jew, the Greek version was not only more accessible but culturally more familiar than the older correspondences, with their roots so far away in the Middle East.

Remember, there is no difference between the Hebrew and the Pythagorean correspondences in the case of the letters that represent signs of the zodiac. The only difference was between two pairs of planets, the pair Jupiter/Sun and the pair Venus/Mars. One pattern represents th Semitic origins of the alphanumeric pattern and the other is a Greek "reform" undertaken in the sixth century BC. We could see them as the eastern and western forks of the ancient alphanumeric Gnosis.

Variant Kabbalah Trees Among the Hebrews

Aryeh Kaplan, in his *The Sephir Yetzira*, briefly mentions several variations that were employed when applying the Paths on the Tree. The first is an offshoot of the Gra Natural Array, which he explains this way: "In practice, for reasons dealing with the basic nature of the Sefirot, they are not arranged in this natural order, but have the middle line lowered somewhat" (p. 32). Kaplan seems to refer to the outcome of "the fall," graphically illustrating that the "heart of creation" has fallen out of contact with the Supernal Tri-

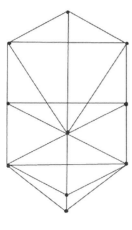

Gra with Dropped Tifaret

angle and into alignment with earthly life. Now that the Sephiroth have become base, they don't sit the same way in the Tree that they did before. This pattern still conforms to the canon of three horizontals, seven verticals and twelve diagonals, so it can't really be called a different system. It is the old Natural Array with a kink, the distortion of our fall away from the Creator. This pattern can rightly be called "ancient" because it came down with the oral tradition from Biblical times.

The Kabbalah Gets Mixed Up

By the tenth century AD, however, laments began appearing in Kabbalistic writings about the many versions of Sefir Yetzirah. Aryeh Kaplan spends several pages discussing how the "literally dozens of different variants" may have appeared (p. xxiv-xxv). Since there were Secret Societies among the Jews just as they existed among the Gentiles, alternate versions became "traditional" in separated communities. Transcription errors were deadly in these short, tightly worded texts, as were errors caused by oral transmission. Commentaries and margin notes from earlier versions got incorporated into later copies. Also, and probably most troublesome for historians, spurious versions were knowingly promulgated, disseminated to confuse the uninitiated. When all is said and done, Kaplan names two main versions, the Short and the Long, as being widely disseminated enough to be relevant to his discussion of Hebrew Kabbalah. Only the Short version enters into our discussion on Tarot.

The other, "older" version that Kaplan gives us for the paths on the Tree (p. 28) represents the Safed School, which is based on the *Zohar*, a small book of essays which is the mystical embodiment of thirteenth century AD Spanish Kabbalism. This pattern is a consequence of errors slipping into the transmission of the Kabbalah as mentioned above, and shows that the Gra version became altered by later developments. In the *Zohar*, the Sefir Yetzirah is extensively quoted, but in this case it is the Short Version of the Raavad (also from the 13th century) that is being referred to. In this version, the planets have become disarranged from the letters as given in the Gra. This obscure little text connects the Sephiroth and the Tree with the cosmos, tying the higher and lower worlds together with hierarchies of angels and spheres and paths that are interrelated through the letters of the alphabet into a theosophical system of the universe. The mysticism it inspired left a lasting impression in Kabbalism.

At this point, the path-pattern which the thirteenth and fourteenth century Kabbalists were trying to reconcile with the *Zohar* and the Short Form can be seen to contain an asymmetry that begs for resolution. In it, the two lowest Paths on either side of Malkuth are removed, and one hugely long one is added to connect Chokma to Geburah. This strengthens and emphasizes the "Lightning Bolt" formation that later Kabbalists/Cabbalists love so much, but it leaves the image short one diagonal, and looks lopsided. Kaplan does not tell us exactly how the letters are arranged

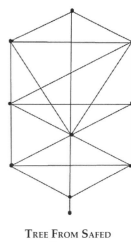

Tree From Safed School

upon the paths in this version. It is this pattern that Rabbi Isaac Luria Ashkenazi (1534-72), affectionately dubbed "the Ari," studied as he strove to rebalance the Tree in light of the *Zohar*.

The Implications of the Ari Version on Tarot Development

The Ari version of the Sefir Yetzirah set a benchmark for the public Kabbalist schools of the 1600s. It utterly departed from the hidden Gra form, either the Natural Array or the "fallen" form for practical application. Because of the great reverence given the *Zohar*, which had become tradition by the Ari's time and which had accumulated significant differing versions, Rabbi Luria worked with the Short Form of the Sefir Yetzirah from 1562 and the lopsided Tree of the Safed School to create his synthesis. Rabbi Luria's contribution to the unfolding of Kabbalistic teachings was immense, but so controversial that its effect was to call into question the monotheistic character of Hebrew religion.

In the context of the tenor of these times, Luria's ideas represent a brilliant and remarkably optimistic response to the miserable conditions his people were experiencing in Europe. There is no room in this essay to expound upon the various details of his teachings (see *Kabbalah* by Gershom Scholem), but essentially in the process of detailing how this world came to be imperfect, he elaborated a whole new structure for the Tree of Life and rearranged the letter/path correspondences.

His was not an effort to prove any other versions wrong (he apparently did not know about the Gra version), but only an account of the difference between Eden at the time of creation and the present world with which we must now contend. Unfortunately, in the process of unveiling his wonderful Hebrew-Gnostic synthesis, he resorted to arguments and illustrations which veered, for many, dangerously close to Gnostic dualism.

There is no doubt that Luria was reflecting themes that saturated intellectual circles during his lifetime. The

Albigensian crusades were already over, and in the course of attempting to suppress the Gnostic heresies, the Catholic Church had unwittingly strengthened and promoted the Gnostic core belief, proving through their viciousness that the mundane world was under the control of a cruel and demented shadow of the One True God. So Luria unfolded an explanation of what had happened to precipitate the "fall from grace" and how it might be repaired. In so doing, he laid out a scenario that paralleled the Gnostic and Hermetic cosmogonies also circulating at the time.

Rabbi Luria did not mean to create another dualist heresy, and even if he did so unintentionally, many people innately identified with his exposition. Intertwined as it was with themes of exile and redemption, Luria's doctrines had emotional resonance with the current life situation of being Jewish in Christian Europe. People also found a basis for hope in Luria's view of the future, when the effects of the fall were to be reversed by the restoration of the world through the spiritual labors of the Hebrew nation.

Before the Fall

To make what Rabbi Luria taught tangible, we have to look at the Kabballah Tree in the ancient Gra form, and then we have to contrast that to the Tree as given in the Ari form from the 1500s. Looking at them back to back makes the issues very clear.

In the Natural Array as dictated in the Gra version, the archetypical human energy-body is shown as a tidy, symmetrical geometric figure that embodies the 3x7x12 structure of the Hebrew alphabet perfectly. This is the structure of human design which links us with higher worlds. In this pattern, the three "mother" letters are corresponded to the horizontal bars of the diagram, the seven planetary letters are the verticals, and the twelve zodiacal letters are the diagonals. Thus the twenty-two letters, as symbols of our inner spiritual energies, weave together the limbs and organs of our bodies with their heavenly correspondents above.

Both the ancient Hebrew alphanumeric system and the Greek Pythagorean alphanumeric system conform to the 3x7x12 rule that places the letters so specifically on the paths. Wherever diagonal paths converge, there is a power-center called

a Sephira (plural, the Sephiroth). These centers each had their own names and attributes from the earliest versions, but the greater practical emphasis had originally been placed upon the paths between the centers, along with practical methods for accessing and circulating these energies for use in healing and magical operations.

Imagine the alphabetical pathways that connect the Sephiroth as if they were veins and arteries in the body conducting energies hither and yon to create connections, feed functions and balance polarities. Much of the earliest strata of the Hebrew Kabballah mysticism was tied up in chanting and meditating to activate consciousness along those internal pathways. One could easily compare this type of practice to a theurgical form of yoga, employing a combination of postures, chants, geometrical visualizations and meditations on the essential nature of reality. The implications are all laid out in detail in Aryeh Kaplan's amazing book.

After the Fall

In comparison, in the diagram of the paths as defined by the Ari, we see humanity in a condition of mortality after "the fall from grace." We have seen attempts to quantify the damage from the fall among even the earliest Kabbalist philosophers, but these variants were not considered dogma, only attempts to talk about what might have happened. But with the Ari version, due to Rabbi Luria's genius and reputation, this pattern became the pattern, both among future European Jews and among the Gentiles of the era.

In the Ari pattern, we see the full tragedy of the fall. Where Tifareth used to stand (the heart center, associated with the feminine part of God, the Shekhina), a hole has opened, now called Da'at. The energy that had filled that place has fallen and has descended to Malkuth (the world of time and space), which is now hanging off the bottom of the diagram like an orphan. Something that was once very elevated and close to the Source is now cast down and stands under all the other forces. From this point of view, "the fall" is not just the loss of Eden but the degradation of the Goddess, who no longer occupies the heart of the creation. She now embodies the low-

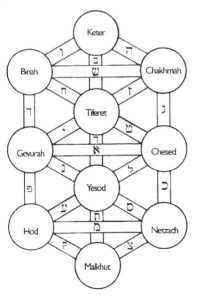

GRA TREE

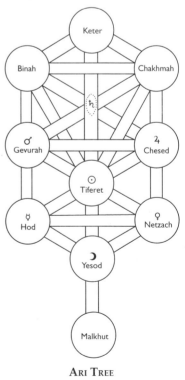

ARI TREE

est world, that of matter, time and space. This is the world we find ourselves in now, according to Rabbi Luria, and we are challenged to find the path back to our former estate.

When we investigate the nature of Da'at, the "new" Sephira, it seems to correspond to the Hindu throat chakra, the power of the Holy Word to create by fiat. So this creative capability, the Word, which used to flow effortlessly from Tifareth, the heart, is now something that has to be earned through effort and striving, by aligning the lower nodes and directing will toward overcoming the distractions of the left and right pillars. Da'at signifies a power-center that a person has to build up to activate, although it exists in potential in all of us born after the fall. This work is necessary to lift ourselves back to our original nature.

The consequence of the fall is chaos in the path structure below the Supernal Triangle (Kether, Chokmah, Binah). The 3x7x12 pattern, dictated by the Sefir Yetzirah, is destroyed, because now the heart triangle (Tifareth, Chesed and Geburah) and the pelvic triangle (Yesod, Netzach and Hod) point downward. Malkuth, "the World," is cast down into a position that didn't even exist in the old system; it now acts like an anchor on the soul instead of like a throne or a wonderful garden from which to draw nourishment.

In the post-fall human, the centers below the Supernal Triangle become increasingly dense and crystallized, and for the first time, they represent the planets of the solar system. Malkuth is Earth, Yesod is Moon, Hod is Mercury, Netzach is Venus, Tifareth is the Sun, Geburah is Mars, Chesed is Jupiter and Da'at is (at least potentially) Saturn. The pathways are no longer arranged in their pristine pattern from Genesis,and this unorthodox development allows for new positions for the planets and paths, increasing controversy between Kabbalistic schools. Saturn, who has fallen to Malkuth but in potential could "rise" to the "new" throat center, is the last visible planet in the solar system, therefore the symbol of limits, discipline, examinations and natural consequences. The ancients used to say that Saturn was the final judge of whether we reincarnated again and again or whether we could pass on from this world into a higher state. This natural association of Saturn with Da'at fits in well with Luria's reincarnational themes, marking another resemblance to Gnostic ideas circulating in his times.

Rabbi Luria, in reaching for a way to explain humanity's fall from grace into the wretchedness of this life, reconceptualized the way the paths connect the Sephiroth on the Tree. He was not attempting to displace the Gra pattern because he did not know it existed. He was looking at the *Zohar* and the skewed Tree of the 1400s, hoping to patch the confusing welter of versions back together.

Luria was simply trying to create a format by which humanity could reconstitute itself and bring the world back to its pristine condition. His philosophy had certain consequences on the Tree of Life diagram, because "the fall" was seen as having changed our primal symmetry, which is to say, having upset the energy grid of our bodies. So the Ari version is a map of the problem awaiting solution, a dam-age report, like a medical x-ray the doctor views before surgery. This is true for every version that has fallen away from the Gra Natural Array. We are not supposed to enshrine this pattern as a way to live, but instead use it as a game plan for self repair. Luria was actually trying to give his people much-needed hope in troubled times, but his approach ultimately generated more confusion than it was able to heal.

Because the Ari pattern of "after the fall" attributions was offensive to old-school rabbis around Europe, a good deal of what one finds on the subject is negatively biased. Much ink is spent bemoaning the way in which Luria unwittingly exposed the monotheist core of Judaism to accusations of harboring the Gnostic dualism (see "The Gnostic Tarot"), a charge that undercuts the Hebrew claim of being the original chosen people of the One True God.

It looked to the skeptical as if he were positing two worlds with two separate administrations, the unfallen "upper face" of the Supernal Triangle (Kether, Chokma and Binah), where the energies are still balanced, contrasted with the "Lower Face" of the planetary Sephira resting on Malkuth, the fallen and chaotic World. This is the dualism that was so loudly disclaimed by traditionalists of the sixteenth century, even though it explained in very convincing terms the reality of the Jewish experience in Europe.

Rabbi Luria was offering a plan for the steps that Kabbalists could take to cultivate themselves and right the balance of Nature upset by "the fall." Unfortunately, it seems that the traditionalists of Luria's day could not get past the appearance of dualism to hear the call. Meanwhile, the literalists among his followers forgot that he was proposing a provisional map, not the final goal.

It is in this controversial and fragmented state that we must leave the Hebrew Kabbalah for now, because it is necessary to investigate intellectual developments in Renaissance Christian culture before we can appreciate the next developments in the history of this ancient philosophy.

Our attention will now turn to the other body of astro-alphanumeric correspondences which has been handed down, like the Hebrew alphabet, from ancient times, the Greek alphabet. It is the Greek correspondences which became standard in European esoteric circles, thus forming the paradigm upon which the first European Tarots were built.

English Letter	Greek Letter	Hebrew Letter (Continental use of Hebrew)	Arcana Number	Gra version SephirYetzirah – From ~1800 B.C. El Gran Tarot Esoterico, Tarot of the Ages	Old Alexandrian, 600 B.C. – Hermetic Etteilla, Falconnier Tarot	Continental Tarots ~1880 A.D. Levi, Wirth, Papus	Marseilles, Spanish Tarot Maxwell's correspondences	Pierre Piobb, 1908 A.D. – Spanish Variant #1 Dali, Euskalherria	Balbi, Spanish Variant #2
			0			Fool △	Fool △	Fool ♏	Fool ש ♏
A	α	א	1	🜁	🜁	🜁	☉	☉	☉
B	β	ב	2	☾	☾	☾	☾	☾	☾
G	γ	ג	3	♂	♀	♀	♀	Earth (♇)	☿
D	δ	ד	4	☉	♃	♃	♃	♃	♃
H	ε	ה	5	♈	♈	♈	☿	☿	♉
V	ς	ו	6	♉	♉	♉	♐	♍	♍
Z	ζ	ז	7	♊	♊	♊	♂	♐	♊
Ch	η	ח	8	♋	♋	♋	♎	♎	♎
T	θ	ט	9	♌	♌	♌	✶	Ψ	Ψ
I	ι	י	10	♍	♍	♍	♑	♑	♑
C	κ	כ	11	♀	♂	♂	♌	♌	♌
L	λ	ל	12	♎	♎	♎	♈	♅	✶
M	μ	מ	13	▽	▽	▽	♄	♄	♄
N	ν	נ	14	♏	♏	♏	♒	♒	♒
S	ξ	ס	15	♐	♐	♐	△ ☊	♂	♂
Ayn	ο	ע	16	♑	♑	♑	🜁 ☋	♈	♈
P	π	פ	17	☿	☿	☿	♉	♀	♀
Ts	φ	צ	18	♒	♒	♒	♋	♋	♋
Qk	ρ	ק	19	✶	✶	✶	♊	♊	♅
R	σ	ר	20	♄	♄	♄	♏	✶	♐
Sch	τ	ש	21	Fool △	World △		World ♍	World ♉	
Th	υ	ת	22	World ♃	Fool ☉	World ☉ #21			World ♇

Table of Correspondences for the Continental Tarots based on Greek and Hebrew astro-alphanumerics

THE ALEXANDRIAN STREAM

If the purpose of this book were just to prove that the teachings of the ancient mystery schools were synchretistically woven together, each with its own vocabulary and symbols but all teaching the same core doctrine, this chapter would be the only one in the book. The time-period this chapter introduces was such a spiritually fertile, creative, philosophically awakened time that we in the modern world are only just now assimilating the results of it.

The label "Alexandrian" is drawn from the conquests of Alexander the Great during the third century BCE. He invaded and subjugated most of the the "known world" of his day, including within his territory not only the eastern Mediterranean lands but north Africa and the Persian empire in Asia Minor as well. Had he not been beaten back by the monsoons of India and then bitten by an infected mosquito in Babylon, the "culture line" between East and West might be drawn very differently today.

But in truth, "Alexandrian" culture is actually the late flowering of seeds planted by Pythagoras in the 6th century BCE. The Pythagorean intellectual legacy includes the most complete ancient teaching on the esotericism of the whole numbers, sacred geometry, harmonic theory, and the Lambda diagram (an infinite multiplication/division table demonstrating the rations and frequencies which govern the fractioning out of colors from white light and the parallel fractioning out of harmonics from any single tone). His mystery school in Samos had the reputation for synthesizing the very best of the mathematical and cosmic understandings from both the Hebrew and the Hindu mysteries, and the broad sweep of his studies embraced the whole of the world as it was then known. A great reference on Pythagoras and the impact of his teachings is *The Pythagorean Sourcebook and Library*, compiled and translated by Kenneth Sylvan Guthrie.

For all the completeness of that volume, the most interesting aspect of Pythagoras' contribution (for Tarot students, that is!) is his involvement with the Greek alphablet reforms, and nowhere does Guthrie mention this detail. I found this information in Book Two of David Allen Hulse's encyclopedic tome *The Key Of It All*. In his chapter called "The Seventh Key — Greek", he puts the importance of Pythagoras' contribution into perspective. In Hulse's own words, "From my own research it is apparent that the Hebrew tradition of ascribing a symbolic and numerical content to their alphabet preceded the devopment of Greek into a numbered language by as much as 1,000 years. The numerical code we know for Greek in the range 1 through 800 was not apparent until 500 BCE, while Hebrew may have contained its innate number code as far back as 1500 BCE....My contention is that this [Greek] code represents the ultimate secret

Pythagoras imparted to his third-degree initiates (though no document survives to substantiate my claim.)....these Greek letter names when first penned, were in imitation of the Hebrew alphabet." (p. 4)

Just to duplicate my sources, I also consulted W. Wynn Westcott's little volume *The Occult Power Of Numbers*, which forms Volume VI of his series entitled "Collectanea Hermetica." I expected a more thorough treatment of the subject, but instead I found this pithy little blanket statement: "The Greeks...did not develop nor use their letters as numbers for mental conceptions, [like Pythagoras and the Kabbalists] yet in the Middle Ages we often find Greek letters used to transliterate Hebrew similars, and so there was formed a bastard Greek Kabalah(sic) on the Hebrew type". No mention is made here of the fact that the Greek astro-alphanumeric system does not exactly match the Hebrew, nor do I find any other sources explaining the discrepancy. Hence we must be satisfied with Hulse's assertion that the Greek correspondences were drawn from the innermost orders of Pythagorean Initiates.

And what is this discrepancy? In the Hebrew set of Correspondences, the number three is connected to Mars, four is connected to the Sun, eleven to Venus, and twenty-one to Jupiter. In the Greek system, the number three is Venus, four is Jupiter, eleven is Mars, and twenty-one is the Sun. In other words, the Sun/Jupiter pair are switched, and the Mars/Venus pair are switched. Everything else is exactly the same between the two systems. It would be fascinating to find a source explaining the theological and philosophical justification for these inversions of the Hebrew tradition, but Pythagorean Initiatates were notoriously tight-lipped, so we may never know.

Hence, at future points of this book when I mention the Hermetic/Alexandrian stream of the mystery tradition, it is this "Pythagorean" reform of the Hebrew alphabet attributions that I am referencing. The entire Greek alphabet is arranged for your viewing pleasure, with all the other variants mentioned in this book, on the two-page table which you will find on pages 118-119 of the Continental Tarot chapter.

The Mysteries of Serapis

Now that we have detailed the Greek underpinnings for the Alexandrian cultural flowering of the final centuries BCE, let me cite some testimony from Manley P. Hall's book *Freemasonry of the Ancient Egyptians*: He is remarking on the heedless way the Roman Legionaires gobbled up the religions of the peoples whom they conquered, without ever examining their philosophical contents. In comparison, he cites the Egyptian culture-center of Alexandria, named after its founder but administered by Alexander's general Ptolemy.

"In Alexandria had blossomed the supernal products of Neo-Pythagorean and Neo-Platonic culture. Ptolemy had imported Eleusinian Initiates, by whose aid the Serapic Rite had been formulated. The Egyptian Platonists were also amazingly lucid. It is highly probable that, in the elements of Greek philosophy, the more highly enlightened of the Egyptian Initiates recognized fragments of their own dead lore, for in the time of [Ptolemy] the great institutions of Egyptian learning were already but faint memories." (P. 17)

These remarks caught me entirely by surprise! I had no idea that the Isis/Serapis Mysteries, which were such a strong feature of late antiquity, were assembled from extinct, ancient Egyptian ingredients by latter-day Greek Initiates. I do remember reading that the Isis/Serapis mythos was a hybrid, a blend of old and new influences at the time that it emerged. I also recollect that the Serapis temples can be found all over Europe, wherever the Romans dominated. But I had not yet seen the bigger picture.

Turning to the tremendous scholarship of David Fideler in his masterwork *Jesus Christ, Sun of God: Ancient Cosmology and Early Christian Symbolism*, I found these remarks right away. In reference to the ancient number-letter connections, he states "The earliest known usage of this practice, known as *gematria*, is recorded on a Babylonian clay tablet....From the Greeks, the Jewish Kabbalists adopted the practice of *gematria*, interpreting the meaning of sacred words and phrases by their numerical values....The word *gematria*, however is based on the Greek word *geometria* or geometry, and, as we shall see...there exists definitive evidence that gematria constituted a sacred language of Greek theology and was used before the time of Plato. It is well known that the Christian gnostics, who claimed to possess a form of secret knowledge (*gnosis*), employed the gematria and mathematical symbolism in their teachings, for such is reported by the early church fathers..." (p. 27-8)

Here are several more amazing statements! Not only are the early church fathers using Greek letter-number connections in their studies of the New Testament (all written in Greek with gematria consciously built in), but the Hebrews, whom the early church fathers were emulating, learned *their* astro-alphanumerics from the Pythagoreans! Here is proof of the Alexandrian synthesis at the root of Christianity, which simultaneously validates the absolute authenticity of the Greek astro-alphanumeric values in Christian Europe, even after the death of the Mysteries.

Once I started thinking about the implications of these remarks, a number of conclusions emerged. Each of them seems to strengthen the basic premise of this work, which is that the structure of Tarot is dictated by its relationship to the Hebrew, and later the Greek, astro-alphanumeric codes of old.

If the Alexandrian Isis/Serapis Mysteries are actually Greek Mysteries in Egyptian dress, then it is more self-explanatory that an "Egyptian" cult could make such inroads into Greco-Roman and pagan Europe. If the Serapian temples were founded upon Pythagorean mysteries, then they would still feel familiar to educated Europeans even after the Church closed down the Mysteries. If the New Testament Scriptures were written with a gematria in mind that parallels the Hebrew equivalent in the Old Testament, then even after the earliest gnostic bishops were excommunicated from the Catholic canon, the astro-alphanumerics would remain in scripture for later mystics to revive.

In future chapters, you will see me constructing elaborate proofs of occult transmission, whereby these Greek correspondences were kept alive despite the dark ages of Europe, preserved by the Arabs and Byzantines, Alchemists, Gypsies, and Kabbalists, revived in the Renaissance and eventually installed in their rightful places on the Major Arcana of Tarot after the church's persecutions finally waned. All those proofs are written for the lovers of detail, like myself. But the simple truth is, the Greek modification of the Hebrew astro-alphanumeric correspondences was constructed right into the Gospels of the New Testament, and every future generation of clergy could have access to the inner secrets if they wanted to take the time to learn the correspondences. Many of them did, because it gave them access to the eternal ideas which have traveled from one mystical cult to another through the ages, surviving translation and misunderstanding because the core truths are expressed in numbers, hidden within the sacred names and words of holy scripture. The more things change, the more they stay the same!

THE GNOSTIC TAROT

The subject of Gnosticism is entirely too large to be dealt with in an essay such as this one. This spiritual path has a history longer than that of Christianity and covers a territory that includes most of western and eastern Europe, the Middle East, North Africa, India, China and the Russian territories.

With so many different cultures and languages involved and the inevitable proliferation, demise and revival of countless versions and variants over two thousand years, there is no one thing called "Gnosticism." We must content ourselves with using this word as an umbrella concept, holding within its broad description myriad offshoots, competing ideas and exotic forms of practice.

"PAPAL TRIUMPH"
BY GIORGIO VASSARI
MID-1500'S
SHOWING THE CHURCH AS THE POPESS

In the remarkable history of this faith, an extensive chapter could be written just on the interactions of Gnosticism and the Catholic Church. The establishment of the Church of Rome in the fourth century AD allowed for three centuries of Christian development before the regulating authority of Rome arose to assert the "party line." Initially, each bishop was free to study, teach and write what he believed, and many were deeply influenced by Gnostic thought. But once the canonical standard for Christianity was set, the Church felt it necessary to posthumously excommunicate several of its most well-respected and influential early bishops for being Gnostic heretics! With an identity crisis like that defining its birth, it is no wonder the Church remained on guard and actively hostile to any traces of Gnostic thought appearing in "Christian Europe."

For those Gnostics who considered themselves followers of the Master Jesus, this exercise in internal censorship illuminated the true character of this new institution called Roman Catholicism. The paramilitary approach of the corporate Church toward its "irregular" members never softened, even though both Christians and Gnostics sometimes used the same scriptures and could be found worshipping together at the same altar.

The difference between Gnostic Christians (only a small group within the larger Gnostic field) and formal Catholics was in some ways a matter of interpretation of the meaning of a human life, the spiritual forces at work in this world, and the place of the feminine in the panoply of Higher Powers. Suffice it to say that this essay only touches a corner of the extensive mosaic that is Gnosticism.

Gnosticism & Tarot

In order to be clear about the relationship between Gnosticism and Tarot, it should be stated at the outset that there are no specifically "Gnostic" Tarots. It would be equally true to say, however, that every Tarot is a Gnostic Tarot. This paradox exists because, as with the difference between the Gnostic reading of Genesis and the Catholic reading of Genesis, the difference lies in interpretation. Tarot artists used this ambiguity to their advantage in the early centuries of Tarot. So, for example, the High Priestess image could be seen as an allegory for "Mother Church" in the eyes of a believing Christian, while a Gnostic might see in the very same image the female pope, a truly heretical concept! In this manner, the Gnosticism of Tarot is "hidden in plain sight," like much of the esoteric content implied in the art of the earliest handmade Tarots.

POPESS
LOMBARDI TAROT
THE GNOSTIC PRIESTESS

The situation gets a bit easier to untangle in modern Tarots because through the centuries, the tensions between the Church and its heretics took on more of the character of a stalemate: the Church came to understand that it could not kill every heretic in Europe and still have a constituency to call its own. As a result less anonymity was required on the part of the philosophers and artists who were working with Tarot, so we are more easily able to learn about the Secret

Society affiliations of those who have contributed most to the development of the Tarot.

Therefore, for purposes of this book, we will assume that there is a Gnostic undertone to every Tarot deck to which we refer. Certainly since the time of Etteilla in the mid-1700s, almost every luminary in the field of Tarot has belonged to either the Rosicrucians, Masons, Martinists or some other Secret Society group. Among the older Tarots, a good indicator of Gnostic affiliation, aside from subtle clues hidden in the artwork, would be the relative vigor of the Church's reaction to that deck, or to its artist, the person who commissioned it or to the region in which it was produced.

We must remember that great variety existed in Gnostic thought. There were Arabic, pre-Islamic Gnostics, Gnostics who remained culturally Jewish, Egyptian Gnostics, Zoroastrian Gnostics and Hermetic Gnostics. They didn't all believe the same things, although most of these ancient cultures based their collective histories upon these first five books of Moses.

These were not merely Hebrew scriptures. All of Western civilization believed in this as history. Many of the stories that Moses codified can be traced back to Babylonian, Akkadian and Sumerian oral tradition. Yet, not every spiritual seeker using the Mosaic texts agreed with his slant on the story. So from the time of Alexander right up to the French Revolution, the Gnostic "underground" has been preserving competing origin stories rejected by "orthodox" Judaism, Islam and Christianity, keeping alive an alternative vision of human nature and destiny.

It is probable that the expulsion of the Moslems, Gypsies and Jews from Spain helped bring Tarot into form as a deck of cards in other parts of Europe. Those expelled minorities flooded Europe with literate, spiritually inclined seekers. The European Secret Societies were providing a place for a meeting of the minds among those who were being marginalized and forced underground by the controversies of the times. I am convinced, and the evidence implies, that the Secret Societies participated in enabling the Hebrew/Hermetic/Gnostic synthesis from antiquity to again see the light of day, albeit in card form.

Gnosticism And The Goddess

One of the things Gnosticism represents is a rebellion within the Old Testament-based (Mosaic) religions against those who used the myth of Genesis to stamp out the ancient Goddess-based mysteries of antiquity. Even as early as the second century BC there were those who felt Moses had distorted the ancient creation stories to eliminate the participation of the feminine side of Deity. The Goddess as co-creator had in earliest times been revered by all Semitic peoples and those memories have never been entirely wiped out despite the Hebrew focus on Jehova (JHVH) as the One True God.

As just one example of the preservation of the Goddess in Gnostic thought, let us look back to the Hebrew tradition about the "daughter of God," called the Matronit of the Kabbalah. Her roots were planted in Talmudic times in the first through fifth centuries AD. They called her by several names in their mystical literature: the Shekhina, Malkuth, the Supernal Woman and the Discarded Cornerstone, among other titles.

In this ancient conception, the FatherGod and his consort exist in such a rarified state compared to humanity that there is no way human consciousness can reach to them and experience their reality. The son and daughter of the Holy Pair, however, extend like shadows of their parents into this fallen world, linking humanity and the "fallen" creation to higher realities. (As this mythic theme came forward in time from Judaism, through Gnosticism and into Christianity, this pair would be renamed Christ and the Sophia.)

In *The Hebrew Goddess* (p. 135), Raphael Patai says "there is a detailed similarity between the life history, character, deeds and feelings attributed by Jewish mysticism to the Matronit, and what ancient Near Eastern mythologies have to say about their goddesses who occupy positions in their pantheons" (for example Solomon's Asherah or Ashtoreth, Ishtar in Addad and most ancient, Astarte in Byblos). Her cardinal attributes, according to Patai, are chastity, promiscuity, motherliness and bloodthirstiness. She is the archetype of ancient women's four roles in traditional relationship to men: sister, lover, mother, mercy killer. He goes on to equate the Matronit who "at times tastes the other, bitter side, and then her face is dark" with the Hindu Kali, who is also black and also feasts upon the dead.

XXXVIII.
MISTRESS OF CUPS

QUEEN OF CUPS
IBIS TAROT

If one were looking for clues to this ancient Hebrew form of the goddess on the Tarot, one could look for images that show qualities of the Matronit on the cards. Taking up the list of her qualities, we could easily see the four Queens having the attributes of virginity (Wands, sister), promiscuity (Coins, lover), motherliness (cups, nursemaid) and bloodthirstiness (Swords, the mercy killer).

We could also look for the quality of blackness, which appears on the Queen of Cups in the Alexandrian/Hermetic imagery of the Ibis Tarot and others that follow the old Falconnier model from the *Fratres Lucis* document (see "The Continental Tarots"). In these Tarots, her cup is covered with pomegranate seeds, another reference to the combined Hebrew Goddess mysteries and the Egyptian Isis cult.

We would also notice those Tarots that crown the coin on the Ace of Coins, a detail in the Tarot by Augustus Knapp and Manly P. Hall. This crowned coin is representative of Malkuth, one of the titles of Shekhina/Matronit, and a symbol for the Goddess in the World among the Merkabah Mystics who were practicing Jewish Gnosticism before the

Kabbalists. For that matter, the World card itself represents the Goddess enthroned in matter, with the four elements doing her bidding and the earth turning under her feet.

I might add that the Knapp-Hall Tarot is an especially interesting deck in this context. Hall was an occult scholar of the 1920s and 1930s who in the process of cataloging the world's great Mystery Schools and their teachings, assembled a wonderful library of images from which to draw when making his own Tarot. Upon close analysis, it is obvious that he is, like the Ibis Tarot and all the others in this stream, reproducing the Falconnier or Fratres Lucis model. The only deviation of the Knapp-Hall from these older, Egyptian-style Tarots is that Knapp-Hall shows the characters in European clothing and situations.

On the Knapp-Hall suit of Cups, Hall shows the royalty in possession of a magical cup, the Holy Grail. The Queen is not black, and the cup is now in European form, but it boils and bubbles with potency in the King and Queen's hands, referring, I am sure, to the theme of the excellent book *Holy Blood, Holy Grail*. This blockbuster details the Gnostic heresy that Jesus of Nazareth was the husband of Mary Magdalen, from which union there were children (see also "The Esoteric Origins of Tarot"). After the crucifixion, Mary and the children traveled across the Mediterranean to Marseilles, and she lived out her last thirty years in Europe.

Susan Haskins's encyclopedic *Mary Magdalen* fleshes out the details drawn from scripture, myth and legend. But it is clearly a traditional theme or else Hall would not so explicitly reference this Gnostic heresy on his Tarot. Nor is his slant a part of the modern rewriting of Tarot's history, since his deck was published in 1929, while all of the above-cited scholarly tomes have only appeared in the last thirty years!

As Gnostic artists and mystics retrieved and revived the feminine aspects of Deity in the imagery of Tarot, we see glimpses again of her many variations coming to us through the ages. It would not be amiss to say that any historical Tarot that has a preponderance of female images in the Major Arcana, and/or adds female images where one would more usually find a male image, could qualify as having a Gnostic slant. I will make direct reference to examples in various Tarot decks as we go along.

Gnosis Means Direct Knowledge

According to the Old Testament-based religions, direct mystical or spiritual experience was not accessible to ordinary humans. In contrast, the Gnostics' credo was to achieve direct experience of the Mystery whenever possible; each group was looking for intimate, personal experiences with godhead, much like those available through the traditional older Mystery Schools.

Drawing upon ancient Hermetic and Jewish gospels rejected by the canonizers of the Old and New Testaments, they challenged the official Judeo-Christian explanations of a monotheistic FatherGod, human origins, and the destiny of the soul. They felt that a straighter route could be found to reunite humanity and godhead without the interference of clergy or priestly heirarchies. In particular they worshipped and championed Sophia, the Wisdom of God (as mentioned in Genesis) who in the beginning co-created the world with the Father. In their societies, women's roles reflected this greater respect for the feminine. As Dr. Lewis Keizer and Stuart Kaplan remind us, the earliest Tarots show a woman dressed in ecclesiastical garb and named "The Popess." In the Mantegna tarocchi, this image is the person at the top of their "stations of man" series, the person who is closest to God, representative of humanity's highest development, and clearly a woman! In the mid-1400s, that is a powerful statement.

Pessimist vs. Optimist Gnostics

Another of Gnosticism's basic beliefs was internally disputed for centuries and is an ongoing philosophical and spiritual debate to this day. This split is well defined in the following quote from *In Search of the Primordial Tradition and the Cosmic Christ* by Father John Rossner, Ph.D., beginning on page 112:

"There is an essential distinction which must be made between 'optimistic' and 'pessimistic' forms of pre-Christian esotericism. The 'optimistic' gnosis views the whole world as good, as a divine and living world because it is animated by the divine effluvia, and capable of being activated by man as a co-Creator with God and as a priest of Nature. In this world, man's function is not to 'escape the world' but to awaken and activate persons, places, and things in Nature to become 'temples of the Divine Spirit.' Man himself develops gnosis in order to 'become or re-become a god,' in order to 'know God' in the existential sense. Like the 'magician' or 'theurgist' in the iconography of the Egyptian tarot card, man is to 'bring down' the divine power and light in order to impregnate and fill the objects of the physical world with their appropriate form of divinity.

"The 'optimistic' form of gnosis may be identified with the ancient Egyptian 'religion of the world,' according to Frances Yates [see her book *Giordano Bruno and the Hermetic Tradition* pp. 20-38]. It was such a positive 'Hermetic' conception of a good, God-given creation (which is to be redeemed and divinized rather than discarded) which indeed may have provided the Egyptian background of both the Hebraic and Mosaic concepts of the creation in Genesis, and a source for the classical Greek metaphysics of Pythagoras and Plato. This earlier Egyptian understanding of gnosis predated the later Hellenistic, world-denying 'religion of Gnosticism' in the early Christian era."

A few paragraphs later, on page 113, Rossner writes that "during the Renaissance, Ficino and Giordano Bruno believed that this 'optimistic' variety of an earlier Egyptian 'proto-gnosticism' had found its way into original Mosaic tradition, and into the works of the New Testament, in the positive metaphysical philosophies of Jesus, John (the author of the 4th Gospel) and Paul. It also found its way into the Neo-Platonic Hermeticists of the early Christian centuries."

When we remember that the Tarots of Etteilla are de-

FOOL
ECOLE D'ESTE TAROT

signed to represent this very same strain of optimistic Hermetic Gnosis expressed in *The Divine Pymander,* we have to again give respect where it is due and return to studying his fascinating Tarots in a new and deeper light.

In contrast to the optimist Gnostics of various stripes, a spectrum of negative thinkers felt that this world of matter and time/ space is a prison instead of an Eden. Those Gnostics viewed incarnation as "the fall," believing it to be a punishment. Others saw our immersion in matter as the result of a war between good and evil in heaven.

Some of these groups refused to reproduce, believing that in being fertile they would be playing into the hands of our captors, the fallen angels. The practice of sexual union has the effect of enticing other souls to leave heaven for this captivity below, an undesirable outcome for these world-denying Gnostics. Among the groups of pessimist Gnostics there were some who were entirely ascetic, choosing to stay maximally detached from the Fallen God's temptations, which would include the entire roster of earthly delights.

Other strains of Gnostics believed that the soul would not be allowed to leave this plane of existence until it had been through every experience available to humans. This belief encouraged all forms of license and excess, the unhealthy effects of which get this group more often classed with the pessimists than the optimists. Their motto was "eat, drink and be merry, for tomorrow you may die."

The Penetration of Gnostic Concepts into European Culture

Prior to examining the visual evidence of three significant Gnostic themes embedded in European imagery and the Tarot, let us first investigate how these ideas managed to penetrate and indeed eventually saturate pagan Europe and become so popular that they survived the turbulent transition to Roman Christianity, the Crusades and the fires of the Inquisition.

Astrological and magical teachings were first carried west by the Jews liberated from slavery by the fall of Babylon. We have to give most of the credit to the Hebrew people for saving much of this early knowledge, because they were the one ancient nation who encouraged the literacy of every adult male in their tribe. Following the lead of Hebrew tradition, the New Testament writers encoded a full set of astrological and numberological codes into their Gospels

through the Greek alphabet. The Jews themselves migrated into Europe around the 900's CE.

The Moors from North Africa moving into Spain and France around 650 AD increased the redistribution of Alexandrian scholarship into Europe and led to the building of libraries and universities in Madrid, Toledo, Seville and Aragon. They brought thousands of manuscripts, reflecting nearly a thousand years of scholarship, out of Egypt and onto the European continent.

As the Roman Church was plunging Europe into the Dark Ages with its book burnings and prohibitions against reading and writing for all but the clergy, most of Europe's cultural memory was either destroyed or collected in the clergy's secret libraries. Pagan, Egyptian, Jewish and Arabic families who had found niches for themselves in Christian Europe were hounded from pillar to post as the Christians destroyed the Mystery sites and practices.

The Jews, and later the Arabs, translated and studied the manuscripts, diagrams and technologies bequeathed to them by history. In them, they rediscovered their own esoteric roots. The discipline of alchemy, originally explored by the Egyptians to satisfy humanity's need for medicines of a physical, emotional and spiritual nature, became a repository of proto-scientific experimentation. In the process, the imagery and symbolism of the ancient Mysteries formed the vocabulary and graphics for the alchemists' journals. The Arabic scholars omnivorously assimilated Egyptian, Hebrew, Hermetic, Gnostic and pre-Nicean Christian gospels, including it all in their experiments and theories.

This helps explain the enthusiasm that gripped the Roman Church to mount the Crusades and try to recapture the Holy Land for Christianity. An educated clergy that had either sequestered or destroyed the cream of European Classical civilization

WORLD
ANOYMOUS PARISIAN TAROT

was getting restless and inquisitive. The Arabs had become famous for their revival of the secret knowledge, and the Hebrews had never left it behind in the first place. Both civilizations co-occupied the Holy Land. How could the pope resist the urge to seize it all, if it could be done?

Of course, the Church didn't succeed. Not only were the Crusades a disaster, but by the time it was all over, Europe had been reinflamed with the very Gnostic, Kabbalistic and Hermetic heresies that Rome had been trying to squelch the entire previous millennium! Among other things, the Crusades awakened Christians to an alternative reading of their cherished gospels, restimulated suppressed heresies about

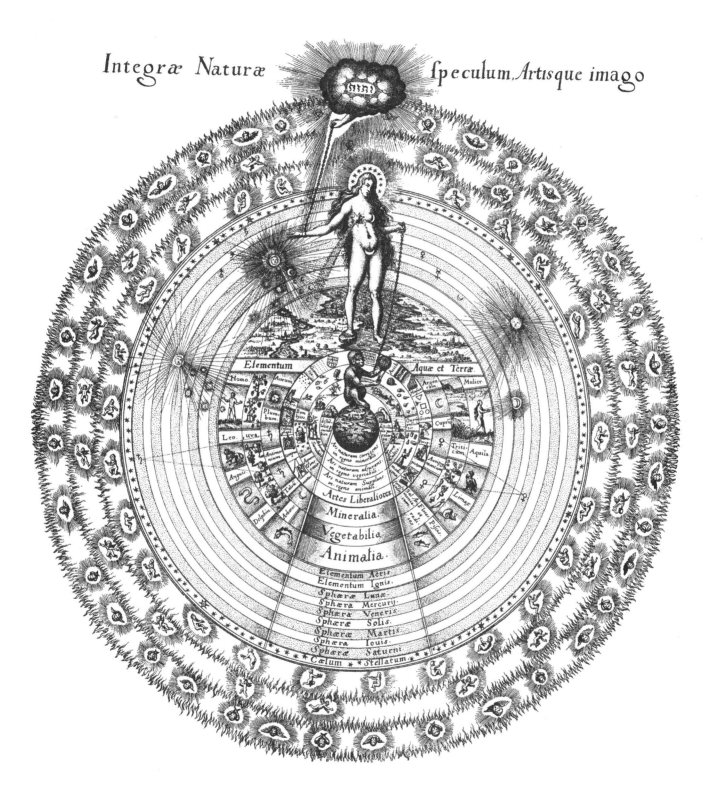

THE MIRROR OF THE WHOLE OF NATURE AND IMAGES OF ART
(ENGRAVING BY JOHANNES DE BRY
FROM *UTRIUSQUE COSMI MAJORIS. . .*
BY ROBERT FLUDD, 1617)

the life, family, and travels of Jesus and the nature of the Grail Mysteries, and provided the impetus for the reawakening of the Gnosis in the underground Secret Societies.

Gnostic Concepts Embedded in European Imagery and Tarot: Three Themes

1. Evolution: The Path and the Journey of the World Soul

Reincarnation was part of the belief system of the ancient world. In a very general sense, the Gnostic gospels assert that when the Creator fashioned the material plane, it was set up in solar system form with seven planets. At that time people thought the planets all revolved around Earth and that Earth was protected and guarded by the rings of the other planets.

What you see illustrated here is Earth and the World Soul surrounded by the circles of the four elements (earth, water, air, fire), in turn encircled by the planetary rings, embraced in their turn by the octaves of angels who make it all go round. This is the exact same concept illustrated by Mantegna's Prima Causa card (No. 50). The two cards that precede it in sequence, called the Eighth and Ninth Spheres, represent the Milky Way (No. 48) and the Vault of the Heavens (No. 49) invisibly turning all the inner wheels like a cosmic perpetual-motion machine. All this wheels-within-wheels creation makes up the Body of God. This conception is not exclusive to Gnostic beliefs. Earliest Kabbalists used the image of a circular reation before they developed the Tree format.

Those who agreed that humanity is "made in the image of God" would then see this cosmic map as the Gnostic model of the soul's challenge to "grow into" its full potential as a spark of the Divine. A soul that wanted to take incarnation in this world had to cross each planet's orbit and make an agreement with that planet's "soul" or intelligent principle (its genius). Each soul would pick up some of the qualities pertaining to that planet, forming its personality for this incarnation out of these different "planetary metals" in their raw state. And that soul's assignment in the course of a lifetime was to extract the pure metal from the raw materials of planetary qualities, purifying these elements so they could be minted into the "coinage" of each planetary realm. When it was time to leave the body and cross those planets' orbits again on the way back off this "mortal coil," one paid the toll owed to each planet and became liberated from further incarnations.

This is the source of the original idea of the planetary alchemical metals. Each planet provides a certain amount of its fundamental substance out of which to build a personality. It is humanity's job to evolve and purify those qualities in the course of a lifetime.

Mantegna card No. 39, Astrologia, illustrates the governing intelligence of this spiritual map of the cosmos. She teaches us the math and science of time and orbital motion, leading us into the understanding of our "cosmic clock" and the process of preparing the soul in this life for the adventure of the next. Remember, the ultimate goal of the soul on this journey up the "Ladder of Lights" is to grow in consciousness and comprehension until it can fully identify and join with the great World Soul, the Sophia or Shekhina, who bridges the gap between humanity and Divinity (revealed so well in the Fabricius illustration). We are to become conscious, individuated cells in the body of the primordial Goddess, spouse of God and mother of this world.

No. 39 ASTROLOGIA
MONTEGNA TAROT

2. The Female and Unfallen Creation

The Gnostics brought the ancient, pre-monotheistic Hebrew idea of the Shekhina, the feminine consort of God, into Gentile vocabulary, although among the Gnostics she was called Sophia, the Wisdom principle. Gnostics fostered the belief that Sophia, the Wisdom element of God, was feminine and represented the mind, meaning the actual conscious thinking that was vested in the making of Creation by the Creator. It is she who takes the creative juices of God and ferments them into the tangible world, the ecology of life. She creates what is actual out of the infinity of creative possibilities inherent in God, the undifferentiated Power.

Because of this important role of the Shekinah in Gnosticism, Gnostic Tarot decks place an especially strong emphasis on female figures, with goddesses appearing where the Christian patriarchy would use male images. My main exemplar of a Gnostic Tarot is a fairly recent deck, the Etteila Tarot, which actually was published in the years just before the French Revolution. As mentioned above, recent scholarship has determined that Eteilla was using as his creation model the Hermetic document called *The Divine Pymander*, one of the Hebrew-inflected Hermetic gospels preserved in Byzantium through the Dark Ages to re-emerge in the mid 1400s.

Etteilla's illustrated Major Arcana make it clear that this is a Gnostic revelation being illustrated in Tarot cards. The High Priestess whom you see in the Etteila Tarot (called the Lady Consultant, No. 8), is the Snake and Bird Goddess, the Great Mother of all the Middle Eastern Goddess traditions including the Hebrew and Gnostic Shekhina/Sophia. The Goddess is portrayed as Eve in Eden, with the serpent depicted as a vortex, a circular coil of energy, like a strong tellurgic aura around her. The tree she stands next to is another symbol of bridging Earth and heaven to draw down

EVE
GRIMAUD ETTEILA TAROT

consciousness into creation. This goddess figure is psychologically and spiritually attuned with every molecule of creation, and all the creatures in Nature are her children.

Although few images of The Priestess as Eve survived the shift of the Arcana from verbal descriptions in ancient documents to European cards, the El Gran Tarot Esoterico uses this same Eve image, this time holding a pomegranate and highlighted by the moon. There is also another Renaissance card game from 1616 (not a Tarot) called Labyrinth, devised by Andrea Ghisi, that shows Adam and Eve in the Garden of Eden with the snake climbing the Tree of Life between them.

Only in Gnostic thought do we find a positive interpretation of the snake in the garden. The card that substitutes for the Hanged Man in the Eteilla deck has left behind the Judeo-Christian idea of human guilt for the "fall of man" and its expiation in sacrifice. The replacement card is called Prudence, No. 12, and pictured is the Goddess again, holding a wand in the shape of a "T" with a snake at her feet. In this image, she is lifting her skirts to the snake as if in invitation, with an enigmatic smile on her lips. The "T" cross refers to the last letter of the Greek or Hebrew alphabet, assigned to the path leading to Malkuth, bottom station of the Kabbalah Tree, and another name for the Hebrew "Earthly Goddess." Manly P. Hall, in his tome *The Secret Teachings,* links the Tav, the Tetractys, the caduceus and the Kabbalah!

PRUDENCE
GRIMAUD ETTEILLA TAROT

We know from the history of symbolism that the snake is a longtime symbol of lifeforce, vitality or what the Chinese call "chi." It has not always been used as a symbol of evil or deception. The Gnostics held that the snake in the garden was a teacher of humanity, educating Eve and opening her eyes to the sexual mysteries. This same theme was explored in the older Mantegna Tarot image of Prudence, but in this one the snake is wrapping itself around the mirror into which Prudence gazes.

The mirror is another symbol for Wisdom as are the two faces looking forward and backward, so we are back with the Gnostic idea of Eve/Shekhina/Sophia as the initiator of humanity into the Mysteries, the Wisdom tradition, through her curiosity, mental reflection and natural magnetism.

Another clue to Gnostic influences in Tarot is the use of a female figure on the Pope card. This would be considered heretical in any Christian context, yet we see it from the earliest Tarots, the Mantegna tarocchi and the Visconti-Sforza pack, right up to that of modern scholar Manly P. Hall. In more modern Tarots, we have diluted her name down to the non-threatening "High Priestess," but her original title and form is that of the Female Pope. It is safe to say that a female Heirophant or Popess is a glaring clue to the spiritual beliefs of a Renaissance Tarot deck's author!

We also find female Chariot cards in three or four deeply Gnostic-influenced Tarots, suggesting that this is the ancient "Triumphant Chariot of Venus," an old mythological and alchemical theme highlighted by the fourteenth century poet Petrarch in his poem *I Triumphi.* The power of Venus lies in harmony, magnetism and the art of raising consciousness through the power of attraction and pleasure. Left alone, Nature rewards right action with joy and fulfillment, implying a trust in instinct and intuition which the Judeo-Christian tradition has rejected.

The optimist Gnostics believed that Eve was *supposed* to bite the apple. This strain of Gnostics (and there were others who disagreed) felt that without the biting of the apple, literal time and space would not have precipitated out of eternity. Hence, in the Eteilla Arcana, we see the Great Mother on the Eve card and then we have her whole creation on the Empress card, teeming with life and creative possibilities. There is no hint that this creation is flawed or less than an expression of Divine Will.

Yet in both the Jewish and the Christian concept, without the approval of God, the whole creation is fallen, in need of redemption, a problem waiting to be solved (see Kabbalah chapter). It's only the optimist Gnostics who felt that the spontaneous creation had virtue of its own because it is an expression of the Sophia force.

3. Sexuality's Place in the Creation

The theme of the androgyne or double-sexed magical entity is a subset of Gnostic speculation which harks back to the old Greek idea that before the soul's "fall from heaven" into a physical body, it had to split into halves, one male and one female, to accommodate the duality of the material plane. These two halves of the same soul then have to search for each other through the rounds of time, to complete each other before they can reascend into the divine realms as one. This is the origin of the idea of soul mates.

Within this story is hidden a teaching about the power of sexuality, the attraction of the male hidden within the female to the female hidden within the male, and the state of divine union which can transform animal sexuality into a source of magical and spiritual power. Given that the ancient Middle Eastern nations considered human intercourse as a microcosmic expression of the Great Union on high of God and his Consort, it would be remiss for a Gnostic Tarot to fail to cite the sexual mysteries in at least one Arcanum.

But different schools of Gnosticism had different opinions about this idea of opposites uniting. Some thought of the sexual urges as part of the conspiracy of the elements to bind human souls to Earth and the limitations of the flesh, therefore something to be avoided. Some felt that as long as the cycle of reproduction is being carried on, drawing more souls to this planet for reincarnation and polarizing human souls, fixating them on their gender differences, the creation would not return to its original innocence and divine order.

Others felt that only through the sex act could the opposites be united and the soul prepared for growth and evolution. The style apparent on any given Devil card of the Gnostic type will show whether the author was of the "sex is the problem" crowd or the "sex is the solution" crowd.

In either case, the Esoteric Devil (called Typhon in the 1700s, Baphomet by the time of Eliphas Levi in the late 1800s) has a body with womanly characteristics from shoulders to waist, although the head and legs are those of a goat. The goat-like characteristics make a reference to the Gnostic Demiurge, a figure cited by some Gnostics as the force in opposition to the ascension of humanity, whose influence on the world's conception spoiled the intended perfection of the creation and enforced the dualities riddling this world—good/evil, rich/poor, dominant/submissive, and so forth.

In this sense, when there is an emphasis on masculine characteristics in the Devil card, it highlights how the unified feminine is divided, split, parted, made from one into two upon the emergence of the Demiurge, also known as the Satan, the "tester," by the Jews. His job is to tempt souls to sin by creating chaos and disorder, then just sit back and see how we behave under stress.

DEVIL
EL GRAN TAROT ESOTERICO

Meanwhile, the Shekhina, whose female breasts the Typhon/Baphomet exposes, is here being assimilated to the seductive force which attracts us into incarnation and makes it so devilishly hard to leave this plane. Not just the violated Bride of the Underworld, dragged down by her immersion in the elements, she is shown as fully merged with the Demiurge, animal and Divine fused together. The Venus Triumphant ideal of the Gnostic Chariot card is now showing its flip side, as a dangerous sensuality which steals immortality even as the soul aspires to sacred union. This is an idea from the pessimistic Gnosis, a sex-negative teaching that infiltrated Judaism and Christianity in the Alexandrian centuries, encouraging all the Old Testament believers to reject pleasure and sensual expressions from their spiritual practices. And by thus demonizing the sensuality associated with the Goddess, which is one of the forces bringing the creation from unconsciousness to consciousness, the entire material world is demonized as well!

The Tarots that are more optimistically Gnostic emphasize the sensuous breasts and wasp waist, sometimes giving her angel wings rather than bat wings, and referencing her body parts to the elements of Nature (fire in the head, air in the breast, water in the bowels, and earth in the legs). Any Tarot that places a caduceus upon the belly of an obviously female Devil card, whether the caduceus is pointed upward or downward, is revealing the sex-positive Gnostic beliefs of its maker (as in the Esoterico, Papus, Etteilla, Tavaglione group).

The Devil image from the Alchemical Tarot reconciles the opposites in a novel way, using an image of a two-headed, two-sided man/woman balancing upon the winged eye of the Mystery. This image is an adaptation from a German alchemical manuscript by Basil Valentinus, published in 1604, and is cleansed entirely of any pejorative overlay from either Jewish or Christian sources. This image managed to escape the notice of the Church censors only because it was buried in an esoteric tome which never came into mass circulation.

ALCHEMICAL DEVIL
FROM VALENTINUS' OCCULTA PHILOSOPHIA

The Tarot, by the 1600s being printed in "catchpenny" versions for mass consumption, had to be more energetically veiled to survive the burning times. Artists became adept at creating ambiguous images which on their surface expressed the evils of fleshly pleasures, while revealing for initiates the inner teachings of the Primordial Goddess, not sacrificed or eliminated, but veiled to protect her essential purity from the misunderstandings of the uninitiated.

One very interesting clue to the complexity of this tricky imagery, wherein ancient mythologems are distorted in their historical transmission and made to serve entirely other meanings, can be found on page 143 of Raphael Patai's exceptionally detailed *The Hebrew Goddess*, in the chapter on the Matronit, an early understanding of the Consort of the King. In this ancient conception, the happiness of the whole creation depends upon the blissful sexual union between God and the Matronit, and each week every Hebrew couple was required to replicate this happy union in their own home in honor of the Sacred Marriage, and to restore happiness to the creation.

In Patai's own words:

"Yet another version, still preoccupied with the times of divine copulation, speaks not of a weekly, but of an annual cycle. Every year, we are told, the people of Israel sin with tragic inevitability which enables Samael, the satan (or Azazal) [our sex-negative Devil], to bend the Matronit to his will. Samael, in the form of a serpent, or riding a serpent, lurks at all times near the privy parts of the Matronit, in the hope of being able to penetrate her. Whether or not he succeeds in thus gratifying his desire depends on the conduct of Israel. As long as Israel remains virtuous, Samael's lustful design is frustrated. But as soon as Israel sins, as they, alas, are bound to do year after year, their sins add to Samael's power, he glues himself to the Matronit's body 'with the adhesive force of resin,' and defiles her.

Once this happens, the Matronit's husband, the King, departs from her and withdraws into the solitude of his heavenly abode. This unhappy state of affairs continues until, on the Day of Atonement, the scapegoat, which is destined to Azazal, is hurled to its death down a cliff in the Judaean desert. Samael, attracted by the animal offered to him, lets go of the Matronit, who thereupon can ascend to heaven and reunite with her husband, the King."

What happens to this myth if we recognize that the Serpent is not evil or a tempter, but the educator of the optimist Gnostics? As a symbol of the life force, the Kundalini or serpent-fire of primal vitality, we might be looking at a perversion of the old Snake and Bird Goddess, who takes great joy in her creation teeming with rich possibilities. The King comes off as punitive and abandoning, discarding his wife just as she is getting initiated into the wild, passionate, uninhibited expression of her natural vitality. The snake heads for the bull's-eye, the sacred site of the original Blood Mysteries, which later degenerated into animal sacrifice and a distorted understanding of the Eucharistic Mysteries.

I suspect that Eteilla is showing us a positive interpretation of the Matronit's experience in his "Prudence" image, with her shy smile and skirts lifted for the serpent! Perhaps he is trying to communicate to us through imagery that it is prudent to study this serpent-force in its various manifestations, to be receptive to these wild, earthy, untamed and vitalizing forces usually demonized in the Judeo-Christian paradigm.

In Summary

This essay merely hints at the great Gnostic riches which lie hidden in the deeper layers of Tarot imagery and philosophy. It is my hope that scholars of the future will begin to take the Tarot seriously as a spiritual and initiatory testament, equal to any of our written Gospels, and embark upon the work of reconnecting the Holy Word to these pictures worth a thousand.

I would like to leave you with one last comment on the gnostic creation story and the events of the Fall. This is from the most excellent Frances Yates, in her peerless book *Giordano Bruno and the Hermetic Tradition*.

" It is true that he falls, but this fall is in itself an act of his power. He can lean down through the armature of the spheres, tear open their envelopes and come down to show himself to Nature. He does this of his own free will moved by love of the beautiful Nature, which he himself helped to create and maintain, through his participation in the nature of the Seven Governors [the Elohim, or planetary Sephiroth].... And Nature recognises his power, the powers of the Seven Governors in him, and is united to him in love.

"It is true that this is a fall which involvs loss, that Man is coming down to Nature and taking on a mortal part, under the domination of the stars, and it is perhaps punished by the seperation into two sexes....But Man's immortal part remains divine and creative....In short, the Egyptian Genesis [she is citing the Hermetic *Pymander* tells the story of the creation and fall of a divine man, a man intimately related to the star-demons in his very origin, Man as Magus." (p. 27-28)

It is no wonder that some persons were attracted away from the fire-and-brimstone Roman church to the Gnostic church of love in the embrace of Nature. The patriarchal Church lost adherants over this schism in every generation, from the early centuries of Christianity through the flowering of the Cathar movement in southern France a thousand years later, and certainly the exodus has not ended yet. A philosophy devoted to Wisdom in her female form ("philosopher" means lover of Sophia!) would have appeal in any generation, which may help us to understand the popularity of Tarot from its first inception, despite vigorous Church disapproval.

HOLY BLOOD, HOLY TAROT

Who is Mary Magdalen?

Legend has it that sometimes she will allow herself to be glimpsed, just a wink of her, moving between the trees at the foot of the cliffs. On particularly bright, moonlit nights, it is said she stands against the scoured rock and lets the southeast winds pound upon her, pinning her in chiseled shilouette. None can name the forces working her at those times.

She fills her eyes, her ears, her skin with the sound, the feel, the wincing saltiness and windiness of the sea, and she is washed over by a wave of Spirit, rising, breaking, and retreating on inner shores, memory shores. Her inner eye ranges across landscapes of time, probing for the "signs" and meaningful coincidences which have shaped her destiny. By what miracle of power did this life unfold so?

In retrospect, her coming-of-age years showed even then that she was unusual. Called to the Work earlier than most, she took her empowerments seriously and received Initiation as fast as her teachers would let her. Her prosperous family had indulged her mystical tendencies, endowing her with a fund from which to support herself as a single woman — an enviable position to be in during such repressively partriarchal times. Even then this wind was blowing inside her, blowing her along to that fateful day when she met The Teacher.

By that time she had cultivated herself to a high degree. She had entered into relations with the spirits of the directions, the elements, the planets, the Sephiroth; her charisma and telesma were finely developed. Yet in the presence of The Teacher she could feel new potentials swelling, inner senses sharpening, a dawning recognition of something new yet very old and familiar. She eagerly entered into training with him, craving his company and thrilled to assist at the Eucharist beside him. Others saw the singificance of her excitement long before she did.

We can go no farther, he had said, until we liberate you from the bondage of your ancestors. There are spirits clinging to you, like mud on a crystal, and you deserve to be cleansed and consecrated for the Work. May I give you this empowerment? So a time was set, and the intention was made, to exorcise her of the sins of her forefathers. In a simple but deep ceremony, she was cleansed of the seven spirits of the Governors, servants of the Demiurge, God of the Lie.

With his hand and his heart he made her new. Lifted from within by the wind of the Spirit, she blew like a kite in the updraft, dancing dizzyingly while held firmly by his heartstrings 'til she came to earth again, touching down into

his deep dark eyes. After that, she knew her calling.

Now they were together more often than not. Some of this students complained, mostly the men, but The Teacher teased them, saying, "Ask not why I love her so much, but ask instead why I don't love you more! " She was not too proud to humble herself for him in the manner of a proper Hebrew wife, though she belonged to no man legally. She doted upon him and he upon her, and their love sweetened the space around them and nourished the onlookers, even those who disapproved.

Alone together they rediscovered the sinless joys of Adam and Eve before the fall, when Nature worshipped herself in the dance of opposites. They practiced the yoga of love, treating each other as God and Goddess in the work of creation. Who could fail to notice the bond they had, the at-onement? The souls conceived and born between these two hearts were vastly blessed, and heavily weighted, by the synergy of this union.

All the time the Spirit-wind would blow around her, making harmonics in her head and pointing her like a weathervane towards an unknown destination. Days and nights would unfold, looking much like each other, with their children to feed and clothes to mend, while the Teacher gave discourse to the slowly-growing crowds. Everything looked normal, but her ears would ring from the sound of her heart surging like a tide. Whither this yearning? This dread?

Sometimes she would ask him if he felt it too. He would look very tenderly right into her and say "Feel me right here with you, take me in and let me live in your heart. I will never leave you, not ever". He would put her hands on his face, his chest, his thighs, reminding her to soak up his physicality and assure herself of his here-nowness. He would hold her tight long into the night if she needed it. Most of the time this would comfort her, but she was occasionally struck with a grief and anguish so profound that she could only sob helplessly, totally swept away by it. He seemed to understand it all much better than she did.

Then came the year of the Sacrifice, and events unfolded quickly to reveal the terrible road that lay before her. The Teacher had come to his time of testing. His path was leading towards certain trouble which he would not sidestep. Even she, the mother of his children, had no leverage to dissuade him from his task. Mary had to quickly rediscover her independence, which had relaxed in the safety of her bond with him.

Now she knew what it was she had been unknowingly grieving. No more did she have the blanket of ignorance to cushion her dread. When she looked into her Teacher's eyes, into her lover's eyes, the father of her children's eyes, she saw deep space. There was no bottom, no limit, no ego or self anymore, and she knew that he had to go on without her now, and she without him. Nothing could relieve her loneliness, because even before it was all played out, he was already lost to her.

Yet she stayed on through the ordeal, imprisonment, humiliations. She stood by him at the foot of the cross, at the tomb, serving him in his darkest hour as she had served him at the altar and in their private rituals, A fountain of compassion flowing through her, moved by forces she had to trust and bow to. She knew that she was his earthly anchor as the Light strove with his broken body, and she freely lent her energy to his monumental struggle.

Only after they took him down did she finally return to herself. Heartbroken, she wept bitterly for the evil in the world, that it could so freely manhandle and abuse the Light in him, in her, in us all. Outrage mixed with horror as the images replayed in her mind, and through it all, beating with her own heart, was the crushing pain of knowing that their life together was over, finally and forever. He had made this clear to her before he was taken — no matter the outcome of the ordeal, she would need to go on without him, as any overt association with him would be too dangerous for her and the children. In this long and terrible night, she wrestled with the paradox that her God, the loving and merciful parent, had somehow sanctioned and allowed this ghastly situation.

The morning after the Sacrifice was over, she rose early to visit the tomb. With her she brought the salve he had instructed her to use when he was laid in the gravecloths. She thought to minister to her husband one last time, to smooth his matted hair, say his name, and put her hands upon his face one more time. How she screamed when she saw that he was gone! The gravecloth was empty! Forgetting what he had told her to expect, she thought the worst and started to raise a hue and cry. Someone she assumed was the gardener responded, and she asked what had been done with the body. Only then did she realize she was speaking with the Teacher himself!

It was a miracle to her how he had done it, even though he had been tutoring and testing her for years in those very skills. Her faith became belief right then and there. And how had he managed to camouflage himself so well that even she didn't recognize him? It was anguish not to touch him, not to grab him as of old and hang on for dear life, but he wouldn't let her. He was truly different, she could see that, and perhaps she was a little awed. But the strangest thing was, she could hear his voice in her mind! He was saying "I live, and I will never leave you," and as the words would emerge in her mind, tenderness and trust saturated her heart like a sponge. Without effort, spontaneously, she was healed from the dreadful spiritual labors of the night before. The devil that had besieged and nearly defeated her the night before shrank down to a wraith that evaporated in the presence of the Light.

She calmed herself, and then they could commune. He told her many things he wanted her to tell the other apostles, things he had not mentioned to any if them before. Having so recently traversed the inner planes, he had many things to report. Eventually she wrote those in a Gospel which now only a few have seen. Some of the apostles later became jealous that she was favored in that way, but he had prepared her to receive certain things that the others didn't know yet, and so she forgave them their ignorance.

As they shared, a few things became clear to her. Were they his ideas or hers? She couldn't tell. But as a woman alone, certain decisions had to be made. And somehow, she felt she had the will and the energy to carry on. During the exchange, at the point when she rediscovered her courage and optimism, he charged her with a solemn mission. As first witness to the transubstantiation, first in him and then in herself, he wanted her to serve as the first apostle of the good news. It would be her mission to keep and teach his practices. As his student, his wife, and his peer, she knew she had to accept the charge.

A meeting was called with her brother and sister and their families, and it was decided. A boat was hired and the plans were laid. The wind within Mary combined with the wind from the sea to blow them all to France.

From then on, when the wind would blow, she would hear his voice, and feel his touch upon her skin. When braced against the cliffs, buffeted by the gusts off the ocean, she could feel pressure as if he were leaning on her, laying on her, visiting her again in their special way. She could merge with the wind, merge with him, up on those cliffs. Eventually they named the spot after her, and for centuries she has been celebrated on her holy day, looking out to sea, feeling and tasting and blowing in the wind with her beloved.

The Context for the Presence of Mary Madgalen's Family in Tarot

The opening story of this chapter, really a musing on a pivotal life in a pivotal time, sets the stage for the mythical drama which Tarot has had the privilege to carry from the Renaissance into the present.

Implicit in this story is the original teachings of Master Jesus to his apostles, with Mary Magdalen as the premier apostle. This tradition has been preserved and kept alive despite the challenges brought by intrigue and politics, even against persecution and holy war imposed by the usurpers of the lineage. The essential ingredient in this story, what makes it relevant to the history of Tarot, is that both Jesus and Mary were Initiates, bringing to their union a marriage of lineages, the Egyptian, the Hebrew, the Alchemical, and the Gnostic. Historians need to fill in the details about who each of them were in their own selves, before they met each other, but from the evidence of history, there can be no doubt that this was an amazing couple.

I did not set out to delve into the Christian subplot in the history of Tarot; as a matter of fact I thought I was leaving Christianity far behind in delving into hermetics and the occult! But space is curved, and so is knowledge — it all leads back around to the beginning, which repeats over and over in a continual coil of events and themes. Hail the Great Mystery!

In the process of overhauling my own beliefs to fit the evidence I have found, I have had to read everything I could get my hands on in the field of Holy Land archeology, linguistic analysis, new translations of old scriptures, and new research in cultural anthropology and the history of religions. I don't pretend to understand all that I have been exposed to, but one trend is clear. It is now well known that canonical biblical accounts of the life of Master Jesus have been heavily expurgated, edited, spliced through with later inventions, and otherwise mutated from the original events as they actually happened, and there is too much evidence of this for the churches which bear his name to suppress any longer. The face of Christianity, in all of it's many and varied forms, will change when the story finally reaches the people.

With all this in mind, the goal of this chapter is to expose, with the help of El Gran Tarot Esoterico, the fusion created when the Gnostic, Goddess-loving mystical Hebrew expatriate community on the south coast of France "adopted" Mary Magdalen and her family, after she had taken the child(ren) and fled the Holy Land after the crucifixion. Her relationship with this community guaranteed the transmission of the underground stream from the Holy Land into Europe.

To do this I have to operate on an assumption which you, the reader, have to keep in mind as you read. That assumption is that there is a special body of teachings, practices, and beliefs that Jesus and Mary were sharing with their inner circle, and these were important enough in the unfolding of the Western psyche to have caused a two-thousand-year wave that has rippled through many different ages and cultures to reach us today. I *have* to take up this assumption, and interpret what I find in it's light, because the shape of history demands it. If ideas about "esoteric teachings" from Jesus for his chosen disciples sound surprising or undocumented to you, try investigating the rediscovered Gospels of the Nag Hamadi collection, also known as the *Dead Sea Scrolls*. The emergence of this ancient library from its' desert interment has spurred renewed interest in the Essenes, the Desert Fathers (and Mothers), and their contribution to early Christianity. The works of Morton Smith, Hugh Schonfield, and Barbara Thiering will help to illuminate the issues for you. On the subject of Mary Magdalen and her place among the apostles, look to the works of Susan Haskins, Margaret Starbird, and Ean Begg, as well as Caitlin Matthews' tremendous book *Sophia*.

My Bias

I feel I should confess my personal biases on this topic. Because of my spirit and temperament, I am not an "impartial witness". I study these issues feeling spiritually called to penetrate the veil of revisionism. My desire is to re-encounter the primitive and original essence of the Christ experience. I want to promulgate the teachings of the world's first non-mythical, historical Global Avatar couple.

Now please forgive me as I launch into a few paragraphs featuring Jesus to the exclusion of Mary and children. In the world of their times, history did not record very many of the doings and sayings of women. Here I am staying with historical assertions which are documentable, so I talk about Jesus, just as the scriptures do. Wherever you read "Jesus" in the next few paragraphs, please imagine his wife standing by his side, teaching along with him.

At the demand of the collective psyche of the times, Jesus provided a physical example of a person whose relationship to God was one of child to parent, in direct communication, responsible and responsive. This form of mysticism is very much the antithesis of the "old man in the sky" image of God, or the "cast out orphan" of fallen Adam. Despite all of the new evidence that modern scholarship can amass, we still don't know enough about his inner life to visualize this perfectly, but we have quite a bit of evidence of what he taught, and the evidence is compelling.

It seems that by Jesus' lifetime, the seed of the idea held secret within the ancient Mysteries — that humans carry the spark of divinity hidden within our earthly selves — had sprouted and bourne fruit in the collective psyche. By the first century of the modern era, humanity was ready for a human exemplar of the divine in mortal form, a person who lived normally, yet was in constant intimate communication with the Holy Parent in a way that was demonstrable to all. The Mysteries had long been teaching this ideal, as portrayed in mythology and art through traditional characters like Dionysis, Hermes Trismegistus and Hercules. But it was not until Jesus' lifetime that we can document historical persons appearing as literal exemplars of this new relationship. There were other personalities contemporary to Jesus who also had reputations as man/gods — Simon Magus is one well-known example — but the movement that grew up around Master Jesus is the one that has captured the imagination of countless generations right up to present time.

This shift to a personal relationship with a parental deity made such sense to so many people that within three centuries all of the ancient Mysteries were dying out and Christianity became the dominant paradigm both culturally and spiritually. Due to one persons's reframing of his stance with God, what had once been Rome's military and economic empire eventually became the Holy Roman Empire of the Catholic Church.

For better and for worse, Christianity presided over the demolishment of the ancient Mysteries, from which it has helped itself freely. Western consciousness had become increasingly ready to envision a God-form that looks like an evolved human being after the Alexandrian epoch reexamined Pythagoras and Plato. I see that the lives of both Jesus and Mary Magdalen, both highly self-realized people, were like comets with long and glowing tails, informing hundreds of generations after them about the broad spectrum of human potential and the desirability of becoming at-one with the Holy Spirit.

Merovingian Claims To the Holy Blood

One point I must make here is about the story that Jesus and Mary had a child, or children, who was/were brought to a Hebrew enclave in southern France, and raised among the Merovingian clan, into whom their "royal blood" then flowed by marriage. From all the evidence I have seen, there is no way to accurately either prove or disprove this supposition, because the records to uphold such arguments are lost if they ever existed at all. It is enough for me that these traditions exist, and persist, and were pervasive enough for the Church to undertake great labors to try and rid themselves of this clan of people and their followers.

What is the legend asserting the existence of a Holy Family, descendents of the progeny of Jesus and the Magdalen? Let me try and state this in as condensed a form as possible. The Merovingian bloodline, as traced by the authors of *Holy Blood, Holy Grail*, is said to originate with the ancient Jewish family of Benjamin, driven from their tribal land to Greece by the sack of Jerusalem in 70 BCE. These exiled monarchs became the ancestors of the royal dynasty of the Franks, a Teutonic tribe who migrated west again after the siege of Troy, bringing with them from Greece the name "people of the Great Bear" (Arkades, referring to the constellation.) From their ancient origins they were famed as priest-kings, magi and occult adepts, sometimes called the sorcerer-kings. Along with their totem, the white bear, this magical acuity and their attachment to their long blond hair were family trademarks.

Wherever this family spread in Europe, (eventually over most of what is now Germany and France right into the Spanish foothills), a friendly climate was created for expatriate Jews (and apparently later, Moors as well). Many Hebrew family-names appear in their generational records. Their tribal laws, codified in the 5th century BCE as the Salic Code, have recently been shown to be derived from a section of the Talmud. The authors of Holy Blood, Holy Grail cannot prove it, but they strongly feel that this is the tribe who took in Mary Magdalen when she fled with her children after the crucifixion. In every statue and icon from this tradition, she is portrayed with her child on her lap, and because her shrines nearly invariably are built upon spots traditionally sacred to the ancient Goddess, there is no reason to separate her significance from earlier incidences of the Great Mother tradition.

In my opinion, the "lineage line" of Mary as an Apostle is at least as important to the unfolding of history and culture as is her bloodline. Whether or not there was a child or children to intermarry with the Merovingians is a moot point. What is important is that Mary Magdalen, first Apostle, carried the secret teachings to Europe, and it is that "line" that has proved potent and spiritually fertile, even despite the Catholic Church's best efforts to wipe it out.

The Response from Rome

Apparently the early Roman church suspected that the story of the Magdalen's arrival in Europe and the establish-

ment of a bloodline was true, because in 496 a Merovingian ruler named Clovis made a pact with the Bishop of Rome, that Rome would convert to the Merovingian form of Christianity. This pact bolstered the Roman church immensely because of it's linkage to this charismatic royal family. The Church pledged to uphold this family as it's special patrons, and serve as the secular administration of it's spiritual authority as the Church of the Holy Family. But within a few generations, the church regretted this pact, and embarked upon a campaign which led to the assassination of the last Merovingian king, Dagobert II. Within a decade, a new king was designated by the Church in the brand-new sacrament called "coronation and anointment," a blatant imitation of ancient Jewish coronation ceremonies. The supposed authority for this creation of "instant royalty" was drawn from a document forged for the occasion, the *Donatin of Constantine*, and from this time forward the Pope certified the coronations of all the kings and queens of Europe, eventually undermining all political and ecclesiastical power which had accumulated in the Merovingian bloodline.

In terms of the dissemination of the Gnosis, other families and bloodlines were involved as well; the Merovingians do not have the sole claim on the so-called "holy blood"! What they had was the foresight to create a contract with the Pope at a politically sensitive time, which put their lobbying for special status in the historical record. However, popes change, and with them the winds of fortune, so their "special status" was usurped anyway. The importance of this family in history is their perpetuation of the feminine Apostolic Gnosis, which provided fertile ground for a merging with the feminism of Celtic Christianity and the Arthurian Grail mythos during later centuries.

In Begg's words; "Triumphant Rome tried to exterminate the Church of Mary, but only succeeded in driving it underground. The rights of women were likewise repressed, though in the Celtic world they retained many of their considerable ancient freedoms. They even, according to Jean Markale [*Women of the Celts*}, took part in the celebration of the Mass in Ireland prior to the Norman Conquest....It was this Celtic Christianity that re-evangelized Europe from Aachen to Lucca in the so-called Dark Ages. From the same lands came the quest for the grail that revivified the spirituality of the twelfth century. Markale writes of the Grail quest that it is inextricable from the quest for woman." (p. 129)

Needless to say, it is not the role of this book to prove or document the existence of a progeny descended from the union of the Magdalen and Master Jesus. It is rather my hope that we can together examine evidence in this particular deck of references to the combined teachings of this priestess of the ancient goddess religions and this master of Kabbalah, as well as images that refer to the Merovingian bloodline.

The Egyptian/Alexandrian Content of Jesus and Mary's Teachings

Historians long have been polarized over the how much validity to attribute to the undeniable evidence, found in both Christian and Hebrew gospels, of an Egyptian origin for some of Jesus's teachings. Evidence such as this threatens the dogmatic idea that Jesus was teaching an entirely new and original philosophy. This idea has long a cornerstone of Christian identity. But how could he be teaching something utterly unheard of? Who can live an entire lifetime immersed in a specific time and place, yet not bear any imprint of that cultural contact? As a matter of fact, it is partially through the specifics of linguistic and cultural detail embedded within the stories of Jesus in Christian and Hebrew manuscripts that historians have been able to discern the roots of Jesus' teachings.

That Jesus was a rabbi and a Kabbalist is held as a given in esoteric circles, supported by the internal structure and vocabulary of both the Lord's Prayer and the Sermon on the Mount. It is also recorded that his followers called him Rabbi. He also grew up in a market town where multiple trade-routes that spanned the known world intersected, giving him the chance to interact with mystics of every stripe.

We find Master Jesus at the hub of a wheel of synchronicities which updates the Mysteries again 600 years after Pythagoras. Jesus grew up in Galilee, a backwater by comparison with Jerusalem, but a hotbed of alternative spirituality, comparable to a modern "new-age" enclave. What Galilee lacked in urbanity and orthodoxy, it made up in multicultural stimulation. Arriving from all directions was a steady stream of traders, working the Silk Route heading east through Persia, across India, over to China, and into Mongol territory to the north and west, across the Mediterranean, to North Africa, southern Europe, and the cold lands of the northern reaches. The Holy Land was as much a melting-pot as Alexandrian Egypt.

The Sephir Yetzirah, foundation-text of the Jewish mystics, was a common denominator for Magi from multiple traditions, because of its' role as the astronomical and astrological textbook of the ancient world. We must also remember that Jesus lived 12 years of unrecorded life, off the record, so to speak. I assume that he most likely would have been following up on his well-known mystical interests. There was plenty of time to travel and study outside of Galilee, if that was his wish.

In the case of Mary Madgalen's Egyptian connection, Margaret Starbird has given us this explanation. "It seems likely that after the crucifixion of Jesus, Mary the Magdalen found it necessary to flee for the sake of her unborn child to the nearest refuge. The influential friend of Jesus, Joseph of Aramathea, could very well have been her protector....If our theory is correct, the child actually was born in Egypt. Egypt was the traditional place of asylum for Jews whose safety was threatened in Israel; Alexandria was easily reached from Judea and contained well-established Jewish communities at the time of Jesus. In all probability, the emergency refuge of Mary Magdalen and Joseph of Arimathea was Egypt. And later — years later — they left Alexandria and sought an even safer haven on the coast of France." (p. 60)

A few paragraphs later, Starbird says "In the town of les Saintes-Maries-de-la-Mer in France, there is a festival every May 23 to 25 at a shrine in honor of Saint Sarah the Egyptian, also called Sara Kali, the "Black Queen." Close scrutiny reveals that this festival, which originated in the Middle Ages, is in honor of an "Egyptian" child who accompanied Mary Magdalen, Martha, and Lazarus, arriving with them in a small boat that came ashore at this location in approximately ad 42....A child of Jesus, born after Mary's flight to Alexandria, would have been about twelve years of age at the time of the voyage to Gaul recorded in the legend." (p. 60-61) So here we have the news that Jesus and Mary had a daughter, and she was "Egyptian", and black.

Ean Begg provides another source of reinforcement for Mary Magdalen's ties to Egypt and to Europe, although his evidence is iconographic rather than textual. *The Cult of the Black Virgin*, is an excellent study of the subject. Here is a condensation of Begg's position on how those Black Goddess images got into Christian churches all over France:

"It is characteristic of Black Virgins that they resuscitate dead babies long enough to receive baptism and escape limbo, and in this they adopt a subversive posture *vis-a-vis* the rules of male-dominated theology. They are also numerous in many areas where paganism lingered or where the Cathars flourished. Quite often there is a cult of Mary Magdalen and a Black Virgin in the same place. The interest apparently shown by the [underground survivors of the Templars] in black Virgins, Lilith and the Queen of Sheba, and literary figures connected with them encourages the speculation that the cult of the Black Virgin has indeed links to hidden, dark secrets of the past. That past, it should be remembered, if the principal conclusion of *The Holy Blood and The Holy Grail* has any justification, includes the descent of Merovee [the Holy Blood-line] from the child of Jesus and Mary Magdalen." (p. 130)

In present time, the Catholic Church, in the attempt to re-enfold the Magdalean worship back into Catholicism, have made every effort to say that the many churches in the Iberian Peninsula that feature Black Madonnas are just local people's folksy way of portraying the Virgin Mary. I believe, along with other named resources that it's the offspring of this black priestess who's being displayed and worshipped, the lineage heir, the potential future spiritual leader who emerged from her womb.

The making over of Jesus, Mary, etc. by dark skinned peoples in their own image is understandable, say, in Latin American countries where the indigenous people who were converted were themselves dark complicated. But in Spain and Portugal the dark skinned people were the invaders, so Mary would not be darkened in their behalf. I can think of no pressing symbolic necessity for her to be portrayed as black in so many European locations. Comparisons may be made with Old Testament references in the Song of Songs to the divine Beloved, who is black and beautiful. But the Iberian Christians who hold the Black Madonna sacred do not identify their icon this way. My guess is that Mary Magdalen *was* dark, in her literal person, and the artists who wanted to make it clear that they were portraying the wife of Jesus instead of his mother, would feature that detail, if true, as an identifying marker of her identity.

Richard Pope, in his amazing restatement of history, detailing the contribution which Black Egypt made to the civilization of Europe (Black Spark, White Fire, pub 1997) has added mountains of evidence to the idea that the Egyptian people were themselves the color of toast, but were mingled through the centuries with darker and lighter peoples who emigrated to Egypt for the relative freedoms Egypt offered. He also thoroughly documents that the Egyptian Mysteries were seminal in the establishment of the Mystery Schools in Europe, from pre-Christian times right through the emergence of Masonry in Europe during the breaking up of the Renaissance. After taking in Pope's encyclopedic survey of the cultural trends of the ancient world, a statue of Mary Magdalen in blackface and paralleling Isis will seem a perfectly obvious development in Europe. As well, our ideas about the later European secret societies having links to ancient Egyptian Mysteries are reinforced. He says not a word about Tarot, but that is a good thing, because we know that he has no ax to grind about it; he's just recounting the evidence he has found for his hypothesis.

We must remember that the life and times of Jesus and the Magdalen were marked by priestly politics and factional fighting, much more than by divinity's halo. Not only the earliest Christians, but the contemporary Jews, Persians, Essenes, Johannites, and every other semitic tribe were all experiencing schism and fallout during these volatile years. Today, with the unearthing of the Nag Hamadi library, the Coptic Gnostic gospels, and other caches of hidden scriptures, we know that sectarian infighting was more the norm than the exception. With this in mind, the survival of the inner teachings of Jesus in any form is near-miraculous.

Nevertheless, in the course of the shift from underdog Holy Land heresy to Holy Roman Empire, the original teachings of the Master got overgrown, like a neglected garden. What he *did* and *showed* became legend instead of practice, what he taught and expected of his students became seen as "miracles of God", unrepeatable by ordinary mortals. Huge segments of his life were rewritten or ignored to serve revisionist interests, including what happened during his "missing" years, his ordination of women, plus his marriage and the birth of children. Many lives were sacrificed because they refused to renounce these and other episodes from the life of their Master, like the persistent heresy that he survived his ordeal on the cross, was smuggled away to heal and continued his ministry anonymously.

The distortions which crept into Christianity over the centuries biased the culture of Europe in measureless ways. Countless men gave up having families because they were told Christ was celibate. The tribal, inherited, aboriginal royal families of Europe, several of whom count themselves as having intermarried with the bloodline of the Master and Mary Magdalen, were eclipsed by "manufactured" royalty appointed by the Pope to rule in their stead. Book burning and

anti-scholastic sentiments, promoted by the church to stop the spread of these same banned gospels, resulted in such profound ignorance that had the Arabs not been avid collectors of western learning, Europe would have lost it's history entirely.

The Schism Between Peter and Mary Divides the Church

History records in no uncertain terms that Jesus was highly educated in the broad stream of Hebrew mysticism. No Jewish person escaped being exposed to the Kabbalistic worldview embedded in the spoken, written and read language. Even with all the above-mentioned controversies competing in the Jewish intellectual marketplace of the Holy Land, everybody agreed that the Hebrew letters were the keys to creation. Every son of the Hebrew nation anywhere in the world learned to read and write, not just to make him literate, but to put in his possession those cosmic keys. Master Jesus was famed for his curiosity and love of learning, even at a young age. He was also quoted, by more than one source, weaving Kabbalist idioms into his parables to the poor, as only "one who knows" could convincingly do.

Latest research points to the fact that the Magdalen was not just Jesus' student but his equal and his partner in the age-old *Heiros Gamos* or Sacred Marriage. And perhaps this special relationship underlay the rivalry and schism between the Magdalen and the disciple Peter.

Here's Begg again:

"Elaine Pagels [in *The Gnostic Gospels*] has drawn attention to the polarity that was seen to exist from the second century between Mary Magdalen and Peter. All the writings that extolled the role of Mary were ultimately excluded from the canon. In the *Pistis Sophia*, Mary tells Jesus of her fear of Peter: "Peter makes me hesitate; I am afraid of him, because he hates the female race.' If we think of this polarity not in personal terms but as two traditions within Christianity, what we see are the church of Peter, Catholic, orthodox, male dominated and victorious, and the rival church of Mary, Gnostic and heretical, worshiping a male/female deity and served by priests of both sexes". (p. 129)

Some of the legends associated with Mary's life portray her as a master healer and herbalist, as well as the inventer of distillery equipment which is still in use today. She is regularly associated with the Isis Mysteries, which stretch back from their last great flowering in Alexandrian Greece to the antiquity of Egypt's pharaonic dynasties.

The Sexual Mary

Historically there is a stream of more prurient stories about Mary Magdalen—as a temple prostitute like the "woman at the well", a woman of loose morals (associated with the culture of her hometown, Magdala,) who engaged in sexual yoga with Jesus. These have been added to her legend over time, for moralistic reasons totally unrelated to the true life of Mary and Jesus.

Yet such stories as these may overlay an ancient truth about their magical and Kabbalistic sexual cultivation as a married couple, which would be a natural development for two such highly-trained and psychically developed individuals. More information on these various themes can be found in *Mary Magdalen* by Susan Haskins, *The Jewish Alchemists* by Raphael Patai, and Margaret Starbird's two books *The Woman with the Alabaster Jar*, and *The Goddess in the Gospels*. It would be no wonder, then, if the Magdalenic Gnostics of the 11th and 12th centuries revived Mary Magdalen in the context of their new conception, the Church of Love. She could serve as an exemplar of what is beloved and cherished by Jesus, the divine lover, evoking ideals of a higher order of human communion.

Maria the Jewess

The emergence of Jewish Alchemy was historically coincidental with the emergence of Alchemy as an art or a discipline in the west. Faivre might beg to differ with the claim that Maria the Jewess was the first historical alchemist, (Modern Esoteric Spirituality, p. 6), but Patai assures us that "the first nonfictitious alchemists of the Western world lived...in Hellenistic Egypt." (Patai, p. 60 of The Jewish Alchemists.) "And the earliest among them was Maria Hebraea, Maria the Jewess..." Maria has a very interesting reputation in the canon of Alchemy, articulating a doctrine which runs like a leitmotif through the generations of Western alchemists who claim her as their founding mother.

Her doctrine utilized the opposite qualities in matter, whether fixed or volatile, corporeal or incorporeal, male or female, to bring about a union between unlike substances and a transformation of the opposites into a higher substance partaking of the best qualities of each. She equated the operations of alchemy upon the elements of earth with human evolutionary stages—birth, metabolism, growth, sexuality, reproduction, and mortality. She extended the metaphor of "man made in God's image" to include "Nature made in man's image", a natural development for one who reads Genesis in Hebrew.

We know that Maria Hebraea's anthropomorphic attitudes deeply influenced many generations of alchemists after her. By equating the action of one substance upon another in terms of a "sacred marriage" or "union of the female and the male," she laid the foundation for a marvellous allegory which has captured the imaginations of alchemists right into the present day. A mythos grew up around her legend after her passing, connecting her by blood or "sacred marriage" to pivotal figures in Jewish culture; as a sister to Moses, student and possibly lover of the Persian Magi Osthenes at Memphis in Egypt (4th century. BCE.), and, more relevant to our study, student of the Jewish Tantra as taught by Jesus.

Ironically enough, it is an early Christian bishop who has kept this story alive for us by his vigorous denouncement of it's authenticity! Epiphanius, bishop of Salamis at the end of the third century CE rails against Maria the Jewess

in his *Against Eighty Heresies*, outraged at he legend, which states that she had a revelation from Jesus in which he taught her about sperm and reversing the flow of semen, "being taken back whence it had gone out." In the legend he was also reputed to equate his future ascension to his Father with the spiritual equivalent of the physical act he was showing Maria. (Patai's *The Jewish Alchemists*, p. 74).

Raphael Patai says that this is the first mention in history of a Jew believing in or knowing about Jesus, but I find that rather hard to swallow, considering how many Jewish Gnostics were numbered among his followers. What I can't ignore is the similarity of the name Maria and Mary (Madgalen), who was also reputed to have been sexually intimate with Jesus. This would seem a slender thread upon which to hang a theory, but it must be taken in context to be understood.

Patai's wonderful book *The Hebrew Goddess* is entirely devoted to the revelation of the feminine principle through the development of Jewish mysticism from antiquity to the Renaissance. The theme which he exhaustively documents as being central to Jewish spirituality, ritual, and national identity, is that of sacred sexuality. God is accompanied by a wife in the act of Creation, identified as the Shekhina-Matronit. The relationship between God and his people was also compared to a marriage relationship. The observance of Sabbath was reserved from work to a large degree to facilitate sacred union between husband and wife at least once a week. The Hebrew mystical urge to experience closeness with "God and his holy Spirit" was embodied very literally in conjugal relations between marriage partners.

So we can assume that a story linking Maria the Jewess with Jesus in the context of secret sexual practices for initiates (sperm retention in this case) is not an anomaly or a piece of spurious Christian anti-Semitic gossip. In the context of his times, Jesus would have had a Jewish wife, would have been taught to observe the Sabbath like all good Jewish citizens, and they would have been taught that his sperm was sacred, precious, to be carefully husbanded, either for conception of children, or, as in his exhibition for Maria the Jewess, for spiritual/alchemical purposes.

This reversal of the flow is a traditional practice in Hindu, Chinese, and Tibetan alchemy, thousands of years old in the East. So it should come as no surprise that Jewish alchemy, too, linked sexuality and spirituality, practising identical techniques. The object of this technique is to feed the higher centers of the nervous system as the male and female vitality commingle in the sexual act, preserving health and lengthening life for both parties. All alchemical traditions hold this teaching to be a part of their canon, by which the simple products of nature can be expertly combined by adepts to produce higher states of matter and consciousness.

In the times of the Master Jesus, the Jewish Gnostics characterized the relation between God and Israel as similar to that of husband and wife, portrayed in very earthy and sensual terms in ancient scriptures. In addition, there existed the influence of ancient Hebrew Goddess-worship, laden as it is with celebrations and observances marking the meeting of God and his consort in the Temple. Further, we note that

Jesus could not have earned status of Rabbi among his people unless he was married, and sure enough, stories of his marriage and the resulting family have been circulating in Christiandom for two millennia. Additionally, we factor in the apostles' recorded protests that Master Jesus had a favorite female apostle by the name of Mary Magdalen, who received special personal attentions and sacred teachings. Finally we consider the first Jewish alchemist, famed for introducing alchemical operations and tools which are explained in terms of coition, fertility, birth and death, and who is linked by an early Christian Bishop with Jesus in a story about a lesson in sacred sexuality... *and* her name is Maria! Can one fail to see a pattern here, even if only dimly?

Fragments from Begg's Insights

Begg's final chapter, "The symbolic Meaning of the Black Virgin" is a treasure trove of ideas and new viewpoints, which I cannot possibly synthesize for you here. Let me just string together a series of pithy quotes, so you will want to run out and get this powerful response to *Holy Blood, Holy Grail.* In Begg's own words,

"The Black Virgin is a Christian phenomenon as well as a preservation of the ancient goddesses and compensates for the one-sided conscious attitudes of the age....Against the frenzied fashion for denying, defeating, and transcending nature, the Black Virgin stands for the healing power of nature, the alchemical principle that the work against nature can only proceed in and through nature". (p. 135)

"The Black Virgins are often associated with esoteric teaching and schools of initiation. Wisdom has always cried on the rooftops or at the street corners, and the spirit of this world always punished those who buy her wares. The great age of the Black Virgin is the twelfth century, but legends about her hark back to the dawn of Christianity, the dynasty of the Merovingians, and the age of Charlemaine. Like the Sleepers of Ephesus, ideas go underground for a few centuries to reemerge when times are more propitious". (p. 133)

" Once women are free to bestow their favors and affections where they will, the whole structure of patriarchal society starts to crumble. In the long spiralling progress of the history of ideas this seems to be the point that we have once again reached. Now it is an idea whose time has come and no crusades have so far been launched by Church and State to quell it. If the Black Virgins really do carry a charge from the goddesses, perhaps now that they have been 'found' yet again, they are whispering in our ears like the female serpent of Eden, 'You won't really die'". (p. 137)

"The literalization of the virginity of Mary, like the literalization of Eve's role as the wicked temptress of Genesis, broke the heart of Christianity and works of reparation to the Sacred heart of Jesus and the Immaculate Heart of Mary have still not wholly healed the wound. Thus the dichotomy of the virgin and the whore, the good mother and the witch, continues to gnaw like an unresolved canker at the soul of modern man." (p. 129)

Linking the Holy Couple with 12th Century Cathars and Albigensians

When I first read Ean Begg and his ideas about the Black Virgins, I didn't know quite what to make of it. I had not yet seen *El Gran Tarot Esoterico,* or read *Holy Blood, Holy Grail*, and was only borrowing the book from a fellow esotericist. But these words stood out to me even then, because I realized that my suspicions of deeper content in the Tarot were not entirely unfounded. Says Begg, "Lest we should seem to be straying too far from our main theme, let us recall that the Tarot is a product of that fourteenth century that saw the destruction of the Order of the Temple, the eradication of Catharism in the Languedoc, the Black Death and the Hundred Years War. [Tarot] presents in symbolic form the concentrated doctrine of heretical, dualist Christianity, particularly Catharism, though it is also associated with the Gypsies, and through its 22 Trumps which correspond to the letters of the Hebrew alphabet, with Cabbalistic Judaism. In such circles, astrology was held in high esteem, and systems, like that of Joachim of Flora, which predicted the coming of the age of the Holy Spirit, were closely studied....But to see Gnosticism principally in terms of divination and prognostication is to fail to understand it. When examined from the standpoint of depth psychology the account it presents of the mystery and tragedy of life is far from ridiculous. Perhaps Gnostics might prefer the term "height Psychology', but then 'altus' in Latin means both 'deep' and 'high'."

At that time, I was marveling throughout Begg's prose at his mature and developed spiritual feminism, which I had not encountered often in my study of the Mystery Schools. His book is a refreshing reminder that there are men in the world who understand the need to involve the body and the heart in one's mystical quest. For purposes of brevity I have had to ignore pages of his conclusions about the Magdalenic Church of Love, the troubadours, the cult of courtly love, and the continuing enmity between the Roman and Gnostic branches of Christianity, but believe me, it is all there in his book.

Also, so that you can see that I am not overstating a discredited bit of heresy, let me point the reader again to the book *The Goddess in The Gospels* by Margaret Starbird. Her simple yet profound account of how she, a devout and orthodox Catholic theologian, discovered the truth about Mary Magdalen, exemplifies the present resurrection of the Goddess in the nave of the ancient Church! I deeply appreciate her courage in presenting this material, backed up as it is by research that has probed the full range of available source materials, and bibliographical references that are state-of-the-art. Her expertise lies in recognizing the themes of the Arthurian Grail cycle, the Celtic Grail mythos, in the Tarot. Both in this book and her previous one, *The Woman With The Alabaster Jar*, Starbird pieces together the story of Mary the Apostle, the Holy Grail, the Sacred Marriage, and other suppressed Christian Gnostic themes, linking them with the imagery of one of the earliest surviving Tarot decks of Europe. In *The Goddess in The Gospels*, she explicitly states that she sees in the Charles VI Tarot "a visual catechism of the Albigensian heresy of the Holy Grail." (p. 82) Her work supports my idea that the Tarot as it appeared in the early fourteen hundreds is a product of Hebrew/Gnostic/Christian/Alexandrian crosscurrents which incubated in Europe for a thousand years before the Roman Catholics became threatened and decided to suppress it once and for all. With this in mind, it is now time to look into El Gran Tarot Esoterico directly and in detail.

An Authentically Jewish Tarot, with Alexandrian Gnostic Elements

The Gran Tarot Esoterico is only one of two Tarot decks I've been able to find that fits with the ancient teachings of the Hebrew people. It is unique in Tarot to find the Hebrew Mysteries handled so respectfully, even though it is being spliced in with the Europeanized arcana and overlaid with the Albigensian heresy. Most European tarots feature one of the later, "corrected" bodies of correspondences rather than the truly ancient version presented by Kaplan in his definitive work on the *Sephir Yetzirah*. And when the publication dates of these cards and Kaplan's book are compared, it turns out that over twenty years separates the appearance of El Gran Tarot Esoterico and Kaplan's much later work. Where did Marixtu Guler get her information?

When I purchased this Tarot, I had not come upon the proofs that would let me recognize the astro-alphanumeric correspondences the author was using. But at that time I was reading *Holy Blood, Holy Grail,* so the Magdalenic and Gnostic subtext hit me right in the eye. It didn't all dawn on me all at once what this deck is; it has been a cumulative revelation. And from that point of view I do not want to posture myself as knowing the whole story. This deck opens up more lines of inquiry and more questions than it answers because it has so many different layers. It's a peasant-style, Kabbalist, feminist, Gnostic, magical deck. I hope that others who know more than I do will come forth and illuminate the sources of this teaching.

As I describe this Tarot, remember that I am featuring a Jewish Gnostic slant on these images and symbols. There are non-Gnostic Jews who could quite accurately debate my reading of these Arcana, as well as orthodox Catholics who might wish to challenge my reasoning based on their own interpretations of these ancient myths and scriptures. The symbols and images are common intellectual property among many peoples, each of whom is passionate about their own version, their own retelling of the story, and this is the root of religious conflict in every age and nation.

Also note that we are doing archeology here, but with ideas and images instead of strata of soil and layers of artifacts. In the following accounting, my focus has been on the alphabet-mysteries and the teachings of the Holy Couple. Begg work highlights the Black Virgin/Magdalenic heresy of Europe's "dark ages." Margaret Starbird's response to the Charles VI Tarot emphasises the Holy Grail mythos of the

Middle Ages, showing how much of the Hebrew content survived into the early Renaissance. We are all operating on the same assumption—that the earliest Tarot authors were aware of a Gnostic/Hebrew subculture in the European population of the Middle Ages, originating from the early centuries of the Common Era.

An Introduction to the Author of El Gran Tarot Esoterico

Maritzu Guler, the author of the Gran Tarot Esoterico, grew up at the foot of the Pyrenees, in Roncal. The image on her Hanged Man is, as Guler says, "to be seen in the town of Lacunza" in Spain. (Could this be the town my atlas calls La Caniza?) The little booklet which comes with this deck gives us a short but impressive biography of her life, and with a little further looking I was able to find several other Tarots on which she has collaborated, most notably a Spanish Marseilles Tarot for which she wrote the booklet, a gypsy Tarot called the Tarot Mitico Vasco (the Mythical Basque Tarot), and the Euskalherria (the Basque Country Tarot.)

However I would consider this deck, The Great Esoteric Tarot, to be her masterwork. Her publisher places this paragraph at the forefront of the booklet which comes with the deck: "Heraclio Fournier has the pleasure of introducing this Tarot—which is the first true and wholly Spanish Tarot in origination and design—on the occasion of the 600th anniversary of the existence of playing cards in Europe." It was published in 1976, but for reasons which I think shall become obvious, I believe that the esotericism that it showcases connects with the Jewish Gnosis of the first century of the modern era.

The Major Arcana

Card number one is the **Magus**, called here El Consultant, the male consultant. (The Magus and the High Priestess are designated significators in the Tarot tradition. These cards were traditionally picked to represent the querent, male or female, in a divination.) Actually what we have here is Adam Kadmon, archetype of collective humanity. In the biblical myth of Genesis, before the seventh day of creation when humans were precipitated into bodies of earth, every human soul that was ever going to be born was together in one cosmic entity—the master human, Adam Kadmon, whose organs were the planets and whose body is the solar system. The process of breaking

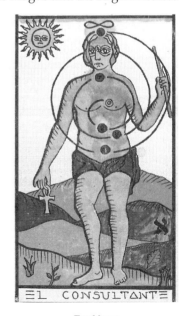

THE MAGUS
EL GRAN TAROT ESOTERICO

Adam up into individual humans has, after the fact, been called The Fall. This is the cosmic first form of the whole human race, all in one body. The earth is below him, but he hasn't yet entered into it—he stands above it.

Adam Kadmon is given in masculine form. The Magus and his consort, the High Priestess, are the prototypes of their gender for the Tarot, the predecessors to all other male and female figures. Here is the first Adam, constituted by the solar system, containing all the potentials of every human who will ever be born into time and space. The collective Soul of humanity is here gendered in the masculine, who takes the stance of an active force in the spirit world. But we will see how the female gender is the symbol for the soul in incarnation, occupying one of the many "little atoms" in human bodies, living out the potentials of Adam Kadmon in practice. A powerful teaching is hidden in this symbolism.

This image in not exclusively Hebrew. Historically it represents the entire ancient middle eastern worldview, which was a thousand years old when Moses wrote out the Pentateuch. What eventually became the Old Testament gospels were originally very ancient creation myths held in common by all the semitic peoples who eventually became the Arabs, the Persians, and the Hebrews. So this Adam Kadmon is a portrait of what the middle eastern world would have thought of as our original state.

This Magus is a unique image; one does not see it on any of the decks that circulate commercially in America. In Fred Gettings' *Secret Symbolism of Occult Art*, we see a Rosicrucian version of this image from Gichtel's *Eine Kurze Eroffnung . . .* of 1799, showing cosmic man and the planetary rulership over the spiritual organs of the body. This must be the prototype for Guler's Adam Kadmon.

The viewer is expected to attribute the traditional planetary vices to Gichtel's image of the fallen Chakras of corrupt humanity, but not so with the version on El Gran Tarot Esoterico! This Magus holds the ankh in one hand and the wand of power in the other, eternal life on the right and directed will on the left, where the hand is raised. He is Adam, but he is also Atom, microcosm and macrocosm, mediated by humanity.

Referring directly to the Old Testament teaching about humanity being constituted "in the image of" God, through the medium of the stars and planets, this image says "See yourself anew, humanity". It reaffirms that our natural psychic, energetic, and physical structure, as a species, is directly related to the laws of nature. In present time, this is one of those things that we have forgotten, having experienced "the fall" (be it mythical or literal) away from unity and towards particularization, away from immersion and towards individuation. We have, unfortunately, lost our sense of identification with the Great Mystery, with the force that put us all here and set things up the way they are, so now we are fated to work out our destiny from the position of separate cells, or selves.

This Esoterico Tarot shows us that each one of us is part of the divine action in this Earthly reality, that we are all actually part of, the individual cells of, this divine entity called Adam Kadmon. We each may circulate around and have many different incarnations within this divine archetype, the Body of Humanity, but each incarnation is still a direct extension of the divine human nature. As Adam Kadmon contains and subordinates all the planetary gods of classical antiquity within his body, so the average person like you or I also contain divinity in our makeup. What an optimistic and uplifting message!

In this deck on each of the Major Arcana a Hebrew letter appears with it's corresponding numerical value from the Sephir Yetzirah. In the case of the Magus, the letter Aleph represents the primal element of "Air", representing consciousness, sentience, the type of awareness that "thinks, therefore it is". Close reading of Aryeh Kaplan's definitive treatment of *The Sephir Yetzirah* shows us that El Gran Tarot Esoterico follows exactly the Gra version of this ancient body of astro-alphanumeric correspondences, another demonstration of its authenticity as a Jewish Tarot. Hence it is imaging our full potential, not just our current limited circumstances

So knowing what we know about the Hebrew Kabbalah, we can "unscramble" the whirling orbs circling Adam Kadmon's body, and envision the Tree of Life mapping the relations of his planets/organs to each other, following the model shown in the Kabbalah chapter. It is not incorrect to say that those planetary centers serve in the western system the same function as the "chakras" serve in the Hindu map of the human energy-body. In the Divine Body, as in Adam Kadmon, these functions aren't divided against each other into competing worlds of divergent actions. In the Divine Body each Sephiroth functions like an organ does in the human body. Each organ carries its' own specialized task to support the survival of the whole. So each Sephiroth has it's own nature and realm it rules, although it takes all of them together to make up the Divine Life.

The work of the Sephirah, or the Chakras, or the organs of an individual, is carried on below the threshold of consciousness. These centers function instinctively, both in humanity and in God, great Nature, or Tao. Our individual life rests upon the autonomic functioning of our organs, and the life of God rests upon the autonomic functioning of the Sephirah. In the genesis narrative, the Sephirah of God are collectively called the Elohim, a female plural title, and now we know them as the Planets as well.

Arcana number two is what we're used to thinking of as the **High Priestess**, but what we actually see here is a naked young woman, overlighted by the moon, most likely Eve, companion of Adam, with an opened fruit in her hand and a gash in the earth beside her which seems to lead down into the ground. Her nakedness conveys vulnerability, but it also implies the innocence of the primal pair before the events of "the fall," when "eden" is still available to humanity. The moon behind her inspires her with intuition, psychic sensitivity, and the nurturing instincts befitting the future "mother of us all," although because of her "irrational" connection with this "emotional" luminary, there is

HIGH PRIESTESS
EL GRAN TAROT ESOTERICO

no telling what she will do next.

Her lack of formal attributes beyond her youth and blonde nakedness make it ambiguous who she "officially" is, as the text explanations are sparse and her name evidences only her divinitory role. But we know this is Eve. There are only two Tarot streams that portray Eve—the Etteilla family of decks, and this one—where she appears as her virgin, naked, primeval self, before she's eaten the forbidden fruit. This unique version of the High Priestess clearly refers back to the Gnostic reading of Genesis, wherein the tasting of the apple brought the knowledge of good and evil into humanity, which was considered the birth of the human race—not the fall, but the birth!

So here she is, the mother of us all, predecessor to reality as we know it about to get the knowledge that will make her fertile and receptive to Adam and start the ball rolling. We don't see her castigated as a fallen creature here. She stands in the midst of the woods, not in the open plane like Adam Kadmon, protected by and identifying with nature. She's on the dark side of daytime, but her hair is blonde, and the moon lends her it's reflected light. She's virginal, or at least young and beautiful, hence governed and led by forces which emanate from her own unconscious, irrational, intuitional, and spontaneous. She is not yet tamed by any externally-imposed hierarchy. Within this image is all the continuity Raphael Patai refers to in his tome *The Hebrew Goddess*, reaching back through earlier forms of the Creation myth, into the matriarchal roots of Judaism, as we shall soon see.

Both of these first two arcana show human potential at its highest, undimmed, standing at the beginning of the flow of history. And it is Eve who responsible for ending the mythic time of "before". Her bold act of eating the forbidden fruit marks the beginning of our mortal, incarnate, human experience of present time. We see her just teetering on the edge of change, before the fateful move is made which creates life as we know it. The fruit in her hand looks suspiciously like a pomegranate, long sacred to both the ancient goddess-mysteries and the later Hebrew priesthood. In the accumulation of symbolism offered here, this Eve is still "virgin", not yet inseminated but ripe and ready, like the earth in spring awaiting the seed. Just as the Magus is all explicit human potential for action, Eve is all of humanity's implicit human potential, our capacity for consciousness and soulful being, for intuition and tidal lunar fluctuations. Innocence and intuitive wisdom commingle in this arcana.

This Eve exists not only as consort to Adam Kadmon, but she also forms a pair with the next card. In the Alexandrian Tarots we find Isis Veiled as the High Priestess and Isis Unveiled as the Empress, expressing a change of state between the Virgin and the Mother, but making it explicit that the two cards represent different versions of the same entity. Read from a purely Christian context, these could be referring to the paradox of Virgin Mary / Mother of Jesus.

But the third arcana in this Esoterico Tarot, the **Empress,** is very visibly an older, matriarchal conception, as evidenced by her attributes. We are looking at a dark haired, bat-winged, Mars-assigned, lion-accompanied priestess of the ancient Great Mother. I take her dark hair to be an allusion to the dark color of the Magdalen's bloodline, and to her underworld connections. We don't see such striking brunette coloring on the Empress in any other esoteric Tarot. But let me elaborate on her persona in the authoritative words of Raphael Patai, as he is describing the first century, Kabbalistic conception of the Wife of God : "The mother is the bearer, nurturer, educator, that is, the establisher and maintainer of order; she, therefore, must be the one who wields the legislative, chastising, and correcting powers which are the attributes of sovereignty.... [she is] the parent who has to be obeyed... a fierce lioness". This image seems to be a perfect match with Patai's stern and no-nonsense Hebrew mother-goddess.

The Empress' shield bears a very enigmatic symbol. This is not the usual eagle, (which is also a Kabbalistic symbol in it's own right) but is instead a symbol for the ancient Hermetic axiom "as above, so below." The shield is bisected by a horizontal line, above which a pyramid stands dark against a light background containing the sun, while below an inverted, light-colored pyramid stands out against a dark sky containing the moon. This is a reference to the reversal of appearances when planes of consciousness are crossed. In the

THE EMPRESS
EL GRAN TAROT ESOTERICO

light of the sun, which could be said to be the light of the ego, the Empress looks dark, but in the darkness of night, of the Mysteries, of the underworld, she is the light. In the inverse world of the spirits, this dark mother is the doorway to life as we know it.

So we don't just have the hermetic "as above, so below," although it's a reference to that. The Empress is the flip side of the Priestess. What looks desirable and attractive in the human world is actually "darkness" to the world of pure spirit, whereas things that appear harsh and stern in the human world are the true benevolent, beneficent forces. This is a very strong tenet in magic that has come forward to us from ancient times. We'll see more of this theme in future arcana.

The Empress channels the divine, terrifying magical forces of the spirit world. But the work must be done under The Empress' tutelage and by her rules. She's accompanied by lions (which are usually assigned to the Strength card.) She wears the bat-wings of the Devil, (and the Devil, we will note later, has the angel wings usually attributed to the Empress.) Surprising to modern sensibilities, she bears the sign of Mars, nowadays given to combative, aggressive sources of power. But in this oldest, traditional attribution, Mars as Gimel on the Empress is the capacity for work, the very energy that drives the labors of nature, the engine of the homestead and the marketplace. My readers who are more familiar with more modern Tarots will be well aware that Venus is the more usual association here. But in the old Hebraic culture, the husband studied the Mysteries, spent time in the temple, was educated and contemplated philosophy, while the wife owned the house, the children and the business and ran the show in the material plane. So seeing Mars on the Empress card is no anomaly, but images forth the cultural sensibility from the times in which the Hebrew alphabet was forged.

On the Tree of Life diagram the materializing energy of the Mother Pillar (named Hyle) moves down the right side, across the Sephira of Mars (Geburah), culminating in Hod, "that through which all converts to inferiors" according to Gershom Scholem (*Major Trends in Jewish Mysticism*, P 209). Conversely, the contemplative energy of the Father Pillar (Azoth) rises from Netzach, "that through which all converts to superiors." (op. cit.) Through her identification with Mars, The Empress is directed towards results in the material plane, symbolized by bat wings, a classic symbol of descent, where angel wings will represent ascent. Her red dress shows her connection with the animal world and the blood mysteries, the mysteries of birth, fertility, and death. This is the force that keeps the material plane open for our habitation. We may be shocked by her dark hair and bat wings, because almost every Empress on the European decks is etherial and fair-haired, not dark and sternly brooding, as we see here. We know that these arcana/letter/sign correspondences from the Sephir Yetzirah far predate the later Venusian attribution, a result of the Greek alphabet reform. The El Gran Tarot Esoterico image, I believe, depicts more correctly the older Semitic and Phoenecian roots of the story.

The Empress has a fierce countenance, and she definitely looks older and heavier and much more powerful than her fair and dewy predecessor. Eve as the unsullied virgin hovers on the doorstep of the unconscious, but the Empress possesses the daily true grit a mother requires to be strong enough to feed and clothe a family. This shift from the idealized Priestess to the stern Empress emphasizes that the former resides in the realm of mythos, while the latter deals with the real-time issues of survival in this difficult world.

This arcana depicts the great Earth mother, whom we now call Gaia, both creator and destroyer. The ear of corn prominently displayed on her card further connects her with Demeter, goddess of the grain crops.

After all, with a good harvest and lots of grain, everybody lives through winter. With a bad harvest, there will be those who will be malnourished and lost to the tribe, failing to make it through winter. This Empress is manifestly the goddess of tough, dark times, with her bat wings and that hole in her skirt that probably goes straight down into the Underworld. But again, her shield says, "You may look at me and see something dark, in the light of ego or in the light of the day. You may see something dark and shadowy, but when ego and reason and our vaunted cultural attainments are eclipsed, I'm all that stands between you and the howling void, so you had better serve me or your existence is moot." Those lions remind us that she's the enforcer of the rules, the rules of nature and the rules of this creation.

Next comes the **Emperor**, who stands as the regent in the place of the Great Goddess. She has no specific locality, as her body makes up the whole material plane as we know it. Nature has laws and she has rules, and she has ways she wants things done, so the Emperor serves as her mouthpiece. He wears her cloak and carries her wand, knowing that his rule is law in this world. But he's sitting on her throne, and when we look more closely at the card, we see that he is completely at her behest.

Notice that on both the Empress and the Emperor there is a little bush in the background. The Empress' bush has no black bird on it, but, ominously, the Emperor's does. That black bird is a traditional symbol from the ancient Mysteries of an emissary from the underworld warning, "Your time is up." The Emperor is the grain king who will be sacrificed at the end of his tenure. He's got the shed deer horns of a seasonal hunter-god, most likely Cernunnos, and a leather hat instead of the usual crown. It is crown shaped, but it's green, so it symbolizes the growing world, not a metallic substance. The Empress, instead, wears a gold crown, with the four phases of the moon on it, indicating that she has the power of life and death. The Goddess is eternal, perpetual, boundless. In contrast, the God blinks on and off; he is born, he serves the Goddess, and when he has done his job, like a drone bee, he is sacrificed.

The attribution of the sun to the Emperor signifies that every one of us as individuated egos in our separate bodies is in the position of regent for Demeter. It is our job to hold

THE EMPEROR
EL GRAN TAROT ESOTERICO

up the role, wear the cape, wield the wand and do her will, so when she comes around to check our work, she doesn't decide that our season in the sun is over. In the very oldest versions of this story, the Emperor is her son, her lover, and her emissary into the Underworld, being recycled every fall and sown as a seed in her womb, to be gestated and reborn again the next spring. In the later mysteries, the regent would just hand over a bunch of goats and bulls to be sacrificed in his stead, while he was heading for the hills!

But while he's still sharing the throne with the Mother that horned helmet on his head has to do with increased intuition and shamanic power, enabling him to receive transmission from her. As her regent he must fathom her will and intuitively know in any given situation just how she would want things handled. If he hasn't studied his natural law enough, then at some point or another, he'll make a decision that will obliterate him. Of course, he sits on the traditional cubic stone, and that's classic Tarot image for sovereignty and authority, but the wand with the cross over the globe traditionally belongs to the Empress. It is a pre-Christian symbol for domination, for the spirit dominating matter, and it belongs to her. It is also a symbol of the Tree of Life, the connection between the material world and the spiritual world. The globe is a big Malkuth, and the cross represents everything above it on the Tree of Life.

Traditional decks tend to give the Emperor all kinds of credit as the boss. But that little black bird over there on the bush reminds us that the Great Mother is watching, and just because he's wearing the hat and carrying the wand doesn't mean he can do whatever he pleases! There are consequences to everything... hence, he's under a death sentence even as he sits there. This is traditional to both folk European and middle eastern mysteries, and definitely pre-Christian. The day the Emperor gets cocky and mistakes himself for his role, he will be recycled, in no uncertain terms!

The next arcana, the **Heirophant,** is dressed in classic papal skirts, but, strangely enough, he wears no hat. On most Tarots, we see a huge crown, the Babylonian Triple Tiara representing the opening of the lotuses above his crown chakra. Here, the crown is missing, because this priest apparently has direct transmission "from above". This Heirophant is a priest in the ancient order of Melchezidek, the traditional designation of self-made priests, without lineage, of spontaneous generation, like the shamans of old. They've been visited by the divine impulse, as you

see happening in this card. Jesus claimed his priesthood from the order of Melchezidek, asserting himself as a self-ordained Heirophant when his detractors complained that he wasn't "Jewish enough". A Heirophant has to have made the choice to open up to an invasion from the divine, unmotivated by the desire for recognition by external human authority. Nonetheless, once his mastery is complete, his authority is self-evident and he becomes the head the school of future priests.

Replacing the triple crown is his triple cross, a sign of having undergone the three levels of initiation. Physical birth is the first level, birth into the celestial (astrological and occult) knowledge is the second level, and birth into the underworld (the realm of the archetypes) is the third level. One must have transcended one's limited ego, possess the freedom to move in and out of various levels of reality, being conscious simultaneously on all three worlds (organic, egoic, cosmic) before becoming a Heirophant or a bishop, the highest order in the outer spiritual community. The Heirophant is self-initiated through a link made with his own inner divinity, thereby staying in communication and communion with the vast web of souls. His status is recognized by the humans around him by their need of him to heal, to teach, and to speak the will of the Gods. And the two neophytes sitting at his feet are oppositely dressed because they represent different aspects of human nature, all of which are subservient to he who has conquered all aspects of the human dilemma

There is a paradox to this arcana which winks at us through the papal trappings. If he has transcended incarnational laws, having conquered the three realms, then he has conquered death as well, and is in possession of his eternal nature. That means he can come and go as he pleases in time and space! We can't know for sure whether the Heirophant is an incarnated human, or whether he's an angel that has taken a body just for this event, just to inject a little energy into the human world and then move on. The Heirophant appears to officiate at the mysteries, but there's no proving that he's a person who's still stuck in time and space with a local identity built up from consecutive human experiences. Because he's an independent contractor, no church can control him, hence the power of mystics and magicians to shake the Holy Roman Empire for the last two thousand years. (In Guler's Euskalherria Tarot, we see the Heirophant with the papal tiara, but it's lifted off his head, hovering above him, and his skirt swirls around his ankles, revealing that his feet don't touch the ground. So he's literally levitating through the world.)

The fact that he raises two fingers instead of one is a nod to Roman Catholic Europe. Many priests and bishops ordained in the lineages which the Church declared heretical, (including those founded by the family of the Magdalen) had to join the Catholic Church to continue practising as priests. According to Kabbalah's teachings, there is no literal difference between divine nature and human nature, but in the human historical world of popes and inquisitions, the people who look to the Heirophant give him the attributes they need to see him having. The Heirophant could be standing there naked, and it wouldn't make any difference to his abilities and powers. But if he shows up in certain clothes or in a certain pose, it's because these are the signs the people need in order to recognize him. Above all, this is a self-realized individual. The attribution of the sign Aries to this card reemphasizes this point, saying "I am self-born and self-initiated".

Moving on, the **Lovers** card shows a single path coming to a place where it splits. This is the traditional Alexndrian-style image called The Two Paths, but it has

THE LOVERS
EL GRAN TAROT ESOTERICO

been altered subtly from the Egyptian model. A man that might be the Magus stands there between two women. The woman with the bound hair signifies an older person, a matron. (Traditionally, hair binding was done after marriage; a maiden wore her hair loose until she attracted her mate). The matron is offering a golden apple to Adam and his companion on the path, a young woman. Instead of the single path splitting, I see this as two paths fusing. This is the Sacred Marriage, not a choice between mother and girl friend, but the sealing of a union in traditional folkways, which would be a hand-fasting at a crossing of

the ley lines, and the fusion of the destiny of the two people by a priestess. They stand at the place where two different powerstreams merge, and of course that augments the power of the ritual that unites them.

The old version of a hand-fasting was a spiritual contract that would last over many lifetimes. This arcanum says, "Don't take relationship contracts lightly. You are joined in relationship for eternity, and you are responsible. You will be not let off the hook if later on you change your mind." The ritual of marriage does more than just call attention of the community to a union. It calls all the angels and the spirits in, hence the presence of the little cherub. Solar rays come out from the aura of the cherub, who is inside a distinctly egg-shaped, radiant bubble. That's the Ain Soph Aur, another Kabbalistic symbol, representing an emissary from the Unknown God, breaking through from the spirit world and laying this karmic bolt down on Adam Kadmon, saying, "I see what you're doing. Don't assume that just because you're doing it in time and space that it doesn't have eternal consequences".

The golden apple is the symbol that comes to us from the Greek Mysteries, the apple being what the more traditional Jews cast as the offending fruit, but what the Gnostics saw as the vehicle by which ignorant, innocent, asleep-at-the-wheel humanity became awakened. When an apple is

cut crosswise around it's middle, what you see inside is a pentagrammatic seed-chamber. The number five represents the transcending of the ordinary sense-world of the four elements, just like the Heirophant, arcanum #5, transcends normal human experiences. So this speaks to us of the magic hidden deep within the ordinary. We ourselves are the fifth element; consciousness is the fifth element that makes magic out of the material plane. This card represents the marriage of two soul's five-element natures into one larger, multidimensional being.

The Lovers is keyed in this system to Taurus, the long, slow unfolding of agricultural, and biological time. It's a fixed sign, indicating the marriage is forever. Breaking these vows brings havoc, not just upon the offender and his or her lineage, but perhaps upon the whole village, because, of course, if Demeter's mad, she'll withhold the grain and the harvest.

The **Chariot** card is fairly standard, though we don't really see the bodies of the horses in this card, we just see their heads. Traditionally the Chariot card references the chariot mentioned in the first book of Ezekiel, piloted by the Word of the Lord. Mounted on this vehicle is a man enthroned, whose lower half is hidden in the glowing, seemingly burning, metal chariot. He is specifically named as "the likeness of the glory of the Lord" (Ezekiel 1:28.)

THE CHARIOT
EL GRAN TAROT ESOTERICO

Of course, there are other mythic chariots to which this arcanum refers as well. For one thing, this is also the chariot of Hermes, the force that comes in and changes ordinary time into mythical time again. This chariot is also Apollo's vehicle, carrying the Sun across the sky in Greek mythology. On the negative side, this could be Phaeton, who one day stole the chariot and ended up getting thrown to his death because he couldn't control the horses. A Talmudic Jew would see in it the chariot of the Merkabah, the Holy of Holies, on wheels due to the diasporah, which we ride to ascend in consciousness to the Throne of the Great One. An alchemist would see in it the Triumphant Chariot of Venus or nature, carrying all lives along to their destinies by her magnetic power of attraction. There are layers and layers of mythos here, all pre-Christian.

The Chariot sweeps us up and forces us to come awake again to our divine prerogatives and be victorious in the fields of time and space, using the divine attributes hidden in our Adamic nature. That could be Adam driving the Chariot, or some part of the divine self enthroned, like the Emperor, but with wheels this time. Aligned with divine Will and prepared for the journey, one's activities will be expedited by those awesome wheels, and the steeds of the gods will be yours to command.

The handful of thunderbolts is an old symbol of the king of heaven coming down from Olympas. When the Chariot card comes up, there's the opportunity available to navigate with the full realization of one's divine nature. Gemini rules this card: one may or may not elect to follow through on the possibilities offered. But those that choose to take the risk and conquer their fears enough to grab ahold of the reins and shoot for something have a chance of a major victory. Spontaneity and adaptability, combined with a warrior's toughness, are the hallmark of this arcanum.

For those who are used to the twentieth-century tarots which have abandoned the old correspondences, you will be surprised to see the Justice Arcanum in the 8th position, and the Strength Arcanum as #11. The opposite ordering has become "traditional" in the last century, but those attributions are thoroughly modern, having nothing to do with the ancient alphabetics or the Alexandrian synthesis underlying our original Tarot archetypes. As we are concerning ourselves here with a deck that portrays the "aboriginal" values of the Hebrew alphabet in visual form, I must stay true to the material at hand. (See the English School chapter for more explanation.)

The next image in the El Gran Tarot Esoterico sequence is the **Justice** card, number 8, depicting Solomon and the ruse he used to find the true mother in the case of the contested baby. Despite the fact that he retained the hereditary power of life and death over all of his people, he chose to try cases judicially, probing for deeper values and taking justice as his standard. In his own lifetime, Solomon was reknowned for his wisdom both in his studies and in his rulership.

This version of the Justice arcana is amplified by the sign of Cancer, the sign of birth and death. It is not amiss to notice that Solomon as Justice also has a crack in his skirt like that of the Empress, which similarly seems to open up into the underworld. The water-sign Cancer contains the ocean of unmanifest being, and souls are fished out of it in order to have incarnations, then cast back into it when they're done.

So this baby has just come out of the unmanifest, and Solomon offers to send it back, which elicits the response he needs to hear to determine the rightful mother. He is dealing with human justice using natural consequences, which in his time set a very high standard of rea-

soning and created legal precedent. Very seldom do we see the Justice card as a male figure. Solomon, listening for the maternal response, determining who cares and who doesn't, is a novel role model for male wisdom in his patriarchal age. His genius is his intuitive way of reading between the lines and revealing the motives behind people's presentations. He is able to separate fact from fiction with his double-edged sword of truth. So again he's serving Demeter. He's serving the female agenda, and he's doing so without disempowering the Emperor's traditional powers as the regent.

Although this version of the Justice arcanum may seem less than sympathetic, we must remember that in many civilizations, the belief in reincarnation was universal and people were less attached to their personal egos. Solomon offered to split the baby, but he did not actually do it! He was fishing for a reaction. And in the moment of realization when it seemed he might actually do it, each mother showed her true motives. For the times that Solomon inhabited, this card shows keen psychological insight, and indicates that motive *as well as* action needs to figure into the application of true Justice.

We see a higher number of male figures in El Gran Tarot Esoterico, but they're still all dominated by the goddess's concerns. Several times we see masculine images given to traditionally "feminine" signs or planets. We also see some very strong female images. As previously mentioned, this apparent genderbend is characteristically Jewish, a strong identifying mark in a tradition surrounded by the virulence of the patriarchal backlash against Goddess culture. One almost suspects the Jews of the Alexandrian era of being the closeted feminists of the ancient world!

This **Hermit** is classical, especially with the deer in the background, possessing horns just like those on the Emperor arcana. I take this as a statement about the Hermit being attuned to and telepathic with nature, immersed in it, with his green cloak and his deep woods background. The deer has been associated with the arcanum of the Hermit since the epic poem I Triumphi celebrated the archetypes of Love, Death, Time (the Hermit), and Resurrection in Renaissance Italy of 1356 - 1374 (the years during which it was written.)

The Leo attribution, in the ancient astrological lore, refers to the branch of the priesthood whose job it was to literally enact the Mysteries at the sacred times. These individuals learned how to create spaces inside of their ego for the overshadowing invasion by the archetypes, from gods and demons, to animals, weather, and fea-

JUSTICE
EL GRAN TAROT ESOTERICO

HERMIT
EL GRAN TAROT ESOTERICO

tures of the landscape. This is considered the oldest, most shamanic strain in the long lineage of preistcraft—the locating of game animals for the tribe for the hunt. This role requires isolation to perform the consciousness-work enabling one to create that space inside of himself to channel the divinities, and in particular Gaia, mother of the ecology. So although he is always and forever to be found working for the people towards their physical, emotional, and spiritual well-being, he is still a hermit, and he just wants to be left alone to do his own thing! In most Tarots, he is clearly masculine and of advanced age, implying perhaps that once one has put in one's time as a respectable pillar of society, there is a time when one wishes to just drop out, responding only to Spirit instead of the demands of the world. He still holds out his lamp, so those who come into the wilderness seeking him will not be lost. But he's established in a position of distance and renunciation, and that gives him the necessary perspective to help and advise those who have no such peace. I think of him as a wise old gramps or crone.

The next arcana is a unique formulation of the **Wheel of Fortune**. We absolutely do not see this anywhere else. We see a tiny fragment of it on the Etteilla Tarot, which shows a crowned monkey in the lineage tree. Here we see this big white bear, rolling a giant calendar-stone, and a mask looking in two directions at once. The mask is associated with the old theological virtue of Prudence, who "looks both ways" in both time and space, much like the analytical view taken by Virgos in the administration of the practical duties of this material life.

What we see in the image is the old Tree of Life, and on it, to the left, a crowned monkey with a pinwheel and a little red cape. This is a hermetic joke; the monkey is the Ape of Thoth (the pretense of knowledge) dressed up as European royalty. The monkey itself is an old figure of the shadow from the Egyptian mythos of Hermes, but for this deck it has been dressed and crowned and "made king", presumably by the Pope, since this is a European deck.

"Those who have eyes to see" would take this whole assemblage as a direct reference to the Holy Family. The monkey represents one of the puppet-kings usurping the Lineage Tree, displacing the royalty of the suit of Cups. His little pinwheel is a pretend signature of authority, mocking the white bear who rolls the Wheel of Time at his feet. The wheel could be viewed as a millstone, or as an ancient calendar. It's definitely the sign of a cycle and something that's moving very slowly. One might also read here an echo of the stone that mysteriously moved from the mouth of the cave that held the body of Jesus.

The little Janus head on the card looks backwards to the past and forwards to the future. That's how the Holy Family had to be. Members of these various families had to think generations ahead in order to keep their lineage and the sacred teachings intact from generation to generation. Once the anti-Merovingian sentiment set in at Rome, the stakes got higher for those who continued to serve the inherited destiny of carrying forward this inner magical, spiritual teaching. Evidently, membership in this bloodline is both a terrible burden and a great gift, and certain individuals were sacrificed to the destiny of the clan.

Meanwhile the secular kings and queens come and go, occupying a stolen throne, wearing the monkey crown, holding the pinwheel, assured by traitorous Popes that they're something special. In the shadows, this sacred tribe of Gnostic Magdalenic priests, like the Cohen lineage of the Jews, waits through generations for the moment when they can finally come forward again and be legitimized. I do not sense that the role of this Great Bear is threatening or vengeful or ambitious for worldly power at all. This is an image of long-suffering survival, waiting, holding back from using tremendous power or magical endowment until the world is ready, until all circumstances can be brought into alignment.

The Wheel of Fortune card shows the fate of the generations following the Magdalen's arrival in Europe. She came, she started this new movement and brought all this energy from the Middle East, but she herself died, and it's her children's children who are suffering from the persecutions and being hunted down through the generations, targeted by the Pope. The writers of *Holy Blood, Holy Grail* have accumulated monumental evidence to document that this suppressed and martyred lineage/faith/family/priesthood is the engine driving the secret history of Europe, and I simply have to agree.

The next arcana is the **Strength**, stripped of lions, a male figure instead of female, with long braided blond hair and a club on his shoulder, marked by the sigils of Venus and eternity. Having a young blonde hero on the letter that stands for Venus seems to be another clue to this Magdalenean connection. In the Holy Grail, Holy Bloodline mythos which these images reflect, it's not the Goddess or Mary Madgalen who is personally important, even in the concentration of Black Madonna churches all over the Iberian peninsula. Her significance is as the mother of these special children. It's

the blood running through her to future generations of children, which is the main fetish object in the Black Madonna worship, the Holy Grail mythos, and the Magdalean reawakening.

This young man who shows up on the Strength card in the place of the more-usual female figure is distinctly blond. This brings back to mind the Frankish (German) wing of the Hebrew/Gnostic/Magdalenic lineage, whose long blond hair signifies magical power and is left unshorn. What is implied here is that this heroic figure is not a particular historical character, traceable to a particular time or place, but an ideal, the archetype of the risen Christ of future humanity. Thus he would have the association with Venus, ruler of all things beautiful, refined, aesthetic, and sacred. He represents that purer strain of humanity that all Old Testament believers feel existed before the Fall, a recapitulation of Adam Kadmon, which we may someday reawaken within us.

This arcana also refers back in time to Samson and Hercules, Moses, Solomon, all of the charismatic leaders of the past who represent natural law and the greater hope of the people to be brought through difficult times and initiated into their higher nature. This is the androgynous young vindicator of the Great Mother, the redemptive aspect of the Goddess' pain at being suppressed by the patriarchy. So he embodies the Promethean role, bringing us gifts from on high—numbers, letters, the sigils and signs of astrology and other forms of learning. As a matter of fact, it's in a hollowed-out club just like the one we see on this card that Prometheus brings down the coals for fire.

He does look a little like a caveman, but that impression is tempered by the assignment of Venus and the eternity symbol over his head. He's the young, virile handsome son of the Great Mother, manly enough not to be sissified by the association with Venus. Venus adds the slant that he can be a romantic hero too, aesthetically cultivated and sensitive to the finer things, a "civilized" man. (We will hear echoes of this theme later, in the chapter on the Renaissance and the secret societies of that later time.)

Of course, there's nothing about this in the book that accompanies the deck. We have to go by very few clues, and I'm making some leaps of faith here. But because the author refers to the myths of classical antiquity in the first few cards—(Adam Kadmon , the Great Mother, the Grain King), I feel justified in stretching beyond jut the short historical moment of the literal Magdalen to see the greater mythological import this card carries. He is a sign of the good things which live in human nature, who will emerge from the shadows when we need him the most.

The Esoterico **Hanged Man** has no human figure but bear**s** a portrait of the village square in the little town close to where Maritzu Guler lived. This is a medieval stocks and gallows that stands in the center of the town square and has been there since the Inquisition. Maritzu lived in the territory to which the very first campaign of the Crusades was launched, in the effort to quell their ancestral Gnostic Albigensian heretical Christianity. Being the inheritors of the Magdalenian legacy, they had an understanding about the

mission of Jesus and the purpose of incarnation in the world which was very threatening to the Roman Catholic Church. These stocks were erected all around this neighborhood as a part of the inauguration of the burning times.

THE HANGED MAN
EL GRAN TAROT ESOTERICO

I have not been able to find a dictionary definition for La Picota, but I would guess it is related to the word "picket", as in picket fence. The prong at the top would serve as a gallows, and it's construction of stone makes it indestructible when the heretic manacled to these loops was being burned. It also could serve as a stocks for public display of the criminal, or as a whipping-post. So without even having anybody attached to it, la Picota displays the fate that awaits heretics who live under the long arm of the church. The Hanged Man can also be seen as a symbol of the dilemma of the descendants of the Magdalen's and Jesus' marriage, whose status made them scapegoats in Catholic Europe during the dreadful years of the tenth and eleventh century.

In this deck, this version of the arcana bears the old symbol of the two trees each with six stumps. Remembering that this is an astrological metaphor, we are directed to Libra, the halfway point in the year, where the year turns back on itself. Spring and summer have passed, the time of waxing and warming; now fall and winter begin, the time of dark and cold. In this sense the Hanged Man is a card of the turning point. The Inquisitional assault on the Cathars was also a turning point in European history. For the first thousand years of the common era, the Roman church grew, but many different dissident groups grew as well. The Cabbalists and the Cathars and different sects and lineages carried on relatively unmolested. However, the baleful eye of the church was watching them accrue wealth and gain popularity, and eventually the threat they presented, and the riches they deployed, became too tempting a target.

So I think this Picota card is making a specific historical reference to that moment when the storm clouds that had been massing for centuries finally broke, and a whole new wave of disasters struck, not only for the Holy Family but for all non-Christians throughout southern Europe.

Next in the sequence, the **Death** card is an especially syncretist statement using, as it does, images from the ancient Hellenic world. Death comes riding in on the underworld's dog, not on a medieval horse, like a knight, but on Cerebus, whom the ancients believed guarded the river that runs between the world of the quick and the world of the dead. The Reaper wears the usual ghoulish grin, evok-

DEATH
EL GRAN TAROT ESOTERICO

ing with his red-lined cape that fear of the plague, of death, of continuously-impending mortality which had the mediaeval folk running to the church on Sunday, only to visit the astrologer on Monday and the crone in the woods on Tuesday. This arcana was deliberately exploited by the Roman church to enhance the general fear of dying without absolution and last rights. Because they claimed to be able to either confer or withhold entry into heaven through the power of the Sacraments, the priesthood could control the people's allegiances, hence their lives.

Rome was not the first Mystery School to mediate over its members' eternal lives. This function of the priesthood goes right back to the oldest mysteries, where the candidates for initiation were told not to mourn for the old self that would be taken away, an experience they should expect during course of the rite. The understanding was, when a soul comes into a body, it actually dies to its spiritual life. Conversely, when the soul leaves the body at the end of it's lifetime, this is seen to be a return to its eternal inheritance, and is celebrated as a great rebirth.

The Mysteries were so arranged as to put the individual through an experience that separates the soul from the body without death, to give that soul a new platform of consciousness from which to contemplate this life, without having to die to "get it." The Roman church, on the other hand, did not have enough trust in its members to offer them this option. It kept its participants in thrall with the idea that they could not die in spiritual safety without priestly mediation.

The cape on this reaping skeleton is a wonderful metaphor for the "veil" between the world of the living and the dead. Its blood-red lining speaks to the lust for life we all feel in our flesh, but on the outside is black as night and studded with the stars of the firmament, representing the vastness of eternal space and time. These two sides of the cape are symbolic of the exchange we make when we cross that threshold. So although this arcanum does to some extent refer to the old medieval plague/death image, because he's astride a steed and wearing this cloak of impenetrable darkness, we do not have to see this figure as a threat or a punishment. Death is only the revolving door between the visible world and the invisible world. Once we get over being afraid of it, we can learn how the seeds of the future are sown by the reaping of the past, in the eternal cycle.

The temple/sepulcher with the ankh on it that appears in the background suggests a revival of what was known when nations were young, before the fall of the ancient Mysteries. Eternal life was well-understood long before the birth of Jesus. This was one of the core purposes of the Mysteries, healing the people of their fear of death. Many people are not free within themselves, to truly understand what they are here for, until they get free of their mortal attachments, their clutching to the outer life and the sensual life as if that were all that is. A person who had undergone Initiation would gain the soul-serenity of knowing that they are already installed in eternal life, with or without the mediation of the priesthood or blessings from the Pope. This adds up to a very non-Christian card for a European Tarot!

The next arcanum, **Temperance**, represents what's immediately beyond the experience of death, following upon the heels of detachment from the fleshly envelope. Here we see the soul in female form, unencumbered by the body's polarities, be they issues of gender, age, race, temperament, or any other spectrum of outer or inner qualities by which one might define the "known self". If the soul is immortal, its very being transcends those qualities of limitation and particularity. As such, the soul has access to *both* yin and yang energy, *both* solar and lunar capabilities, mediating all opposites with its infinite flexibility. All of our qualities are putty in the hands of the higher nature, who mixes up the personality in any given incarnation just like an alchemical recipe. With a dash of this planetary metal, and a dash of that moon phase, a really interesting lifetime is created, perhaps one in which the soul can get some learning done.

Here we have the soul in its lab blending the opposites to create the Master Medicine, the alchemical elixir of eternal life. The waters of life are being rebalanced and renewed in preparation for the distillation of cosmic fluids into earth substances. Later these same waters will be poured out upon the creation, in The Star.

I experience the two vessels as the left brain and the right brain. This is the result of shamanic work, especially in the context of the Mysteries where the initiate is shocked and/or paradigm-shifted. In the process of being tempered via this method, the competing brain chemistries of "fight or flight" versus "rest and digest" encounter each other and merge. This stimulates the corpus colosum, and then one is no longer working in either/or mode. This is an "and/and" mode, inclusive of all possibility. One's being is no longer compartmentalized, and all of reality is flowing together and fusing into a new higher order. This process is supervised and mediated by the "angel of the sun" or the higher self, the sun-self.

TEMPERANCE
EL GRAN TAROT ESOTERICO

In all Tarot decks, the Temperance gives the message to take the time and learn the practices enabling one to adjust brain chemistry at will. The fact that this arcanum follows right after the Death card is no accident. In the Mysteries, the initiates ate some massive dose of psychedelic ergot or wild mushroom or some soma mix, and was blasted right out of their normal minds as a part of the Mystery experience. Even in the Christian services after the Mysteries folded, harmonic singing, vast darkness punctuated by flickering candlelight, hypnotic movements and repetitive chants, fasting, and incense were used in long ceremonies that went on into the night and through the next day. This would have that same effect of massively altering consciousness to promote the opportunity for direct experience of the intimate presence of God, heralded by the angel's presence.

Such experiences sometimes occur spontaneously at pivotal times, when facing the Grim Reaper or one's potential immediate demise. All of a sudden there's this extra-intelligence, this extra clarity, as the higher nature clicks on. But somebody who didn't handle the death card correctly, would never encounter the angel because of their attachment to the material plane preventing this higher octave of consciousness illuminating the psyche. This extraordinary vision only appears to people who are working on a higher frequency, who know the self to be energy beyond form.

The **Devil** arcanum represents the state of the individual who has shed human limitations and recognized him- or herself as an incipient God in the making. This concept in ancient times was called the Demi-Urge, and it signified the "unconscious" operations of God, the aspect of the Elohim (previously mentioned as the "chakras of God", which humans also participate in) which takes over the intimate administration of the material plane when the first seven days of creation were finished. Think if it as the metabolism of God, the "autopilot" features which uphold this creation. Like the Emperor stands in for the localized presence of the imminent Great Mother, the Demi-Urge serves as regent for the administration of the Cosmos, with the understanding that the Creator and Originator is now concentrating on other things. When a human soul evolves to a certain point, it can influence the Demi-Urge by becoming one with it and directing the flow of the collective Unconscious with personal will. This is the goal of every practicing magician, ancient to modern.

The Demi-urge is a regular feature in Gnostic, Hermetic, and Persian cosmologies, and would not have been unknown to Jesus and Mary Magdalen either. Some Hebrew Gnostics believed that Jehovah was actually the Demi-urge, who cast Adam Kadmon into the bondage of fleshly life out of fear that humanity would evolve beyond him eventually. No wonder the orthodox Jews of the time hated them! But for us living in these more psychological times, the Devil, Demi-urge, Typhon, or whatever else one might call it is a fascinating archetype of humanity's magical potential to affect the flow of circumstances *from within*, through a strategic application of consciousness to the collective unconscious. And to follow this line of thought a little further,

THE DEVIL
EL GRAN TAROT ESOTERICO

then the demi-urge, who is the administrator of the fallen or the post-Eden creation, is the rightful ruler of the material plane and set there for divine reasons by the over-god, the unknown God. That this is not a tragedy, this is not a torture, this is not a punishment- this is the plan. The Demi-urge is our baby-sitter and role model until we grow up and assume this role ourselves, in our spiritual maturity.

Heaped upon that already-formidable pile of paradoxes, the Devil card also carries all the freight of doctrinal differences that have provided the justification for holy war over several thousand years duration. Here we see the primeval ancient earth goddess, related to the Great Mother of the Empress card through the bat wing/angel wing switch. She is made up of the four elements (earthy legs, watery abdomen, airy breast and wings, fiery head), and as well she has been" scapegoated", made to wear the mask of a goat or donkey, a shaming symbol since ancient times.

But it's more than just a goat's head. This is a very unique formulation, the face of this Devil card, and to me it looks like aspects of human female genitalia, like a clitoris and its labial folds. The face on this Devil card is just unprecedented. Additionally, we see this feminine force associated with the letter Mem, which is explained in Hebrew calligraphy books as a snake eating its own tail. What is less often explained is that this circled serpent is also an old symbol for the yoni, the vaginal opening among the Semitic tribes!

This Devil card also shows also shows a distinctly female form, which in our chapter on the Major Arcana I explain is a more "esoteric" take on the Devil. It all serves to make explicit the fact that this Devil is aligned with the Goddess Mysteries. To top it off, she makes the same hand signals we traditionally find on the Heirophant, with a crescent moon above and a dark moon below, referring back to the old lunar mysteries. There's a lot of emphasis on blood and menstruation here as well, with a caduceus running down her spinal column and culminating in an exaggerated second chakra, a great throbbing red uterus of some kind, as if her inner organs are exposed.

What a combination of symbols! The demi-urge is equated with a feminine force channeling descending energy, sending something to earth, along lines of occult transmission. She's apparently totally unstoppable, as she's already slipped thorough the fingers of the Wheel of Fortune, the Hanged Man, the Death card... all of the social controls belonging to the collective mind used to rein us in, hold us down, and keep us from believing the heresy that we're part of God. All of that collective control has been left behind, and the initiated individual functions as the demi-urge, controlling the environment. The demi-urge dominates the foreground, while a sketchy little church fades into the background, totally dominated by this force. When all the layers of acculturation have been peeled back, what we find is the divine power within us, still fully capable of changing the world at any given moment through personal will and magic, through self-empowered acts of Sagittarian expression and freedom.

For our discussion, the important factor is how literally genital and blood-mystery oriented this card is. Here we have the goddess, the female principle, as the genatrix of creation, the literal genital generator. And also from the point of view of the Magdalen myth, she is the Holy Grail, the vessel who carries the bloodline from the past into the future, so that holy blood is seen here accumulating around the genitals of the Devil card. There's something sacramental about this, that somehow we go from red as blood, the carnage of the Death card, through the mixing up of an sacred elixir in the Temperance to the accumulation of this terrific potency in the womb of the Devil.

Without the proper spiritual cultivation at this level of initiation, however, there is the possibility of immediate self-destruction through the stupidity of bad choices. Once external limits are removed, if we can't set limits on ourselves, we'll just explode from our own inflation. Ordinary human laws and even natural laws no longer hold for the individual who has fused with the demi-urge, but, at that point, the temptation is present to attempt everything in the world, to risk everything, to exceed all possible limits. Sagittarius wants to fly as fast as the arrow, but if he does not use foresight when he releases his bow, the curve of space makes him shoot himself in the back!

The person who at an energetic level is working in the realm of the Devil arcanum as the demi-urge is free of the karmic delay that allows them to do something rotten now and not hear the consequences until later. One of the things experienced with the Devil card and everything afterwards is instant karma, instant response, instant accountability. The center of gravity has shifted out of the human ego, so when the ego wakes up with the demi-urge's capability, its response if it is immature would be, " Oh, wow! Now I can do anything!" In truth, the soul is much more culpable at every level, because it has shifted to being an actor rather than a reactor in life. That's part of the test of the Devil card. Can you handle that capacity and not get yourself in trouble with it?

And obviously the very next card is the **Tower** where the consequences of any action whatsoever in the Devil card come down. Once the lightning bolt is loosed, the material plane will change. The Tower card is the immediate response to any action taken.

One of the challenges, for the initiate is to be impeccable in decisions and choices without becoming ego-inflated, and so the transition from the Devil card to the Tower warns against the over inflation of the ego, against assuming owner ship of that flow of energy which the Initiate

merely mediates. The forces of Nature are much stronger than any human agency.

We know that there are a lot of associations with the Tower that go back to biblical times. One old myth is that during the three days that Jesus hung on the cross, the great temple, the Synagogue in Jerusalem, was hit by lightening. Another myth relates to the tower of Babel and the smiting of *language* into different tongues because of the hubris of trying to build a tower to heaven. We do know that the Tower built of bricks represents a human construct instead of an organic growth, and be-

The Tower
El Gran Tarot Esoterico

cause its a construct it's an imposition on the landscape. The tension it generates in nature eventually makes it a lightening rod, primed for destruction.

The figure exiting from the bottom of the Tower symbolizes both emergence from oppressive cultural constructs that benefit the few by enslaving the many, and also, in this Magdalean context, the destructive struggle between different religious hierarchies, while the incognito, without dramatic alignments, are preserved and maybe even liberated. So there is something here that may be part of the fulfillment of the prophesy implied in the Wheel of Fortune card, that with time and cultivation of the sacred blood line, the false hierarchies of power will crumble of their own deficiencies and self-inflation, allowing the keepers of the sacred trust to once again emerge publicly. There's been more controversy and more exploration and more in print on this sacred family in the last twenty years than there was in the previous 1400 years. This arcanum is assigned to Capricorn, the traditional sign of rulers and lineages that are able to carry teachings, power, money and authority through several generations.

In the Tower card there is a sub theme about orgasm. Remember that in the strict reading of the Bible is the injunction to be fruitful and multiply. In the remnants of the Gnostics that had to go underground in Europe there were alchemical practices such as coitus interruptus or cunnilingus/fellatio, as well as non-ejaculation, which helped to prevent impregnation. So the Tower card, following as it does upon the Devil arcanum with its emphasis on female sexuality and the second chakra, is to some degree connected to the act of non-procreative sexuality. It's the big bang, orgasm without the expectation of traditional family and all concomitant mundane consequences. And this of course was a part of Gnostic practise that deeply threatened Roman Catholicism, which taught that people were to remain celibate and enter nunneries and monasteries or they were to marry. What did St. Paul say ? "Better to marry than to burn". Any other form of contact between men and woman that might lead to ecstasy or joy or higher states of consciousness that wasn't immediately tied to reproduction responsibility was also part of the Devil's work.

In the **Star** we see the dispensation of the alchemical elixir that was mixed up in the Temperance card. While we find the gold and silver vessels traditional to the Star, here they are both being poured into the water, where a more traditional Star would show one part falling on the earth and one part falling in the water. The color of the fluid is blue. It isn't blood or wine or sacrament, but rather an indigo blue like the night sky. I take this to refer to a stellar consciousness being poured down into the water, an element that is common to all life forms. This is not a sacrament being poured out just for the few; this is being given to the whole creation, as depicted by his pentagram in the center of the sun , and the solar flare bearing the glyphs of Jupiter, Mars and Saturn, the outer three visible planets in the solar system. (The personal planets are the ones inside the orbit of the earth-Moon, Mercury, and Venus, while the visible ones outside the orbit of the earth are considered to be social or collective planets.) So, again that's a implication that this sacrament is being poured out, not just for human souls or certain selected individuals but for the enlightenment of the entire creation, a Gnostic conception because the Shekhina residence in every thing. Matter itself is made of her body and the liberation of the world is the liberation of the light in everything.

Though the Star is traditionally a female figure, one could read the long flowing blond hair as a reference to the heroic Strength figure. The breasts first appeared on the Devil card, and we will later see the hermaphroditic World card as well. My tendency is not to see them as naturalistic attributes of a youth in the woods, but as symbols of powers accumulated which the soul wields in the work of redeeming the world. Those who remember their New Testament studies will remember the teaching Jesus gave, that in the Kingdom (among the coming humanity), there would be no gender separating women and men. I think that at this later stage of the cycle, the polarities of the soul are beginning to fuse back together into the Hermetic Androgyne, with attributes of both male and female.   This Star is presaging the hermaphroditic World card to come, image of the Regenerated Human, all in

keeping with the theme of redeeming the tragic consequences of the "fall of Adam." The ongoing goal throughout the Major Arcana remains to provide a path for self-initiation.

The presence of the pentagram on this arcanum is the symbol of humanity in the spirit world. Because human consciousness is the fifth element (the first four are the obvious material elements, earth, air, fire and water) we supply the fifth element which is imagination, creativity. Therefore when we use consciousness to mix the traditional four elements we actually invent new substances and invent new technologies. The pentagram is the symbol of our curiosity and human persistence in augmenting the creation with modifications and experiments . So that Pentagram is the image of the positive but also feared aspect of humannature. This is why the Church had to demonize it. So, it simultaneously represents what's unique about human species and what gets us in trouble all the time-our imagination. So, here then, to put the pentagram in the middle of that sun is to say that it is a divine quality of ours, it's part of our innate Godhead, our mandate from heaven and from that point of view that goes back to that optimist reading of Genesis that of course Eve was told not to eat the apple *so* that she would.

Another interesting little detail is the little bird on the bush. The last time we saw a bird on bush is was on the Emperor card, as the blackbird of the underworld. This is the white bird, the dove, from the higher world. So, there's a communication being extended from outside the solar system or from the supernal triangle on the Kabbalah Tree from the realms of super-consciousness and the realms of the Divine Archetype to the human world and a prepared individual is able to distill that fiery energy. This is not just a Christian conception, but an ancient belief handed down from the Mysteries that everything has to be re-illuminated by brightening the sparks of the divine within until they penetrate the illusion of the material plane. The Gnostic approach is to assume that even God is evolving, through creation's evolution. We are the act of God evolving in consciousness. So this a very optimistic message, that any moment that we can be licked by these divine tongues of flame and awaken just a little bit more or push ourselves a little farther along in terms of coming to consciousness and be seized by the spirit of that which is higher within us to become good servants, good stewards, tenders and keepers of the garden.

As a follow up to the Tower, in terms of Tantric sexual practises, that image of the flame can be taken as the orgasm that doesn't inseminate in the sense of creating a child, but instead illuminates consciousness and is applicable to the entire world .

The next arcanum, the **Moon**, is rarely seen formulated this way. Instead of two towers in the background, we find the two pillars of Hercules, which were like gate markers to enter into the Olympian realm of the gods. Hercules, because he was half human and half god, had to prove to the gods that humans had some redeeming values. Unlike the traditional pathway cutting between two towers, symbolic of the opposites of reason and imagination, we have here a watery path where what is usually dry land has been overtaken by this watery inundation. In the tradition this card is called "The Eclipse of Reason", and one can view that full moon in the sky as blotting out the sun. The resulting high tide obliterates daylight reasoning and brings up the dreamtime, turning the world into a ghostly realm of shadows and illusions, implying that it's spiritual intuition or the psyche that is the vessel and vehicle for moving between the opposites of reason and non-reason or science and magic. And of course we have already seen that the water is mixed with this sacred elixir that has been generated through the Temperance card and disseminated through the Star card. We know that water is the common denominator of all carbon based life forms, for all of us who have grown through evolution from single celled organisms up to higher mammals. This is again a clue that it is planetary consciousness that is attempting to evolve, not just human consciousness.

Here also we find droplets of multiple colors, rising towards the moon instead of the more usual falling pattern. The droplets are returning to the moon, being pulled like the tides, so this implies the soul getting ready to go back to its celestial origins. Earthly gravity is no longer so binding, and this spiritual or psychic force is starting to draw us towards something higher. Where the average Moon card is laden with negative associations, I see those etheric droplets as a hopeful image that we might be "raised to a higher state", to rejoin the celestial ocean of consciousness.

THE MOON
EL GRAN TAROT ESOTERICO

The little bay appears to be marked by the Pillars of Hercules, which stand in for the more usual two towers. If this is the author's intention, then perhaps this bay is the Mediterranean Sea, around which the cultures of the Mystery Schools flourished. The moon, symbol of collective spiritual intuition in its many forms, draws the waters of inspiration into the bay, and later she will pull them back out again, symbolizing the fortunes of the ancient Mystery teachings through the cycles of history. Some centuries are hard on those souls who chose Magian ways rather than more conventional religious paths. Other eras are marvelously supportive of the spiritual quest, resulting in great cultural flowering like that of the Renaissance, or that of our own time. In every generation, some hardy souls will even find themselves swept from the sheltered bay of local tradition, into the boundless deep, physical symbol for the ocean of cosmic space from which we may have come so long ago and to which we are told we

will eventually return. We call such cosmic surfers "mystics", and they push the envelope of human consciousness for the sake of collective evolution.

The moon, with her grey face and her spiky, straight rays was first seen on the High Priestess card, in this deck called Eve, La Consultante. Now that we understand that Eve is not "fallen" but is the mother of us all, we can also see this Moon as a benign, nurturing matrix of divine instincts and intuitions, calling us back to our primordial depths. The Moon doesn't have to be an image of fear. Recalling the four quarters of the Moon on the Empress' crown, again we are linked to the great Goddess and her cyclic ways. In this arcanum we come to terms with our fear of the unknown, which in the Roman Catholic paradigm was considered infested with demons, but which the Gnostic Kabbalists knew as the domain of the Great Mother.

The **Sun** from El Gran Tarot Esoterico is depicted with wavy rays, as opposed to the straight rays of the moon. In the foreground below the Sun, we see the Gemini twins, portrayed as androgynous or gender-neutral figures. The two of them are sitting under this very interesting sun with three coiled snakes of black, red and green. I see this is an alchemical reference to the three different states of being believed to underlie the makeup of humanity, that is the animal, vegetable and mineral worlds. The animal world is red, for the red of blood. The vegetable world is green. The mineral realm is black. These three serpents come together and cross their heads at the center, implying that the Sun is the source of all the life-forces and life forms on the planet. The Sun radiates these three colors outwards. Those drops, as on the Moon card colored gold, red and green, are ascending toward the sun, again portraying the gathering up of the different sparks of light and life that were scattered upon the mythical "fall of man".

I have not see this picture in any other Tarot, although my hunch is that we will find its prototype among the journals of the alchemists, who retained the old Gnostic myth of the constitution of human beings from the planetary metals. Here it is, combined with the Hebrew idea that each one of us is a spark of the sun. So this pictures the return of human nature to its original state, wherein humanity embodies not only the special gifts of our own species, but also occupies the pinnacle of evolution overall. This is neither a Christian nor a Jewish conception. From the Biblical point of view, we were invented on a certain day as a separate entity. But from the Gnostic point of view,

THE SUN
EL GRAN TAROT ESOTERICO

humans are a composite of every life form with which we share the planet. The evolution of God itself happens through the agency of the mineral/vegetable/animal and, hopefully, human layers of consciousness. So this is not just the awakening of an individual soul. This is the Great Light containing everything that has gone before and gathering up all the fruits of all those incarnations now finally becoming conscious of its own fullness, having unfolded all those potentials. This is God, emerging from unconsciousness into consciousness, not just the illumination of an individual human consciousness.

The alchemists understood that all matter was made up of the same base elements, but they didn't have the scientific terminology that we use nowadays. Their concept, even at the material level of turning lead into gold, had to do with untying the bound core units of matter and then reassembling them at a higher level of expression . This version of the Sun arcanum is that same metaphor taken to the levl of the macrocosm, including all forms at all ages in all stages. Human consciousness is meant to be the midwife assisting in the process of disassembling the unconscious creation and reassembling it in a more lucid form, in the light of consciousness. Through this image a link is being asserted between the alchemical creation of gold and the metaphysical return to the light.

An alternative reading of the three snakes would be the three Mother letters of the Hebrew alphabet. Or, this could be Father/Mother & Divine Child, because the Gnostics understood the godhead in terms of the Holy Family. In the Hebrew Kabbalah, the supernal triangle makes up the divine presence above Daath, the throat chakra, the abyss. Together they make up the original manifestation of deity, which still exists in perfect balance above the firmament. A Hermetic take on the triplicity would reference Pythagoras' theory that the number three is the first "real" and stable number, because one is the great All, the Monad full of everything, and two is a state of transition between unity and polarity. Three is the first true state of individuation, a balanced harmony between thesis, antitheses, and synthesis.

Next we encounter **The Cycle** (usually called Judgement), which has a unique image reminiscent of the Etteilla Tarots of the late seventeen hundreds. Here we see the lintel and frontispiece of the Parthenon, adorned with the symbol of Venus. The temple itself is gone, already an archeological relic by the time of Jesus and Mary. In an arc across the sky stretches a path along which travel the signs and planets of the zodiac, so this would be the band of the Milky Way along the plane of the ecliptic. In the distant part of the arc the sign of Pisces is setting, while at the closer end is elevated the sign of Aquarius. I take this to be a reference to the precession of the equinoxes, which accomplishes the passing of the Age of Pisces and the starting of the Age of Aquarius. The planet Saturn, who rules this card through it's Hebrew letter attribution, is "hidden in plain sight" in a mound of earth at the bottom of the card. The moon and the sun are also shown moving along the zodiac, an image of the turning of the years and of the millennia.

Venus, meanwhile, symbolizes the ancient values of harmony, proportion, ratio and perspective, the one who is naturally true and good and beautiful. She has the power of attraction, making us resonate to our highest frequencies, that which inclines us all to make our best and sincerest efforts. She is also the action of natural cycles, the law of eternal return. At the time of the establishment of the Roman Church, these Greek temples were already ruins, and yet they still stood for something noble in human character that continues to attract us and inform us about the values held by our higher natures.

On the surface, it may seem a paradox that the card

JUDGEMENT
EL GRAN TAROT ESOTERICO

bearing the Ankh of Venus is dedicated to the planet Saturn. Yet in classical astrology, Saturn is exalted in Venus' sign Libra. Saturn's other name is Chronos, the cosmic clock ticking and turning the wheel of karma. His orderly and inexorable ways guarantee the eventual enactment of nature's laws. This combination of symbols superimposes the linear experience of sequential time (Saturn) with the eternal experience of sacred time (Venus), showing both as being true simultaneously. Apparently the sizzle between the two experiences of time is part of the meaning of this card, which shows a radical departure from the more normal "resurrection" image.

The next card is not numbered on its face, but it has been assigned the next-to-last letter in the Hebrew alphabet, Shin, making it correspond to number 21. This is the **Fool.** Visible here is a very specific formulation of the Fool as scapegoat, the well-known yearly sacrifice who atones for the sins of the people. This scapegoat tradition started with the Hebrews in the Holy Land. At the new year, they would assign all the negativity that had happened in the village to a goat, giving to it the role of the devil, the vessel that held all their sins. Then they would chase it around the village throwing sticks and stones and calling names, eventually driving it out to expire of its wounds in the desert. In this way the villagers would then feel relieved of all their year's sins.

By the time this tradition trickled into Europe in the Dark Ages, it was transformed, and the carrier of the village sins became the village idiot rather than livestock. At this point it could be some old crone who was getting demented with age, or a child with a birth defect. This person would be singled out and designated the scapegoat. You can see on the card, his clothes are stuffed with straw. He's wearing bells on his belt, like a leper. He's the straw man who gets blamed for everything. The leper's bell, the goat ears and the dunce cap with the horns on it are all clues, not only to the medieval scapegoat tradition, but to earlier Hebraic roots.

The corn wand refers back to the Empress card, and to pre-Christian mysteries of the Holy Fool. He is an emissary of the Great Goddess who enters this world to gather intelligence for his patroness on the state of the human experiment. Yearly he is sent back to the Goddess carrying messages from the people saying, "Accounts are closed. We have paid for our sins, and now the year is cleared".

The Fool
El Gran Tarot Esoterico

Notice that the Fool's bag is red and black, symbolizing the blood of life and the obscurity of the underworld. His life force is packaged up neatly, with no loose ends, in anticipation of his journey "beyond". He's being used in a very specific ritual format to release the people from their sins by carrying them away, and as such he's also the pied-piper, because the bad spirits of the village follow him out.

The letter Shin is the Divine Fire, karmic or celestial fire. He's carrying the sins of the village into the furnace of the gods to be melted down and reborn. (The word hell derives from a Germanic goddess who was the goddess of the underworld. She received the souls of the fallen warriors, put them in her cauldron, cooked them down and reforged them into new warriors. Her name was Hel.) This pre-Christian conception details the process of taking the past, breaking it up, recombining it and recasting it as the future. The Fool stands in the doorway between the visible and the invisible worlds.

The Fool steps off the edge of the mountain as if the Spirit were bound to hold him up. After the long, twisting path of the Major Arcana, having just reawakened to his eternal spiritual nature in the cycle, he now has a choice whether to reincarnate again or not. He has won his way back up to higher ground, but it looks like he will sacrifice it all again, tumbling back down into another body and another incarnation. I see this Holy Fool as being on the Boddhisattva path, bound to life after life for the service of humanity, not satisfied with personal liberation until all souls are rescued from the Wheel of Time and Incarnation.

The final major arcana, The **World**, is perfected humanity, the future Adam, gathered back in again after the great fragmentation, with all the different personalities of the divine entity, the different reflections of the face of God, reunited. At the center of the four angels of the Apocalypse, those four exemplars of the cosmic elementals, is a beautiful and androgynous entity that is the symbolic fulfillment of all human potentials actualized. This card celebrates the awakening of a conscious divinity, evolved from an ancient,

The World
El Gran Tarot Esoterico

half-aware creation into a self-conscious Godhead. Here stands revealed the composite of all animal, vegetable, mineral and human experience gathered together. This pictures the future god that we haven't yet become, but is the goal of our communal project here on this Earth. In this arcanum, all the opposites are resolved, all darkness illuminated with self-conscious awareness, and the little, temporal sense of self fuses with the Self of the whole creation, never to feel lost, isolated, or abandoned and purposeless again. Although the Fool will continue choosing incarnation lifetime after lifetime with or without illumination, the World is forever living, never dying, fully identified with the outworking of divine will and evolution. This is the final goal for the human soul, ageless, timeless, all-wise and serene, dancing the cosmic dance in eternity.

Summary

As we pause to look back over the intellectual and historical structures which underpin the Tarot proper, it is hard not to be impressed by the survival of the ancient Wisdom Tradition throughout the eons and against all odds. The Mysteries appear and disappear in continuous cycles of growth, flowering, fruiting, decadence, and dormancy, followed by a renewal of growth again from a hidden source. We are currently in the midst of a synchretist revival as well.

Amidst this revival has emerged the suppressed story of the sacred marriage between Jesus and Mary Magdalen. It has appeared both from sources utterly uninvolved with Tarot, and from sources totally involved with Tarot. This seems to be a subject whose time has come. I, like Margaret Starbird and Ean Begg, see the Tarot as a repository of traditional lore about both the "bloodline" aspect and the "Arthurian quest" aspect of the Holy Grail mythos. But no one Tarot holds the answer alone.

Despite that fact, I am still moved to submit for consideration as a Gnostic, Kabbalistic, Magdalenic Tarot, El Gran Tarot Esoterico. This *is* a modern deck, not one of the originals. But with the coincidence of it's match-up with Kaplan's explication of the Sephir Yetzirah, the special treatment of the Cups cards, the plethora of details referring to Hebrew, Gnostic, and Magdalenic/Merovingian mysteries....there is nothing like it! I think we can derive from it some ideas about the survival of the Mysteries among the Gnostic Spanish Kabbalists, and I dearly hope that the entire subject receives the attention it deserves among the scholars of the future, to make up for the ignore-ance of the scholars of the past.

THE ICONOGRAPHERS OF THE MIDDLE AGES

The above title is a blatant ripoff from Oswald Wirth's wonderful book published Paris in 1927, called *Le Tarot, des Imagiers du Moyen Age* It's modern title is uninspiring by comparison — Tarot Of The Magicians. I borrow this title because I want to highlight the concept of iconographers, the makers of icons, who in every generation provide the people with representations of sacred scenes, God-forms, angels, magical animals, themes from myth, and culture heros. Icons have always been popular, especially among non-alphabetical peoples, since they are often embellished with symbols that enrich the image with mythic and magial depth. Found on altars and walls around the world, Icons link the worshipful soul with the energy-entity depicted in the art. The individual attributes of the image each symbolize qualities and motives of this energy-entity at work in this world. The meditator studies the image and is educated in the true sense of the word.

My dusty Doubleday dictionary gives me two definitions of icon. The first one refers to holy pictures or mosaics of Jesus, Mary, or saints and scenes from the Eastern Orthodox Church. The second one points back to an old Greek word for image or likeness. To get a real sense for what an icon is, however, one needs to pick up an art book on Medaieval or Renaissance sacred art, and look at everything, from the image to the theme to the symbolic overtones to the materials from which the art and its details are made.

The religious standard for making sacred art is informed by the magician's standard for making any talismanic object — that the created object have the necessary qualities that make it suitable to hold, store, and carry the uncreated energies called into it, either by the artist or the person for whom it was commissioned . Toward that end, the materials that comprise it, whether pigments, fragments of glass or tile, even the plaster or paper the image is impressed upon, must be of highest quality. Plus the ideas it portrays must be of the most inspirational type, drawing the highest possible emotional and spiritual response from the viewer.

Toward that end, an icon will often have a gold-leaf background, with pigments made of ground gemstones and rare earths, themes of great sanctity and exquisite technical mastery of the chosen medium. The earliest "art" tarots from the workshops of Benefacio Bembo absolutely meet this standard, as do the 22 Lazarelli Arcana in the Vatican, the Mantegna cards,the Charles VI Arcana, the Ercole d'Este Tarot, as do Lombardy I and II, among others. In more modern times, the Oswasd Wirth Tarot and the Medaieval Scapini both self-consciously present themselves as a pack of icons.

These collections of "divine images" make it very clear that their originators were intending to attain the religious standard of iconography in their Tarots.

The Path of Transmission

In his chapter on "The Origins of the Tarot," Wirth briefly lays out the path by which the subject matter of the iconographers came down through history to appear on the icons of middle-ages Europe. Inevitably, along with every occultist since *Monde Primitif* was published in 1787, he begins with a recounting of the legendary Egyptian origin of the arcana as "hieroglyphic paintings" used in ancient, secret initiation rites in the great Pyramid of Memphis. Much controversey has attached itself to this account in the twentieth century, but as with many other "myths and legends", there may be a kernal of truth yet to find at the heart of the matter.

The story goes that Christian persecutions forced the priests of Memphis to create miniatures of these paintings before fleeing for their lives, and "...once reproduced on portable tablets, [they] were passed on to the gnostics, then to the alchemists, from where we have inherited them."(p.22) In the next paragraph, he reminds us that "these ideas are timeless, they are as old as human thought, but they have been expressed differently according to the climate of the age. The philosophical system of Alexandria gave them verbal expression, whereas the Tarot was later to present them in the form of symbols." So he's saying this is ancient oral and artistic tradition concentrated into symbols, which then are passed on through miniatures used in card form.

Those doing the "passing on" were the Masons, Rosicrucians, and Martinists, of which Oswald Wirth was an initiated member. In a few sentences, he has named all the lines of transmission providing imagery for iconographic expression in Europe except the Gypsies. The jury is still out on the theory of Egyptian origins, but as I hope these chapters show, the historically European Tarot contains multiple layers of Gnostic, Kabbalist, Alchemical, Gypsy and Astrological imagery hung upon the framework of the Alexandrian astro-alphanumeric philosophical system. Let's remember that the oldest stream of astro-alphanumeric *correspondences* is the Hebrew alphabet pattern. But the oldest *Tarot decks* in Europe would have been keyed to the Greek astro-alphanumerics, because by the time of the Renaissance, the ancient Hebrew pattern had been lost or hidden. All 78-card Tarots before our present century were keyed to variations on the Greek alphabet correspondences.

Magic in the Middle Ages, Before Tarot Emerged

For those who are used to looking to the Renaissance for the sources of modern magic, let me cite Frances Yates' wonderful book *Giordano Bruno and the Hermetic Tradition*. "Magic had never died out during the Middle Ages, in spite of the efforts of the ecclesiastical authorities to exercise some check over it and to banish its more extreme forms." (p. 57) The Sephir Yetzirah existed in various editions, with it's highly developed astro-alphanumeric codes and correspondences and the Tree of Life diagram. The rapid expansion of Islam brought about a wave of new cosmogonic esoteric speculations, inspired by Neoplatonic and Hermetic text being translated into Arabic. And ca. 825 c.e., the first version of the *Emerald Tablet* appears in a manuscript called *De causis*.

By the twelfth century, Antoine Faivre says in his *Access to Western Esotericism* , "If this Roman period favors esotericism because of the importance of correspondences, imagination, mediatations, Nature, and pathways of spiritual transformation, the Franciscan spirit in the thirteenth century reinforces this tendency through its love of Nature." (p. 53) This is the century of the amazing mystico-theosophic (Faivre's word) texts of Hildegard of Bingen. When you add these influences to a still-strong peasant belief in the earth and the natural forces, you have a description of the tinderbed that the spark of Ficino's translation of the *Corpus Hermeticum* ignited.

Due to the stream of dualist, demon-fearing thought being preached from the pulpits , framing the Middle Ages experience of life, people felt spiritually safer when they attended Church and received the Eucharist. But then they also went home and duly lit their candles and made their prayers at the family altar, which would be decorated with an icon of a saint or deity from the pre-Christian days of their forefathers. Tradition cannot be erased by edict, only driven underground for a time.

As an example, Yates points to the *Picatrix*, a twelfth-century Arabic hermetic gnostic magical work in four volumes."...an extremely comprehensive treatise on sympathetic and astral magic, with particular reference to talismans..."(p. 49). She tells us"...there is a good deal of evidence that this *Picatrix*, though it was never printed, had a considerable curculation in manuscript during the fifteenth and sixteenth centuries. Since there is no manuscript of it earlier than the fifteenth century, it is possible that it began to circulate in the same century as that which saw the apotheosis of Hermes Trismegistus." (p.51) By this Yates is referring to Ficino's translation of the *Corpus Hermeticum*, when Europe's exposure to Alexandrian and Greek Gnosis grew from a trickle to a flood.

Hermes is Taken for One of the First Theologians

The Roman Church had been vigourously cleansing itself of heretics, gnostics, and magicians since the first Crusade to wipe out the Albigensians. So how is it that the church did not suppress the *Corpus Hermeticum* once it re-emerged? Aside from the fact that a Pope commissioned it's translation, there were other reasons. Because of the Renaissance misdating of the era of Hermes Trismegistus, attributing him to hoary antiquity, he was classed with Orpheus, Zoroaster, and other "prisci theologi" (first theologians) who were also Magi, and whose works were okayed by the Church. Because of their purported antiquity, they were "grandfathered in" to the Church's view of history, and hence were considered legitimate to study.

Another factor in favor of a warm reception for the *Corpus Hermeticum* is the personality of it's translator. Ficino took such great pains to introduce this revived Hermetic magic as a means of overcoming the influence of "fate" (read; Astrology), that he could curry the favor of a clergy who taught that calculating with the stars was heresy.

Ficino was also offering up his very mild, and very Christian form of astral magic as a path of redemption, as a self-cultivation art, towards a more unimpeded contact with the Christ within. This was especially easy to do because to its Renaissance readers, an echo of Christian theology and locution were discernable in the *Corpus Hermeticum*, (being a second-century product for the most part). This caused it to be seen as predicting or prefiguring Christianity. Hermes effectively became one of the Church Fathers, an ancient guidepost along the path to Christ.

So the context was all in place, embedded in tradition for hundreds of years already, with an understanding of the world that included elements, zodiac signs, planets, angels, demons, and the use of magic. Especially popular were talismantic practices for concentrating subtle energies onicons and other objects made to hold the operator's intention over time. In this type of magic, symbols, glyphs, and images are inscribed, applied, carved, painted, or impressed upon the magical media at special, astrologically-chosen times. All the aforementioned books were the magician's library for this type of work.

The person who is moved either to study my sources or to refute my assertions need look no further than the two excellent sourceworks *The Art of Memory* and *Giordano Bruno*, both by the peerless Frances A. Yates. I only stand in her shadow and point in the direction of her monumental scholarship. Withouut her willingness to devote her life to the history of ideas from classical times to the present century, our knowledge of the milieu in which Tarot appeared would be immensely impovershed. Athough I have never seen her mention Tarot once in any book of hers, she has such a good grasp on the political, social, and metaphysical climate of Europe, especially from the Middle Ages to the Enlightenment, that her books answer questions she didn't know people would be asking!

Introducing Petrarch into the Discussion

In *The Art of Memory*, Yates dedicated a few pages to the position of Petrarch, author of the "Triumphi" (a landmark poem in the documentaion of Tarot's early history.) She leads up to this topic by introducing "An Italian illustrated manuscript of the early fourteenth century [which] shows representations of the three theological and the four cardinal virtues seated in a row; also the figures of the seven liberal arts similarly seated. [here she footnotes the source and mentions several other similar illustrations] The victorious virtues are shown as dominating the vices, which crouch before them. The liberal arts have representatives of those arts seated before them." (p99-100) Yates goes on to say, "The iconographer will see in these miniatures many of the normal attributes of the virtues. The art historian puzzles over their possible... "[connection to other similar works footnoted before.] I invite the reader to look at them as *imagines agentes*, [impactful, magical images as required by the art of memory] active and striking, richly dressed and crowned." (p100)

These images bear the same titles and ideas which were traditional visualization subjects for the Art of Memory. This Art was a popular and venerable technique for memorizing, suitable for allowing a person to store a whole Renaissance education, with all it's related arts and sciences, under a visualized outline of places or things, onto which any number of ideas and teachings could be projected. In her words, "Such images would be both artistically potent corporeal similitudes arousing spiritual intentions , and yet also genuinely mnemonic images..."(p. 101) A person who had taken the time to set up and furnish an internalized "castle of memory" would have an awesome resource of both intellectual and mythopoetic resources to work with!

In other words, these illustrations Yates is introducing from the early fifteenth century were traditional mnemonic devices used by generations of intellectuals to organize their bulging brains, replete with learning. Remember, the first formal Tarot decks appeared in the mid-fourteen-hundreds. But mnemonic images of the cardinal and theologicalvirtues, the signs and the planets, all subjects of later Tarot arcana, are the classic contents of a long and venerable tradition, employing themes and ideas passed through time by a lineage of philosophers and theologians stretching back into the classical world,. This tradition very clearly contains much of the imagery we observe from the very first Tarots.

Now notice where Yates takes the discussion next: "Petrarch is surely the person with whom we should expect a transition from mediaeval to Renaissance memory to begin, and the name of Petrarch was constantly cited in the memory tradition as that of an important authority on the artificial memory." It is very interesting to find Yates bringing Petrarch into her discussion, because despite all of the research that has been done on Petrarch's later poem *I Trionfi*, and the impact that poem had upon the earliest Tarots, little mention has been made in Tarot circles to his connection with the Art of Memory. Why not?

Yates' continues; "Petrarch wrote a book called "Things to be Remembered" (*rerum memorandarum libri)*, probably about 1343 to 1345. This title is suggestive, and when it transpires the the chief of the 'things' to be remembered is the virtue of Prudence under her three parts of *memoria,*

intelligentia, providentia, the student of artificial memory knows the he is on familiar ground. The plan of the work, only a fraction of which was executed, is based on the definitions in Cicero's *De inventione* of Prudence, Justice, Fortutude, and Temperance." (p 102) ..."I suggest that these references to artifical memory in a work in which the parts of Prudence and other virtues are the 'things to be remembered' would be enough to class Petrarch as belonging to the memory tradition..." (p. 103) This is a powerful statement to the Tarot community, saying "get visually literate if you want to *see* your cards!"

So now we can assume that the likely date for the initial assembly of a collection of memory-images analoguous to the Tarot arcana could be pushed back at least a hundred years from when the first Tarots were themselves made. Even then, these images and concepts constitute "familiar ground." Anyone who doubts this can pick up any compendium of early Alchemical art, and they will see the prototypes of the Tarot arcana fully developed, posessing all the attributes of magical images or icons. One great place to look is in the wonderful oversize paperback *Alchemy* by Johannes Fabricius, which is liberally illustrated with woodcuts and line drawings from alchemical works spanning from the Middle Ages to the Renaissance.

An Overview and Timeline of Dates Relevant to Tarot

Yates' book traces this *Art of Memory* from Alexandrian culture onward to the birth of the scientific method in the late 1600's, with an aim towards showing how each era contributed to the great magical self-cultivation discussion going down through history between the scholars, the clergy, and the creative practitioners of these arts. One of the themes she is developing throughout is the path by which the classical memory images of old became visual, drawn out and published for all to see. This very process is crucial to understanding the continuity of the Underground Stream during the burning times. (As a companion volume to Yates' wonderful work, investigate *The Survival of the Pagan Gods: The Mythological Tradition and Its Place in Renaissance Humanism and Art*, by Jean Seznick. This contains a very illuminating chapter on the Mantegna cards).

These images were originally never drawn or illustrated, only described, so that each practitioner would construct their own in imagination, using striking, emotionally-charged details which would cause them to be retained well in the mind. But the emergence of woodblock printing and moveable type made the reproduction of manuscripts infinitely easier, encouraging the revival and proliferation of the art-of-memory masters from classical times. Remember, this is also the period after the Templars had brought back some of the treasures of Arabic and Hebrew esotericism. The resulting explosion of new insights and imagery had the effect of mulitplying the mystical and magical options available for the educated seeker.

Here is Frances Yates considered opinion about the transition between the Middle Ages and the Renaissance. "Is the proliferation of new imagery in the thirteenth and four-teenth centuries related to the renewed emphasis on memory by the scholastics? I have tried to suggest that this is almost certainly the case."(p104) So let us look at the evidence assembled here to see if a pattern emerges.

In this timeline I am letting chronology lead the way. These events are gathered from various sources, some of which are noted, in hopes you will go look them up. I am highlighting these overt and documentable events in hopes that you will be able to see the covert development of Tarot taking place between the lines. Because Tarot was forced into becoming an underground stream for several centuries, we have to sharpen our minds, become occult detectives, and learn to recognize the signs and clues of esoteric hands at work! Some parts of history are explicit, and other parts can be derived from the amassed evidence.

Timeline

10th century CE — excavations of Isis/Serapis temples begins in Italy, revealing the old Mystery centers and fascinating Italians with their own history. The Serapian rites were created by Elusinian Initiates from Greece recycling Egyptian symbolism and lore, then later exported back to Europe during the Roman expansion. As such they are only superficially Egyptian, but instead are solidly Alexandrian and synchretistic.

1118 (or 1119) — The founding of the Order of the Knights of the Temple of Soloman, (Templar for short), in Jerusalem, ostensibly to keep the roads to Jerusalem open for pilgrims from Europe, traveling to and from the Holy Land. Within two centuries the Templars had grown into such a huge finantial and political enterprise that King Philip of France and Pope Clement V felt the need to crush them utterly.

1095 to the 1300's — the Crusades are embarked upon, with the first intention being to win back Jerusalem from the Moslems. The mandate to eliminate Christianity's competitors expanded into Christendom with the Albiginsean tragedy in the first decade of the 1200's. While crushing Gnostic culture in the south of France, the Church exposed its most adventurous generations to a new wave of evidence that Jesus was an Initiate in the Isis mysteries, among others.

Before 1236 — The Book of the Angel Raziel is created by either Issac the Blind or Elezar of Worms, attributed to the "angel of mysteries or secrets", containing "...all celestial and earthly knowledge, as well as the secret to decoding 1,500 keys to the mystery of the world." (from Guiley's *Encyclopedia of Angels*, p. 169.)

1220 — Wolfram von Eschenback creates the Parcival legend, which quotes Astrology, Alchemy, Kabbalah and possibly even the Tarot! (see Malcom Godwin *The Holy Grail*.)

1215-1500 — the Inquisition: a war on women, the Goddess, priesteses, midwives, healers, believers in the Old Ways, Gypsies, Jews, other undesirables.

Friday the 13th October, 1312 — the Templar leadership are all burned at the stake together. The power of the Church to suppress dissidents is consolidated.

Raymond Lull (1235-1316) was contemporary with the Spanish Kabbalists who published the *Zohar*. He was a courtier and troubadour in his youth, and never had any regular clerical education. A Franciscan friar, he was overtly trying to reach out to the Jews and the Mohammedans, using ideas universal to all Old Testament peoples. He used a letter-based system rather than the images-for-ideas style of old, which would appeal more to the anti-iconographic "people of the Book" (all the Semitic peoples.) Using the divine names from the Old Testament and the Kabbalah, he created a rotating method for combining them in triads to illustrate the formation of the Elements of Matter. He is also the one who set the scheme "in motion" visualizing the changing interactions between the letters as wheels within wheels, like gears in a watch. Lull presents Christian Cabbalah quintessentialized, all set in alphabetical order, with ascending and descending letters working to bring the Astral Order down to Earth. With this he hoped to convert Jews and Moslems to Christ.

1343-1345 — Petrarch's "things to be remembered," the memory-treatise for which he was reknown throughout the Renaissance. *I Triomfi*, the poem for which he is famous among Tarotists, was written later, from 1356 through 1374.

1430's-70's — Bembo's studio makes sumptuous icon-style Tarot decks for the Visconti-Sforza families in Italy. In his university textbook *Access To Western Esotericism*, Antoine Faivre says "Playing cards, appearing around 1375, began from the early fifteenth century to be symbolic repositories for the gods and the planets."(p. 56-57)

1440 — Guttenberg creates the first movable-type press in the West, in Germany. The Chinese had invented block printing, and made the first movable-type presses in 1405, but the immense number of unique characters in Chinese made movable type unwieldy. In Europe metal plates were used first in the late 1300's, then woodblock printing emerged in 1423, and by 1456 the Guttenburg Bible was published. From here on, laborious hand-copied manuscripts with minature icons at the heading of each chapter became a thing of the past, replaced by copies that are "run off" the press in bulk.and assembled mechanically. Demand for books of all kinds, on all subjects, has not flagged ever since.

1453 — Constantinople invaded by the Turks, entrapping a delegation of Eastern Orthodox negociators in Italy. They came to Italy attempting to craft a truce with the Roman Church. As a resultof this historical accident a number of "new" influences come into Italy from Europe's Greek and Alexandrian past, including the *Corpus Hermeticum*.

1463 — Marcilio Ficino's Hermetic Christianity — When the Hermetic writings were rediscovered and translated into Latin by Ficino, a new wave of educated spirituality appeared, called "Renaissance occult philosophy". Hermes was already "positioned" as the ancient philopher who presaged the Christ (the true chronology of antiquity had not been untangled yet.) The Christian theorists latched on to the aspects of the newly-translated Hermetica which were compatable with their agenda; the names of God are derived from the Sephiroth of the Kabbalah Tree, and the Gentile world discovers the Elohim. Ficino is constructing a specifically Christian hypostasis upon the skeletal structure of the Kabbalah, and using the "Pymander" from the *Corpus Hermeticum* as an alternate Genesis.

1450-1480 — Rosslyn Chapel built outside of Edinburgh by Masons/Templars. The entire interior in every detail swarms with symbolism of the Grail Quest, the lost Goddess, the hierarchies of entities from angels to demons, ancient godfoms, myths and magical imagery linking it's makers and patrons with the Secret Societies, Gypsies, Islamic and Jewish mysticism, Gnosticism, Alchemy, and magic.

1470 — Mantegna Arcana created - Its structure of five ranks, designated by letters, expressed in ten steps, expressed in numbers, may show an influence from Lull and his "ars combinitoria"

1471 — The Vatican aquires twenty-two Mantegna-style arcana in folio form, by Lazarelli. This is not the only instance of cross-pollination of the Mantegna Arcana and the more recognizable Tarot with only 22 Major Cards, but it is quite intriguing!

1480 — Cathedral of Siena is built with a mosaic pavement of Hermes Trismegistus at the entry. Quote from Yates: "The representation of Hermes Trismegistus in this Christian edifice, so prominently displayed near its entrance and giving him so lofty a spiritual position, is not an isolated local phenomenon but a symbol of how the Italian Renaissance regarded him..."(p. 43,. *Giordano Bruno*)

1486 — the young Pico della Mirandola goes to Rome with his nine hundred theses, which he intended to prove in public debate to be internally consistent. The debate never happened, but the upset these nine hundred theses raised defined his career. These theses were derived from the traditions of astrology, natural magic (Ficino's Christian Hermeticism), the Orphic and Chaldean magics, and Hebrew Kabbalah. It is that latter ingredient that was especially important to Pico, who was contemporary with Ficino, only younger. Pico took great pains to assert that without the inclusion of the Kabbalah, history's other magical paradigms were disempowered. He even asserted to the Church that

Magia and Kabbalah help to prove the divinity of Christ! It was Pico who asserted that the Natural Magician makes the marraige between heaven and earth, using the names of the angels, archangels, Sephiroth, and the angels of the Name of God (the same 72 as given with their *signacula* by Reuchlin). We recognize the sacred marraige as a theme from earliest times, but Pico is taking it to it's highest Gnostic Christian conclusion, with the Magus as officiant in the ceremony linking Heaven to Earth, the Eucharist. It was Pico who first articulated the concept of Silent Invocations, made up of Hebrew letters, names, signs, and such. (See the entry of 1517 for Reuchlin's explanation of them.) We now see these exact symbol-sets on several Continental decks and one English Tarot, keyed to the seventy-two traditional Names of God/ Zodiac Angels, which collectively span the zodiac and therefore the suit cards.

1489 — Ficino published his *Libri de Vita*, an astrological medical book.

1490 — First Marseilles Tarot, of which many versions and variants were made, eventually settling down into a mostly-standard pattern by the late 1660's.

1492 — Spain expells Jews, and those who won't leave are "converted by the sword."

1493 -1541 — Paracelcus' lifetime of influence. I happen to own the Selected Writings of Paracelcus from the Princeton Bollington series, and it is a knockout for Tarot enthusiasts! The images include that of the Wheel of Fortune, on the lap of Blind Justice, who sits opposite Prudence on twin thrones, all in one picture! The art is half the fun of this book, especially as it is nearly all drawn from his own times. Paracelcus was a mystical physician who perfected the art of talismans as medicine, concieving of it as the "new alchemy". Yates says "The new Paracelsan alchemy thus derived its stimulus from the Renaissance Hermetic-Cabalist tradition....He is the Magus as doctor.(p .150-152, *Giorgano Bruno*) Paracelcus is the father of the classical homeopathic method in medicine.

1517 — Johann Reuchelin's Cabbalistic treatise *De arte cabalistica* introduces Hebrew mnemonic signs in association with the angels, "...who are voiceless, [and who] are better communicated with by '*signacula memorativa*', then by using their names." (p102 of *Giordano Bruno*) Later we will see those very "*signacula*" appearing on the Minor Arcana of Tarot, linking the cards with the seventy-two Angels who were said to collectively form the name of God. "...Through Reuchlin, Pico's Cabalist magic leads straight on to the angel magic of Trithemius or of Cornelius Agrippa, though these magicians were to work it in a more crudely operative spirit than the pious and contemplative Pico."(p. 102).

1533 — the publication of Henery Cornelius Agrippa's *Die occulta philosophia*, twenty-three years after it was finished. Agrippa's work took the whole magical paradigm a giant step further, in that he "...provided for the first time a useful and — so far as the abstruseness of the subject permitted — a clear survey of the whold field of Renaissance magic."(p. 130 *Giordano Bruno*) What is unique to Agrippa is that his manual was for the proactive Magus, one whose ambitions included working magic that could influence or expedite the operator's will. Bursting the bonds of Ficinian discretion, Agrippa's intent is to use humanity's divine resemblance as a point of leverege to maximize the results of a magical operation. His goal was to instigate developments instead of just refining the personality of the operator. With Agrippa,the attitude of humble witness to divine wisdom gives way to the desire to manipulate the laws of causality through theurgical ceremonies calling upon angels, planets, guardians, elements, and forces all aimed at creating designated effects in either the operator or his/her fortunes.

1534-72 — Rabbi Isaac Luria Ashkenazi, called "the Ari", proposes a new synthesis for the Kabbalah Tree, to reconcile the teachings of the Zohar with the Short version *Sephir Yetzirah* of the Ravaad. His revision is called the Ari Tree or the Ari version, and he is trying to portray the consequences of "the fall" on the human soul and Sephiroth. His impact is largely confined to the Spanish Kabbalists, amongst whom he created acrimonious controversey because of the resemblance of his thinking to gnostic dualism.

1548 - 1600 — Giordano Bruno amalgamated all of the above into his version of religion, and got burned by the inquisitors for his trouble. To quote Yates; "Bruno's practical magic therefore consists in drawing spirits or demons through "links". The linking-with-demons method was mentioned by Ficino....though he protested that he was not using it. Agrippa has a chapter on the links, and this was Bruno's basis though he greatly elaborates it. One way of linking is 'through words and song', that is incantations....another way is by attracting demons with images, seals, characters, and so on. Another way is through the imagination, and this was Bruno's chief magical method, the conditioning of the imagination or the memory to recieve the demonic influences through images or other magical signs stamped on memory." p. 265-6 *Giordano Bruno*) Bruno entirely abandoned trinitarianism, his guides in religion being four; Love, Art, Mathesis (his word, meaning number-mysticism) and Magic. In his enthusiasm for all things Egyptian, he abandoned the "Christainizing" of Hermeticism, which may have helped provoke his downfall with the Church. Frances Yates opines that Freemasonry is the outcome of Bruno's work in England (p.274)

1582 — Splendour Solis Published - a set of twenty-two exquisite paintings accompanyed by matching Alchemical Treatises, purported to be by Solomon Trismosin, Adept and Teacher of Paracelsus. In the preface a writer of "explanatory notes" known only as J. K. states "Their mystic meaning seems to be identical with that of the 22 keys of the Tarot, and they observe the same order."(p.8) although that is all

that is said on the subject. The artwork displays great intricacy and symbolic depth, although mine is a reprint by the Yoga Publication Society, and is therefore in black and white. The essays are extremely subtle, requiring a good deal of preparation on the part of the reader, and it's all in strictly Alchemical terms.

1614-1615 — Publication of two broadsides or pamphlets, together called the "Rosicrucian Manifestos", in Cassel, Germany. Their long titles have been abbreviated as the *Fama* and the *Confessio*. These present themselves as the first public announcements from a secret Order or Fraternity. "The hero of the manifestos is a certain 'Father C.R.C.' or 'Christian Rosencreutz' who is said to have been the founder [of this order], now revived, and which the manifestos invite others to join. These manifestos aroused immense excitement, and a third publication, in 1616, increased the mystery. This was a strange alchemical romance, the German title of which translates as *The Chemical Wedding of Christian Rosencreutz....*The hero of *The Chemical Wedding* seems also connected with some Order which uses a red cross and red roses as symbols....The author of The Chemical Wedding was certainly Johann Valentin Andreae. "(p 30 *The Rosicrucian Enlightenment* by Frances Yates) Yates remarks that "...the idea that the Rosicrucian movement was rooted in some kind of alliance of Protestant sympathizers, formed to counteract the Catholic League, is one which would accord well [with the premise of her book.]" (p.35)

Late 1602-1680 — the long and productive lifespan of Athanasius Kircher, last of the Renaissance polymaths. (This is Yates' word, but I take it to mean a person who is fluent not only im several sacred languages, but also in the number and astronomical codes and calculations that associate with letters and words in each language.) He was trained as a Jesuit, which meant his life was regularly upset by the vehement and sometimes deadly disputes arising between Catholics and Protestants all over Europe. But because of his immense curiosity, he used every relocation to learn another branch of knowledge and become expert in some new art or skill. He is so important to our narrative because his study of Kabbalah has become the definitive gentile conception of this ancient Hebrew mysticism, from his lifetime right up to our own. His linguistic and archeological studies confirmed in his mind that Egyptian culture formed the foundation of Greek and Roman religion, the culture of the Hebrews, and even into the East, a belief which he communicated emphaticaly to future generations of occultists. (We know now that this is an oversimplification, but in his day, the chronology of the transmission of the Mysteries was not yet fully understood.) Because of his incredible artistic talent, we also have a giant catalogue of occult diagrams, maps of mystical places, art of memory illustrations, gods and demons of mythology to look into and see the mind of a Renaissance Magus at work. It is my belief that some of his visual conceptions found their way onto the Tarot in the reform of the Marseilles Tarots in the early 1660's.

1662 — The Royal Society of London is founded under Charles II in England, which provided a Protestant haven from the dungeons and flames of the Inquisition, for those European Magi who had not yet been jailed and executed. It was at this time that the fateful decision was made to separate what we now call "the sciences", (mathematics, optics, astronomy, chemistry, medicine, and the rest), from "metaphysics", (as in astrology, alchemy, theurgy, sacred geometry and it's application in music theory, etc.) This decision has improved the material lives of humanity manyfold, but at the expense of all of nature. This schism severed conscience and ethics from science, leading to the enviornmental catastrophes and soulless technology which devour our world today.

1662-1665 — In this very short span of time, dramatic and unique changes appear in the Marseilles Tarot consistent with an unseen set of Egyptianized Hermetic or Alexandrian Major Arcana, which "occult rumor" indicates has been sweeping around the underground stream in manuscript form since the Middle Ages. (see the foreward to *Egyptian Mysteries: An Account of an Initiation*, published by Weiser, 3rd imprint in 1993.) Along this line of thought, Manly P. Hall quotes Madame Blavatski (in his little but fascinating *Freemasonry of the Ancient Egyptians*), herself citing a book entitled *The Ritual of Initiations* (by Humberto Malhandrini, published in Venice in 1657). Blavatski asserts that Malhandrini's book is one of the sources for the reconstructed seven-stage Alexandrian-style initiation ritual eventually published under the title *Crata Repoa* in Germany in 1778. Could the manuscript form of the pre-publication *Crata Repoa* be the as-yet-unseen prototype for the radical changes on the Marseilles Tarots emerging at this pivotal time? Madame Blavatski, says Hall, "accepted the antiquity and integrity of the ritual, a point of considerable significance to all students of metaphysical philosophy." (p. 79) I believe that it is from this reconstruction of the "Initiations to the Ancient Mysteries of the Priests of Egypt"(the *Crata Repoa* subtitle) that the Tarots sponsored by Madame Blavatsky, those of the Hermetic Brotherhood of Luxor and the Brotherhood of Light, are drawn. Knowing what we now know about the ubiquity of the Greek astro-alphanumeric correspondences in Europe, we should not surprised to see the Alexandrian/Hermetic decks (Falconnier, St, Germaine, et al) using the Hebrew Alphabet to express the Greek correspondences.

1666 — The French government bans the study of astrology in the universities.

The events and publications listed above comprise a severely limited selection of the cultural flowerings emerging from the persecuted underground stream despite the torturous setbacks of the Albigensian Crusade and the Inquisition. Just searching out and reading the sources named above will be a wonderful tour through a magically fertile time in the western imagination.

I personally identify with the life of the Renaissance Magi (without the persecution, of course.) They were studying and practicing the most sacred magic of their ancestors, as well as they could understand it. They were culturally and spiritually eclectic enough to enfold within their Christianity themes from the Gnosticism of Islam, Judaism and Hermeticism. Their self-cultivation included meditation, use of sacred sound technologies (then called "orphic singing", nowadays dubbed "overtone singing"), magical visualization, astrology, alchemy, incence and essential oils, tinctures and essences, gemstones, icons, archetypes, theurgy and liturgics, colors, flowers, fruits, precious metals, sacred geometry and magic squares, among other things. What wonderful preoccupations!

So you can imagine my delight when I ran into this confirmation in *Giordano Bruno* (p. 104): "The operative Magi of the Renaissance were the artists... it was the magic of a highly artistic nature, heightening the artistic perceptions with magical procedures" Here Yates is citing one of her favorite sources, D. P. Walker's book *Spiritual and Demonic Magic from Ficino to Campanella.* , which I have not yet seen but which sounds indispensable to the modern Magi.

Timeline Emphasis

I have placed a lot of emphasis on philosophies and manuscripts, because such phenomena leave discernable "footprints" in the sands of time. But certain other activities or beliefs connected to those phenomena may go unrecorded due to their ephemeral nature. One of those more subtle products of the Renaissance was a revival of the mathematical magic within music, which had been taken over for centuries by the Church.

Pythagoras and the Neoplatonsts had left quite a literature on harmonic theory and the natural ratios that create magical special effects both in different types of instruments, and in the human voice. The hymns of the ancient Orphics fascinated the Renaissance magi, and starting with Ficino we see musical considerations rating high with the Magi right through to Giodano Bruno. We have in the literature evidence of musical regimens for healing and spiritual attument, magically composed pieces for special astronomical alignments, discussions about modes and tunings and which planet is attracted by which style, and performances of the "music of the spheres" by mathematicians on their own unique harmonic instruments. Since we lack recordings, however, and the state of musical notation was still evolving in the Renaissance, we are less than sure about the actual practice of these and other "mathemusical" speculations. We can, howsever, be sure that our Renaissance Maig did not skip this aspect of their educations!

Tarot Cards as Icons as Visual Talismans and Silent Invocations

When you look at high-quality reproductions of the earliest art decks, with their gold backgrounds and splendid images of royally-clad, godlike figures, Tarot cards look like nothing so much as a pack of icons, each one a complex set of picture-symbols, then all of them together harmonized with meaningful numerical, astronomical, and elemental relations between them. With the help of Frances Yates and our other scholars, we can see unmistakable evidence that the Tarot Arcana, the Major and Royalty cards in a Tarot deck, even the numbered suit-cards in some cases, were conceived to be used as magical emblems or visual talismans, each one attracting and reflecting the essential energy of one of the Cosmic Forces constantly at work shaping this world.

This concept of magical objects being used to anchor spiritual forces was not new in Europe, and is in fact the core shamanic method underlying all magic everywhere. Once the cultural trends surrounding the transition from the Middle Ages to the Renaissance are examined, and the relevant dates are corelated to the big events in the history of Tarot, it is hard to miss the conclusion that the Tarot cards have been the tools of both the Speculative and the Operative types of Magi from their very inception as a collection of palm-sized icons.

And Now Back to Tarot, Specifically, the Marseilles

It is true that in the very literal historical sense, the symbols of signs, planets, Hebrew or Greek letters, and numbers have only appeared on the faces of the cards since the late 1700's. However, this should not blind us to the traditional history of these images, which have been correlated to the gods of the zodiac, the Virtues and Vices, the elements and states of matter, the whole esoteric and occult paradigm, for many centuries before Tarot. The Magi of the Renaissance only reconfigured what was already explicit in the historical body of memory-imagery. From their fabulously cultivated imaginations (I-magi-nations), they exteriorized a pack of interlocking, angelically-keyed icons to use as "silent invocations" during their workings. This is Tarot. It's as simple and as complicated as that!

But what were the common people doing? This whole chapter so far has been about the highly-educated, well-off, intellectual clerics, doctors, and noblemen who were working at the "high end" of the magical arts. Frances Yates mentions in her book *Giordano Bruno* that the daily experience of the Renaissance Magus was enviable in any age, containing a steady stream of pleasures and consolations, from gemstones crafted into magical jewelry, to flowers out of season, to hours spent playing magical music in clouds of incense meant to put the magician into contact with divine intelligence. But, much like in any age, very few people get to live that life, statistically speaking, and the rest of us spend our time chasing scaled-down versions of that blissful state.

The same was true with the use of Tarot. Rich families who could afford to patronize the best artists commissioned icons of consummate and lasting beauty. The poorer townsfolk went to the printshop where the woodblock images were run off in sheets. Perhaps it was partially colored by a few well-placed smears of red, blue, and green, and perhaps a patterned sheet of paper was glued onto the back, wrapping around the edges to frame the image on the front. But the least expensive Tarots would be printed in black and white only, and this economy would not diminish their value as Silent Invocations one whit..

Costing nearly nothing compared to the handmade art Tarots, these decks were also disposible when they got too beat up. A treasure-trove of old Tarot cards was discovered when the cisterns and wells of Sforza castle were cleaned at the beginning of this century. A most interesting collection of these are shown in Volume II of Stewart Kaplan's *Encyopedia of Tarot*, most of them identifiable through their resemblance to the early French Marseilles Tarots, although the Italian art style shows more grace and skill. (p. 289)

In the Marseilles style of Tarot we can see the model which became the "lowest common denominator" Tarot for Europe, suitable for the full range of Tarot applications from simple card games to a full art of memory excercise. What we now call the Marseilles Tarot is actually a stream of consensus decks, crafted in both France and Italy but as if cut from the same cloth philosophically. They were continually produced with small variations from the late fourteen hundreds to the first years of the 1660's, and then a paroxism of change seized the archetypes, which I document card by card in the chapter describing the Major Arcana. It is my assertion that an underground manuscript about an Alexandrian form of these arcana emerged at this time, perhaps through the agency of or with the assistance of Athanasius Kircher and/or a Secret Society called the Fratres Lucis (extant for the century before the French Revolution, according to Dr. Keizer, see Chapter 4).

Looking again at the entry for 1662-5 in the Timeline, we see Blavatski asserting that a book on Egyptian Initiations had just been published by Malhandrini in Italy. She draws the link between it and the *Crata Repoa*, giviing her very valuable endorsement for the veracity of both texts. Manley P, Hall himself says "The Crata Repoa belongs to the class of documents which may be said to have the activities of a secret society for their origin. A comparison of the *Crata Repoa* Rite with St. Germain's ritual, the Cagliostro initiation described by de Luchet, the mystical rituals of Martinism, and the Rosicrucian rituals described by Magista Pianco leaves no doubt that all these works are from a common source and are sustained by a common inspiration." (p. 75, *Freemasonry of the Ancient Egyptians*.)

Take note of these names and orders, because in the Continental Tarot chapter we shall hear of them again. The Count de St. Germaine and Caglostro were secret-society contemporaries of Etteilla, creator of the first mass-market Tarot which carried signs and planets on the Major Arcana, and was pictured to represent a Hermetic creation-myth rather than the Hebrew one. The *Crata Repoa* may very well have been the "Egyptian Tarot Manuscript" which both de Gebelen/de Mellett and Etteilla were referring to when they each were writing about the Egyptian Book of Thoth.

And let me state right here that my awareness of the *Crata Repoa* and Manly P. Hall's book about it is 100% attributable to Mary K. Greer and her great intellectual generosity. By persistantly refering me back to this little goldmine of a book, she has very kindly strengthened all of my arguements asserting an Alexandrian/Hermetic prototype standing behind the emergence of Tarot proper. The change impacting the Marseilles Arcana in the early 1660's is one of the "footprints" of this branch of the underground stream, and the Crata Repoa is another.

Two Different Bodies of Correspondences Possible

In its earliest forms, the Marseilles Tarots have both numbers and names, but no astrology until after the Etteilla Tarots broke ground for that development. Even then, the clues one would find would not be astro-alpha numeric. If anything resembling number-for-letter correspondences were being used, they did not stretch to include astrology. The Hebrew or Greek letters themselves were never shown directly on the earliest Marseilles Tarots, but later they would occasionally appear in the form of the Persian Magical Alphabet, one of the many ciphers employed by the Renaissance Magi to convey yet conceal their inner truths. It is when these symbols start apearing that we can see a formal system of correspondences being applied to this deck, but by this time it is nearly the dawn of the twentieth century.

A wonderful little book called *The Tarot Trumps, Cosmos in Miniature* by John Shephard proposes a set of correspondences for the earliest Tarots based upon the doctrine of the Fall of Man through the rings of the planets (see chapter on The Gnostic Tarot), amplified with the astrological tradition of the Essential Dignities of the Planets. In brief, the astrological attributes of the Major Arcana show the seven planets ruling the the "day signs" (Aquarius through Cancer) in the first seven cards, then visiting their corresponding "night signs" (Leo through Capricorn) in the second seven cards, and thirdly occupying their "exaltations" in the last seven cards. (pp. 66 and 71 of Shephard's book) This conception is a wonderfully optomistic Gnostic approach.

The other documentation that we find for astrological connections with the Marseilles Tarot comes from a Frenchman of Scottish extraction, Joseph Maxwell (1858 - 1938). His book *The Tarot* was published posthumously because he was a judge in the French courts and was concerned about the possible effect on his work if he was exposed as an occultist. In his compact but pithy book, he reveals a set of correspondences that is obviously connected to European aboriginal mythological astronomy. It contains not a shred of Hebrew, Greek or Persian astro-alphanumerics, being purely folk Tarot.

In this pattern, the Magus is called the Juggler, and carries the meaning of the Sun, the Self. The High Priest is Mercury, refering to the Hermetic Priesthood of Melchezidek. The Chariot is powered by Mars, and the Wheel of Fortune is Capricorn. The Moon card is assigned to the sign of Cancer because of the presence of the crab in the pool at the bottom of the card. The Death card is given to Saturn because of the scythe on the card, sacred to that planet These attributions are folksy and obvious.

The Emperor literally sits in the Jupiter shape, facing left in profile, right leg crossed over left. Libra is on the Justice card with the Sword of Truth and the balancing scales. The twins on the Sun card are the sign for Gemini. The Lovers is assigned to Sagitarrius, because of the bow and arrow brandished by the cherub overhead. Virgo matches the World card, because the image is of the Virgin of the World. This use of the traditional smbolism evoked a certain feeling of familiarity for the people using these cards. The World card spoke directly to people's lingering memories of the ancient mysteries with its purely gnostic depiction of Sophia, the Shekinah, the feminine consort of God.

A few of the connections may feel a little strained, such as the Hermit with Pisces or Taurus with the Moon, but on the whole the set of correspondences feels workable. There are none of the three newest planets here, so he puts the North Node (of the Moon) on the Devil card leaving the South Node for the Tower. The Fool card he leaves out of the system entirely, but one could find a way to distribute Uranus, Neptune, and Pluto among these three cards to satisfy the requirements for a complete system.

At first I looked at Maxwell's book as an obscure approach with little relevance to the ancient tradition. Then I started making graphs to study the relationship of one body of correspondences to another, and a very interesting thing becomes clear in this way. If Maxwell is indeed stating an established tradition, then these are the correspondences which were being studied and experimented with when both the English lineage and, simultaneously, the new Spanish lineages were appearing at the end of the eighteen-hundreds. One can easily see connections between the Waite pattern, the pattern on the Dali and Euskalherria Tarots, and the Balbi deck, as if they all possessed Maxwell's book. But they couldn't have, because it was published in Europe at mid-twentieth century! This is another mystery that the European Tarot experts will have to research and solve for us, because these fascinating correspondences deserve more thorough documentation.

The 10 that Vanquished the 12

When the Renaissance mentality encountered Lull's Hebrew Kabbalah emerging from Spain, an entirely new set of considerations was created for Christian occultists. Now the Christian Cabbalists would make the claim that "the 10 have vanquished the 12" (p.270 *Art of Memory*, p.108 *Giordano Bruno*) This referrs to the superiority of the self-created Hermetic/Kabbalist Magus, who has organized his interior life according to the ten-stage Tree of Life in a way that creates a superior climate for spiritual growth and the acquisition of immortality. A claim is being made of primacy over all previous forms of magic. The implication is that the "natural" person of this earth is ruled by planetary ebbs and flows, moved by intuition and instinct ("the twelve" being the signs of the Zodiac). Such a person is therefore less conscious, less self-directed, less refined, and generally inferior to the person of the Tree, who has used will and art to cultivate the Self into the Divine Resemblance.

Although the Magi who took this position were not actually intending to offend the church, their efforts to highlight the evolutionary results of their practices made it seem as if they were glamorizing magic above the salutory effects of mass and the Eucharist. In truth, the schism had been introduced by Pico dela Mirandola's "discovery" of the Hebrew Kabbalah. Enmity between the Church and the Renaissance Magi as a group was greatly increased by Agrippa's astral medicine (based in the signs and planets), and by Agrippa's omniverous intellectual attitude, (Agrippa valued what worked over what the Church wanted no matter what the consequences, because he was a doctor.)

The fact that Agrippa got away with it did not make the path easier for those who followed him, unfortunately. Eventually the Church Fathers boiled over in Italy, targeting Giordano Bruno as the scapegoat meant to send a message to all of his kind. (This book, and others along these lines, are proof that Bruno did not die in vain!)

We can now shift our focus back to the subject of Kabbalah, only this time we will look through the lens of the Magical Christians in the Renaissance, and we will use the Cabbalah spelling to differentiate their treatment of the subject from the ancient Hebrew approach.

THE CHRISTIAN CABALLAH

Let us recall what we have covered so far in the history of alphabet-mysticism in the West. History has preserved for us two "core versions" of the ancient connections between the astrological signs and planets and the letters-which-are-numbers. These interlocking mysteries dictate the structure of Tarot as we know it. One pattern comes from the original, ancient Phoenecian and Hebrew usage, and the other is a much later, slightly variant version in Greek. The first version was sequestered among the Jews, so agressively hidden that it disappeared from sight for hundreds of years. The later version became the model for the European systhesis that eventually emerged as Tarot. I call these Greek correspondences the Hermetic Alexandrian version throughout this book, because the term "Greek Kabbalah" creates a false impression.

Whatever it is called, this is the pattern well-known in Europe by the appearance of the first esoteric Tarots, and it is the pattern of correpndences being used by any Secret Society member frm the Renaissance to the late nineteenth century. Whenever you read about Cabbalah (the form the Christians and Gnostics worked with) as opposed to Kabbalah, (the Hebrew form, unchanged from its middle eastern inceptions), you can be sure that it is the Alexandrian correspondences being referred to. Remember, in both variants, A always equals #1, B always equals #2, and so forth down the alphabet.

The Non-Hebrew Kabbalah, Called Cabbalah

History shows us that some Gentile scholars interested in Hebrew themes picked up the Ari pattern and built it into their worldview. Gathering momentum in the century prior to the first Tarots, a reawakening of classical wisdom was dawning upon Europe from both the Arab world and the eastern Mediterranean. Then, in 1492, the Spanish throne declared its nation Catholic, exiling all Moslems, Jews, Gypsies and whoever else would not profess the faith. This great loss to the culture of Spain produced more stimulation for the cultures of continental Europe. And in the middle of it all, the first fourteen treatises of the Corpus Hermeticum were found, a momentous event in European scholarship.

Simultaneously, and as a result of this wonderful return of the ancient wisdom to Europe, the Secret Societies began to reemerge into visibility, producing the "Rosicrucian Manifesto" in the early 1600s. The subsequent publishing revolution embraced sacred literature from all the traditions of antiquity. The Masonic societies appeared, who over several generations constructed a Hermetic synthesis of the Western Mystery Tradition and eventually cast that construction into the form of playing cards.

Some Context for the Renaissance

Frances Yates states, in her chapter "Pico della Mirandola and Cabalist Magic" from her wonderful book *Giordano Bruno and the Hermetic Tradition*, "names of angels, names of God in Hebrew, Hebrew letters and signs, are a feature of gnostic magic in which pagan and Jewish sources are inextricably mixed. . . .thus both the Renaissance Magia and its Cabala could be regarded as reformed revivals of magics ultimately derivable from pagan and Jewish gnosticism" (p. 108). As during the Alexandrian era, the Greek stream and the Hebrew stream often ran parallel, and in the Gentile world, the correspondences used for the Hebrew letters were those of the Alexandiran variant.. So even though the bulk of the texts from the Alexandrian period had been lost to Europe for over a thousand years at that point, they were embraced with great spiritual enthusiasm upon their reemergence and taken to heart by the most talented and visionary intellectuals of the day.

Although the return of learning to Europe was gradual, certain themes remained perennially of interest. Greco-Roman culture was physically engraved in the landscape around the southern Europeans, and the tradition of Hermes had a persistent hold upon the imagination of learned Europeans. The Jews and Gypsies were feared, romanticized and depended upon for their many "exotic" skills. Medicine especially was still largely magical and depended upon non-Christian (pagan) methods, some of which were nasty and disgusting or alternately, merely ritualistic, the true meanings often lost in time or corrupted in the transmission. Losses to superstition-induced illnesses and occasional bouts of plague provoked intelligent people to keep searching for better information, even if it came from non-Christian sources.

As part of the gradual shift that replaced the Middle Ages with the Renaissance, the quality of magic and mysticism, therefore the entire culture, became more refined. As more of the classics of antiquity were rediscovered and people had the luxury of using their brains for more than survival again, we see a new optimism, a sense of spiritual and intellectual empowerment and a return of the synchretist urges stamped out by earlier Christianity. As history's mystics and sacred philosophers became available to European intellectuals, their narrow-mindedness and superstitiousness began to evaporate, replaced by awe and reverence for the intelligence and understanding of antiquity.

The Renaissance Magi and Tarot

Around 1460, the aging Lorenzo de Medici of Florence received a Greek manuscript from Macedonia that contained a nearly complete copy of the *Corpus Hermeticum*. He had a scholar in his employ whose work he especially valued: Marcilio Ficino, who had been assigned to the translation of the Plato manuscripts. De Medici was afraid of dying before he had an opportunity to read the books of Hermes, so Plato was set aside, allowing Ficino to translate Hermes posthaste.

What Ficino found in the *Corpus Hermeticum* and developed throughout the rest of his career was the first Renaissance statement of NeoPlatonism, an amplification of the Alexandrian synthesis of the first and second centuries. Through his agency, the entire astro-alphanumeric structure of the ancient Mysteries came pouring into the magical imaginations of these inspired and brilliant linguists.

Due to Ficino's regard for the Church, the whole synthesis was explained and experienced from a Christian outlook. He was careful to explain that he was using only the God-given "natural sympathies" that exist between visible and invisible things in the great chain of being. He attested to be merely connecting the upper and lower worlds through their innate lines of relationship, and he sincerely hoped the Church would not feel threatened. As this Christian, Gnostic-leaning antiquarian encountered the Alexandrian synthesis of Greek and Hebrew mysteries, a movement was born.

In particular, Ficino brought talismanic and theurgical practices back to Christian mysticism under the aegis of Hermes, mythical author of the *Corpus Hermeticum*. He felt that by strengthening the affinities between higher and lower things, he could help annul the effects of "the fall," permeating time and space with divine energies channeled by his astronomical talismans. To quote again Dame Frances Yates, "When Hermes Trismegistus entered the Church, the history of magic become[s] involved with the history of religion in the Renaissance."

Ficino's younger friend and colleague, Pico della Mirandola, wittingly or unwittingly contributed another huge boost to the impetus toward the Tarot. Pico added Cabbalist magic to Ficino's Christian NeoPlatonism, opening a fertile field both for study and for controversy. He extolled the virtues of the magical signs, sigils, numbers, images and other devices inherited from Hebrew antiquity and that form the literal link between celestial and terrestrial things. He asserted, quite firmly, that by bringing in the Hebrew mysteries, especially the seventy-two angels who connect the earthly realms to the zodiac (which we eventually see on the Minor Arcana), we can empower the natural symbolistic magic of Ficino with the extra charge of genuine Biblical tradition.

All these new correspondences emerged from close reading of the *Corpus Hermeticum* and related studies, and they produced a tremendous mystical surge not only in della Mirandola but in his whole milieu. Della Mirandola continuously reminded his readers/listeners that this was Christian Magic, not only because it was meant to be used toward and dedicated to the Trinity, but because it came from the Hebrew/Alexandrian synthesis within which Christianity is grounded. History shows us, however, that Pico della Mirandola was not as well-received as he would have liked; he suffered regular persecutions and detractors because of

how closely he skirted the line between scholarship and religion as defined by the Church.

Without straying too far from the topic of Tarot, let me emphasize that Pico della Mirandola also imprinted the Renaissance imagination with the idea of the magus as an agent of the Sacred Marriage, uniting the heavenly and earthly realms through theurgical workings. Using focused consciousness, the Holy Word, sacred sound and the powerful Hebrew talismans that della Mirandola taught that embody the formulae for cosmic values, the world can be impregnated with celestial energies much more efficiently that with Ficino's natural magic alone.

It is also della Mirandola who first articulated the concept of Silent Invocations composed from Hebrew names, letters, signs and sigils, and through this concept, the numbered suit cards received another layer of meaning. To this day, on the esoteric Tarots of the French School from Ettiella forward (and in some of the later English decks), one can see the sigils of the zodiacal angels progressing on the numbered suit cards. (Eliphas Levi called these angels the "Shemhameforesh," a bad transliteration of the Hebrew but a brilliant idea for making Tarot into Silent Invocations.) Tavaglione's Stairs of Gold Tarot details all these angels in the back of its booklet, all aligned with their various degrees of the zodiac for your magical convenience.

To sum up the contribution of this extraordinary person, we should look at the grand design of his mystical conception. For the Gentiles, Pico della Mirandola explained how what he called the "Twelve Punishments of Matter"— the signs of the zodiac—are driven out (actually, harnessed to the Paths) by the "Ten Good Forces" of the Sephiroth. In other words, if the domination of the astrological universe (fate and destiny) over the soul of humanity could be broken, then the Tree of Life can grow back up the Sephiroth (chakras). In this way, the mortal soul is secured, the Ogdoad (eighth sphere, Da'at) comes together, and "the powers sing in the soul the 'ogdoadic hymn' of regeneration." When the Tree conquers the pagan zodiac in the soul, the soul becomes immortal. It is here that we see the unifying thought that binds della Mirandola to the Christian Cabbalah above all other teachings and makes him the enemy of the astrologers of his time. His was a system that a person could use with free will and self-determination, undaunted by the stars or the elements of earth.

Pico della Mirandola and his philosophical peers (Marcilio Ficino, Cornelius Agrippa, John Dee, Paracelcus, Francesco Giorgio, Giordano Bruno, Johann Reuchlin and others) were at the crest of the Renaissance wave, fusing their scholarship with their art and their religion. They made it their business to investigate the philosophies and practices used by our multicultural ancestors. (It is a mystical experience just to read about these people in Yates's meticulously researched tomes.) They were deeply devout Christian, Gnostic and Hebrew scholars, passionately writing volumes and debating about ancient philosophy, filling folios with art and imagery and practicing theurgical rituals designed to put the soul in contact with our higher

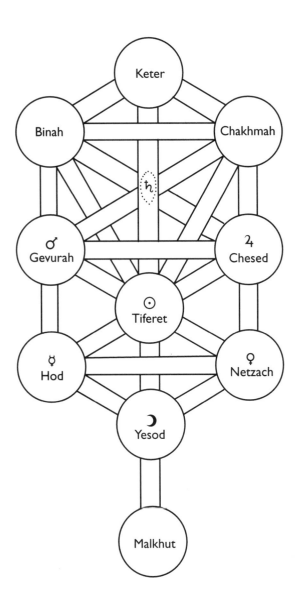

OUR ADAPTION OF KIRCHER'S TREE WITH SATURN AT DA'AT

Kircher's Christian Cabbalah

When we left the Hebrew Kabbalah to look in on the Renaissance magi, we had brought the Tree and the Paths up to the reforms of the Ari. His version of the Tree was an attempt to synthesize the Path attributions of the Short Version he had in his hands with the awkward Tree of the Zoharic Kabbalists of the 1300s.

We saw that in the Renaissance, Christian applications of the Kabbalah were being discovered and synthesized from new translations of ancient manuscripts, and the Gentile world was getting a history lesson. (They did still think that Hermes predated Moses, however, causing them to promote the Alexandrian Mysteries even more than the Hebrew. It took more scholarship yet to untie that intellectual knot!)

Athanasius Kircher was born in 1602 and lived until 1680; his was a long and productive life. As a priest, he was not engaging in his studies with the aim of practicing magic or reviving the Mysteries, but his combination of scientific interest and spiritual respect for the ancients caused him to treat all his subjects respectfully, keeping in mind their best attributes. He was an artist, a linguist and a Cabbalist and had many other areas of expertise. I have no doubt his voracious intellect and voluminous writings and images influenced Tarot profoundly.

With all the sincerity of his Christian training and the scholarship that made him the last Renaissance polymath (he created the first Coptic grammar), Kircher "reformed" the Kabbalah Tree into the renamed Christian Cabbalah pattern. We see this pattern now throughout Tarot, alchemical and magical literature. It is he who decided to count out the alphabet along the paths in top-down order, an approch that has nearly completely supplanted the 3x7x12 ordering of the *Sefir Yetzirah* as reported in Aryeh Kaplan's master work.

Kircher's is also the final and loudest voice in the Renaissance chorus that attributed the wisdom of antiquity to Egyptian culture. He had no way of knowing the truth in the way that we do now, in our age of scientific archeology and linguistic analysis, but the force of his conviction, that Egypt is the source of all the oldest magic, continued to reverberate through the Mystery Schools for several more centuries, stimulating the Rosicrucians and later Masons—Etteilla most notably—to incorporate Christian NeoPlatonist Cabbalah into the Silent Invocations that Tarot embodies.

In the sequence of Renaissance magi from Ficino to Kircher (and through many fascinating characters whom I regrettably cannot mention here), we see the force that drives Tarot into expression. The ancient Mysteries were already in place, although episodically forgotten and re-remembered with the cycles of history. The rediscovery of the bone structure of the Mysteries at the cusp of the publishing revolution made the creation of Silent Invocations in card form possible for the masses. How could Tarot not emerge as the "flash cards of the Mysteries"? It was the next logical step!

Source. It is too bad that the Church eventually felt too threatened to let this wonderful flowering carry on. But while it lasted, we all benefited, because in the sweep of the expansion the Tarot appeared, and on the momentum of the Renaissance, Tarot soared into the esoteric empyrean.

As a matter of fact, it is from the notebooks of the last Renaissance magi, a German Jesuit named Athanasius Kircher, that I believe the images which brought overt esotericism into Tarot were eventually drawn. Kircher is discussed in the essay "The Continental Tarots" as well, but for this chapter, we must acknowledge his contribution to the Christian Cabbalah content of Tarot.

Conclusion

In this brief and incomplete scan of this fascinating stream of Kabbalah/Cabbalah knowledge, I have tried to keep the focus upon the details relevant to the formation of Tarot. This approach cannot help but leave some readers annoyed at what I left out, while others will wonder why I dragged so much detail in. My only defense is that I have learned to find it fascinating, and I hope you will too.

Just tracing the ins and outs of the evolution of the letters/numbers, astrology and paths on the Tree of the Kabbalah is a life's work in and of itself. I have attempted only to present the results of my own delving and scholarship in order to assist in untangling the conundrums that have arisen around Tarot and its number/letter associations through the centuries. I pray that my superficial presentation of this material will provoke insights and answers from other scholars who have also found these topics compelling.

THE CONTINENTAL TAROTS

In the chapter titled *The Major Arcana* I have repeatedly stated that "something happened" to the Tarot in the late 1600s, when a new trend emerged in the images of the Major Arcana. I point to the Marseilles family of decks and the Etteilla Tarots to illustrate my point. The images shown by Antoine Court de Gebelin in his book *Le Monde Primitif* further underscore this idea. The remainder of this essay is about exploring "what happened."

For context, let's review the situation of Tarot in the first half of the 1600s. Since the early 1400s, both handmade and woodblock Tarots showed a remarkable constancy of internal structure even though some packs were either edited or expanded to meet the needs of the various games for which they were created. Tarot appeared in 72-card form in Italy around 1450, although this model may represents "splice" between pre-existing symbol sets: the twenty-two Hebrew alphabet-keyed set called the Major Arcana, and the Turkish Mamluk cards of unknown provenance, a 15th century version of which can be seen in Volume 2 of Stuart Kaplan's *Encyclopedia of Tarot* (see chapter on the Minor Arcana).

THE MOON
CARY YALE/SCAPINI TAROT

Kaplan also explains that the numerical order the Arcana appear in now is drawn from the French pack by Catelin Geofroy, published in 1557 (Vol. 1, p. 65). Kaplan presents evidence of various other styles of orderng the Major Arcana, some in Volume I, some in Volume II, but my friend Mary Greer assures me that the issue of which order is the first or "correct" ordering has gotten more complicated as the state of the reserch has improved. I have no stake in this discussion, because my belief is that from the beginning, Tarot has been attempting to format an Art of Memory system relating the Macrocosm to the Micorcosm. Once the Hebrew alphabet (the format of 22 Major Arcana) was settled upon, then the Arcana gravitate to the letter they were created to represent, and that is why the Arcana have the numbers and order that they have today.

Many of the earliest decks did not show either Roman or Arabic numerals, titles or astrology sigils. Some of the images do, however, utilize traditional scenes and characters from the signs of the zodiac, the personae of the planets and other traditional mythic themes familiar to the culture of the times.

A look at these oldest packs reveals images from the per-

secuted Cathar movement as well as Hebrew, Greek and Gypsy occult symbolism. The vehemence with which the Church attacked the cards and their makers only reinforces the evidence that Tarot was the repository of heretical wisdom preserved in imagery. Close study of the excellent book called *Tarot Symbolism* by Robert O'Neil exposes the falsity of the belief that there were no esoteric associations with Tarot imagery before Eliphas Levi.

The Marseilles family of Tarots began to appear in the late 1400s or early 1500s, slowly evolving and becoming more distinct as versions were reproduced and a their popularity spread. The deck we are featuring from this family is based on the classical Italian-Piedmontese tarot of Giusep Ottone, first published in 1736. Dr. Lewis Keizer considers this family of decks to be the best reproduction of the earliest Arcana to have survived the Inquisition (see "The Esoteric Origins of Tarot: More than a Wicked Pack of Cards").

O'Neil suggests that the Marseilles Tarots were actually the original "folk" pattern, but since most copies were woodblock-print "catchpenny" decks, not expensive works of art like the handmade decks of the Milanese ducal families, they more easily became worn and were discarded and replaced. (I agree to the extent that I too think the earliest extant Tarots are probably not true to the sources that originally inspired Tarot.) This helps explain the uniqueness of the Visconti Sforza and related Tarots, which have more in common with the Mantegna Tarots than the Marseilles.

MONTEGNA'S THEOLOGIA
SHOWING THE ANDROGYNOUS
SOUL

Most of the differences from one pack of Marseilles Tarots to another were simply local details entered into the standard image to identify the maker and the region in which the given version was produced. But in the early 1660s, two decks appeared that permanently changed the look of several Major Arcana. Subsequently, those changes "leaped out" of the Marseilles mold, appearing in the works of de Gebelin and all the Etteilla variants of the following century, effectively obliterating the older versions of these cards except in the case of a nostalgic few Tarot makers who preferred the archaic form. The two Marseilles-style decks that date this telling change in the Tarot canon are the Tarots by Jacques Vieville and Jean Noblet, both Parisian cardmakers in the Marseilles tradition.

A Glance At the Cards in Question

Two defining characteristics of the oldest Tarots were a Lovers card that shows "The Union of the King and Queen" theme, and a Devil card that shows the image of a traditional werewolf or lamia from European pagan antiquity. After the change in the late 1600s, those two cards are drawn to entirely different models, called the Two Paths and Typhon (or later Baphomet). These amendments to the Arcana can first be seen in the aforementioned two French Marseilles Tarots which appeared in the early 1660s. A century later these same amendments appeared as illustrations in Le Monde Primitif by Court de Gebelin, and Etteila's Tarot also followed them faithfully. By the beginning of the 19th century, all schools of Tarot used the "new" models despite their other differences. Adjustments were made at the same time to several other Major Arcana, but the Lovers and the Devil serve as perfect "markers" in Tarots that accepted this new influence.

In Volume 2 of Stuart Kaplan's Encyclopedia, we have an excellent illustration of the development of these two "new" Arcana as they appeared in 1660 in Jacques Vieville and Jean Noblet's decks. Kaplan was kind enough to put them on opposite pages, and we can actually see the ideas developing. Apparently Vieville liked the new version of the Lovers, but rejected changes to the Devil, while Jean Noblet went all the way and changed them both. It is uncanny how they form the line of demarcation--before them, only the old forms appear, but after them, entirely new images take over. It's hard not to wonder "what happened here?"

Introducing Athanasius Kircher

One way to answer the above question would be to ask the parallel question, "What else was happening in Europe during the second half of the 1600s that might cause a ripple of change in the Tarot?" This question is easier to answer. In a general way the answer is "the closing years of the Renaissance." But the more specific answer, very relevant to Tarot, is "Athanasius Kircher." One has only to find a copy of Joscelyn Godwin's wonderful presentation *Athanasius Kircher: A Renaissance Man and the Quest for Lost Knowledge* from Thames and Hudson to realize that this German Jesuit scholar is a key to many riddles in the history of esoteric Tarot.

In our chapter on Christian Cabbalah, an entire section is devoted to Kircher's Cabbalah paradigm. It is he who adapted the paths of the Tree of Life into the form that modern magicians and Tarot practitioners are familiar with. It is also Kircher who was so convinced of the Egyptian source of the ancient mysteries, and so learned and literate in the

exposition of his ideas, that the sheer force of his certainty impregnated esoteric thought for centuries afterward. And I think it is he who, either directly or indirectly, affected the look of the Tarot forever after.

As you gaze upon his illustration called Pan or Jupiter on the next page, it is difficult to miss how closely the "new" Devil image that appears in the 1660s resembles Kircher's conception. This image is surprisingly modern, presaging what the Devil will look like by the 1800's. A shift in gender is in evidence by Levi's time (late 1880's), in which the Devil gravitates from a masculine form, through a form with attributes of both genders, to the final female form. This gives us the Baphomet image favored in the esoteric schools all over Europe. (see chapter on The Major Arcana)

Taking our educated "Tarot eye" beyond the strict Tarot canon, we might find evidence in Kircher's work, or that of his contemporaries, for the shift that happened in the Lovers card simultaneously with the Devil adjustment, and possibly other details as well. Unfortunately, my catalog of Kircher's work is not extensive enough to let me point to such a striking parallel image in the case of the Lovers. Interestingly enough, a remark by Hall in *Freemasonry of the Ancient Egyptians* indicates that Kircher described Typhon, the Alexandrian Devil, as having the head of an alligator and

THE LOVERS
JEAN NOBLET'S TAROT

the body of a hog, (p.16) Where did he learn that? His own images of Typhon are very different, and that description is specific to the *Fratres Lucus* manuscript. It is definately not an image natural to European sacred art of the Renaissance!

Meanwhile, the article by Dr. Keizer points to the mid-1700s as a pivotal time in the history of Tarot, because that is the time of the Fratres Lucis or Brothers of Light. In essence, Dr. Keizer says that the books published by de Gebelin and Etteilla, lauding the Egyptian origin of the Tarot Arcana, were not original in their ideas at all, but were "already common understanding in French occult circles, which were essentially Freemasonic" (p. 12). Keizer sets forth that the "Egyptian Initiation" manuscript that was translated and published by Paul Christian (aka Jean Baptiste Pitois) in 1870 is actually a Fratres Lucis initiatory document from before the French Revolution (which started in 1789). Keizer does not say at which point the Fratres Lucis got the document or when the images were created for it. Upon exmining the book Dr. Keizer refers us to, called *Egyptian Mysteries*, anonymously published by Weiser in 1988, we find in its foreword "... *Egyptian Mysteries* was probably translated into French by Christian, *though not from the original manuscript*....but from a handwritten copy, many of which had been circulating in the occult world from the Middle Ages up to the 19th century." (italics the author's.)

DEVIL
JEAN NOBLET'S TAROT

Once again we recall the evidence, laid out in the previous chapter, demonstrating the existence of a reconstructed Egyptian Initiation rite, pieced together from clasical sources, published in Venice by Malhandrini 1657, then appearing as the *Crata Repoa* in Germany in 1770. Paul Christian uses illustations from the Masonic artist Lenoir, (whose work on Egyptian Masonic rituals was "certainly influenced" by the *Crata Repoa* according to Hall,) in the section "Book Two: the Mysteries of the Pyramids" from his fascinating *History and Practice of Magic*, in which the full text for the Hermetic/Alexandrian Arcana is published for the first time. Who can doubt that all these things are related?

We can now see a theme emerging: In the late Renaissance Kircher amalgamates the Ari version of the *Sephir Yetzirah* with the Pythagorean astro-alphanumeric code, and the basis for Christian Cabbalah is born. Kircher may have also been exposed to the *Fratres Lucis* document, or its predecessor the *Crata Repoa*, which by then was available to occultists in Europe, and which reinforces his aliegence to the Hermetic astro-alphanumeric varient. He declares in no uncertain terms that the entire occult canon of the Renaissance comes from Egypt. The stream of Marseilles Tarots shows sudden and characteristic changes that could easily reflect the mammoth catalog of sacred art Kircher both created and commissioned.

The Freemasonic community availed itself of Kircher's works, stimulating the enhancement of the already existing Gnostic-inflected folk Tarot with his fabulous and extremely occult images. Secret initiatory documents would then be emerging, further illuminating the teachings contained in both his images and the available sources on Egyptian Initiation. Court de Gebelin and Etteilla (both Freemasons) each publicized the story of the Egyptian origin of the Arcana just as Kircher and the ancient initiates assembled in the *Crata Repoa* asserted it. However, the resulting initiatory document, which became associated with the Fratres Lucis by the time of the French Revolution, was not revealed to the general

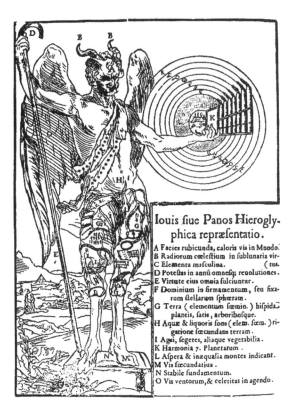

KIRCHER'S PAN/JUPITER

public until 1870, by Paul Christian.

Why is it that this range of fascinating changes appears spontaneously in the Marseilles family of Tarot in the early 1660's? I draw the conclusion that the inspirations for those changes are to be found in Kircher's obsession with Egypt, the assembly of the *Crata Repoa,* and the resulting *Fratres Lucis* manuscript traveling through the underground stream of the Secret Societies. And if Kircher himself did not have a hand in mirroring the *Fratres Lucis* concepts into the Major Arcana of Tarot, then the Rosicrucian and Masonic community who followed in his immediate footsteps did.

Tarot historians have never seen the original models for the changes that appear in the Vieville and Noblet Tarots, but that may be just because we are not studying the Renaissance magi carefully enough. The telling fact that details from this lineage first appeared on Tarot cards two centuries before Paul Christian's publication of the *Fratres Lucis* document, and Hall's treatment of the *Crata Repoa* means that we have to reevaluate the current theory that the "Egyptian-style images" on some Tarots are late developments in Tarot art.

The very first of these Egyptian-style Tarots to emerge after Christian's publication was the Falconnier/Wegener Tarot of 1896. Gareth Knight, in his fascinating book *The Treasure House of Images*, tells us "Designs for the Falconnier Tarot were taken from original frescos and bas-reliefs in the Louvre and the British Museum, but they nonetheless retain a very French flavour" (p. 20) In the article written about this deck in Volume 2 of the Encyclopedia, Kaplan says "Interestingly, he [Falconnier] cites the 1760 Tarot of Marseilles by

N. Conver [see Vol. 1 of the Encyclopedia] as one that is closest to the 'traditional' Tarot." Perhaps now we can understand why Falconnier would make such a comment!

The catalog of Egyptian-style Tarots, with art that matches the *Fratres Lucis* manuscript, also includes the Papus Tarot, the St. Germaine Tarot, the Ibis, the Brotherhood of Light Tarot, Egypcios Kier, Tarot of the Ages and that of the Hermetic Brotherhod of Luxor, a group associated with Madame Blavatski in her early years. The information accompanying these Tarots all create the impression that their images come to us from sources far anterior the first historical decks of the 1400s, and yet each shows the Two Paths and Baphomet rather than the earliest "European" images. We cannot prove such an early date as the origin of the manuscript or the images that have become associated with it. But it's clear that those who say it's "proven" that Pitois/Christian made that manuscript up for his book are simply not looking at the cards themselves.

Dr. Keizer also reminds us that the images that have become associated with the Fratres Lucis document might be influenced by the Isaian/Serapian cult that existed in Italy during Alexandrian times (until the 400s AD). The Italians were excavating and studying Serapian temples by the 10th century (see the essay "The Esoteric Origins of Tarot"). Kircher spent the later decades of his life in Italy, and was known as an omnivorous thinker and student of the world. Can we really imagine that he missed out on visiting one of those Serapis temples during his decades in Italy, when Egypt was his passion?

To summarize, although the temptation for modern historians has been to look at the pivotal 19th century and the work of Eliphas Levi as defining the epoch of esoteric Tarot, upon closer examination, the situation is not so easy to characterize.

A Bit of Secret Society History

The term Secret Societies is used to refer to an underground affiliation of esotericists deemed heretical by the Catholic Church since the 1100s, made up of pagans, Jews, Arabs, Gnostics, Gypsies and other people of minority beliefs in Christian Europe. The Church's abuses drove them into each other's arms over time, and by the earliest publication of Tarot there were sophisticated international organizations within which mystically and philosophically inclined people, including Christians of a tolerant ilk, could associate and cross-pollinate their ideas.

A particularly important group in the history of Tarot is the Rosicrucians (having their public beginning in Germany in 1614), whose membership was always kept secret, and who were dedicated to keeping aspects of ancient wisdom alive despite the Catholic overthrow of pagan Europe. Over time the Rosicrucians created various Masonic Orders to serve as a doorway through which to attract new menbers. Masonry became tolerated as the only legitimate non-Christian "religion" in Catholic Europe, providing a haven of refuge for alternative thinkers who were spiritually inclined but

would not bind themselves to the Pope and all he stood for.

The Order of Elect Cohens (established in the second half of the 1700's by Martines de Pasqually) is the more recent origin of a lineage whose members have included many esoteric scholars pivotal to the history of Tarot, including Court de Gebelin and Etteilla. A century later, this lineage produced The Martinist Order, named after the philosophical stream of Martinez de Pasqually and Louis Claude de St. Martin and started by Papus in 1891.

So we can confidently assert that, from the time of Etteilla, the first to popularize a Tarot with overt esoteric content in the 1780s, virtually all the pivotal writers and makers of esoteric Tarot decks in Europe have been Secret Society members. It may prove true that the Tarot is itself a Secret Society creation, although the conditions of persecution under which it originated make that assertion difficult to either affirm or deny.

It is possible to find many books of Tarot "expertise" professing to recount the known history of Tarot but that entirely gloss over the Secret Society connections of the people who have been most pivotal in the history of Tarot. This results in a view of Tarot development with holes big enough to swallow an entire esoteric lineage! Thus I am infinitely grateful to have in my possession, due to a simple twist of fate, a three-volume restatement of the history of the European lodges, (called *The Book of Rosicruciae*, published in 1947) which puts an entirely different spin on the situation.

The author, E. Swynburne Clymer, also asserts that many of the people whose names are intertwined with the 18th and 19th century Tarots were members in the remarkable, multilayered web of connections linking the mystical intelligentsia of Europe. In his giant Book, he starts with the publication of the seminal document "Fama Fraternatis" in Germany, around 1614. From that event he moves forward in time with biographies of all the leaders through the generations who were willing to have their names go down in history (many more are mentioned, but anonymously).

I have been greatly enriched by reading the esoteric biographies of St. Germaine, Cagliostro, Stanislas de Guaita, Eliphas Levi and Gerard Encousse/Papus. All these names are familiar to students of Tarot, but the public record on these people is in some cases scant, in others distorted. Clymer's information has given me a less lopsided perception of these dedicated and cultivated persons. Although some have felt that Clymer is a less than unbiased source and therefore his word is not taken as gospel, we cannot correct his excesses or gain perspective on his contribution unless his work is republished in accessible form for all.

When I looked for confirmation of Clymer's excellent volumes, I found Isabel Cooper-Oakley and her book *The Count of Saint-Germaine*, (as derived from the Masonic Archives, with all sources cited). Cooper-Oakley affirms that a whole cohort of magical personalities — St. Germaine, St. Martin, Etteila, Mesmer, Cagliostro and others — collectively represented the French at the Masonic Convention in Paris in 1785 (see pages 108-9). By the end of the chapter she has supplemented that quote with similar remarks from other contemporary sources. As in the previous paragraphs, we are seeing the names of people who have featured heavily in the history of the Orders, in the history of occultism, and in the history of Tarot.

Manley P. Hall helped me finally lay my doubts to rest about Cagliostro and St. Germaine in his fascinating *Fremasonry of the Ancient Egyptians*. On p. 74 he states "The impulse behind Masonic scholarship in France during the period of the revolution and immediately thereafter is entirely obscure. It is quite possible that St. Germain, Cagliostro, and Claude Saitn-Martin were the moving spirits behind the sudden interest in Egyptian and Oriental metaphysics. Certainly, St. Germain's TRINOSOPHIA and Cagliostro's EGYPTIAN RITES stand out as the albest products of the French recension."

I find it fascinating to imagine just what the chemistry of those times and this group was like. It has piqued my interest that in this century, Tarots have emerged bearing the names of St. Germaine and Cagliostro. Subtle details on these Tarots point back to this exciting moment in history when Etteilla, Cagliostro, St. Germaine and their Brothers were fanning the flames of the Tarot revival begun in the previous century.

The Older Alexandrian Stream

In addition to the revolutionary reemergence of the *Fratris Lucis*-style images of the Devil and the Lovers (among others), the European Lodges also popularized the traditional astro-alphanumeric correspondences of the Alexandrian Hermetic system set into place by Pythagoras around 600 BC and revived during the flowering of Alexandrian culture after 300 BC. These correspondences, slightly different from those given in the Sephir Yetzirah of the Jews, are the only other version of the letter/number/Arcana correspondences we can be sure are truly authentic and founded in antiquity. Etteila taught these correspondences in his books published in the late 1700s, but the correspondences printed on his decks are a blind. Levi made subtle modifications in the late 1800s, and all the European Rosicrucian and Masonic lodges used them, with the exception of the English, right up to the 20th century. Etteilla's Tarot became the most famous deck in Europe in the century after its inception. Its offshoot,

"LE TYPHON"
AKA THE DEVIL
FALCONNIER TAROT

the Catalan Tarot, became the first 78-card Tarot deck published in Spain in 1900, according to Fournier's playing card encyclopedia. Etteilla-style Tarots became more ornate in the 19th century (see Kaplan's Encyclopedia, Vol. 1, p. 141-144 and Vol. 2, p. 400-410). A shortened version was also printed in France at the end of the 19th century to simplify it for fortune telling. In Italy, the 19th century Cartomancia was the homegrown response to Etteilla, and that Tarot has made it considerablly easier to unscramble which of Etteilla's images go with which Arcana of the usual Tarots, as both of the sources mentioned below have only partial information in their lists. After and over two centuries of reprinting in various countries, the Etteilla cards began to show considerable corruption in the letter/astrology corresponcences, making a confusing situation even more difficult to unravel.

The two lists I am citing to detail Etteilla's astro-alpha-numeric correspondences are the one given by Papus in the late 1800s, and Stuart Kaplan's version in Vol I of his *Encyclopedia*. Although I cannot read French to confirm those earlier connections, I know that Papus was the recognized expert of his time and he was quoted by all English, French and Spanish Tarot writers of his day. I trust his opinion, although his information only goes so far as to link Etteilla's Arcana to the more usual versions from the Marseilles Arcana. Stuart Kaplan shows a differently organized version of the same set in his Encyclopedia of Tarot, Vol. 1, having taken the trouble to supply the astrology correspondences from Etteilla's books. These correspondences became standard for all of Europe's Secret Societies and their Tarots by the time of Levi.

That would make Etteilla the harbinger of the late-appearing Egyptian-style decks, which include the Falconnier/Wegener Tarot, its modern cognate the St. Germaine Tarot, the Ibis, the Egypcios Kier and the Brotherhood of Light Tarot. All these Tarots bear Egyptian-style images (which I stated earlier could be Serapian-inspired, reflected through A. Kircher's synthetic genius). The texts of these decks reference, to a greater or lesser degree, the *Fratres Lucis* text translated and published by Paul Christian in his *History and Practice of Magic*.

Again, the numbers and signs printed on Etteilla's' cards exist in their own little universe, as they are purposefully rearranged compared to any previous Tarot ordering. This body of attributions is a blind. What is true to the Alexandrian stream are the astro-alpha-numerology connections published in his books.

Why Did Etteilla Modify the Major Arcana?

It seems that Etteilla was attempting to realign the images of the Major Arcana with a Greek creation story, a later, Alexandrian modification of the ancient Hebrew mythos of middle-eastern origin. Recent research shows that in changing the images of the Major Arcana, Etteilla was drawing from a Hermetic book, *The Poimandres*, a Greek treatise on the creation of the world and the fall of humanity into Eros.

Essentially it's a Greek version of the Genesis story, but with differing names and an altered ordering of events. It fits the standard type of a hypostasis narrative.

The hypostasis is a detailed recitation of the stages that The Creator used to step down universal power so it can be organized into a time-space world peopled with creatures.

"THE BIRDS AND THE FISHES" AKA EMPRESS, ETTEILLA TAROT

The Kaballah Tree is one hypostasis narrative, evident when you follow the angles of the Lightning Bolt as it descends through the planetary Sephira into matter. Such presentations are a recognizable feature of a Mystery School format. This is the classic "how the world came to be" narrative (see *A Wicked Pack of Cards* by Dumett et. al.).

Etteilla's Tarot assimilated the seven days of creation theme directly from The Poimandres (or "Pymander"; there are several spellings). This is one of the manuscripts returned to Europe from Byzantium in the 1500s. By so explicitly detailing a seven days of creation theme that is not the Judeo-Christian version, he is waving a red flag, stating without words that "this is not the folk Tarot that can be passed off as Catholic." Perhaps the workings of democratic groups like the *Fratres Lucis* emboldened him to tell his truth, if only in veiled form, and only in the pictures. In hindsight, he was getting away with a lot!

Along with referencing the Greek and Hermetic stream of Gnosis as the source of his Arcana, Etteilla also reintroduced certain themes that were present in the earliest handmade and woodblocked Tarots but which had been suppressed through the efforts of the Church. Etteilla put back the earliest Goddess images that had been replaced by male figures like Hercules (Strength), Mars (The Chariot), the Hanged Man (Prudence), not to mention any extra Popes and Emperors.

To my eye, Etteilla attempted to revive the more blatant representation of the Sophianic, Hebrew Goddess-based suppressed Gnostic and Holy Grail mythos so threatening to the Church five centuries earlier among the Cathars. Gershem Scholem asserts this very theme in many places in his excellent works--that the Gnostic religion of the Cathars was by no means a purely Christian phenomenon, but instead was imprinted by the Jewish Gnosticism fermenting locally at the same time. Remember, the earliest handmade Tarots (from the mid-1400s) prominently feature the Popess card as a woman in full ecclesiastical garb, intimately identified with the Cathar heresies. Perhaps by clothing these oldest

Gnostic images in Hermetic garb, he hoped to cement the link between Alexandrian culture and Gnosticism in Tarot tradition. It is too bad that the layers of veiling he applied to his Arcana have obscured them for so long!

Etteilla also put the signs of the zodiac on his first twelve Arcana, although again following no previous traditional ordering system, but superimposing his own logic, then claiming it was from the Hebrew. However, as we have seen above, he was, in fact, working with the Hermetic/ Alexandrian variation, which dates back to the Pythagorean corrections to the Greek alphabet in the 7th century bc.

Reassessing Etteila's Work

Elizabeth Cooper-Oakley's book *The Count of St. Germaine* names Etteilla as a compatriot to Masons and Martinists in his time. We also can see that he was using Kabbalistic correspondences that are in line with what we know of Pythagorean and Hermetic teachings. As well, his Tarots became the most popular and influential of the world's Tarots in the century following their publication. Why, then, do Tarot historians invariably skim over him so lightly? It is a measure of his success as a lodge member that the popular press has never seen the esoteric merit of these Tarots. "Hidden in plain sight," indeed!

It is more than likely that the Etteilla Tarot is the "blind" that the English writers from the early 20th century were warning students against getting caught up in. I can appreciate the thicket of considerations the Etteilla Tarot raises, appearing as it seems to, "out of the blue" and stealing the show so completely in its century that some scholars of his day feared Etteilla's Tarots would push out all the other decks on the market.

But if Papus, Kaplan, Decker, Depaulus, and Dummett are correct, and the similarities between Etteilla's arcana images and the Fratres Lucis astro-alphanumerics are not accidental, it becomes clearer how important Etteilla's Tarot is for transmitting historical values, like a fly in amber, until we could finally decode them. His correspondences, both in the images and in the occult attributions, reach back to an ancient strata of magic, theurgy and mysticism refering us to Alexandrian sources rather than the older Judeo-Christian ones.

It is important to note that in the Arcana which Etteilla chose to rework to his own liking, he shows a high degree of literacy in the canon of magical art and the original Tarots. This suggests that the portrayal of Etteilla by exoteric history is another aspect of the "blind" around his Tarot. For all of Levi's bluster about the imperfection of the Etteilla Tarots, it is no accident that a century later, Papus would borrow the entire framework for his own Minor Arcana from Etteilla!

One Century Later: Eliphas Levi

Returning to Secret Society lore, let us note that Clymer spares no pains in mentioning, among those rosters of illustrious lodge members and esoteric scholars, that Eliphas Levi was the Supreme Grand Master of the Fraternitas Rosae Crucis of Europe (with the exception of England) from 1856 until his death in 1875. This makes him a distinctly more interesting person than has yet been admitted by his translators or biographers. The public perception of this man and his life work would have one believe that his importance to the transmission of the esoteric paradigm was mostly in his own mind! Some modern Tarot scholars seem genuinely puzzled that he commanded such respect from the European intelligentsia of his day, a huge oversight in view of the facts as stated by Clymer.

Whatever aspersions have been cast by the dubious upon the name of Eliphas Levi, esoteric tradition reveals his steadying influence in the chaos which the Secret Societies were experiencing during his tenure as Supreme Grand Master. Not only did he serve as Grand Master for over twenty of the most difficult years the combined orders had faced in his century (the siege of Paris during the Franco-Prussian War), but his name and writings were the turning point for esoteric Tarot, making it more accessible for the masses after the century of Etteilla's confusing tarots. Clymer also names him as a Kabbalistic and Magean Initiate, and a member of L'Ordre Du Lit.

The books for which Levi is most known appeared during his earliest years as the Grand Master. In them he indicated the Sephir Yetzirah, Pythagoras and Court de Gebelin (among others) as sources for the letter/Arcana/astrological codes and correspondences used within the Fraternitas (Levi's *History of Magic*, p. 76-7). In an article called "The Science of the Prophets" found in *The Mysteries of Magic*, a digest of Levi's writings translated by A. E. Waite (p. 275-288), Levi lays out his Hebrew letter/Arcana correspondences very clearly, with no ambiguity. If his attributions were spurious or mistaken, there was plenty of time for the world to critique his assertions when he was still alive. But no such controversy ever erupted, because these were the common correspondences all over Europe and had been so for over a century. Only after his death, upon the disposal of his papers and the translating of his works, did the efforts at revisionism begin.

Levi's Significant Contributions to Tarot

It is clear that Eliphas Levi's monumental scholarship and high status in the Secret Societies made it easier for his attributions to become the standard European pattern from the late 1900s until today. Yet a few Tarots continued to follow the older pattern represented by Etteilla. The switch is subtle, because nothing changes between the Hebrew letters, their numbers or their astrology. But Levi's work and the decks that grew out of his work show the letter Tav on The World and Shin on The Fool. The element/planet correspondences with the letters stay the same, but the Arcana themselves switch places in the alphabet.

It is possible that while working with Charles Nodier

and Jean Baptiste Pitois (aka Paul Christian) on the spoils of Napoleon's sack of the Vatican, cataloging and translating manuscripts from disbanded heretical monasteries of earlier centuries, Levi discovered the fact that the Hebrews (before the Greek alphabet reforms) correlate the letter Shin (#21) with the primal Fire element. He was passionately devoted to the Hebrew Mysteries, so it would make sense of he wanted to restore that correspndence to resonate more closely with the Hebrew understanding. This he did by switching the last two Arcana without changing the letters or their order in the alphabet.

In his introduction to Oswald Wirth's insightful booklet *Introduction to the Study of Tarot*, Stuart Kaplan states that Wirth was following Levi in putting the Fool between Judgment and the World, while "in the Arabic sequence, The Fool was designated 22 or 0" (p. 9). This is the one and only time I have seen "the Arabic sequence" mentioned, but it suggests a period when the astro-alphanumeric correspondences were diverted to the Moslem libraries and there lost to the west. After the waning of Alexandrian culture, they reappeared in Europe in the late 1600s to effect the "correction" that the Marseilles and Etteilla Tarots represent.

Levi's work on the Vatican treasures stolen by Napoleon made him and his co-workers, Nodier and Pitois, privy to materials that had been out of circulation for centuries already, materials we would give our eyeteeth to see again today. Quite likely it was all very carefully arranged to enlist Levi and his student (Papus) when the time came to catalog it all—who else at that time would have known what they were looking at? With access to these remarkable papal treasures as well as to the archives of the Rosicrucian and Masonic societies they each belonged to, they were "insiders" in the most inside sense of the word! (This, by the way, shows one possible path the *Fratres Lucis* manuscript could have taken to reach Pitois/Christian, although it is certainly not the only possible way.)

We can now attribute to Levi the pattern of correspondences leading to the decks by Papus, Wirth and the one named after Cagliostro. The lion's share of modern European esoteric Tarots seems to be informed by this style of connecting the letters to the Arcana, no matter whether or how they splice on the astrology after the fact.

Reinstating Levi

Eliphas Levi was not the only person to suffer postmortem redactions and come out looking significantly reduced in the translation. I believe an unwritten mandate within the Societies states that when a member comes out with a book, deck or course of training that is too power-packed with the real teachings, or if it looks like it might be misunderstood or misapplied, several generations of lodge members following after them will be assigned to disclaim them. Etteilla disclaims de Gebelin. Levi disclaims Etteilla. Levi's Golden Dawn translators play havoc with him. Papus disclaims Christian/Pitois, and Waite repudiates them all.

This is all part of the ancient debate over how much of

the inner teachings should be shared with the masses. Built into the Secret Society paradigm is the notion that "our group is privy to esoteric truths that others lack." The Church was continually trying to infiltrate the Secret Societies and criminalize their activities, so Society members could not freely share their teachings even if they had wanted to. Many occultists were also scientists, mathematicians, doctors, inventors and the like who rightly feared that their experiments and inventions would fall into the hands of those who would exploit them materially without adequate moral or spiritual guidance. (This is exactly what has happened in the nineteenth and twentieth centuries, with the rise of secular scholarship disconnected from religious frameworks and ethical considerations.)

So even those who were seen by Secret Society members as teaching the esoteric paradigm (Etteilla and Levi, for instance) felt they had to resort to a bit of obfuscation, retaining the innermost secrets for "those who had eyes to see." Even though Levi states in public that he thinks of Etteilla's Tarots as misguided and erroneous, in truth he is using the very same system, with only the slightest amendments. And neither he nor Etteilla were entirely truthful about where the attributions came from. We must try to keep this trend in mind when we see how disparaging the English Tarot writers were about Levi just forty or fifty years later (see "The English School").

Interestingly enough, both Etteilla and Levi were educated occultists who would most likely have been exposed to whatever versions of esoteric correspondences were being taught and used in the widespread Secret Society groups of their respective times. Yet they chose not to specify that they were each representing the Alexandrian/Hermetic branch of the Hebrew tradition rather than the considerably older Semitic branch as originally tabulated in the Sephir Yetzirah.

In Conclusion

In light of the above, we can now define the Continental Tarot as comprised of a lineage of lodge brothers collectively committed to the survival of the Hermetic/Alexandrian Gnosis, already old and revered at the time of the founding of the Fraternitas. The first, handmade Tarots revealed the Hebrew/Cathar/Gnostic origins of the Arcana, but those Tarots were eventually either lost or misunderstood, resulting in the promulgation of mass-produced decks with little but folk meanings, taking the place of the original flash cards for the Mysteries (see "The Confluence of Ancient Systems").

Kircher, the Fratres Lucis, Etteilla, Levi and other Tarot reformers eventually imprinted a more esoteric version of the ancient Arcana into the collective consciousness. This was largely an underground endeavor until Levi laid it out in a systematic way for the whole of the Fraternitas. We have seen that this stream of Tarots has formed the riverbed in which most modern European Tarots (not of the English stream) are flowing.

My meta-theory that underlies most of what I'm work-

ing with here is that the Rosicrucians, especially the Martinist Lodge, has made it their business to save and revive the Inner Tradition of Tarot. The Continental Esoteric Tarots perpetuate representations of the ancient Hermetic/Alexandrian Mysteries, of the earliest proto-Tarots, and of the secret documents from the Middle Ages. This is one reason for calling the nineteenth century the French Occult Revival. Most sources point to Levi as the figurehead, but the dates prove that he was coasting on the previous century's momentum.

As mentioned earlier, the crowd that has followed Levi's "adjusted" correspondences, from the late 1800s to this day, places the Tav on the World card, while the letter Shin is on the Fool (see the essay "The Confluence of Ancient Systems"). I think we can use this variation as another marker to show which Tarots were constructed by Fraternitas members after Levi and which were drawn from the Fratres Lucis document from the 1600s.

For further insight into the more recent esoteric decks that promote the assignment of Shin to the Fool, see Valentine Tomberg's priceless *Meditations on the Tarot*. Tomberg tells us that this correspondence was given to him from a "Martinist-Templar-Rosicrucian" confederation he belonged to in St. Petersburg, Russia in 1920. The modern occult writer Mouni Sadhu uses a redrawing of Court de Gebelin's images with Levi's correspondences in his extraordinary manual, *The Tarot*. Irene Gad's very valuable *Tarot and Individuation* also teaches this arrangement. I hope that this book will stimulate more scholarship to emerge on the European esoteric paradigm.

From Levi's *Transcendental Magic.*
BAPHOMET, THE GOAT OF MENDES.

LEVI'S DEVIL IMAGE
"THE SCAPEGOATED GODDESS"

English Letter		A	B	G	D	H	V	Z	Ch
Greek Letter		α	β	γ	δ	ε	ς	ζ	η
Hebrew Letter (Continental use of Hebrew)		א	ב	ג	ד	ה	ו	ז	ח
Arcana Names	Fool	Magus	Priestess	Empress	Emperor	Pope	Lovers	Chariot	Justice
Arcana Number	0	1	2	3	4	5	6	7	8
Gra version SephirYetzirah – From ~1800 B.C. El Gran Tarot Esoterico, Tarot of the Ages		🜁	☾	♂	☉	♈	♉	♊	♋
Old Alexandrian, 600 B.C. – Hermetic Etteilla, Falconnier Tarot		🜁	☾	♀	♃	♈	♉	♊	♋
Continental Tarots ~1880 A.D. Levi, Wirth, Papus		🜁	☾	♀	♃	♈	♉	♊	♋
Marseilles, Spanish Tarot Maxwell's correspondences	Fool △	☉	☾	♀	♃	☿	♐	♂	♎
Pierre Piobb, 1908 A.D. – Spanish Variant #1 Dali, Euskalherria	Fool ♏	☉	☾	Earth (⯓)	♃	☿	♍	♐	♎
Balbi, Spanish Variant #2	Fool שׁ ♏	☉	☾	☿	♃	♉	♍	♊	♎
↑ **ABOVE** this line, Hebrew alphabet is used in the ancient manner.									
English Use of Hebrew	A	B	G	D	H	V	Z		Ch
English School Waite/Case	Fool 🜁 ♅	☿	☾	♀	♈	♉	♊	♋	♎
Crowley's English Variant	♅ Fool	☿	☾	♀	♒	♉	♊	♋	♎
Arcana Names	Fool	Magus	Priestess	Empress	Emperor	Pope	Lovers	Chariot	Justice
Arcana Numbers	0	1	2	3	4	5	6	7	11

T	I	C	L	M	N	S	Ayn	P	Ts	Qk	R	Sch	Th
θ	ι	κ	λ	μ	ν	ξ	o	π	φ	ρ	σ	τ	υ
ט	י	כ	ל	מ	נ	ס	ע	פ	צ	ק	ר	ש	ת
Hermit	Wheel	Strength	Hanged Man	Death	Temperance	Devil	Tower	Star	Moon	Sun	Judgement		
9	10	11	12	13	14	15	16	17	18	19	20	21	22
♌	♍	♀	♎	▽	♏	♐	♑	☿	♒	✷	♄	Fool △	World ♃
♌	♍	♂	♎	▽	♏	♐	♑	☿	♒	✷	♄	World △	Fool ☉
♌	♍	♂	♎	▽	♏	♐	♑	☿	♒	✷	♄	Fool △ #0	World ☉ #21
✷	♑	♌	♈	♄	≈	☊	△ ☋	♉	♋	♊	♏	World ♍	
♆	♑	♌	♅	♄	≈	♂	♈	♀	♋	♊	✷	World ♉	
♆	♑	♌	✷	♄	≈	♂	♈	♀	♋	♅	♐		World ♇

↓ **BELOW**, modern adjustments prevail.

I	C	L	M	N	S	Ayn	P	Ts	Q	R	Sh		Tav
♍	♃	♌	▽ ♆	♏	♐	♑	♂	≈	✷	☉	△ ♇		♄ World
♍	♃	♌ Lust	♆	♏	Art ♐	♑	♂	♈	✷	☉	♇		♄ World
Hermit	Wheel	Strength	Hanged Man	Death	Temperance	Devil	Tower	Star	Moon	Sun	Judgement		
9	10	8	12	13	14	15	16	17	18	19	20	21	22

CONFLUENCE OF THE THREE GREAT SYSTEMS

In this chapter we will examine the most esoteric, interior architecture that connects Tarot to the historical stream of Mystery School teachings passed down and grafted together from most ancient times. We will compare and contraste the details of the most ancient Babylonian astrology model, the Hebrew Mysteries of Kabbalah, its Pythagorean adaptation in Greece, the Ari redaction of the *Sephir Yetzirah* (which changed the form of the paths and settled the Planetary Governors upon the Sephiroth), and Athanasius Kircher's resulting efforts to redefine the paths and the letters upon them. So this "confluence" to which I am referring is the result of three thousand years of ancient lore, refined in the fires of the European Renaissance. This chapter contains the key to it all.

Once we can grasp the idea that the Arcana of Tarot have been organized around a blend of Hebrew Kabbalist astro-number theory and Pythagorean sacred geometry, we can appreciate what the Renaissance Rosicrucians might have seen in the Taro—flash cards for drilling on the curriculum of a Hermetic University course of study.

WHEEL OF FORTUNE
BRAMBILLA TAROT

No such university could exist in public by Kirscher's lifetime, which spanned much of the 1600s. The Church had forbidden the universities from teaching the subject of astrology, the last trace of the ancient Mysteries, by the fourteenth century. Only the Secret Societies were keeping the ancient lore alive, and in some generations, there were only a few isolated scholars to pass it along. Luckily for us all, among them were a few truly enlightened members of the clergy, who used their privileged positions, excellent educations, and access to Church archives to study and illuminate the teachings of the ancients. Athanasius Kircher was one of those, as we have seen in the chapter on Christian Cabbalah).

The Tarot, like all esoteric paradigms before it, outlines the Grand Plan, an overview of life at every level, with all its related mystical arts and sciences. As it has come down to us from history, we can see clearly how Tarot embodies the confluence of astrology/Kabbalah/number mysteries of antiquity. The goal of these schools was to redeem the soul of humanity after its fall from grace into eros, returning us to our primordial wholeness and immortality. Therefore we should expect to see a healthy trace of the Mystery School agenda still shining through the Tarot, despite its many superficial permutations in the last few centuries. Given what we now know about history, it would be more surprising if such values could not be found in the Tarot than if they could!

The Major Arcana, these twenty-two sophisticated and multileveled symbolic packages, have more often than not been presented in an order that parallels the numerical values of the Hebrew alphabet. Tables found in the first chapter of Stuart Kaplan's *Encyclopedia of Tarot* (Volume 1) confirm that since at least the mid-18th century, the Major Arcana have been publicly associated with the Hebrew alphanumeric system on a card-for-letter basis. Few people realize that this body of correspondences carries within it several other symbolic formations that would be familiar to a Renaissance Hermetic synchretist. These secondary internal structures link the Arcana to the Hebrew Kabbalah, the Seven Planetary Governors, the Hermetic Caduceus, Pythagoras' Tetractys and the Astronomical Wheel of the Year. In the chapter on the Minor Arcana, some of those themes were taken up to explain the internal structure of the suit cards. In this essay, we will take on related themes to be found within the Major Arcana.

Internalized Structures of Tarot

• *Astrological Correspondences*

The first internal configuration to examine is the ancient astrological underpinning which serves as the foundation for Hebrew Kabbalah, Pythagorean Numerology and Christian Cabbalah of the Renaissance, much less the relatively recent Tarot. If you were a Renaissance magus, you would have this model internalized at the foundation of your learning.

The Hebrew letters link astrology to the Major Arcana, which then assume the role of pathways between the Sephiroth of the Kabbalah/Cabbalah Tree. We will see these correlations further investigated when we return to discussing the Tree later in this chapter.

First, witness the ancient figure of the Wheel of the Zodiac, showing the Seven Planetary Governors apportioned around the signs. The essentially Gnostic character of this diagram is revealed by the fact that starting from Aquarius and working sunwise to Cancer you see illustrated the descent of the soul from heaven to earth, picking up the "planetary metals" from the Archons as it sinks to physical Earth. (This corresponds directly with the descending motion on the left-hand side of the Wheel of Fortune in most Tarots.) Then starting with Leo at the bottom and working sunwise

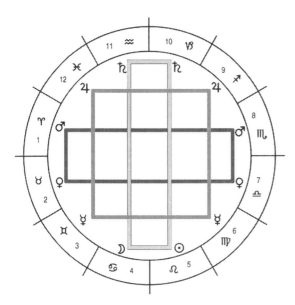

WHEEL OF THE ZODIAC

back up to Capricorn, you see the regeneration of man, the soul's repayment of his debt to the Archons (planets), who then liberate him to return to eternity on the rising motion of the right side of the Wheel. When lined up thus, we see the "Ladder of Lights" formed by the planets stacking up around the Sun. (Remember, when this diagram was created it was thought that the sun, moon and the other planets all revolved around the earth. Nowadays we can see this as a psychological model, where each ego thinks that the rest of life is revolving around it.)

These sign/planet correspondences have been in place since the time of Babylon (2200 BC). The fact that the axis of the diagram puts the midheaven/nadir axis on the cusps of Aquarius and Leo could indicate it was composed in the "Platonic month of Leo," 10800 BC to 8000 BC, as the vernal equinox precessed.

A friend with whom I have enjoyed sharing metaphysical speculations pointed out to me that in this rulership diagram, you can see not only the rulerships themselves, but also along the left diagonal bias you can see the pattern of "exaltations," while along the right diagonal you see the pattern of "falls," as named in the ancient rulership relations. (Connecting the "detriments" makes a beautiful star in the center of the diagram.) I would never have seen this pattern if he had not mentioned it, because I don't use exaltations, detriments or falls in my astrological practice. He added that those same diagonal patterns prevail in astrological homeopathy as well, where the "exaltations" are thought of as the "sympathies" and the "falls" are seen as "antipathies," both to be used as remedies depending upon whether you want to strengthen a condition or disrupt it. C.C. Zain in the Brotherhood of Light teachings discusses this in his volume on medical astrology.

• *The Three Septenarys*

Another of these internal formations within the cards is the 7 by 3 division of the Major Arcana that expresses the

three worlds paradigm within which the human soul must seek initiation to return to its original estate (see chapter on Gnostic Tarot). Different modern Tarot teachers have highlighted this "three sevens" approach in which one sets aside the Fool card and arranges the rest in three horizontal rows of Arcana numbered 1-7, then 8-14, then 15-21. Since Papus's tome *The Tarot of the Bohemians* emerged, in which a great deal of space is given to this topic, and despite the fact that modern teachers may disagree on what values to attribute to these three septenaries (or seven triplicities), this internal symmetry is too compelling to ignore.

I will here attempt the briefest explanation of the system, but any interested party will have to seek further for detail.

The first septenary corresponds to the acquisition of an individuated self, separate from the mass mind, separate from one's personal historical background, suitable for carrying forward into eternity. The Magus, Priestess, Empress, Emperor, Heirophant, and Lovers give us six primal dramas the ego can try on and learn about the Self with. This septenary culminates in the Chariot, one's vehicle for psychological mobility in the Self's expanding reality.

The second septenary represents the work of learning to operate in the collective world of human family, society, and group psychology. Here we become responsible to and for our tribe and our times, acting for the greater good of the whole rather than just looking out for ourselves. The sequence Justice, Hermit, Wheel of Fortune, Strength, Hanged Man, and Death puts us through the experiences we need to find our moral structure, our rules for living, and our aspirations for this life. This septenary culminates in the Temperance card, the Art of Healing, where we regenerate and restore what was lost from human potential due to our "fall from grace" so long ago.

The third septenary is the circuit of deification or apotheosis, where the Self becomes assimilated to the Great Beings of the expanded Cosmos. The sequence Devil, Tower, Star, Moon, Sun, and Judgement shows the larger-than-human forces the human soul has to conquer to win its immortality. This septenary culminates in at-one-ment with the Virgin of the World, Sophia, who is also the Matronit, Wife of God and ultimate Great Mother. The goal of the whole sequence is to become assimilated to the source again, to the point where "to be born or not to be born" is transcended, and exististence at all is existence in all.

• *Numbers: The Decave*

Another internal esoteric structure to be found within the Major Arcana is the embedding of the ancient Mystery of the Decave into both the Major and the Minor Arcana (see the chapter on the Minor Arcana as well). The divinity of the numerals one to ten is a long-established feature of the Mysteries. The Egyptians surveyed their fields and squared out their temples and homes with a thirteen-knotted string rather than manhandle the sacred numerals with addition, subtraction, multiplication or division. The Hebrews fitted their ten-based number system into their alphabet, making each word a number and an astrological spell as well as a name.

The Greeks and Hebrews are known to have studied each

other's alphanumeric systems in Alexandrian times. It should come as no surprise that the Arcana were constructed with the intention that a one-to-one identification be drawn between the Greek and Hebrew letters/numbers and Tarot Arcana which are numbered in single digits.

The Tetractys (see Minor Arcana chapter) expresses another revelation of this same Decave mythos, and there is every reason to place those same Arcana into that glyph with a rightful expectation of significance. You can easily see the symmetry between the Numbers 1-10, the Arcana 1-10, their stations within the Tetractys diagram, and their stations on the Tree. This is deliberate, not an accident.

So even though there are twenty-two Major Arcana in all, the first ten are customized to play this double role, just as the stations of the Kabbalah Tree of Life do, to embody and reflect this ancient reverence for the principles behind the first ten numbers.

• The Hebrew Letters and the Tree of Life

The arrangement of the Hebrew letters on the paths of the Kabbalah Tree was established in antiquity when the manuscript Sephir Yetzirah was formalized around the second century AD. The Hebrews had alphabet mysteries before this time (see Hebrew Kabbalah chapter), but the Tree did not appear with named Sephira and paths until this manuscript. The connection between the letters, their number values and their placement on the paths of the Kabbalah Tree persisted unchanged in history from 1800 BC to the Middle Ages, when the Ari began to speculate about the consequences of "the fall" (see below). Even then, it was only the pattern of the paths that was changing, not the letters and their associated numbers.

Whenever the Tarot Arcana have been associated to Hebrew, Greek or any set of magical letters derived from those two alphabets, one can expect those path numbers to carry over unchanged to the Arcana, giving the paths definite images to which they would innately belong.

A glance at page 30 of Aryeh Kaplan's great work *The Sephir Yetzirah* will illustrate the original ordering which the ancient Hebrews kept among themselves from ancient times, and which was recently reaffirmed in the 18th century by the Gra, also known as Rabbi Eliahu, Gaon of Vilna. This pattern is dictated very specifically in the *Sephir Yetzirah* text, with careful attention to detail.

We seldom see this form in modern occult literature or on Tarots of the last five centuries, however. This is because, from the 10th century AD forward, differing variants slowly crept into the tradition, some of which Kaplan suggests were released with deliberate errors to befuddle the ignorant.

In Kaplan's own words, "Since the Gra Version was considered the most authentic by the Kabbalists, this is the one that we have chosen. . ."(p. xxiv). Because in this book we are focusing intently upon the ancient tradition in relation to Tarot, we stand with Kaplan in taking this pattern as our baseline from which other patterns diverged over time.

Two modern decks have taken up the correspondences as outlined in Aryeh Kaplan's *The Sephir Yetzirah*. The first is El Gran Tarot Esoterico from Spain, and the second is

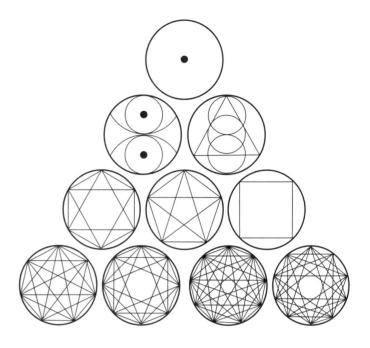

TETRACTYS

Tarot of the Ages, published in America. The Esoterico has the distinction of having been commissioned by cardmaker Fournier on the six hundredth anniversary of Tarot in Europe and has the look of an old Marseilles Tarot "with a twist." The Tarot of the Ages has Alexandrian-looking Major Arcana and fully illustrated Minors. They seem to have appeared unbeknownst to each other, the first in 1977, the second in 1988. One can think of these as our two truly Hebrew Tarots (see "The Spanish School").

More research is needed to "type" the details on the Marseilles-based Major Arcana of El Gran Tarot Esoterico, although they are intensely suggestive of the ancient Hebrew Goddess mythos as chronicled in Raphael Patai's wonderful book by that name. Both this deck's pedigree, and its exact correspondence to the ancient Hebrew astro-alphanumeric infrastructure, cement El Gran Tarot Esoterico in the Tarot canon as an authentic representative of the Hebrew Gnostic Tarot tradition, parallel in importance to the Alexandrian/Hermetic stream, the Etteilla decks or the Marseilles Tarots.

• Christian Cabbalah: A New Set of Correspondences

When the Ari (title of the Rabbi Isaac Luria, late 1500s) set out to make sense of the Zohar in light of the older, idealized Gra format, he was attempting to explain to his followers how we humans had become trapped in our bodies, alienated from heaven and our original selves. This is the point when the planetary attributions of the Sephiroth become concrete, in response to the belief that the human soul is now caught in the karmic web woven around us by the planets. Now that the abyss has opened at Da'at, it is nearly impossible for the fallen and divided soul to return to the primordial state of the supernal triangle. I have taken the liberty of placing Saturn at Da'at, as I think the ancients would have, to express humanity healing from the Fall.

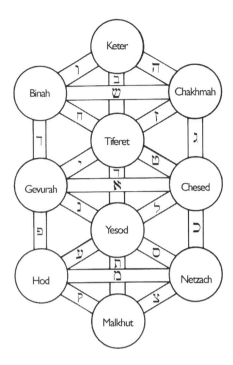

THE GRA TREE

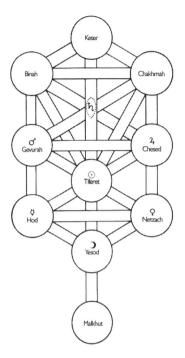

THE ARI TREE

As Rabbi Luria speculated and studied the versions and explanations available to him, he was inspired to alter the paths on the Tree to reflect the whole creation's tragic "fall from grace" after the sin of Adam as detailed in Genesis. From his time forward, various asymmetries can be seen in the Tree diagram, as the later Hebrew philosophers grappled with the consequences of living in this imperfect world. They were also attempting to deal with considerations raised by the Zohar, a thirteenth century addition to the Kabbalah canon, which forced extensive adjustments to the original Sephir Yetzirah pattern (see the chapter the Hebrew Kabbalah). This new pattern was eventually responsible for the creation of Christian Cabbalah through the esoteric insight of Athanasius Kircher.

Linking the Systems

As we compare these crucial Hermetic diagrams, we can see how that shift on the Tree made possible the late Renaissance synthesis by Kircher. This was then handed down through the Secret Societies, appearing more visibly on the Tarot cards after the persecutions of the Church died down in the 18th century.

We know from the Gnostic myth (see chapter on Gnostic Tarot) that when the Shekhina is displaced from her original seat (at the heart spot in the Gra pattern), the upright heart and pelvic triangles turn downward, and Malkuth is shoved out on its own, below the others. In other words, the Shekhina takes residence in The World, Malkuth, and dwells

with her creatures instead of the Creator. From the myth of the Matronit, we know that the departure of the Divine Con-

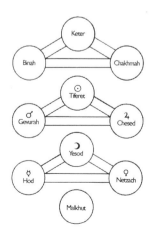

THE UNFALLEN HUMAN

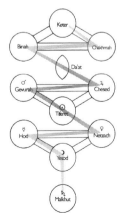

THE LIGHTENING-STRUCK TREE

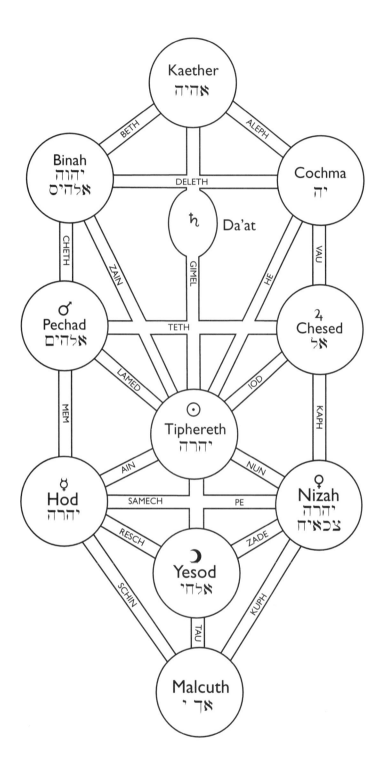

OUR ADAPTATION OF KIRTCHER'S TREE
(WITH SATURN AT DA'AT)

sort makes Jehovah cranky, and leads to difficult times for the people. The Hebrew nation had been celebrating the Sacred Marriage every Shabbat for thousands of years to assist in the reunification of the Goddess and the God, but the world has not mended yet.

No doubt mystics who contemplated this situation were looking for teachings and techniques to begin the process of mending the breach. The problem mythologized by the fall of the Shekhina away from the Supernal Triangle corresponds to an ancient Creation moment when matter was externalized from spirit and the link between them was broken. A discontinuity broke the order of the emanations (the Sephiroth), creating a hole called "Da'at" in the pattern of the Tree and dropping the Goddess out of heaven. How would a Renaissance Magi construct the solution?

Piecing It Together

Compare and contrast the Wheel of the Zodiac diagram (on page 121) with the Kircher Christian Cabbalah Tree diagram below. They have a central theme in common, which is the ancient rulership pattern that links the Planets to the Signs in the Zodiac, as detailed above.

By looking back and forth between this rulership of the zodiac figure and the Kircher Christian Cabbalah Tree, you can see that the Tree diagram holds within it a wheel of Planetary Sephira ranged around the Sun at Tifareth. Drawing a spoke between Venus and the Sun, and another from the Sun to Mars, links the same planetary pairs that are joined in the rulership diagram. (Mars and Venus together cover the rectangle of Aries/Scorpio/Taurus/Libra.) A similar spoke exists between Jupiter, Sun and Mercury on the Kaballah Tree (Jupiter and Mercury rule the Mutable Square in the rulership diagram).

The only unmatching correspondence between the Astrological Wheel and the Tifareth wheel is the fact that Kircher placed Saturn upon Binah in the Supernal Triangle instead of on the Middle Pillar, where it would complete the pattern. If it were placed either at Malkuth or at the throat station, you would then have Moon, Sun and Saturn all conected along the Middle Pillar, just like they are up the center of the astro-rulership diagram. I submit that the post-Ari Christian Cabbalah stations of the Middle Ages Tree are constructed to reflect this ancient rulership diagram.

In light of the Hebrew tradition that precedes the appearance of the Renaissance magi, it seems obvious that the placement of Saturn on Binah is in error. Frances R. Yates, in her masterful tome *Giordano Bruno and the Hermetic Tradition* (p. 100, footnote 3), indicates that this misattribution was made by Pico della Mirandola in the late 1400s. He was probably copying Irenaeus, a 2nd century anti-Gnostic Christian who was not likely to have been vouchsafed the secrets of the Kabbalists of his time. This error has apparently stood uncorrected since. (Following the logic of the Hebrew Kabbalists on this matter, we would find Saturn with the fallen Matronit at Malkuth, where she awaits redemption and restoration through a rise to Da'at. (see The Christian

Cabbalah chapter).

The Wand of Hermes

The relationship between the Tree and the Planets becomes even clearer when you then look at the Kabbalah Tree's links to the Wand of Hermes. This image, also known as the caduceus, is usually portrayed as a straight rod with two snakes twining around it. Occasionally the snakes are winged. This is yet another symbol, like the Tetractys, that served as an organizing principle in the ancient philosophers'

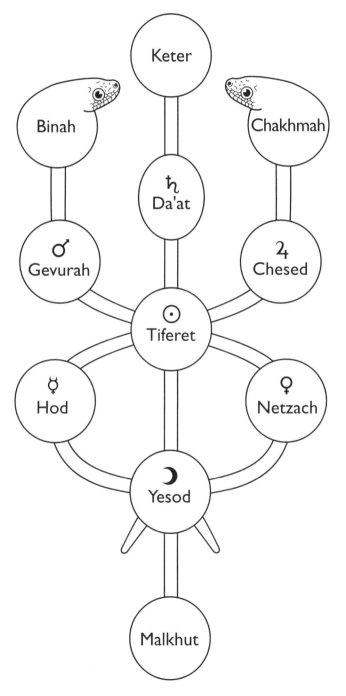

HERMETIC CADUCEUS ON
THE TREE OF LIFE

thoughts. Looking at the caduceus with the Kaballah Tree overlaid, we see Moses' rod and serpents with the serpents' bodies crossing at Tifareth, dividing the Tree into the Macroprosopus and the Microprosopus, the "upper face" and "lower face" of Deity, as developed by the Hebrews.

The Tifareth wheel, seen in purely Hebrew terms, shows a rotary movement just like that on the Wheel of Fortune Arcanum due to the Mother Pillar's downward attraction toward Malkuth, the Earth, balanced by the Father Pillar's upward longing for Kether, the Unmanifest. But when the caduceus is overlaid, one sees a new and more sophisticated kind of movement, more suitable to express the interplay of yin and yang around the center pole of androgyny (again, made up of Malkuth, Moon, Sun, Saturn and Kether). The two complimentary energies do not remain separated, each on their own pillar, but intertwine across the hub of Tifareth. The top of the Father Pillar is the head of the yang serpent, whose tail wraps around Hod to end in Malkuth, while the top of the Mother is the head of the yin serpent, who wraps around Netzach to end at Malkuth.

Each serpent is unique in its Supernal Triangle origins, but they each show seemingly opposite characteristics in their material extension at the bottom of the Tree. This pattern portrays the inverse reflection between "above" and "below," the mirror-image effect that happens when the soul falls "through the looking glass" from supernal or eternal reality into the material or reflected world, or inversely, rises up to transcend the ego and merges with Higher Self. The caduceus, symbol of the Hermetic Gnosis, comes from the same tradition as the Rulership Diagram showing the ascent and descent of souls on the Ladder of Lights. The Kabbalah molecule, the Wheel of the Zodiac and the caduceus are all that same Ladder, and we can only wonder at the marvelous minds who were able to design this interlocking mystical puzzle.

Flash Cards of the Mysteries

Now that we have investigated the layers of the Mysteries in relation to each other, we can see the place of the various "schools" of Tarot in the transmission of those Mysteries. The El Gran Tarot Esoterico relates the Arcana to the pre-fall state of the Original Human, so it and the Tarot of the Ages give us instructions from the point of view of our immortal origins. One could most properly use them with the path-

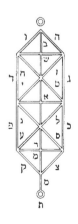

THE PATHS DEFINED BY THE GRA,
(WARSAW 1884, TAKEN FROM
KAPLAN'S SEFER YETZIRAH)

pattern on the cover of Aryeh Kaplan's *The Sephir Yetzirah*, as that pattern was proposed by the Gra at the same time as he restored the letter-to-planet correspondences. The unique feature of this Tree is that it closes the gap at Da'at without drawing Malkuth back up into the diagram. (See Hebrew Kabbala chapter).

The entire Continental group of Tarots, from the reformed Marseilles of the 1600s through Etteilla, Levi, Papus, Wirth and all others who follow either the "old Alexandrian" correspondences or Levi's subtle adjustment, are designed for the work of the Christian Cabbalists, who would be basing their theurgic rituals on the model inherited from the Renaissance magi (see the Christian Cabbalah chapter) and codified by Kircher. These are the Tarots that partake in the confluence I have detailed in this essay.

Tarots that have departed from this order or were never created in respect of it, cannot be used esoterically with the fullness of the decks created between 1660 and the late 1800s. For whatever reason, they lack the interior architecture we have explored above. Because of this, modern "esoteric" Tarots have had to work extra hard to justify their "corrected" systems. They have parted company with the Renaissance magi who gave us esoteric Tarot.

Now You Have Eyes To See

Whenever I examine a new esoteric Tarot, these are the kinds of tests I put its correspondences through. I look to see if the creator is in touch with these bedrock alignments which are built into the interior structure of the Hebrew alphabet, the Kabbalah molecule, the numerals, the astrological rulership pattern and the Arcana. I hope to see that all the internal linkages hold up—that if the deck shows Hebrew (or Greek) letters linked to signs and planets on the Major Arcana, then this symmetry between systems is held sacred. Of the Tarots available today, only those of the Continental Esoteric Schools (including the decks mirroring the *Fratres Lucis* manuscript) and the (unscrambled) Etteilla Arcana pass this test, although most of the very earliest handmade and woodblock Tarots can be used as if they were aware of these connections. Certainly since the "reform" of the 1660s (see "The Continental Tarots"), Tarot has been an esoteric document with a developed body of correspondences, and quite likely this has been true since its beginning.

For better or for worse, the modern Tarots with their reinterpreted correspondences are not representing historical Tarot, other than just the history of the twentieth century. I include here the Spanish decks taking off from Maxwell, the Golden Dawn group of Tarots, the BOTA Tarot, the Egypcios Kier and my very first real deck, the Church of Light Tarot.

These decks or "schools" of decks have all moved on from the Renaissance paradigm of Christian Cabbalah, much less the older tradition of Hebrew Kabbalah. In all cases, the "corrections" to the ancient interlocking system undermine the position of Arcana within this family of related paradigms. This will be true of every other New Age attempt to reinvent the alphanumeric-astrologic connections of old, unless it is grounded in a thorough knowledge of the longstanding tradition Tarot rests upon. There are only a few ways one can adjust the correspondences without shattering the system, as we have seen.

THE SPANISH SCHOOL

A few years ago, I was very excited to acquire the *Catalog of Playing Cards* from Fournier, the Spanish cardmaker whose archive "must be the most numerous collection of its type in the world." The author, don Felix Alfaro Fournier, grandson of the founder of the press, aserts that his book is "the most complete graphical repertoire of playing cards which has been published to date, with 4,000 illustrations in full color and 2,000 descriptions of packs."

According to Fournier, early mentions of the Tarot in official documents first appear in Spain in the Municipal Archives of Barcelona in 1378. Unfortunately by 1382, card games were being prohibited by decree, first in Barcelona, then in Castile and Turia (Valencia). These warnings from the Church were meant to be taken seriously, following on the heels of the Albigensian crusade, waged from 1208 to 1229 by the Catholic Church against Cathar heretics affiliated with contemporary French and Italian papermakers and printers' guilds. It would not be surprising at all if the savagery and destruction that the Church perpetrated in the south of France a century and a half before had a dampening effect on the industry's freedom of expression in Spain.

The Spanish never stopped playing the card games, however, and instead experimented with and developed a rich artistry in their cards. The Fournier chapter on the Spanish cards shows 923 packs of playing cards just in Volume 1! What it does not show is a single Tarot pack being published in Spain until 1900, the Catalan Taroccos, and that one was a Spanish adaptation of the earlier Etteilla Tarot from eighteenth century France.

Considerable evidence tells us that the Spanish Jewish mystics kept in close touch with their colleagues in France, sharing consensus in interpretation and practice of their common faith. This may have been the reason that a Tarot from France, the Etteilla Tarot, appeared drawn with Spanish art before the Spanish produced a truly original deck of their own.

Just as we do with images from Etteilla's Tarots, we have to take his writings with a grain of salt, too. On the faces of his cards, Etteilla printed various words, numbers, astrological glyphs and Hebrew letters, but they belong to the category of "veils" concealing his true correspondences. He was producing his works in a time when it was still necessary for him to disguise the content so as not to violate the boundaries set by the sources he was using or the oaths he had sworn upon becoming a Mason. In his books about Tarot, on the other hand, Etteilla passed on a body of astro-alphanumeric correspondences which he claims to have received from the *Sefir Yetzirah* of the Jews (see chapter called The Hebrew Kabbalah).

We know now that he was dissembling on this point, because the astro-alphanumeric correspondences he used were actually a variant that had emerged with the Greek alphabet reforms of 600 BC. The confusion created by this misdirection has been a major obstacle that has deprived Etteilla of due credit for his contribution to Tarot history. The correspondences Etteilla published in his books are indeed related to the ancient Gra tradition detailed in *Kabbalah* by Gershom Scholem, but "related" does not mean "the same as." Etteilla was actually teaching the Hermetic/Alexandrian variant, a later product of Pythagorean numerical mysticism. One could think of these correspondences as being Greco/Roman, a later development of the Hebrew pattern, itself derived from the Phoenician of antiquity.

But the Spanish Tarot decks as a whole are not characterized by the Etteilla Tarot alone, borrowed as it is from France and a hundred years old already in 1900. The one truly original Spanish Tarot, which like all others was printed in this century, is El Gran Tarot Esoterico, commissioned by the Fournier card publishing company in 1977 to honor the six hundredth anniversary of Tarot's appearance in Europe. We have described this Tarot in great detail in the chapter called "Holy Blood, Holy Tarot."

El Gran Tarot Esoterico

The Esoterico Tarot could be mistaken for a spin-off of the Marseilles Tarot to an unpracticed eye, but it is loaded with telling detail that links it with very ancient Hebrew legends about the Goddess, Eve, Sophia and the Wife of God (see chapter called The Gnostic Tarot).

Additionally, when the astrological sigils on the Majors and Minors of this deck are analyzed, they correspond exactly to a pattern of astro-alphanumeric correspondences of origin in biblical times. This pattern, called the Gra arrangement of the Sefir Yetzirah, was written down in the first or second century AD, late in history relative to its true age. Evidence of its antiquity can be found in the fact that the Sefir Yetzirah was mentioned by name in the Talmud, which can be traced back to at least 300 BC.

It is also true that Pythagoras, Greek number mystic of the 600s BC, studied with the Hebrews, adapting their number theory to his own. So again history tells us that the roots of this pattern are considerably older than any others, although Marixtu Erlanz de Guler, author of El Gran Tarot Esoterico, was the first to print them on a Tarot deck.

Recent Hebrew scholarship from Aryeh Kaplan's *The Sefir Yetzirah*, published in 1990, highlights the reasons why the Gra version has to be at the root of the Hebrew alphabet mysteries (see the chapter called The Hebrew Kabbalah).

This version has been confirmed in its authenticity and antiquity by no less a light than the eighteenth century Rabbi Eliahu, Gaon of Vilna, whose honorific, "The Gra," was given to this version. Aryeh Kaplan also reminds us that the Sefir Yetzirah is one of the primary ancient astrological texts, which strongly implies to me that its earliest form would have shaped a "world standard norm" from which future traditions would be drawn or against which later redactions (i.e., commentaries) would be contrasted.

Seeing El Gran Tarot Esoterico using the Gra correspondences, and noticeing that it was published two decades before Aryeh Kaplan's definitive research proved the historical validity of its astro-alphanumeric correspondences, made me sit up and take notice! Marixtu Guler, author of the Esoterico Tarot, clearly has her finger on a rich vein of esoteric, occult tradition in this Tarot.

In light of what we now know, that the Etteilla cards were designed to be used with the Alexandrian/Hermetic astro-alphanumeric attributions (despite what he had printed on the cards), it is even more noteworthy that seventy-seven years later, after the Catalan Taroccos had become Spain's "traditional" esoteric Tarot, El Gran Tarot Esoterico would be prestigiously commissioned to represent an even older, more venerable and largely unsung set of attributions. This indicates to me that there was not as homogeneous a situation in the Spanish Secret Societies as on the rest of the Continent.

One impression that is hard to miss with the Spanish playing card decks is that the Spanish culture has been the most multicultural, colorful and open-minded of all the European cultures when it comes to playing card imagery, especially the closer we get to modern times. People from Africa, China, the Middle East and the Americas appear in their native dress, right along with the expected Europeans, often standing for "the four corners of the world" through their suit attributions.

Perhaps we should expect to see this variety since the path that papermaking took to reach Europe was from China via the Arabs, up through North Africa and into Spain. In these Spanish playing card decks, costumes are ornate, the figures are most often caught in various action poses (the Spanish royalty do not sit, unless astride a horse) and occasionally one of the royalty will suggest a Major Arcanum. The King of Cups often looks like a minor pope, while the King of Swords sometimes holds the crossed orb known from the Empress and Emperor Arcana. I am sure more resemblances could be found if we had the full decks to look at, instead of just a few "representative cards" from a catalog.

This multicultural trend continued as new Tarots began to appear in Spain. What the Spanish lacked in Tarots before 1900, they make up for in the late twentieth century!

Modern Spanish Tarots

The first seventy-eight card Tarot published in Spain, as previously mentioned, was the Catalan Taroccos, possessed of every feature that we would expect from an esoteric Tarot,

although in an unusual arrangement. This deck demonstrates detailed and pleasing numbered Arcana inspired by classical archetypes, Hebrew letters, symbols purported to be Egyptian hieroglyphics, and in the case of the Minor Arcana, the faces of both the Catalan and French playing cards.

Starting with this deck, all the Spanish Tarot images show the modifications we have come to associate with the *Fratres Lucis* Egyptian-style pictures first published on the Falconnier Tarot of 1896, as discussed in the chapters The Esoteric Origins of Tarot and The Continental Tarots. Perhaps the Spanish found the Catalan Tarocco uniquely satisfying, despite its unorthodox arrangement of the Hebrew letters on the (reordered Etteilla-style) Major Arcana. Or perhaps they were supplementing their experience with French and Italian Tarots that made their way in from abroad.

We do know from books on Tarot published by Spanish authors at the beginning of the twentieth century, that the Falconnier Arcana (or some other source of Alexandrian-style Major Arcana) had appeared in Spain. We know this because we see their titles listed in a table in Pierre Piobb's *Formulary of High Magic*. This table, and an essay on the Minor Arcana by Eudes Picard, appears in *The Encyclopedia of Occult Sciences*, which was published anonymously in English in 1939. Both Piobb and Picard were originally published in the first decade of the 1900s, and can be found listed in the annotated bibliography at the back of Volume 2 of Kaplan's *Encyclopedia of Tarot*.

In this article on Tarot from the *Encyclopedia of Occult Sciences*, Picard's section is illustrated with the Minor Arcana from the Etteilla Tarot, although the descriptions make it clear that what he was writing about was acutally a deck much like, if not identical to, El Gran Tarot Esoterico. On the table from Piobb, the astro-alphanumeric correspondences given for the Hebrew letters are marked "as given by [Paul] Christian." (This is another reference to the *Fratres Lucis* manuscript that Christian translated and printed for the first time, although the correspondences on those decks are those of the Old Alexandrian stream.) These correspondences are exactly as now used on the Dali's deck and the Euskalherria Tarot today, with one exception. In Pobb's table, #21 is the letter Shin and the Fool Arcanum, and the next is #0, Tav, and the World. Dali and Euskalherria have those swtiched, just as Levi did with the Continental Tarots, putting the World on # 21 with Shin, and The Fool on #22 (or #0) with Tav.

The illustrations documenting these Major Arcana correspondences are made from an unnamed Spanish Marseilles deck. The labels for Arcanum # 21 and #0 are switched compared to their pictures (p. 425), which was probably a typo, but one never knows. Talk about an eclectic mix of influences! With so many themes appearing in the literature about Tarot upon the appearance of the Catalan Taroccos, it is no wonder that no other Tarots were published in Spain for seven decades.

The very next Tarot published in Spain was the "007 Tarot" created for the 1973 James Bond film *Live and Let*

Die. Someone else will have to review that deck, because I have never owned it (I don't like the art, and it is not esoteric either).

The Spanish Marseilles

The Spanish Marseilles emerged in 1975, based on the 1736 Italian-Piedmontese Tarot of Giusep Ottone. We know that the Marseilles family of decks consisted of "esoteric Tarots" not only because of the many artistic references within them to myth and magic, but also from the telltale changes instituted upon the Lovers and the Devil Arcana in the late 1600s (see "The Continental Tarots"). However, most Marseilles Tarot decks do not have any sigils or glyphs that indicate Hebrew letters, astrology signs or other overt occult correspondences. If one were just trusting in the momentum of "tradition" in Spain, one would expect the Spanish Marseilles to have correspondences like the Catalan Taroccos.

But I am inclined to believe that the most common astro-to-Arcana correspondences used in Spain with the Marseilles cards, at least by the turn of the twentieth century, were the ones presented in Joseph Maxwell's posthumous book called *The Tarot*. These correspondences clearly aren't derived from Hebrew sources, but are just as decidedly linked to traditional portrayals of the zodiac, the planets and other mythic figures, partaking more of the nature of European folk associations than true "occult" technology.

I include these correspondences in this essay rather than in the Continental essay because it appears from the available evidence that the Spanish esotericists were the ones experimenting with various versions of the set published by Maxwell, while the French were sticking with those of Levi. One can see a version of Maxwell's correspondences on the illustrations included in The *Encyclopedia of Occult Sciences* (published anonymously in 1939), in the section about High Magic called "The Tarot, the Supreme Symbol." The Marseilles-style Tarot used as illustrations in the *Encyclopedia of Occult Sciences* as illustrations for the essay includes astrology correspondences clearly related to Maxwell's version, published after his death in 1938. Dali's Tarot and the Euskalherria by Marixtu Guler, both mentioned below, also use nearly these exact correspondences.

1976 saw the publication of the Balbi Tarot, a Marseilles offshoot using a body of Arcana/astrology connections that's another variant of Maxwell's system. This deck gives us the most accessible and sympathetic esoteric Devil card (Baphomet) in my collection. Balbi's Arcana present a blended combination of complimentary and clashing colors, creating powerful optical effects when used for meditation and "scrying." They also look very lively when laid out for a spread.

In 1977, on the six hundredth anniversary of the appearance of playing cards in Europe, Fournier commissioned the very first Spanish Tarot, the aforementioned El Gran Tarot Esoterico, created by Marixtu de Guler and rendered by Luis Peña Longa. This is the only Tarot I have ever been able to recommend to my Jewish students, who want a Tarot that will be respected by their rabbis.

The fact that this definitive Tarot also has Minor Arcana that exactly match the essay on the Spanish Tarot written by Eudes Picard in 1908 gives us another assurance that El Gran Tarot Esoterico is not a "fad" Tarot. It would be so helpful if Picard's book, *Manuel Synthetique et Pratique du Tarot* were translated into English with all illustrations reproduced so we could study more about the Tarot situation in Spain at the turn of this century.

In 1980 the English school was represented in Spain with the publication of the Hermetic Tarot by Godfrey Dowson. This Tarot is especially valuable for its inclusion of the spelling and zodiacal degrees of the seventy-two Angels of the Name of God, the Shemhameforesh, drawn from Old Testament sources and invoked through theurgy. Being of the English model, the angels are arranged differently on the suit cards than was traditional from the eighteenth century French decks that introduced them. The images on Dowson's cards seem strangely hallucinatory, and the black-and-white format is a bit ominous compared to the brightness of other Spanish packs of cards.

Also in 1980 the Secrets of Tarot deck was reprinted in Spain following a 1955 first edition in Italy under the title Il Destino Svelato Dal Tarocco (aka the Cagliostro Tarot). This deck presents the Continental School alphanumeric pattern, but with Alexandrian/Hermetic Major Arcana imagery. The images on these Arcana are adjusted to portray more female figures, in the spirit of the Etteilla and the earliest handmade Tarot decks. The pity is, the Minor Arcana look utterly unrelated artistically, having only a little character of their own, and are printed top and bottom with divinatory patter, also like the Etteilla Tarot. I am sure this defect affects the circulation of these interesting Arcana.

The Basque Mythical Tarot followed in 1982, with scintillating designs by Angel Elvira and support material written by Marixtu de Guler. This wonderful deck has undeservedly lapsed out of print, a situation that needs to be rectified due to the artistic and occult value of this unique deck. Ms. Guler also wrote the booklet for the next Tarot to emerge in Spain, the Marseilleise Tarot, which also seems to be unavailable at present. (Is there a Spanish-speaking student of Tarot who can account for the genius of this modern Tarot magus, Marixtu Guler? No doubt the history of Tarot would be greatly enriched if we knew more about her sources, her inspiration and the process she went through to create the monument to esoteric Tarots which comprise her small but powerful collection of decks.)

In 1984 the Universal Dali Tarot emerged, created by the famous artist to please his Russian-born wife's love of the cards. In his Tarot he mostly follows the alphanumeric pattern revealed in the *Formulaire de Haute-Magie*, published in 1907 by Pierre Piobb (a pseudonym of Comte Vincenti) and footnoted as being "according to [Paul] Christian." From this roundabout clue I assume that Dali (and Maxwell) were reproducing a pattern known by Christian to have been common in Spanish esoteric Tarots during the eighteenth century. The Dali Tarot, along with the aforementioned Balbi Tarot, show more alphanumeric relation to Joseph Maxwell's correspondences than to any other version.

Artistically, the Dali Tarot shows a direct correlation to the Royal Fez Moroccan Tarot, which was commissioned in the late 1950s though not published until 1975. Imitating the Waite-Smith Tarot, the Fez Tarot has very similar pictures card for card, replacing the geometrical arrangements of suit symbols that were traditional. In that sense, the Dali could be considered a hybrid Spanish/English/folk Tarot.

An interesting note on the Spanish Tarots is that the deck made by Augustus Knapp and Manly P. Hall in 1929 looks and feels distinctly like a Spanish Tarot except that the royalty are seated. These inspired versions of the Major Arcana display the Pope and the Charioteer in feminine form, like the oldest Gnostic-leaning decks. Yet Knapp and Hall employ the alphanumeric pattern of the *Fratres Lucis* archetypes, which seem to be the avenue through which the Alexandrian correspondences survived in Europe (see The Continental Tarots). This makes the Knapp-Hall Tarot a scholarly splice between the Hebrew Gnostic and the Pythagorean streams coming from antiquity.

A modern Tarot with the Hebrew (Spanish) correspondences of the Gra is the Tarot of the Ages. This looks like a divinitory deck because every one of the suit cards is illustrated with a scene of human experience instead of showing geometrically arranged suit emblems as El Gran Tarot Esoterico does. The Major Arcana look Egyptian (modern interpretations of the Falconnier Tarot), but the astrology is old Hebrew. Nowhere is it explained why this combination of images, correspondences and cultures was chosen, but that is not a defect because all the imagery makes the deck more accessible to beginners. The fact that it matches El Gran Tarot Esoterico, though the two appear to have no direct relation to each other, seems to mean that the world of Tarot is maturing and becoming more scholarly about our traditions, even in decks prepared for the mass market. This is a development we can all applaud!

More could be written on the Spanish Tarot stream, especially as it concerns the cultures of Mexico, and Central and South America. Kaplan's *Encyclopedia* shows that versions of the Alexandrian, Etteilla and Papus Tarots have remained popular among Spanish speakers of the world, despite their lack of commercial impact in North America. More research is needed to put this fascinating and eclectic group of Tarots in proper perspective relative to the larger history of Tarot.

English Letter	Greek Letter	Hebrew Letter (Continental use of Hebrew)	Arcana Number	Gra version Sephir Yetzirah – From ~1800 B.C. El Gran Tarot Esoterico, Tarot of the Ages	Old Alexandrian, 600 B.C. – Hermetic Etteilla, Falconnier Tarot	Continental Tarots ~1880 A.D. Levi, Wirth, Papus	Marseilles, Spanish Tarot Maxwell's correspondences	Pierre Piobb, 1908 A.D. – Spanish Variant #1 Dali, Euskalherria	Balbi, Spanish Variant #2
			0			Fool △	Fool △	Fool ♏	Fool ♏
A	α	א	1	△	△	△	☉	☉	☉
B	β	ב	2	☽	☽	☽	☽	☽	☽
G	γ	ג	3	♂	♀	♀	♀	Earth (♁)	☿
D	δ	ד	4	☉	♃	♃	♃	♃	♃
H	ε	ה	5	♈	♈	♈	☿	☿	♉
V	ς	ו	6	♉	♉	♉	♐	♍	♍
Z	ζ	ז	7	♊	♊	♊	♂	♐	♊
Ch	η	ח	8	♋	♋	♋	♎	♎	♎
T	θ	ט	9	♌	♌	♌	✷	Ψ	Ψ
I	ι	י	10	♍	♍	♍	♑	♑	♑
C	κ	כ	11	♀	♂	♂	♌	♌	♌
L	λ	ל	12	♎	♎	♎	♈	♅	✷
M	μ	מ	13	▽	▽	▽	♄	♄	♄
N	ν	נ	14	♏	♏	♏	♒	♒	♒
S	ξ	ס	15	♐	♐	♐	△ ♋	♂	♂
Ayn	ο	ע	16	♑	♑	♑	△ ♋	♈	♈
P	π	פ	17	☿	☿	☿	♉	♀	♀
Ts	φ	צ	18	≈	≈	≈	♋	♋	♋
Qk	ρ	ק	19	✷	✷	✷	♊	♊	♅
R	σ	ר	20	♄	♄	♄	♏	✷	♐
Sch	τ	ש	21	Fool △	World △		World ♍	World ♉	
Th	υ	ת	22	World ♃	Fool ☉	World ☉ #21			World ♇

TABLE OF CORRESPONDENCES FOR THE CONTINENTAL TAROTS BASED ON GREEK AND HEBREW ASTRO-ALPHANUMERICS

THE ENGLISH SCHOOL

Many histories have been written to clarify the people and events connected to the founding of the Hermetic Order of the Golden Dawn, the most familiar of this century's Secret Societies and source of most of the Tarot decks on the market today. The best of these written works is Mary K. Greer's *The Women of the Golden Dawn*, which details not only the well-known outer events that attended its founding, existence and eventual collapse, but examines the role of the powerful and magical women who have been neglected in previous treatments of the subject.

From personal experience, I know Ms. Greer to be a scholar and a gentlewoman who is evenhanded to the extreme. Most of her published work has been either about the Order or the Tarot decks that have emanated from it, yet she retains her objectivity about their place in the history of Tarot. So it was to her book that I turned first in order to gain an overview of the events that created, and later destroyed, this association of talented, inspired, highly educated occultists who changed the face of Tarot for the twentieth century.

That said, I must add that I could not possibly present these events with a fraction of the understanding that Mary Greer shows. My primary focus for this book has been on the ancient Mysteries that Tarot preserves. Therefore I must leave the fascinating topic of the modern Tarots to future books, where they can be given their due. The goal of this chapter is only to relate in the simplest terms those portions of Golden Dawn history that pertain to that group's treatment of the Tarot Arcana and their body of correspondences to the Hebrew letters, astrology, numbers, paths, angels and the rest of the panoply of Mystery School tradition inherited from our ancient and Renaissance esoteric ancestors.

A curious person can reference plenty of sources to find a fuller treatment of these fascinating artists, magicians and scholars and their tumultuous times. The bibliography of *Women of the Golden Dawn* makes an excellent starting point for your research.

A Brief History of the Golden Dawn

Eliphas Levi made quite an impression on the English Rosicrucians in 1853 when he visited Rosicrucian friends in London. One of those friends, Fred Hockley, decided to send his young apprentice, Kenneth R.H. MacKenzie, to visit Levi in Paris and find out more on the state of Levi's research into the mysteries of the Tarot. The two men visited several times over the course of a few days in the winter of 1861, and MacKenzie took copious notes.

Four years later in England, a Rosicrucian group was formed called the Societas Rosicruciana in Anglia, and it was made up of master Masons only. Kenneth R.H.

MacKenzie was one of its earliest members, along with the Rev. A.F.A. Woodford (co-compiler with MacKenzie of the *Masonic Cyclopedia* published in 1887), W. Wynn Wescott and S.L. MacGregor Mathers. Twenty years later, this same group (minus Woodford) were still associates, between them founding the Golden Dawn.

Even in these early years before the Golden Dawn, MacKenzie was fascinated with Eliphas Levi, so when he went on that visit to Paris in 1861 he made every effort to cultivate a personal relationship with Levi despite their language barrier. In the detailed notes he kept about their meetings, he enthused that theirs was a profound meeting of occult minds and that they shared ideas and compared experiences like old friends.

A decade later he published an article about their meeting in the *Rosicrucian*, the short-lived magazine of the Societas Rosicruciana, describing a number of the subjects they had covered in their wide-ranging discussions. This meeting had taken place before any of Levi's work had been translated into English, so MacKenzie was in effect helping the English Masons and Rosicrucians "discover" the important contributions that Levi was making through his publishing and teaching in France. At the point the article was published, Levi had been the Supreme Grand Master of the Fraternitas Rosae Crucis of Europe (with the exception of England) for over sixteen years already, and was to hold the position for two more years until his death.

Because of their imperfect French/English communications (neither spoke each other's language), the exchange was bound to be a bit inexact. MacKenzie, well known as a creative ritualist and connoisseur of magical codes and cyphers, had wanted to show Levi some correspondences he had worked out for the links between Tarot and the Christian Cabbalah. It is not entirely clear whether Levi was responsive to these ideas or not because the only version of events ever reported was MacKenzie's.

For whatever reason, somewhere in the decade between the meeting and the publication of his article MacKenzie conceived the idea that Levi had intentionally "blinded" the astro-alphanumeric correspondences he used when talking about the Major Arcana of Tarot in his books. This is actually true of Etteilla, an earlier member of Levi's esoteric "lineage" in France, so perhaps this seemed a logical assumption at the time.

But in truth, as we have shown in other chapters, Levi was faithfully reporting the correspondences as they had come down through the Hermetic/Alexandrian writers of the first and second centuries AD, which then were picked up by the Renaissance magi during the Hermetic Revival. Levi did insert one correction into the ancient pattern of correspondences, but it was subtle and did not change the ancient number/letter connections, only two Arcana that were switched between the last two letter/numbers (see "The Continental Tarots").

MacKenzie Devises His Own System

Recalling that MacKenzie, Wescott and Mathers were lodge members in the Societas for years before the Golden Dawn was ever conceived, we probably can assume that they would talk to each other about their studies and their personal spiritual work. It is through this friendly association that Wescott learned of MacKenzie's project of "adjusting" the system that Levi had taught. Eventually MacKenzie's adjustment blossomed into an entire system of his own, but in his lifetime he never shared the details with Wescott and Mathers. It came into their hands only after MacKenzie died in 1886, when his impoversed widow was forced to sell the manuscript to Wescott.

The official story goes that in 1885, after the death of Fred Hockley, (MacKenzie's mentor), a "cypher manuscript" was "discovered" among his personal effects. Because Hockley, the man who first introduced MacKenzie and Levi, was an avid collector of ancient magical texts, the Golden Dawn founders were able to claim they had discovered a cache of esoteric rituals and teachings that seemed ancient, authentic and more accurate than those of the French lodges. Among the papers was found a set of astro-alphanumeric correspondences that appeared to them to correct the "blind" they felt existed in Levi's work.

Three years passed between the "discovery" of the cypher manuscript and the founding of the Order of the Golden Dawn. Ostensibly, in that interval they were translating the manuscript, deducing that it described the workings of a German lodge, gaining permission to convene an English branch of this lodge, and fleshing out the quasi-Masonic rituals for their own use. The first lodge of the new order was founded March 1, 1888.

Let us remember what Dr. Keizer mentions in his chapater "The Esoteric Origins of the Tarot": "The synthesis they created for the Golden Dawn rituals combined Rosicrucian and Christian Cabbalistic doctrine with the kind of layout used on a Masonic floor. The floor and officers represented Sephiroth, and initiation from 0=0 to 5=6 represented the upward ascent from Malkuth to Tiphareth." If we review the essay "The Confluence of the Ancient Systems," we can see what a challenging and sophisticated task they set themselves to.

The Story Comes Apart

Occult scholar R.A. Gilbert eventually managed to see through this myth of origins, revealing that MacKenzie (possibly with the aid of his old friend Rev. A.F.A. Woodford) had superimposed the new correspondences onto the Renaissance Christian Cabbalah model (see Christian Cabbalah) in such a way that they could present the "correction" as another historical tradition. Then, when it came

into the hands of Wescott and Mathers, it was fleshed out into an entire lodge and grade system based upon the new correspondences. In this way, their new Secret Society had genuine traditional-seeming secrets of its own.

The deception was revealed to the rest of the members of the Order of the Golden Dawn in 1900, upon the appearance of an American woman calling herself "Madame Horos." She was passing herself off as the fabled German source of the cypher manuscript, the woman who had supposedly obtained for Wescott and Mathers the charter for their English lodge. Madame Horos presented herself to MacGregor Mathers as having come to help them with their "Isis movement" (the mother lodge of the Golden Dawn was called the Isis-Urania Temple). He formally introduced her to his group, the Ahathoor Lodge, as the very woman who had been their contact with the original German lodge. It is not at all clear why he would do such a thing, as subsequent events show that he knew she was a fraud.

The very day that Madame Horos was introduced to his group, Mathers wrote a letter to Florence Farr, one of the most active of the founding women of the Golden Dawn, denouncing Wescott and calling into question Wescott's avowed connection with the Secret Chiefs of the order. Mathers was clearly rattled, angry and feeling betrayed by the appearance of the impostor Madame Horos, as well as by internal difficulties that were threatening to break up his lodge from within. In the state of mind he found himself in that day, he must have felt he had nothing to lose.

Upon receiving this devastating news, Florence Farr, who was a scrupulously honest soul, meditated on what to do. She formed a seven-member committee to investigate the matter. Together they wrote a letter to Mathers asking him to either prove or disprove these very serious allegations. He refused to answer any questions, pro or con, and dismissed Florence summarily from the Order.

Over the next few years, amidst much acrimony, the Golden Dawn flew into fragments, with each founder accusing the other of intellectual dishonesty of various kinds. MacGregor and his wife Moina Mathers were expelled from the Golden Dawn, Florence eventually resigned, and the movement, so illustrious at the outset, became principally a legend in its own time.

Twelve years after the dissolving of the original lodge, Aleister Crowley, himself a member, published the Golden Dawn astro-alphanumeric correspondences along with their grade rituals and other materials that had previously been kept private. People have responded warmly to the system as set forth by Crowley, so it has continued in use and has spread around the world.

Aftereffects of the New System

The eighteen-year life span of the Golden Dawn is merely a passing hour in relation to the history of Tarot. But in this case, it was a very significant hour. The effort the Golden Dawn undertook to create the impression of having an authentic body of teachings and practices was so convincing and so thorough that they singlehandedly managed to call into question the veracity of the two previous centuries of esoteric scholarship.

How were they able to so convincingly package their version as part of the historical record? For one thing, parts of the cypher manuscript were inscribed upon antique paper, giving it the right look of venerability. Also, its creator used a great deal of the older Christian Cabbalah paradigm that had been inherited from the Renaissance magi and the first and second century Hermeticists. In all honesty, however, the changes the Golden Dawn founders and followers instituted upon the Renaissance model rendered it no longer either Christian or Cabbalah.

Translate and Conquer

The main method used by English esotericists to insert their new version into the historical record was to become the primary translators of Eliphas Levi's works into English. In this way they were able to carefully craft footnotes and explanatory insertions into his works, thereby casting doubt upon Levi when his teachings diverged too far from those that the Golden Dawn was promoting. For example, the preface to the second edition of *The Mysteries of Magic*, a digest of the writings of Eliphas Levi collected by Waite, illustrates the typical commentary laced all through this compilation (available through Kessinger Publishing Co. in Kila, Mont.).

In his preface, Waite justifies the new ordering he has imposed upon Levi's writings. Waite abandoned the one-chapter-per-Arcanum structure which Levi favored in his magical writings, and which Levi's students felt "cast great light upon the mysteries of magical interpretation." Waite counters with these remarks: "While I in no way deny that there is weight in this objection from the Kabbalistic standpoint, I submit that the great light mentioned exists mainly for those who are in possession of the true attribution of the Tarot keys, which attribution neither was nor could be given by Eliphas Levi in writing". (p. xiv-xv).

Furthermore, Waite complains that he has "incurred . . . some unpopularity for a time among extreme occultists by tabulating a few of the discrepancies and retractions which occur in the writings of Eliphas Levi, and are either typical of different stages in the growth of his singular mind, or difficulties willfully created for the express purpose of misleading the profane." He means us, dear reader; Waite says that Levi is willfully creating difficulties for us, the profane.

He continues: ". . . it is rather generally admitted by those who consider themselves in a position to adjudicate upon such matters, that Eliphas Levi was not a 'full initiate,' a fact which might account naturally for his occasional deflections from the absolute of infallibility." In light of what we now know about Levi's Supreme Grand Mastership of nearly twenty years, about which Waite was fully aware, I just wonder what accounts for Waite's "occasional deflections from the absolute of infallibility"? "Those who consider themselves in a position to adjudicate upon such

matters" must be Waite's own cronies and students.

In Levi's *The Key of the Mysteries* as translated by Crowley (published in 1959 by Rider & Co.), we reach a segment where Levi wants to talk about the construction of the Hebrew alphabet according to its three divisions—the three mother letters, the seven double letters and the twelve single letters. Levi had just launched into the line "Now, this is what we find in all Hebrew grammars" when we run into a footnote by Crowley. His insertion reads, "This is all deliberately wrong. That Levi knew the correct attributions is evident from a manuscript annotated by himself. Levi refused to reveal these attributions, rightly enough, as his grade was not high enough, and the time not right. Note the subtlety in the form of his statement. The correct attributions are in Liber 777—A.C." Crowley makes it sound as if Levi kept a private list of the Golden Dawn's "correct attributions" which he could not share "because his grade was not high enough." Or is Crowley perhaps implying that the cypher manuscript contains Levi's annotations? Absurd! Note the subtlety of the form of *his* statement!

Following is a quote from W. Wynn Wescott in his preface to *The Magical Ritual of the Sanctum Regnum Interpreted by the Tarot Trumps, Translated from the Manuscript of Eliphas Levi* (this too is available through Kessinger): "The twenty-two Tarot Trumps bear a relation to numbers and to letters; the true attributions are known, so far as is ascertainable, to but a few students, members of the Hermetic schools: the attributions given by Levi in his *Dogme et Rituel*, by Christian, and by Papus are incorrect, presumably by design. The editor has seen a manuscript page of cypher about 150 years old which has a different attribution, and one which has been found by several occult students, well known to him, to satisfy all the conditions required by occult science" (p. ix).

We can guess who those "several occult students" are. And in these few sentences, we can see the device by which all Levi's writings as well as those of his published followers, each scholars in their own right, are called into question—on the "prior historical claim" of the cypher manuscript, which they each knew was a fake as they were writing those footnotes! This was not a simple misunderstanding among friends. Wescott, Waite and Crowley are not saying "we like our correspondences better" or "there are other versions than Levi's". No, they are saying that Levi and his followers deliberately misinformed their public, and the English fellows have "the correct attributions," known only to "full initiates" like themselves.

These quotes are just the tip of the iceberg, I assure you. I have read many translations through the years and have never encountered a phenomenon like this anywhere else. In the innocence of my first studies in the 1970s, I could not understand why a person would bother to translate a book if they felt the author was a humbug! Little did I know the issues—and the egos—that were involved.

I possess two books written by Levi that were translated by W.N. Schoors and published by Weiser in the 1970s, *The Book of Splendours* and *The Mysteries of the Qabalah*. These volumes do not have all the extra commentary, so annoying and disparaging, that is found throughout the books translated by the English group. I would hope that future printings of these earlier translations will include a disclaimer about the commentaries, so that sincere students reading them in present and future times don't have to wade through the thicket of "attitude" without a context.

A Lesson For The Future

To me, the real cause of the propagation of erroneous esoteric history is the fact that the English-speaking world, as a rule, does not feel the need to research what our "experts" tell us about the Tarot. William Wescott published several books before he cofounded the Golden Dawn, and in them he actually reveals the Hermetic/Alexandrian correspondences, presenting them without guile in their proper historical context. But few people compare those books with the Golden Dawn version and notice that the story had changed. Mathers had published a booklet in 1888, on the eve of the founding of the Golden Dawn, referring to the French Occult Tarot and employing the sequence and enumeration taught by Eliphas Levi. No one inside the Order seemed to question how different the Golden Dawn sequence was from the Continental mode. Aleister Crowley dropped many hints to lead his readers to the writings of Levi (which he, Wescott and Waite worked hard to translate into English), but very few people bother to look Levi up and read him for themselves. I am assured as well that Waite encouraged his students to look beyond his writings to see the truth for themselves, but most lay readers would not have the knowledge or motivation to question the legacy left by these turn of the century esotericists.

I encourage you to acquire and read the English translations of Levi's works that are currently available, but if you do, be prepared for the fierce editorial commentary if the translator is affiliated with the Order of the Golden Dawn. Occasionally these translators will grant him a point, but the overwhelming impression is that Levi was not the magus he was thought to be. To achieve the true value from Levi's work, one has to learn how to read through this overlay, which seems also to have been carried over into those works of his which are currently available on the Internet.

Another way to finally clear up all this controversy would be for a non-aligned scholar of the Secret Societies to publish a book detailing the change of relations which emerged between the Continental lodges and the English ones. Such a project could also address the emergence of the modern Spanish school of Tarot, which also appeared at the turn of this century. Dr. Keizer mentions the French/English rift in his chapter "The History of Esoteric Tarot," but I am sure a full exposition of the interior philosophical, political and personality dynamics would help us all see those pivotal times in a clearer light.

Tarot Users Who Love Too Much

We in the West may be guilty of loving the fad of Tarot too much and the history too little. Because we crave novelty,

something new and different, we overlook the ancient and long-term traditions that give Tarot its very form and content. Those systems of thought and spiritual practice have not lost their value just because fashions have moved on! As a matter of fact, those most ancient strata of the Tarot mysteries, the Astrology Wheel, the Hebrew Kabbalah and its Hermetic/Alexandrian counterpart, and the astrological angels of the Minor Arcana have been at the foundation of all the Mosaic religions—Judaism, Christianity and Islam. These are truly the Western Mysteries, and they are just as relevant today as in Biblical times.

We also have to be clear about the "magical theory" we are bringing to the Tarot and the operations we might do with the cards. If we believe that these ancient letters, Arcana, numbers and angels refer to something real in the worlds within worlds that is this life, then perhaps the ancient correspondences, either the Hebrew or the Alexandrian/Hermetic, are worthy of study and deep meditation. At least we know that generations of souls have walked this path and smoothed the road before us, working out the kinks and throwing light into the dark night of the soul. We have a developed and profound wellspring of philosophers, artists, magicians and healers to study and emulate in the work of becoming our own God-selves.

Of course there will always be pioneers, those who steer a course into uncharted waters, who refuse to stay between the lines. Innovative souls exist in every generation. We see these characteristics in the founders of the Golden Dawn, who like the Spanish School(s) departed from the Hermetic/Alexandrian model at the turn of this century. Again, perhaps all the questions can only be answered by someone who has cordial relations with all the relevant lodges, someone who can shine a light on the revolutionary tendencies that were shaping Tarot at the end of the 1800s and the beginning of the 1900s.

In the future, let us not be such passive consumers of Tarot but instead take the time to learn about the various systems available so we can evaluate them intelligently. Tarot is such a powerful tool that we should want to know what our options are, philosophically and spiritually. As we create a Tarot culture wherein imagination and inventiveness can be coordinated with the true history of the Western Mysteries, we will see scholarship and innovation become better partners rather than working at cross-purposes, as they sometimes seem to at present.

My hope is that in the twenty first century we can complete the excavation of this intellectual monument and see once again the beautiful architecture of Tarot still strong and true to its Hebrew/Alexandrian/Gnostic/Renaissance roots. This project has only just begun. When we have more fully fathomed this treasure from our ancestors and more correctly apprehended its stature as a spiritual and philosophical vehicle of highest subtlety, we will be better able to evaluate its variations and see their best applications within our lives.

PART IV
PERSONAL APPLICATIONS

THE MAGUS. WOODCUT BY HANS WEIDITZ, FROM FRANCESCO PETRARCH, TROSTSPIEGEL, AUGSBURG, 1532.

HOW TO TELL WHICH SYSTEM WORKS FOR YOU

With all this welter of correspondences, varyances, lineages and their branches, it is easy to become confused and wonder how you might ever determine which Tarot lineage and deck would be the best for you. I myself have never felt competent to decide this for another person, but I have devised several methods which can be utilized by anyone wanting to make their choice based upon more than just whim and art styles. This chapter will furnish a series of tests that you can use on any Tarot that demonstrates signs and planets (and/or Hebrew/Greek letters and/or their numeric equivalents) on the Major Arcana.

What if your Tarot has none of these trappings? In that case you can freely choose which lineage you wish to embrace, and mentally add those meanings to the author's explanations of your cards. Once you have found your "correct Tarot", suited to you for both esoteric and artistic or emotional considerations, there is no end to how accurate and insightful the cards can be for you. The time it takes to examine and choose the right Tarot at the outset of your studies is repaid a thousandfold in terms of serenity, trust and spiritual bonding with your deck. Don't skip this step if you can help it.

I also need to say this before we start this process: it doesn't matter what you have learned in the past about Tarot. It doesn't matter that respectable sources teach that the Emperor is this sign or the Magus is that letter. It doesn't matter what my opinions are about it either. There is more than one correct system, some of them extremely old and venerable, and they each hold a part of our cultural heritage. These processes are undertaken to find the best operative working magical Tarot for *you*, and the results do not prove anything for anyone else. Using these experiments, you will be able to discern to which "tribe" of Tarot mystics you belong!

The Philosophical Method of Triangulation

The program that I first learned in undertaking metaphysical studies is summed up in one word: triangulation. Think about your subject in triangles, as in thesis, antithesis, synthesis. This keeps your mind from polarizing and getting stuck on the opposites, the stage of two-ness.

To triangulate, you need three points of reference: 1) yourself, your viewpoint, your good sense and life experience 2) a known "other" that is fixed, measurable, and relatively unchanging, and 3) your unknown "other", which you are studying. The method is much like the act of judging the size of an animal you are observing in the wild, by

comparing it's height and length to a feature in the background you are familiar with. You are gaining perspective on the unknown by studying it "in the line of sight" of something already known and understood.

Each of the following assesment methods depends upon the use of three ingredients with which to triangulate — 1) your own life experiences and self-knowing, 2) a deck that you can use to provide you with standard, unchanging illustrations for the Major Arcana, and 3) the astro-alphanumeric correspondences of the lineage you want to investigate (this is your unknown variable, taken from the big astro-alphanumeric graph you'll find on pages 118-119).

In some cases you will also use your birthchart as another "standard value," which personalizes the process just that much more. At those times you will be examining these various Tarot usages in the light of your unique personality and destiny, looking for the lineage and deck which most accurately captures your experience and vision for yourself. Even if you eventually come back to the same Tarot you have been using already for years, you will have a new appreciation for the philosophy passing through the generations of Tarot, and you will greatly increase your self-knowledge, your understanding of what you believe and why.

I reccomend that you do these exercises with the most visually "neutral" Tarot you possess, a deck with old-fashioned looking Major Arcana, and suit cards that do not have people on them except for the royalty. That way, you will know that you are not being influenced unduly by emotion-inducing artistic variations as you examine each body of correspondences.

Test One: If Astrology is a Language You "Speak"

If you are comfortable with the signs, planets, and houses of astrology, you have a great head start in determining which Tarot speaks to you especially. Of course you have to determine to which "family" your deck pertains: the Hebrew, the Greek, the Levi variant, Maxwell's Spanish pattern, the Spanish variant, the English version of Waite and Case, or Crowley's variant. They are all on the two-page graph on pages 118 and 119.

That done, separate the Major Arcana out of your Tarot deck, and then sort them again, separating the arcana that stand for the signs from the arcana that stand for the planets. Then put the signs in zodiacal order, starting with *your* ascendant sign. Draw or imagine an equal-house circle of twelve compartments, and starting at the left side of the circle, lay the zodiac out counterclockwise, matching your rising sign with the first house cusp, the next sign with the second house cusp, the next sign with the third house cusp, and so on around the circle. Ignore any interceptions in your astrology chart. This excerise is not that sophisticated, at least on the first try. Just get the circle of the zodiac drawn in arcana, with three cards to each quadrant.

What you have left is the planets (or the seven visible planets and three "esoteric elements", if you're working with the oldest Hebrew or Greek correspondences.) They need to be apportioned to their proper houses, as near as you can replicate the pattern in the birthchart within the equal house format. Sometimes you can't replicate your birthchart in cards exactly without leaving the equal house format behind, so this exercise requres that you bring a little astrological savvy to it for the most complete experience.

The pattern of sign-planet combinations made by the arcana will illustrate your various archetypal functions (planets), utilizing the energies of the signs they occupy, driving the activities of the houses in which they appear. Each esoteric school will change the lay of the arcana around the houses of your chart, and those differences can profoundly impact your "self-talk" and the interpretations of your Tarot readings as you navigate through your life. In other words, you are using your birthchart, and your life experience with it as the "constant" against which you will test each of these Tarot lineages, looking for the deck or family of decks which best supports who you already know yourself to be. There is no profit in turning to a Tarot for advice which has an estranging or offensive approach to your sun, moon, or ascendant sign, for example. You will always feel criticized by a deck constructed that way, and that can eventually drive you away from using your cards at all!

By laying out your chart in each of the "family" modes, you can begin to get some objectivity on your chart. Perhaps you have a pattern of aspects that you have always been bothered by, or that gives you trouble. When you investigate that pattern by illustrating it in Tarot cards, first from one lineage, then from another, what happens? While doing such an exercise you will be discussing with yourself different views you can take on that part of yourself, different ways you can understand the dynamics of that pattern in your psyche and in your life. The contrast between one set of Tarot correspondences and the next will come into high relief when you start taking it personally in the context of your own chart.

Test 2

(Best used by a Kabbalist, or one familiar with Hebrew ideas about the Tree of Life and the human energy-body; or if you do Yoga or Tai Chi or a similar body-centered practice.)

This method requires a little intellectual knowledge just to set up the visualization at the beginning, but once the map is internalized results are in direct proportion to the power of your imagination, the quality of your concentration, and how much time you can make in your life for uninterrupted internal exploration. The meditative context of

this exercise requires a deep interior stillness and keen powers of observation, much like that of the birdwatcher. But the elusive creatures you seek are living their lives just below the threshold of your ordinary consciousness, inside your own psyche! Any flare-up of ego, emotions, or opinions will disturb your perceptions and scatter the objects of your study. The best approach is one of detached awareness and curiosity, with no "agenda".

With this method, you are learning to apprehend and track your energy-body, by moving through it's internal wiring and circuitry. Different traditions will describe the mechanics with different vocabulary (chakras, channels, meridians, Sephiroth and paths), but every tradition has a body of practices which selectively stir up, circulate, and redistribute life force within the practitioner. This is often called The Alchemical Work, and has literally endless variations throughout human cultural history. I choose the Hebrew version because it is intrinsic to the western model of consciousness, upon which Tarot is built.

According to the *Sefir Yetzirah*, the Hebrew alphabet is the roster of sounds (the Holy Word) with which God created the world. The letters relate to the pathways between the ten great energy-centers of the Tree of Life. This Tree with its centers and paths is repeated in microcosm in every human body and when we can get ourselves back in touch with it's fullness, tradition says we can live the life of the Divine Human. This is in essence the Kabbalist alchemical quest, to order one's energy along the divine pattern as given in the *Sefir Yetzirah*.

This alphabet exists or was created in three movements, with three different kinds of letters. The first sounds, called the "Mother Letters," are Aleph (A), Mem (M), and Shin (Sh). Within that understanding, these first three letters fall into the three horizontal levels in the body; the level between the left and right eyes, the level made by the shoulders, and the level described between the left and right hipbone. (See illustration page 53.)

Start your meditation by installing the Major Arcana representing these three letters into the relevant planes of your body. This is probably best done while seated, as this can become quite a long excercise. Once you start adding in the next and subsequent steps each in their order.

The next group of letters given in the Hebrew alphabet were called the "double" letters, because they each are written, sounded, and enumerated differently depending upon whether they appear in the middle of a word or at the end of it. These letters represent the planets, each of which has both a natural foreward motion in space, and a distorted appearance of backwards motion when it occasionally contacts the sun along our line of sight. In the energy-grid of the Kabbalah, the planets fall in along the vertical bars, two spanning the Sephiroth of the Mother Pillar, two uniting the Father Pillar, and three linking the Sephiroth on the Middle Pillar. Feel the Pillars holding up your physical, emotional, and mental bodies with interior chrystaline light. Pay attention to your experience when you place those arcana on the pillars and in the sections where they belong.

Now, upon the framework of the three horizontals you have built the vertical structure, stabilizing Mother energy, Father energy, and the Divine Child created between them. You may like this part of the exercise enough to do it several times just to "feel your parts falling into place" and study your potentials from this point of view.

The final group of cards/paths represents the twelve "simple" letters filling the diagonal paths, representing the signs of the zodiac and the cyclical energies unfolding through the years. Just as in the construction of a building, the diagonal members add strength and stability to the squared-out original framework of verticals and horizontals that came before. They weave a web of cross-links between the pillars, carrying information from the opposites to the middle and vice-versa. With the addition of these paths, whether you study their individual arcana or not, you can begin to experience and experiment with the circulation of your life-force through the regular geometric figure made by these interlocking elements. Continue to study the planets on your pillars "from inside," so to speak.

When you have a good grasp on the Hebrew arrangement, reassemble it in the Greek system of correspondences (switching the arcana on the Sun/Jupiter and Mars/Venus pairs), and "try that on for fit!" And, finally, assemble Levi's adjustment within your body (moving the Fool to #22/Tau and the World to #21/Shin).

The above are the three "schools" or lineages about which I am empowered to teach, and I can vouch for their relative safety for new students. The English system, it's variants, and the Spanish families are better explored with experienced teachers, I think, because they are extremely new systems and, to my mind, still experimental. Given the power of both applied imagination and these ancient archetypes from the collective unconscious, I like to introduce my students to the well broken-in, bedrock tradition before they open themselves to the winds of the unknown!

You can, of course, branch out into imagining and exploring the other ways of associating the paths on the Tree. Eliphas Levi envisioned the human energy-body as comprised of the Supernal Triangle of God-consciousness hovering timelessly above the Wheel, which is constantly churning around the heart, while Malkuth, the Earth, holds firm from below. You can also experiment with the intertwined snakes of the cadeuceus climbing around your Middle Pillar. You can take your energy-body through the consequences of the later permutations of the Tree, the path-patterns which emerged in Spain in the 1300's and later were standardized by Kircher, one of the last of the Renaissance Magi. That will lead you into the Lightning Bolt pattern, which modern occultists use to designate their levels of initiation. Each of these approaches will yield a wealth of customized information for your particular situation if you will "try them on" energetically, meditating and circulating your energy within them. No amount of intellectual studying will give you the insights of the Kabbalists—you have to go there experientially, in very focused meditation.

This is one way you can make your Tarot work for you,

to help you envision the unfolding ideas and schools which have characterized the history of Kabbalah. The arcana provide you with "flash cards" of the constants in Kabbalah — the astro-alphanumeric combinations of letter/astrology/image. El Gran Tarot Esoterico is actually set up perfectly to reflect the best modern scholarship on this subject, but any Marseilles Tarot will do. The different arrangements of the paths linking up the Tree is the variable you are studying. Your direct experience is the fulcrum upon which you balance tradition with innovation across the historical spectrum.

Remember, if you are a Kabbalist or any type of energy-meditation practitioner, you must be ready to live out in your body whatever belief system you study deeply and believe in. If you beliefs are accumulated around your "shoulds" and "ought to's" rather than your true nature and your innate divine pattern, this type of meditation with the archetypes in your interior spaces could provoke surprising, though ultimately healing, dreams and visions. I recommend starting a journal when you begin a series of exercises like these, as a way to affix and concretize the experiences you will have working in this deep interior way.

And as a sidebar, let me mention a special feature in Aryeh Kaplan's *Sefir Yetzirah*, above and beyond the details of the astro-alphanumerics. Kaplan very kindly translates the sections of the *Sefir Yetzirah* which contain a set of instructions for chanting, intoning, or sounding the alphabet, first as single letters, then in pairs, sets and special orders, as part of the traditional Hebrew cultivation of higher consciousness. Those instructions are just as profitable to follow today as they were when first codified so long ago, and when combined with elementary skill in harmonic overtone singing, comprise a wonderful course in occult liturgy. The arcana can be brought in here too, where every letter combination can be viewed in imagary while being sounded and meditated upon simultaneously.

Test Three: If you are an Operative Magician/Priest or Priestess

In this case you might "interview" the different families or lineages of Tarot by just picking out of the Major Arcana the cards corresponding to the sun and your sun-sign, and the moon and your moon-sign, plus any other planets which conjunct sun or moon in your birthchart (that is, if you can hold all that in your imagination at once!) By doing this you highlight what are arguably the most crucial cards of any Tarot deck for you personally. Now you can conduct an "operation", a mass, soul retrieval, or whatever you already do in your spiritul practice, as a context for contacting the energies of these crucial cards. In the context of your sacred space and time, evoke, awaken or embody any one or any combination of these archetypes you have singled out, and in the course of the experience you just might intuit what sort of influence those archetypes would exert upon you if you allowed them to became your standard values.

By putting this investigation in the form of a sacred ritual, you delineate boundaries to contain the energy you are studying, using the strength of your already-established spiritual connections to keep the experience positive and uplifting. By ritually calling in your allies and helpers and the benevolent forces of the universe, you have protection to help you filter out negative suggestions should they come up through the lineage you are studying. Remember, this exercise, like the first, is personal — about yourself and who you are in your internal mythos and symbolism. It is not as abstract and universal as the Kabbalah excercises are, or others that follow, so the tendancy to emote and let opinions color your reactions is always there. Do not either edit these responses or judge them, as they contain in their natural state the very information you are seeking, namely "how do these energies impact me in my innermost being"?

You may find with one or another version of your sun and moon energies, that you are having a reaction that reminds you of primal relationship struggles or ethical tangles you have experienced in the past. Use the ritual context as an opportunity for forgiveness and healing of those old, unfulfilling patterns, and recognize that you should probably not use that deck or group of decks for yourself at this time. Next time, ritualize with a different combination. Remember to keep a journal, so your breakthroughs can remain in consciousness for when you really need them!

I like this approach because it is so personal, since you consciously acknowledge *how* you want your Tarot to speak to you about yourself. There is no "should" here that will fit everybody across the board. This process is an entirely unique experience for each Tarot user, and I daresay that as you are experimenting with different combinations of the arcana, searching for the most authentic expression, you will also be in a way "trying on" different personas and self-images. Your intuition will be working to portray through each combination of arcana, the probable future awaiting you if you accept that version of yourself.

You may also come to understand better why people tend to see you in the light they do, or make certain assumptions about you, or use you in certain standard ways in their personal dramas. You will quite likely come away with a new respect for how we are all complex enough to have more than one possible "self". I have had many students become astounded to realize that every different possible combination of sun and moon cards was relevant to them at a different stage in their lives. The trick is to decide what deck is relevant *now* in your life! And to forgive and bless those other versions of you, ones you may have previously been through and outgrown, or ones that have not yet come up for you in this lifetime, without being judgmental towards yourself or the cards. The goal here has nothing to do with right or wrong, and everything to do with authenticity and acceptance of your true divine nature right now.

Test Four: The Method(s) of the Philosophers

The word "philosopher" is made up of two root concepts; philo=lover of, and soph=Sophia, the wisdom principle of the ancients, imagined as a Goddess, the feminine mate of the Old Testament God. So a philosopher is one who so loves the ancient wisdom that s/he is happy to contemplate wisdom, seek wisdom, practice wisdom, and otherwise be involved with the principles of wisdom every day and in every way. For such a soul, ordinary pleasures no longer satisfy. The philosopher longs to replace the mundane thoughts in her head with the immortal thoughts of wisdom, sacred to the ages. Such people want to order and refine their aboriginal human nature with the help of wisdom, rather than just "coast" with the qualities they started this life with.

Pursuant to this goal, a traditional philosopher will attune his or her consciousness to a transcendant ideal, something permanent and unchanging, which then gives the ebbing-and-flowing mood swings of the personality and ego a centerpost around which to constellate. Traditionally, this ideal was more often a phenomenon such as the marking of the seasons on the wheel of the year, or the abundant fertility of the Great Mother, rather than an abstraction like "faith" or "belief". Our ancestors were nothing if not practical!

In the Western classical tradition, one such universal constant was derived from the changeless mathematical and geometrical properties of the whole numbers 1-10. This teaching was summarized by Pythagoras, a Greek philosopher of the 7th century BCE, into a compact and revealing little glyph which he called the Tetractys. In it are represented the geometric figures created by each ascending whole number inscribed within a circle, and they are arranged to fill a wedge or pyrimidal shape with 1 at the top, resting on 2 and 3, resting on 4, 5, and 6, resting on 7, 8, 9, and 10.

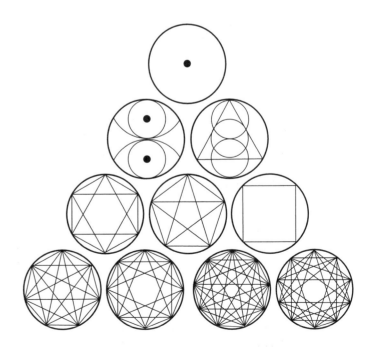

THE TETRACTYS

The Tetractys is a worthy object for the work of contemplation upon as an ideal, because it accurately represents the process by which the laws of number and frequency play out all through nature and cosmos. As the numbers increase in volume from digit to digit, they descend in purity from the heights of oneness to the depths of complexity. Many insightful teachings are built into this figure. The philosopher is rewarded for her efforts of contemplation with wordless insights delivered by Nature herself in the immutable language of numbers.

To bring Tarot into the picture, the first ten arcana (beginning with the card that stands for Aleph or Alpha) of the esoteric Tarot you are examining can be laid out in the Tetractys pattern, being sure to note in each case the astrological correspondences (which will be the parts that change from system to system.) Within any of the Tarot families we have examined in this book, the first ten cards will show the Sun or Jupiter card, the card of the Moon, one more planet card and half the zodiac. In this way you can get a good sense of the philosophy of that Tarot author, measured by the universal ruler of the Tetractys.

Once you have familiarized yourself with the Tetractys model in itself, without Tarot values overlaid, then you will become sensitive to the "spin" imparted to the ideal by the application of arcana from the different lineages. You will be able to see the areas where one system or another is accurate to the geometry of the numbers, according to your own experience and inclinations. This sort of "rational analysis", (literally, examination by the ratios of the whole numbers,) is what the ancient Greek mystics used to train themselves in, to reduce their subjectivity and learn to "think like nature." It is an extention of our original concept of triangulation, bur using each of the whole numbers up to ten. As Einstein said, God geometrises, and the Tetatrys is Pythagoras' illustration of that.

Another philosophical device to contemplate would be the natural zodiac, with the planets overlaid in the Ladder of Lights pattern (see illustrations at the end of this chapter, where the universe of each Tarot family is detailed). This model is a condensed version of the Gnostic and Kabbalistic cosmology, not intended to represent any person's chart, but abstracted to show the ancient rulership pattern revealed to the worlds' astronomers in the *Sefir Yetzirah*. In one glance it summarizes the labor a human soul undertakes when once it becomes ensnared by the Wheel of Rebirth.

I have constructed for you the "universe" of each of the schools or lineages of Tarot being examined in this book. There is one extra, blank zodiac for you to use with any decks you may run across, to see what system it follows. When you fill in the positions of the signs, planets, and elements (in modern times attributed to the invisible outer planets) with their corresponding Major Arcana from the deck under examination, you get an instant picture of this group's view of the cosmic order, within which we all live and move and have our being.

This excercise does not specifically emphasize ones' personal constellation of signs and planets, but it does illustrate each lineage's position on the human condition overall, within the larger context of nature and cosmos. It shows that group's general bias about the natural course of the "average" human's life. In that sense, it is a perfect snapshot of that lineage's philosophy, and represents therefore an integral way of examining a Tarot for it's esoteric or occult content. If you cannot make a zodiac of signs and a set of planets out of your Major Arcana, it is just not an esoteric Tarot!

After the Tests Are Over

Once you have chosen your lineage or Tarot family, you often will have several decks from which to choose that reflect those correspondences. It is at this point that aesthetics matters, and it can make quite a difference for some people. I have noticed for myself that an artist's choice of colors will make a lasting impression upon me if I use that deck often or during emotionally charged times. Some Tarots are so blatantly sexist (repeating negative stereotypes or objectivizing the female body) that one may choose to pass these decks over even if the correspondences are perfect. Some decks have such decadent artwork that they are spiritually unhealthy to look at for long. This may be the very deck which all your other Tarot friends love and study, but do not be swayed by peer pressure! Only you can decide on this point.

In such cases it is best to find a handsome printing of the Marseilles Tarot and impose your own best correspondences upon the arcana, rather than to use a deck that hurts your feelings or subtly irritates you every time you look at it! I tend to gravitate to the old-fashoned Tarots with simple geometry on the suit cards, but modern tastes seem to to turning to the muscular, energetic style reminiscent of comic book art, where beautiful specimens of both genders act out the drama of the cards. In any case, pick a deck for what it conveys "between the lines" through the colors, choice of images, and emotional authenticity, as well as for it's occult lineage.

Remember, unless your tastes run to the gothic and the dark, you do not want to be confronted with a pessimistic or bullying deck when your are grappling with life's big questions. You want the art and the sensibllity to be conducive to your emotional and spiritual serenity, to say the least! Disturbing, artistically distorted, way-out Tarots may be fascinating in a creepy sort of way, but I cannot imagine that it is actually helpful or therapeutic to do readings that talk about your inner and outer life with such a slant. So I encourage you to seek far enough afield to find the special deck that truly speaks to you, both intellectually and emotionally. This effort will greatly repay you by making it infinitely easier to form comfortable, openminded associations with the cards as your experience with them grows.

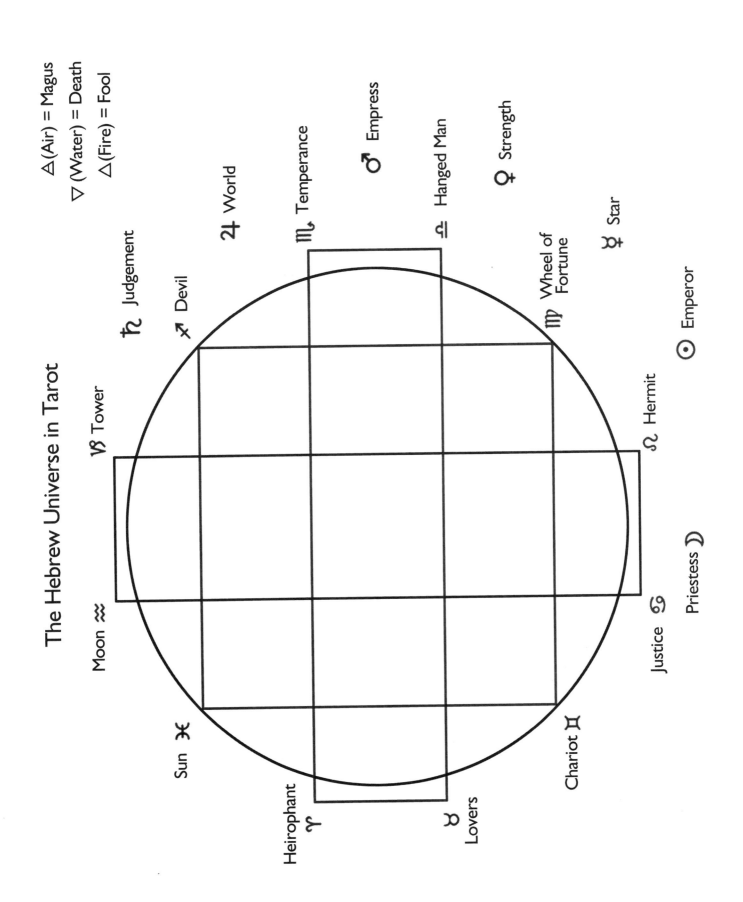

The Hebrew Universe in Tarot

△ (Air) = Magus
▽ (Water) = Death
△ (Fire) = Fool

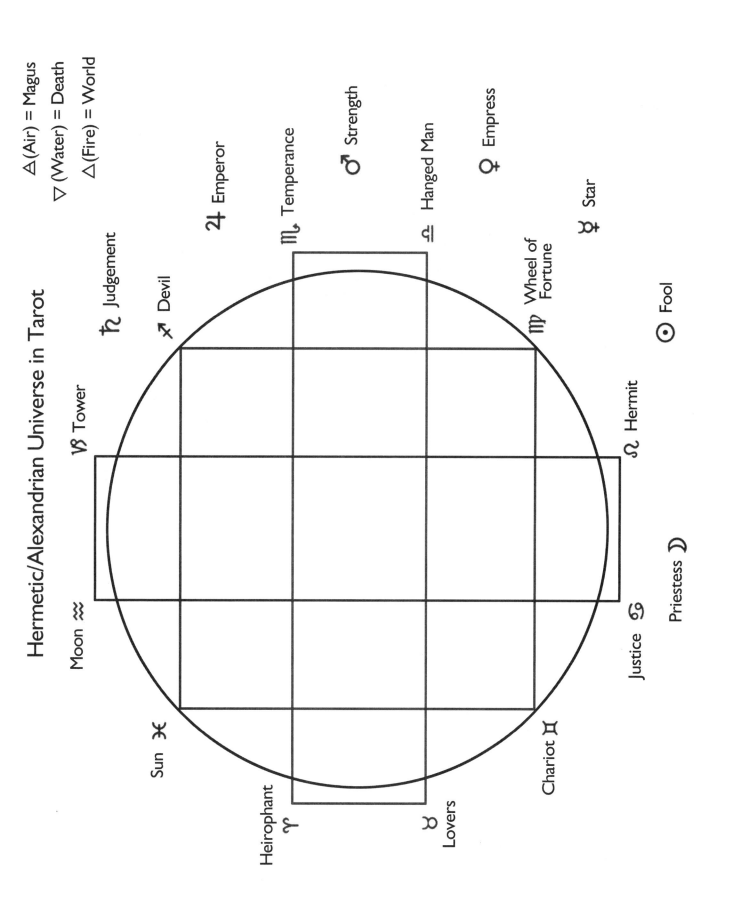

Hermetic/Alexandrian Universe in Tarot

△ (Air) = Magus
▽ (Water) = Death
△ (Fire) = World

Moon ♒

♄ Judgement

♐ Devil

♃ Emperor

♏ Temperance

♂ Strength

♎ Hanged Man

♀ Empress

♆ Star

☉ Fool

♍ Wheel of Fortune

♌ Hermit

☽ Priestess

♋ Justice

♊ Chariot

♉ Lovers

♈ Heirophant

♓ Sun

♑ Tower

Levi and The Continental Scholars Universe in Tarot

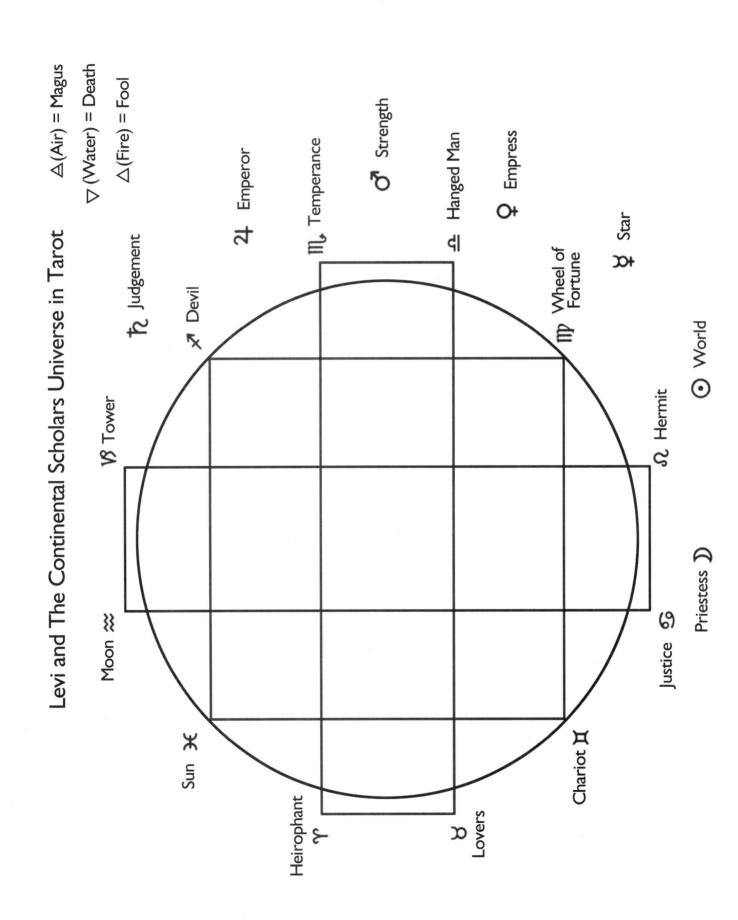

△ (Air) = Magus
▽ (Water) = Death
△ (Fire) = Fool

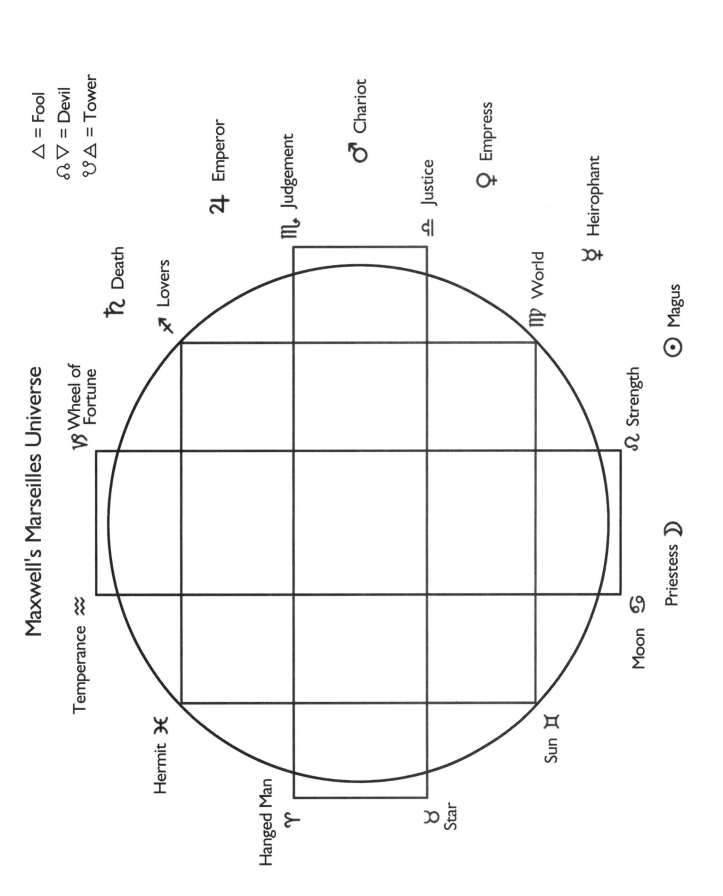

Spanish Variant #1 - Dali & Euskalherria Universe

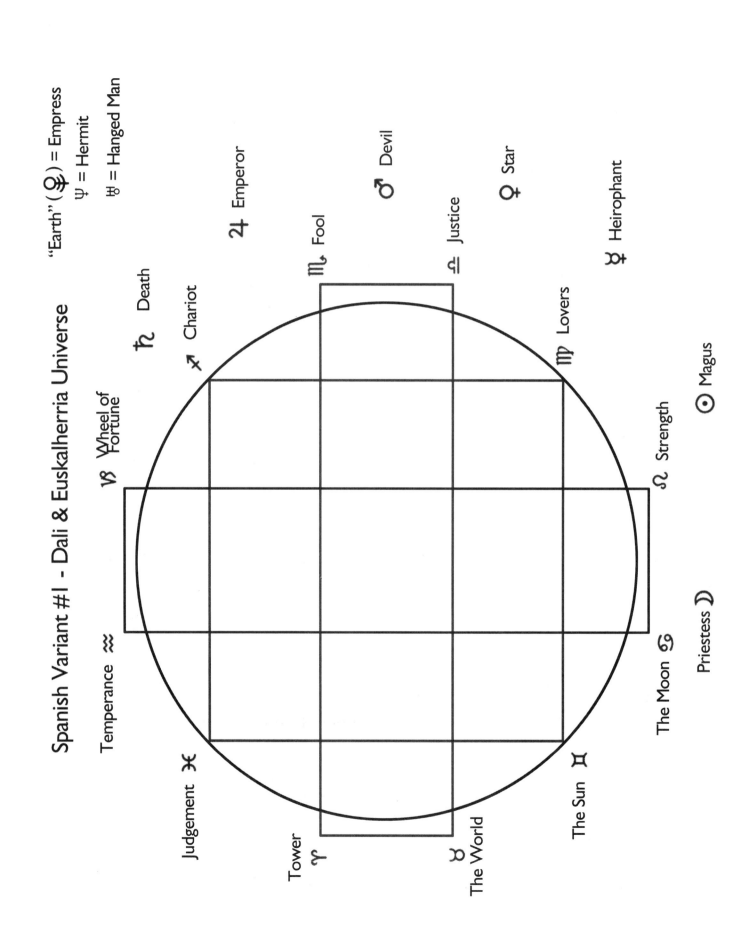

"Earth" (♀) = Empress

Ψ = Hermit

♅ = Hanged Man

♃ Emperor

♂ Devil

♏ Fool

♎ Justice

♀ Star

♉ Heirophant

♓ Death

♐ Chariot

♑ Wheel of Fortune

♍ Lovers

♌ Strength

☉ Magus

♒ Temperance

♒ Judgement

☐ Tower ♈

♉ The World

♊ The Sun

♋ The Moon

☽ Priestess

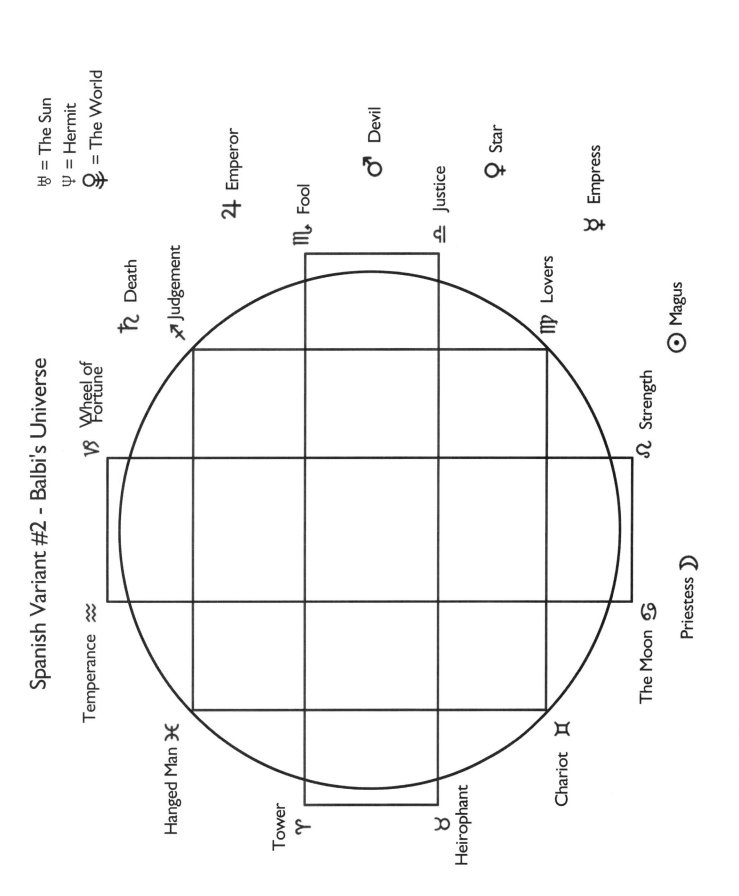

Spanish Variant #2 - Balbi's Universe

♅ = The Sun
Ψ = Hermit
⚵ = The World

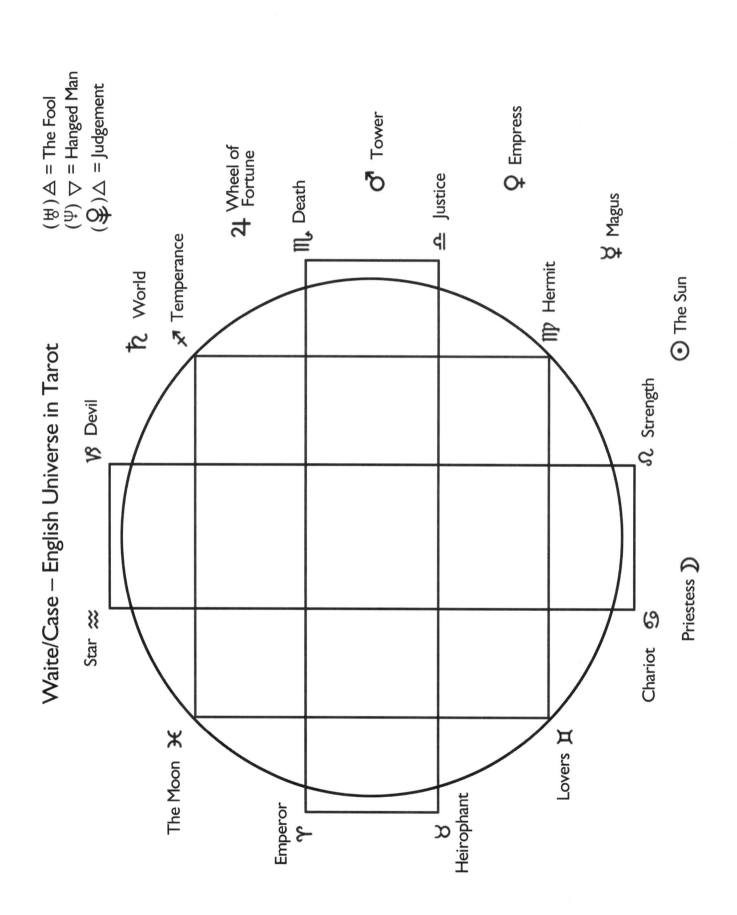

Waite/Case – English Universe in Tarot

(♅) △ = The Fool
(♆) ▽ = Hanged Man
(♀̣) △ = Judgement

Wheel of Fortune ♃
Tower ♂
Empress ♀
Death ♏
Justice ♎
Magus ☿
Temperance ♐
World ♄
Hermit ♍
The Sun ☉
Devil ♑
Strength ♌
Star ♒
Chariot ♋
Priestess ☽
The Moon ♓
Lovers ♊
Emperor ♈
Heirophant ♉

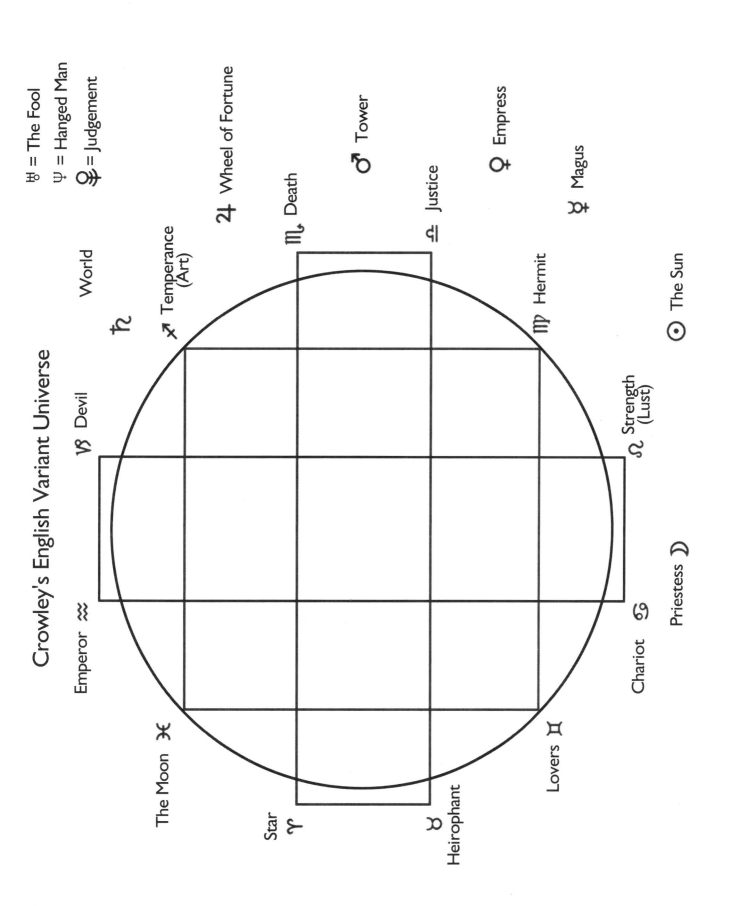

Crowley's English Variant Universe

♅ = The Fool
Ψ = Hanged Man
♇ = Judgement

♃ Wheel of Fortune
♂ Tower
Empress ♀
Magus ☿
Temperance (Art) ♐
Death ♏
Justice ♎
Hermit ♍
World
♄
Devil ♑
Strength (Lust) ♌
The Sun ☉
Emperor ♒
The Moon ♓
Star ♈
Heirophant ♉
Lovers ♊
Chariot ♋
Priestess ☽

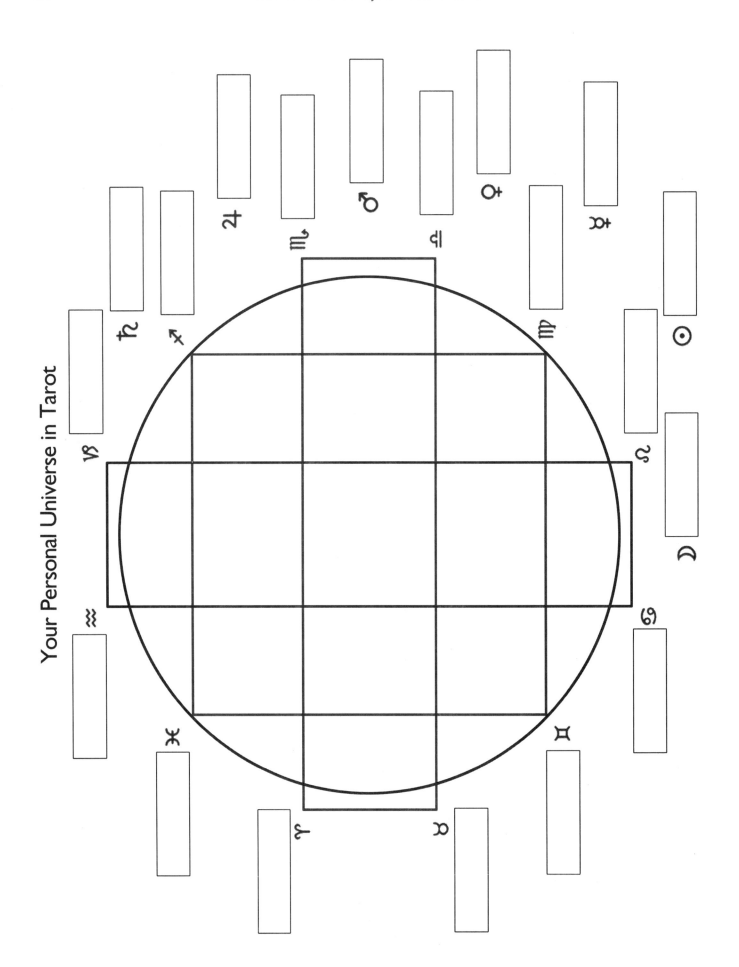

WHAT DOES IT MATTER WHICH CORRESPONDENCES I USE?

This question is at the heart of my lifelong quest to find and study every Tarot lineage with an esoteric bent. I want to know how each serious Tarot is linked to the traditional mysteries it either explicitly or implicitly represents. Much has been made in advertisements and reviews of the "traditions" behind certain modern lineages, as if such things made a great deal of difference to the "authenticity" of a given deck in daily usage. Yet, over the years, when I have taken the time to explain the documentable, historical lineages which *can* be traced to the early centuries of Tarot's existence, the response from the users of those modern decks is invariably "What does it matter what correspondences I use? If I study it in sincerity and do the meditations and rituals, and if I get the results I seek, isn't that enough?"

Well, maybe it is and maybe it isn't. The answer to that question depends upon your intent, what you are trying to accomplish. There are a wide range of reasons why a person would use a Tarot deck, and not everyone is equally invested in the occult correspondences. So I will use this chapter to explain what may or may not be the issues associated with "authenticity" and "historical lineage." You can decide for yourself if these things matter to you.

At the Most Superficial Level...

Nobody needs to worry about lineages, Tarot history, competing claims, or which version is "right," to do a reading with the cards. Every Tarot is a self-contained unit, endowed with all the necessary values with which to accomplish a reading. As a matter of fact, you could do a perfectly good reading with playing cards if you didn't mind the missing Major Arcana. The truth and applicability of a Tarot reading is not a function of the deck, but the interpreter. If you as a Tarot reader have done a good job of educating yourself about both the deck author's opinions on the peculiarities of his/her deck, and the structure of Tarot in general (meanings of the suits, the numbers, the personalities of the royalty and the Major Arcana), you could read with 3x5 cards scrawled with your own homemade titles! The "magic" aspect to Tarot is the thorough shuffle and concentration put into the cards by the person asking the question. The quotient of truth and relevance to the question is handled by the reader. The cards themselves are just a medium to highlight certain universal themes, which come up due to the questioner's focused attention, and are translated into advice by the reader.

If you are a collecter like me and have a large selection from which the querent picks a deck, in such a case, the deck the querent picks is always "perfect" for that reading. Invariably it will contain one or two cards uniquely pictured in that deck, and you will see those very cards come up during the reading putting just the right "spin" on it for that person. I try never choose a deck for my clients because I might not pick the one they need to see today! Some may feel confused when confronted by the embarrassment of riches on my table, but they are never sorry about the deck they picked by the end of the reading. (For the person recieving a reading, the visual experience is very impactful. Tarot readers who can provide their clients with a photo or printout of their spread are greatly aiding the client's retention of the session.)

So feel free to use any deck that comes to you, new or used, gifted or bought for yourself, official or unofficial, as long as it is not overtly pessimistic or negative. The more information you have in your head about the cards, the less dependent you are upon the author's or artist's understanding of the "bigger picture." And once you get some experience under your belt, you will find your own strongest associations with this or that card, and the limitations of the creator(s) will matter less. But never settle for a deck you actively don't like!

If You Want to Use the Astrology on the Cards...

This is the first case in which the issue of the "right" correspondences may matter to you. Many people have made themselves conversant with more than one esoteric system, the most popular parallel to Tarot being astrology. When I first used the cards professionally in the late 1970's, many occultists felt that astrologers belonged in a separate camp than Tarot readers, because Tarot is worked by intuition and astrology is a science. This approach is just too limiting. The two are different manifestations of a larger worldview, which is simultaneously keyed to events in the natural world (the planets moving around us in the heavens) and to psycho-spiritual archetypes within the unconscious of humanity (the Tarot arcana.) A Tarot deck is the flashcards for the cosmos of the Mystery Schools. It portrays in imagery the ancient, time-honored links between the inner life of humans and the larger cycles of nature and the planets. Tarot is astrological by nature and design.

So in the section on *How To Tell Which System Works for You*, I mention various tests you might put a Tarot through which will reveal to you astrologically the best deck for you. By comparing the pairs of cards that represent your sun and it's sign, your moon and it's sign, to your own experience, you will see which cards are appropriate for you and which are not. After all, you are not a blank slate, where your fate is being written by a throw of the cards! You have self-knowledge, you have talents, you have preferences, you have lessons to learn, and you have aversions too. What the cards do for you astrologically is provide you with pictures, especially the Major Arcana, which you can connect with the planet/sign/house placements in your chart.

This is how I actually learned astrology, which has since made up half of my metaphysical private practice all these years. A friend made up my daughter's chart and mine, and at first I couldn't make sense of it because astrology is so condensed, the symbolism was not evocative enough for me to hold it in my imagination. But since I was already studying Tarot, and I saw the signs and planets from the chart on the cards, I laid my cards down around the chart and memorized the planets and signs with the images of the Arcana all together. It instantly helped me to feel and visualize what sorts of impacts the planets had in their combinations, because I could imagine the two or more Arcana "conversing" and making their aspects. Adding the pictures and the mythos they represent fleshed out Astrology for me, and you might want to give it a try yourself. The arcana were designed to provide an edifying addition to your mythic imagination.

When you are Working with a Deck for Magical Purposes...

I want you to ask yourself, very deeply, in your heart of hearts, who or what it is that you are attempting to contact? What are the energies or entities towards which you are making outreach? What convinced you that such energies or entities exist? What place in the creation do you feel that they occupy? Are you naturally in contact with these kinds of energies through your ordinary sensibilities or are you taking somebody's word for it that they are out there for you to contact through magical practices? Would it be healthy for you to remain linked to the energies and influences that you are calling upon, as often happens, after the ritual is over? Do you have the power to direct their action to the desired effects only?

Some of the named entities called upon in magical rituals are from extremely ancient sources; they have had vast, stable existence for thousands of years in the collective unconscious and are relatively nontoxic psychically for a striving soul to encounter. We usually have enough historical information on them that we can see what parts of the human soul they touch, as well. One perfect example to cite is the Great Mother, who wends her way from ancient times foreward, with different names for different millennia, but always the same Holy Mother. Those archetypes, which are held sacred across cultural, temporal, and sectarian lines, are the ones upon which we can rest our souls in trying times.

Other types of entities and energies that the more experimental magicians call upon are not as time-tested, nor as trustworthy being used as objects upon which to focus your personal psyche. But without an educated mind and a researcher's bent, how would you know to separate the one

from the other? You have to take the time to learn where your ideas, your rituals, your correspondences have come from, and see if you trust that source, and if that source is compatible with your highest nature. That means taking less information on faith from the commercial magical manuals which abound these days. It means doing more of your own homework into those earlier cultures, their core beliefs and their actual practices. We are too trusting of our experts, failing to ask the hard questions of ourselves, namely, where do my beliefs come from? How many of my ideas are experientially testable? What makes me think I can get anything done through the avenue of magic if I can't get it done any other way?

Magicians whom I have met over the years, at least those who would admit it, seem to fall into two broad categories, the "speculative" magicians, and the "operative" magicians.. There are not extremes — I see them as the edges of a continuum. The more speculative magicians like to study the subject, collect books and manuscripts, compare, theorize, write rituals and teach, and their specialty is representing the past. The more operative magicians like to create experiences and initiations for themselves and others, fearlessly mix traditions, questioning authority and pushing the envelope of the future. Both types have a lot of energy for their dimension of the subject, despite the different outcomes of their devotion.

This amount of energy and attention is very attractive to some of the inhabitants of the invisible worlds, who are by nature users and conscience-less. We share our evolving universe with entities and energies that are de-volving, slowly breaking down and recycling themselves. This is not in and of itself a bad thing, or an unnatural thing, and in fact this has always been the case, since humanity's first sense of self-consciousness. The danger lies in our temptation to get personally involved with energies that are degenerative, and therefore poisonous to us in subtle or obvious ways. We each have opportunities every day to become host organisms for devolving energies, thoughts, and entities, and it it our misfortune if we let them latch on to us. This happens even under the normal conditions, like our daily lives, through our own black-and-white thoughtforms we have not yet resolved. But during focused rituals or intense visualization, where so much will-power and lifeforce and imagination are concentrated, the results are just like turning on the porch light on a summer night. *Everyone* comes, not just who you were calling!

More to the point for modern ritualists, who are often aligning their ceremonies to astronomical events, the only body of correspondences which will accurately link you to the planets as conceived in the ancient world is to use the ancient astro-alphanumeric correspondences of the Hebrews, whose astronomical treatise, *Sefir Yetzirah*, was the world's astrology textbook for the thousand years before the modern era. Even the Greek order, still over two thousand years old, is a corruption from this root paradigm. The Hebrew alphabet was the universal astro-alphanumeric canon for the ancients in the civilizations around the Mediterranean. Hebrew titles for God and the angels, the planets and signs, the Sephiroth of the Tree of Life, can be found throughout Christian scriptures and liturgies, though in slightly disguised form, because of the Greek Gematria utilized in the creation of the New Testament.

So, for example, the fact that we "automatically" link Nogah (Venus) with the Empress is an overlay from Greek thinking. The original correspondence with the third letter of the Hebrew alphabet, as with the third arcanum, is Madin (Mars). The Martian Empress refers us back to Demeter as the engine of nature, the backbone of all the work done to keep our world alive. She is the life-force pulsing through us all, and she is red with blood. The number three is also the top of the Mother Pillar in the Kabbalah pattern, concerned with keeping a watchful eye (Binah) and an iron grip (Geburah) on the business of the world (Hod). The Great Mother is diminished and disempowered in the trade the Greeks made between Madin and Nogah. Even though the Greek correspondences became the cultural norm for Europe, the very signs and planets themselves were originally "born" and named in the older Phoenecian-based languages, and even the spellings of their names in Hebrew are magically crafted to express their energetic and mathematical interior nature. These facts are very old, and deeply embedded in the roots of our collective consciousness.

So what happens when we have the intent to call upon Nogah, the energy of the Divine Beloved and the inspiration for all works of art and self-improvement, but then can offer her only Madin totems referencing the work of the Great Mother? Do you think the Nogah energy of beauty and proportion and the delecate balance can be at its' most harmonious in that setting? Is that really the best way to honor Nogah? When we want to contact the Madin energy why do we assemble the symbols and talismans of The Tower? This does not happen because we are intending to cross our wires, but because we have studied with one of the English schools who took it upon themselves to "correct" the ancient tradition, and we have no clue what the basis of that correction is. In what way does that rightly address the Empress, Demeter, or Gaia, the Mother of us all? We are failing to meet her energy on her own home ground, and we are also imposing distortions upon her, creating confused experiences which we then take as our norms. Could this bear any relationship to the experience that many women have in our own times, when beauty and femininity too often result in biology-as-destiny (Nogah harnessed to the fertility of Demeter), and the mature, strong, self-sufficient matriarch is viewed as a disaster in the making (Madin as the Tower)?

Remember, it is one of the oldest maxims in magic that to have any impact in the invisible worlds, one has to call things by their real names. And can we not take it as a maxim that the older the name, the closer it is ito the authentic original? "New and improved," as applied to magical workings, may not inspire the greatest confidence in a person who is trying to link up with and reanimate their cultural heritage and lineage-links.

So I am not doubting that everyone who creates rituals and invokes and evokes various cosmic and elemental energies is having a valid experience. With the amount of will and imagination and desire and belief that gets built into those rituals, something meaningful is bound to happen. "New" experiences are being had every day, for better and for worse. What I am saying is that some of those experiences are a mixture of subjectivity and expectation, set up by the forces commericalizing magic right now, whom the buying public trusts too well.

I have no doubt that many users of these modern magical methods are powerfully stirred by contact with the energies evoked. My concern is that the energies evoked may or may not be what you were intending to contact, and may or may not have the nature you expected them to have. We have so mixed our metaphors in the Western Magical Tradition that it requires detective work to untangle the sticky threads of mistranslation, deliberate obfustication, revisionism, and other distractions. Magic is not governed by the same laws as consumerism, where one brand is nearly as good as the next!

The core principle operative here is that like attracts like. Be sure your daily being is on the wavelength of what you are trying to attract in your ritual experiences. It is much easier to draw in coarser energy-forms than the more refined ones, just as it is easier to make noise than harmonious music. This is why a set program of self-cultivation is essential to all serious ritualists.

If the Tarot Actually Becomes Your Spritual Path...

This was my situation in the late 1970's. I had already discovered the cards themselves but the years immediately after my daughter was born were pivotal for my destiny, and I was not getting objective insights from other sources in my life. Even friends with a spritual perspective, my therapist, family members, all had an idea how to "fix" my life. In particular, I was living closely with people who were in the midst of a conversion to Protestant Christianity of a fundamentalist strain. Battle lines were being drawn. I tried to support my friends in their faith and even accepted baptism and Christ coming into my heart, but I did not give up the Major Arcana as my neutral advisors in an otherwise highly-charged time. Nor did I ever see them as Gods or replacements for God I knew them as archetypes, and allies, for and of this life.

At the time, I was warned that I was taking a path antithetical to Christianity, the faith of my anscestors. But subsequent study has shown that to be a mistake. One has only to look into Margaret Starbird's excellent books *The Woman With The Alabaster Jar* and *The Goddess In The Gospels* to see evidence of a robust, Kabbalist-inflected Christianity which included the training and ordination of women like myself. Variations of this strain of Christianity survived in Europe right up to the creation of the first Tarot cards, which show images drawn directly from the Gnostic Christian canon. Images just like those on Tarot are carved into Christian churches, engraved in the hand-lettered Bibles, and painted by the Church's old masters from the eighth century to the twelfth, right up to the first Crusade and the burning times in the Lanquedoc region of France. The Rosicrucians and the Masons preserved this path through the persecutions, so that those of us living in more enlightened times might not miss out on the wisdom and faith of our ancestors.

Therefore, it is incorrect to portray Tarot as an anti-religious tool of corrupting forces from the dark side. And simultaneously, I was wrong to think that I could avoid dealing with the faith of my ancestors by turning my back on the Judeo-Christian paradigm to study Tarot. The more I studied it, the more I saw that the creators, producers, and users of Tarot had for the most part been the most pious, God-loving souls you would want to know either within or outside of the Church. The vast mjority of them were Christians, just of a non-Roman type. A few of them were even "hiding out" within the clergy, traditional ordinations hiding clandestine Secret Society affiliations. With the paradoxical twist of a good koan, the good guys and the bad guys in the religious-persecutian dramas in Europe were often all guys from the same team, just trying to make the best of a diffiicult situation. We in the twentieth century can barely imagine the challenges facing the magically-inclined before the last two centuries.

The reason that I am a Bishop today is that in my research years ago, I discovered the Gnostic Christianity of the Martinists, whose lodge in the late 1800's comprised the most advanced esoteric scholars of their time, and whose labors created the most comprehensive Tarot decks I had ever run across. When the living representatives of that lodge found me and I them, there was no question. The waters of my soul, which had been forced to part around the boulders of modern, revisionist Christianity and modern, revisionist Tarot, came back together again on the other side, reinspired by the certainty that the Christ and I had never really parted, and the Hebrew and Gnostic foundations supporting my spiritual being were not a fluke.

I have taken this detour into my own personal history to illustrate a point that may also pertain to the reader's own situation. In a case like this, what correspondences you use will matter a lot. The Martinists use the Greek or Alexandrian corresponcences, which had been traditional in gentile Europe since the writing of the New Testament in Greek. So all of their insights and teachings are developed upon that framework. This is what I am calling the Continental order, and I personally accept the adjustment that Eliphas Levi put into the system during his tenure as head of the Continental heirarchy of mystical orders. (Levi and the Martinists did not have access to the Gra version of the *Sefir Yetzirah*, so they built beautifully upon what they had.)

And for this reason, if I feel a conflict between whether a card is to be read in the Hebrew mode or in the Greek mode, I look at my motive or intent. I need the Hebrew when I am trying to contact the planets transiting my chart right now, and when I am trying to meditate with the astro-alphanumeric formulas of the arcana or the planets or the

angels. I will reference the Greek, however, when I'm operating as a Martinist, or getting philosophical in the mode of Alexandrian Hermeticism. In both cases the relationship to the universal Gnosis is provided by the images on the cards, changeable though they may be between decks. I am satisfied to "triangulate" between the Hebrew and Levi's variant of the Greek, leaving the various "new" lineages from England and Spain as interesting sidelights for occasional contrast.

The Impact of Making Changes to Tradition in Sound and Music

Bearing this in mind, we must each think again about how our "lineage" affiliations will redistribute the sounds of the letters along the span of the arcana, for better or for worse. I have often been amazed at the fidelity with which ancient teachings have been carefully husbanded from one era to the next, preserved with undying loyalty and handed along virtually unchanged for centuries and millennia. I used to attribute this changelessness as a lack of creativity or an excess of superstition, but now I see it all differently. Those forms were carefully crafted to evoke and resonate the particular frequencies one is calling upon, and they are composed in a very scientific way. This is not just a philosophical difference, but a distinct material difference which has to have magical consequences when you work with them.

What's true is that traditional forms are preserved and revered because they were "built" specifically to provide a means whereby people can contact their ancestral allies in the spirit world. The thinking is, this is how my parents and grandparents addressed the deities, and so shall I. In the magical interface between the spoken word and the Word of Power, the ancient names and phrases are more often than not rich with harmonics, containing the sacred ratios, elegant in their mathematics as well as their expression. Their sound-structure alone provides a tremendous channel of power for the magician/performer to tap into.

As in all traditional, lineage-based teachings, it is a good thing to "go to the well" and get some experience in the sound and feel and workings of the older patterns and correspondences, before getting your mind set on any of the modern versions. For any aspect of vocalizing in the formal Western Magical Tradition, as a general rule it is prudent to ascertain if there is a Hebrew word or phrase for that entity, value, concept or frequency, because that will be the word holding the "original" energy defining it.

Greek is the language of second recourse, but remember that there is no gender in Greek so you already have lost one dimension of magical value in the translation. But Greek is the language which carried the Hebrew alphabet-mysticism to the West, and it has a lot of spiritual history in it too. Any generation in which the church seemed even a little open towards this ancient magical approach to spirituality, the gematria embedded in the Old and New Testament became irresistable to alchemists, occultists, and talismanic magicians. Alexandrian-style synthesis was the intellectual norm until the sixteen hundreds, when Giordano Bruno and

Athanasius Kircher championed Egyptian culture and language as the oldest and most worthy ancient tongue. These sorts of arguments are still echoing among occultists today.

To take this idea to its logical conclusion, we must recognize that words are things in the practice of magic, and in some senses, words themselves are entities. Extremely old words have long generations of meanings, feelings, ideas, and images attached, and when they are sounded, all of those attachments ring just like the harmonics of a Tibetan bowl. If you think that the impact of your words in a ritual is limited to just what you *think* you mean, you may be surprised by the outcomes of your workings!

Make sure you fully understand just who or what you are calling upon in a sacred way, right back to the earliest roots of that energy in its original language. And do take the time to learn to pronounce or intone these powerful words correctly, as well. Remember, the utility of magical names is in the very specific mathematical and sonic frequencies they evoke. The name is nothing if you don't learn how to say it!

In Conclusion

I hope I have made it clear to my readers why I am so concerned with the pedigrees and lineages of Tarot. I see this wonderful archive of magical images as a grand summation of many generations of sincere spiritual effort. As a part of that stream of esoteric transmission, I want to clear up some misconceptions which have been plaguing modern Tarot students. If I can help clear the path to the well, more souls will be able to drink, and I think that's a good thing! I take refuge in the wisdom of my ancestors.

Bibliography

Anonymous. *Egyptian Mysteries, An Account of an Initiation,* York Beach, Maine: Weiser, 1988. (often attributed to Iamblichus)

Anonymous. *The Encyclopedia of Occult Sciences,* New York, NY: Tudor Publishing Co., 1968.

Begg, Ean. *The Cult Of The Black Virgin,* New York, NY: Penguin, 1985.

Biagent, Michael & Leigh, Richard & Lincoln, Henry. *Holy Blood, Holy Grail,* New York, NY: Dell Publishing Company, 1982.

Cavendish, Richard. *The Tarot,* New York, NY: Crescent Books, 1975.

Clymer, R. Swinburne. *The Book of Rosicruciae,* Quakertown, PA: The Philosophical Publishing Company, 1947.

Cooper-Oakley, Isabel. *The Count of Saint Germain,* Blauvelt, NY: Steinerbooks, 1992.

Douglas, Alfred. *The Tarot: The Origins, Meaning and Uses of the Cards,* New York, NY: Penguin Books, 1984.

Elbert Benjamine [pseudonum C. C. Zain]. *The Sacred Tarot,* Los Angeles, CA: The Church of Light, 1969.

Fabricius, Johannes. A*lchemy, The Medieval Alchemists and their Royal Art,* Wellingborough, England: The Aquariun Press, 1989.

Faivre, Antoine & Needleman, Jacob. *Modern Esoteric Spirituality,* New York, NY: Crossroad, 1995. (Vol 21 of *World Spirituality: An Encyclopedic History of thed Religions Quest.)*

Fideler, David. *Jesus Christ, Sun of God: Ancient Cosmology and Early Christian Symbolism,* Wheaton, Il.: Quest Books, 1993.

Fournier, Felix Alfonso. *Playing Cards: General History From Their Creation To The Present Day,* Vitoria, Spain: The Fournier Museum, Vol. I, 1982, Vol. II, 1988.

Gad, Irene. *Tarot and Individuation: Corresondences wth Cabalah and Alchemy,* York Beach, MN: Nicholas-Hayes, Inc., 1994.

Gettings, Fred. *The Book of Tarot,* London, England: Trewin Copplestone Publishers Ltd., 1973.

—————— *Secret symbolism in Occult Art,* New York, NY: Harmony Books, 1987.

Giles, Cynthia. *The Tarot, History, Mystery and Lore,* New York, NY: Simon & Schuster, 1992.

Guiley, Rosemary Ellen. *Encyclopedia of Angels,* New York, NY: Facts on File, Inc., 1996.

Godwin, Joscelyn. *Athanasius Kircher: A Renaissance Man and the Quest for Lost Knowledge.,* London, England: Thames and Hudson, Ltd., 1979.(From the Art And Imagination series.)

Godwyn, Malcolm. *The Holy Grail, Its Origins, Secrets & Meaning Revealed,* New York, NY: Viking Studio Books, 1994.

Guthrie, Kenneth Sylfan. *The Pythagorean Sourcebook and Library,* Grand Rapics, MI: Phanes Press, 1988.

Hall, Manley P. *The Tarot,* Los Angeles, CA: The Philosophical Research Society, 1978.

—————— *Freemasonry of the Ancient Egyptians,* Los Angeles, CA: The Philosophical Research Society, 1971.

Haskins, Susan. *Mary Magdalen, Myth and Metaphor,* New York, NY: Riverhead Books, 1992.

Hulse, David Allen. *The Key of It All, Book II: The Western Mysteries,* St. Paul, MN: Llewellyn Publications, 1994.

Kaplan, Aryeh. *Sefer Yetzirah, The Book Of Creation,* York Beach, ME: Samuel Weiser, 1991.

Kaplan, Stuart R. *The Encyclopedia of Tarot,* Stamford, CT: U. S. Games Systems, Vol. I, 1978; Vol. II, 1986.

Knight, Gareth. *The Treasure House of Images,* Rochester, VT: Destiny Books, 1986.

Levi, Eliphas. *Transcendental Magic: Its Doctrine & Ritual,* translated by A. E. Waite. York Beach, Maine: Samuel Weiser, 1981.

—————— *The Key of the Mysteries,* translated by Aleister Crowley. London, England: Rider & Co., 1959.

—————— *The Book of Splendours,* translated by W. N. Schors. New York, NY: Samuel Weiser, 1973.

—————— *The Mysteries of the Qaballah,* Translated by W. N. Schors. New York, NY: Samuel Weiser, 1974.

—————— *The History of Magic,* Translated by A. E. Waite. Kila, MT: Kessinger Reprints (no date)

—————— *The Mysteries of Magic,* a digest by Arthur Edward Waite. Kila, MT: Kessinger Reprints, (no date).

—————— *The Magical Ritual of the Sanctum Regnum,* Edited by W. Wynn Wescott, Kila, MT: Kessinger Reprints, (no date).

Markale, Jean. *Women of the Celts,* London, 1975.

Maxwell, Joseph. *The Tarot,* London, England: Neville Spearman, 1985.

Matthews, Caitlin. *Sophia, Goddess of Wisdom,* London, England: Thorson's, 1991.

McIntosh, Christopher. *Eliphas Levi and the French Occult Revival,* New York, NY: Samuel Weiser Inc., 1974.

Moakley, Gertrude. *The Tarot Cards Painted by Bonifacio Bembo,* New York, NY: New York Public Library, 1966.

Moore, Thomas. *The Planets Within: The Astrological Psychology of Marcilio Ficino,* Great Barrington, MA: Lindisfarne Press, 1990.

Olsen, Christina. *The Art of Tarot,* New York, NY: Abbeville Press Publishers, 1995.

O''Neill, Robert V. *Tarot Symbolism,* Lima, OH: Fairway Press, 1986.

Pagels, Elaine. *The Gnostic Gospels,* New York, NY: Vintage Books, 1981.

Papus [pseudonym of Gerard Encausse]. *The Tarot of the Bohemians,* New York, NY: Arcanum Books, 1958.

———— *Astrology for Initiates,* York Beach, Maine: Samuel Weiser, 1996.

Paracelcus Selected Writings. Edited by Jaolade Jacogi. Princeton, NJ: Princeton University Press, 1988.

Patai, Raphael. *The Hebrew Goddess,* Detroit MI: Wayne State University Press, 1978.

———— *The Jewish Alchemists,* Princeton, NJ: Princeton University Press, 1994.

Pennick, Nigel. *The Secret Lore of Runes and other Ancient Alphabets, London, England:: Rider, 1991.*

———— *Sacred Geometry: Symbolism and Purpose in Religious Structures,* Wellingborough, England: Turnstone Press Ltd., 1980.

Pitois, Jean Baptiste, [pseudonum: Paul Christian]. *The History and Practice of Magic,* New York, NY: Citadel Press, 1967.

Poe, Richard. *Black Spark, White Fire: Did African Explorers Civilize Ancient Europe?* Rocklin, CA: Prima Publishing, 1997.

Rossner, Father John. *In Search of the Primordial Tradition & The Cosmic Christ: Uniting World Religious Experience with a Lost Esoteric Christianity,* St. Paul, MN: Llewellyn Publications, 1989.

Sadhu, Mouni. *The Tarot,* No. Hollywood, CA: Wilshire Book Co. 1968.

Scholem, Gershom G. *Major Trends in Jewish Mysticism,* New York, NY: Schocken Books, 1961.

Seznic, Jean. *The Survival of the Pagan Gods: The Mythological Tradition and Its Place in Renaissance Humanism and Art,* New York, NY: Harper Torchbooks, 1953.

Shephar, John. *The Tarot Trumps: Cosmos in Miniature,* Wellingborough, England: Aquarian Press, 1985.

Smith, Morton. *The Secret Gospel,* Clearlake, CA: The Dawn Horse Press, 1982.

———— *Jesus The Magician,* San Francisco, CA: Harper & Row, 1978.

Schonfield, Hugh. *The Essene Odyssey,* Rockport, MA: Element, Incorporated, 1993.

Starbird, Margaret. *The Goddess in the Gospels: Reclaiming the Sacred Feminine,* Santa Fe, NM: Bear & Co. Publishers,1998.

———— *The Woman With the Alabaster Jar: Mary Magdalen and the Holy Grail,* Santa Fe, NM: Bear & Company Publishers, 1993.

The Divine Pymander and other writings of Hermes Trismegistus, translated by John D. Chambers. New York, NY: Samuel Weiser, 1972.

The Gospel of Mary, from *The Nag Hammadi Library,* edited by Robinson, James M. San Francisco, CA: HarperSanFrancisco, 1990. Third Edition.

Thiering, Barbara. *Jesus & The Riddle Of The Dead Sea Scrolls,* San Francisco, CA: Harper San Francisco, 1987.

Tomberg, Valentin [Anonymous]. *Meditations On the Tarot: A Journey Into Christian Hermeticism,* Amity, NY: Amity House, 1985.

Trismosin, Solomon. *Splendour Solis,* London, England: Kegan Paul, Trench, Trubner & Co. Ltd., Reprinted by Yoga Publication Society, (no date).

Walker, D. P. *Spiritual and Demonic Magic from Ficino to Campanella,* The Warburg Institute, University of London, 1958.

Wasserman, James. *Art and Symbols of the Occult: Images of Power and Wisdom,* Rochester, VT: Destiny Books, 1993.

Wescott, W. Wynn. *The Occult Power of Numbers,* North Hollywood, CA: Newcastle, 1984.

Whitchead, Nicholas. *Patterns in Magical Christianity,* Albuquerque, NM: Sun Chalice Books, 1996.

Wirth, Oswald. *The Tarot of the Magicians,* York Beach, MN: Samuel Weiser, 1985.

———— *Introduction to the Study of Tarot,* York Beach, MN: Samuel Weiser, 1983.

Yates, Frances. *the Rosicrucian Enlightenment,* Boulder, CO: Shambhala, 1978.

———— *The Art of Memeory,* Chicago, IL: University of Chicago Press, 1966.

———— *Giordano Bruno and the Hermetic Tradition,* Chicago, IL: University of Chicago Press, 1964.

Index

0 El Loco
        Mercury. Magic manifester.

I El Consultante

II La Consultante

III La Emperatriz
        Aries.

IIII El Emperador
        Taurus.

V El Maestro
        Gemini. Challenges of choosing
        a partner. "Integrate 2
        realities or letgos of one
VI Los Dos Caminos   Big romance/love.
        Cancer.

VII El carro de Hermes
        Libra.

VIII La Justicia
        Virgo.

IX El Anciano

X La Rueda de la Fortuna
        Leo.

XI La Fortuleza
        Neptune. Lack ability to be
        oneself. Devotion to cause. Man
XII La Picota dom. Energ is arrested, wait
        Scorpio.   judgment

XIII Death
        Sagittarius

XIV La Templanza
        Capricorn.

XV Aker

XVI La Torre
        Aquarius.

XVII El Astro
        Pisces.

XVIII La Luna

XIX El Sol

ABOUT THE AUTHOR

El Cielo

El Mundo

Christine Payne Towler has made a lifelong study of the imagery, history and practice of the Tarot, Astrology, Kabbalah, Alchemy, Hermeticism, and other traditional branches of the Western Mystery Schools. Starting in 1970 with the purchase of a used Tarot deck in a Salem, Oregon, her interest in occult imagery has burgeoned into a book and deck collection that spans centuries and continents. Contemplation upon those images over time has led to an understanding of the older Classical and European traditions of Tarot which have been nearly eclipsed by the modern trend for innovation and eclecticism..

During the course of her studies, Christine has supported herself as an occultist using Tarot, Astrology, and Kabbalah, in their traditional role as parts of the larger program of Self-Initiation. The West inherited this process from the ancient Mystery Schools which were eliminated by the Roman Church. Her conviction that Tarot is indeed the "flash cards of the Mysteries" has been a motivating force throughout her studies.

In the early 1990's, Christine was initiated into a Templar lodge with Martinist affiliations, allowing her to further investigate the traditions associated with the imagery and esoteric content of Tarot. Happily, the Secret Society movement is still alive and well, and continues to provide a framework within which striving individuals can align themselves with the great work of human evolution going on in all places at all times. Christine was made a Bishop of the Apostolic Succession in 1995, completing the cycle that was begun a quarter of a century earlier.

Christine is presently celebrating the release of her collaboration with Visionary Networks, called *Tarot Magic; The Classical Decks*. This interactive CD-Rom for personal computer showcases the decks and ideas of the Esoteric Tarot's originators from the Renaissance to the 20th century. This program allows owners to use their own decks, or a virtual deck from within the program, to first create a reading for themselves, then have it interpreted by Christine in the light of the historic Tarot tradition. Sixteen original essays detail the primary lineages or families of Tarot, plus the related arts and sciences which underlie the structure of Tarot. A personal journal is also provided so users can record their readings along with their own or Christine's commentary. To visit the website and sample *Tarot Magic* for yourself, search for tarotmagic.com .

At present, Christine continues in private practice in Oregon, and can be reached for readings, consulting or tutoring at 1-800-981-3582.

INTERACTIVE TAROT WILL CHANGE YOUR LIFE !

TAROT MAGIC *will empower you and your friends with the ability to accurately interpret the cards.*

Thousands of years old, the wisdom system known as Tarot is again recognized as a rich source of intuitive guidance and practical insight, powerful for resolving dilemmas and situations that logic can't handle. But Tarot takes a long time to learn and it is almost impossible to evaluate the expertise of those claiming to have mastered it.

Imagine you had a 1000-page encyclopedia that provided all the nuances of every card in every position in every spread, as well as the history of each card. Think of how much you could learn from such a useful tome! But such a book doesn't exist — in print, it would weigh a ton and flipping through it for one spread would take hours. Our solution: Make all that knowledge easy to access by putting it on an interactive CD-ROM!

Managing volumes of non-linear information is what computers excel at — which is why the TAROT MAGIC CD-Rom makes perfect sense. Now you can access a deep repository of Tarot wisdom that's never been available before. Tarot scholar Christine Payne-Towler's expertise is unsurpassed. Her poetic and insightful interpretations, incorporating new historical research, reflect an encyclopedic knowledge of classical Tarot.

TAROT MAGIC is a perfect companion to your favorite deck. It will help you get the most out of Tarot, while adding 11 new (virtual) decks to your collection. Giving yourself and your friends readings with TAROT MAGIC will be a source of fascinating pleasure for the rest of your life.

Take advantage of the most thorough Tarot system ever created now. As soon as you receive TAROT MAGIC, you will experience the personal power that regular access to deeply relevant insights will add to your life!

INTERACTIVE TAROT CAPABILITIES

POSITIONAL READINGS 2000 interpretations that relate specifically to each card's exact position in any spread.

EXPERT INTERPRETATIONS by Christine Payne-Towler, noted Tarot scholar, author and bishop of the Gnostic Church.

ELEGANTLY NARRATED no need to read or take notes.

10 DECKS, 10 SPREADS built in… or use your own deck. Program includes Rider-Waite, Stairs of Gold and eight other beautiful decks that represent authentic classical Tarot at its best. Flip between decks and spreads with just a mouse click.

PRINT AND SAVE READINGS including color graphics.

ANIMATED CARD SHUFFLING programmed to capture exact mathematical properties of physical shuffling and cutting (or you can use a physical deck, if you prefer manual shuffling).

A MYSTICAL FEELING arises as beautiful art, sound track and special effects create an immersive Tarot ritual experience.

GUIDED TOUR shows you how to frame a question, pick an appropriate spread, shuffle and cut the cards.

AN ESOTERIC HISTORY OF TAROT with essays by Christine Payne-Towler on the history of Tarot and each card.

TAROT MAGIC RUNS ON WINDOWS 95 OR 98 OR NT, OR MACINTOSH.